ANGUS LOUGHRAN'S

GUIDE TO

WORLD CUP 2002

ABSOLUTE PUBLISHING LTD

ANGUS LOUGHRAN'S
GUIDE TO
WORLD
CUP 2002

First published in Great Britain in 2002 by Absolute Publishing Ltd.

© Absolute Publishing 2002

ABSOLUTE PUBLISHING LTD
197-199 CITY ROAD, LONDON, EC1V 1JN, UK

Printed and bound in Great Britain by Cox & Wyman, Reading, Berkshire

ISBN: 0 9542304 0 X

AUTHOR ANGUS LOUGHRAN
PUBLISHER PETER LEVINGER
SERIES EDITORS GLYN WILMSHURST, ANDY TONGUE
SUB EDITORS ROB FURBER, MATT WEINER, GUY WOODWARD
ART EDITOR JOHN PAUL YETTON
DESIGNER DAMON COGMAN
IMAGES ALLSPORT

SPECIAL THANKS TO BOB TANNER, CHRIS RHYS, DAVE FARRAR,
MICHAEL CHURCH, SHAW BROWN, RAOUL SIMONS & SPORTY FROM SCOTLAND

CONTENTS

FOREWORD BY
JOHN MOTSON

England go into the World Cup full of optimism as ever. The impressive friendly win over Paraguay proved that even without David Beckham we have two world-class players in Michael Owen and Steven Gerrard.

They are very special players. For England to do well we need those two, plus of course Beckham, to be fit and firing on all cylinders.

Group F has been nicknamed the 'Group of Death' and looks tricky but not insurmountable. England should beat Nigeria and should edge out Sweden, although that one will be harder than many people think.

Of course England vs Argentina is the crunch game. It's a chance for England to gain revenge for 1986 and 1998. The World Cup is the acid test for Sven-Göran Eriksson.

He was slightly lucky in a couple of qualifiers like Greece at home as well as the great result in Munich.

He has enjoyed mixed results in friendlies, though these were due in part to injuries and the excessive use of substitutions.

In Japan and South Korea we will find out how good Eriksson is as he pits himself against the best international coaches in the world.

There is less pressure on the Republic of Ireland as they don't suffer from the same burden of expectation.

Germany will be tough opponents – they are never easy in competitive football – but I think the Republic have every chance of beating Cameroon to get through. Mick McCarthy has a very settled team, though Roy Keane must be fit for the Republic to progress.

The draw is somewhat lop-sided, with Argentina, France and Brazil all joining England in the tougher half.

Argentina are rated favourites by the bookies on the basis of their form in the South American qualifiers and the fact they have so many talented players performing successfully in the major Euopean leagues.

On paper they and France are the top sides. The only question is: Is it a bridge too far for the French? They could be even better than in 1998 because that side won the World Cup without a recognised world-class striker: now they have Thierry Henry and David Trezeguet. They will be in the final reckoning provided the rest of the side has the motivation and the legs.

Italy are one of my fancied sides. They are in the easier section of the draw and they have had some rotten luck in the World Cup.

They have gone out of the last three tournaments on penalties, not losing a knockout match in open play since France in the second round in Mexico '86.

Italy need Del Piero to hit form – he flopped in Euro 2000, which cost them, but they have always been one of the best sides in the world defensively and if the midfield can

6

provide some creativity they will go a long way.

Brazil are not the team of old but if Ronaldo and Rivaldo are fit they can't be discounted.

Spain, the perennial under-achievers, should make the last eight, especially as they are in the weaker half of the draw, as should Portugal. Raul and Figo are the key men for those two sides respectively.

I think two dark horses to watch out for will be Japan and Turkey. The Japanese have the benefits that come from home advantage and will be used to the climate and the humidity.

Turkey have two strong club sides in Fenerbahce and Galatasaray, who have done consistently well in the Champions League over the past few years, and probably don't get the credit from the British media they deserve. Striker Hakan Suker is their star man and could get amongst the goals if you are looking for possible Golden Boot candidates.

Players that I'm particularly looking forward to seeing include Raul and Zinedine Zidane, Owen of course and Robbie Keane. There's always a player who comes from relative obscurity to take the tournament by storm and Robbie Keane could be the man.

Vincenzo Montella of Italy has had a great season in Serie A and looked to have that touch of class in the recent friendly win over England.

Also worth keeping an eye for is Zahovic of Slovenia, who was one of the stars of Euro 2000.

This is my eighth successive World Cup for the BBC – beginning in Germany back in 1974 – and it promises to be the most exciting ever as the tournament will undergo something of a cultural revolution.

It's the first time the competition has been staged in that part of the world and the first time it has been jointly hosted by two countries.

It will also be a new experience for fans back home as they will be watching the games over breakfast and lunch with comprehensive highlights every evening.

I'm counting the days down to the opening match in Seoul on May 31st and I'm sure you are too.

John Motson

WORLD CUP FACTS

Liverpool, Arsenal and Manchester United could all make history this summer. Until now, no England World Cup squad has included more than four players from the same club. But United (Butt, Beckham, Scholes, G Neville, P Neville), Arsenal (Seaman, Keown, Cole, Campbell, Parlour) and Liverpool (Carragher, Murphy, Owen, Heskey, Gerrard) will all be crossing their fingers that that changes.

Jairzinho of Brazil netted seven goals in six games in the 1970 Finals in Mexico.

WORLD CUP GROUPS

GROUP A

FRANCE
DENMARK
URUGUAY
SENEGAL

GROUP B

SPAIN
PARAGUAY
SLOVENIA
SOUTH AFRICA

GROUP C

BRAZIL
TURKEY
CHINA
COSTA RICA

GROUP D

KOREA
PORTUGAL
POLAND
USA

GROUP E

GERMANY
REP OF IRE
CAMEROON
SAUDI ARABIA

GROUP F

ARGENTINA
ENGLAND
SWEDEN
NIGERIA

GROUP G

ITALY
CROATIA
MEXICO
ECUADOR

GROUP H

JAPAN
BELGIUM
RUSSIA
TUNISIA

WORLD CUP SCHEDULE

GROUP STAGE

(TIMES BST)

FRIDAY 31 MAY
1. FRANCE v SENEGAL (Seoul, 12:30) Group A

SATURDAY 1 JUNE
2. IRELAND v CAMEROON (Niigata, 07:30) Group E
3. URUGUAY v DENMARK (Ulsan, 10:00) Group A
4. GERMANY v SAUDI ARABIA (Sapporo, 12:30) Group E

SUNDAY 2 JUNE
5. ENGLAND v SWEDEN (Saitama, 10:30) Group F
6. PARAGUAY v SOUTH AFRICA (Busan, 08:30) Group B
7. ARGENTINA v NIGERIA (Ibaraki, 06:30) Group F
8. SPAIN v SLOVENIA (Gwangju, 12:30) Group B

MONDAY 3 JUNE
9. CROATIA v MEXICO (Niigata, 07:30) Group G
10. BRAZIL v TURKEY (Ulsan, 10:00) Group C
11. ITALY v ECUADOR (Sapporo, 12:30) Group G

TUESDAY 4 JUNE
12. CHINA v COSTA RICA (Gwangju, 07:30) Group C
13. JAPAN v BELGIUM (Saitama, 10:00) Group H
14. SOUTH KOREA v POLAND (Busan, 12:30) Group D

WEDNESDAY 5 JUNE
15. RUSSIA v TUNISIA (Kobe, 07:30) Group H
16. USA v PORTUGAL (Suwon, 10:00) Group D
17. GERMANY v IRELAND (Ibaraki, 12:30) Group E

THURSDAY 6 JUNE
18. FRANCE v URUGUAY (Busan, 12:30) Group A
19. CAMEROON v SAUDI ARABIA (Saitama, 10:00) Group E
20. DENMARK v SENEGAL (Daegu, 07:30) Group A

WORLD CUP SCHEDULE

FRIDAY 7 JUNE
21. SWEDEN v NIGERIA (Kobe, 07:30) GROUP F
22. SPAIN v PARAGUAY (Jeonju, 10:00) GROUP B
23. ARGENTINA v ENGLAND (Sapporo, 12:30) GROUP F

SATURDAY 8 JUNE
24. SOUTH AFRICA v SLOVENIA (Daegu, 07:30) GROUP B
25. ITALY v CROATIA (Ibaraki, 10:00) GROUP G
26. BRAZIL v CHINA (Seogwipo, 12:30) GROUP C

SUNDAY 9 JUNE
27. MEXICO v ECUADOR (Miyagi, 07:30) GROUP G
28. COSTA RICA v TURKEY (Incheon, 10:00) GROUP C
29. JAPAN v RUSSIA (Yokohama, 12:30) GROUP H

MONDAY 10 JUNE
30. SOUTH KOREA v USA (Daegu, 07:30) GROUP D
31. TUNISIA v BELGIUM (Oita, 10:00) GROUP H
32. PORTUGAL v POLAND (Jeonju, 12:30) GROUP D

TUESDAY 11 JUNE
33. DENMARK v FRANCE (Incheon, 07:30) GROUP A
34. SENEGAL v URUGUAY (Suwon, 07:30) GROUP A
35. CAMEROON v GERMANY (Shizuoka, 12:30) GROUP E
36. SAUDI ARABIA v IRELAND (Yokohama, 12:30) GROUP E

WEDNESDAY 12 JUNE
37. SWEDEN v ARGENTINA (Miyagi, 07:30) GROUP F
38. NIGERIA v ENGLAND (Osaka, 07:30) GROUP F
39. SOUTH AFRICA v SPAIN (Daejeon, 12:30) GROUP B
40. SLOVENIA v PARAGUAY (Seogwipo, 12:30) GROUP B

THURSDAY 13 JUNE
41. COSTA RICA v BRAZIL (Suwon, 07:30) GROUP C
42. TURKEY v CHINA (Seoul, 07:30) GROUP C
43. MEXICO v ITALY (Oita, 12:30) GROUP G
44. ECUADOR v CROATIA (Yokohama, 12:30) GROUP G

WORLD CUP SCHEDULE

FRIDAY 14 JUNE
45. TUNISIA v JAPAN (Osaka, 07:30) GROUP H
46. BELGIUM v RUSSIA (Shizuoka, 07:30) GROUP H
47. PORTUGAL v SOUTH KOREA (Incheon, 12:30) GROUP D
48. POLAND v USA (Daejeon, 12:30) GROUP D

SECOND ROUND

SATURDAY 15 JUNE
49. WINNER E v RUNNER-UP B (Seogwipo, 07:30)
50. WINNER A v RUNNER-UP F (Niigata, 12:30)

SUNDAY 16 JUNE
51. WINNER F v RUNNER-UP A (Oita, 07:30)
52. WINNER B v RUNNER-UP E (Suwon, 12:30)

MONDAY 17 JUNE
53. WINNER G v RUNNER-UP D (Jeonju, 07:30)
54. WINNER C v RUNNER-UP H (Kobe, 12:30)

TUESDAY 18 JUNE
55. WINNER H v RUNNER-UP C (Miyagi, 07:30)
56. WINNER D v RUNNER-UP G (Daejeon, 12:30)

QUARTER-FINALS

FRIDAY 21 JUNE
57. WINNER 50 v WINNER 54 (Shizuoka, 07:30)
58. WINNER 49 v WINNER 53 (Ulsan, 12:30)

SATURDAY 22 JUNE
59. WINNER 52 v WINNER 56 (Gwangju, 07:30)
60. WINNER 51 v WINNER 55 (Osaka, 12:30)

SEMI-FINALS

TUESDAY 25 JUNE
61. WINNER 58 v WINNER 59 (Seoul, 12:30)

WEDNESDAY 26 JUNE
62. WINNER 57 v WINNER 60 (Saitama, 12:30)

3rd/4th PLAY-OFF

SATURDAY 29 JUNE
63. LOSER 61 v LOSER 62 (Daegu, 12:00)

WORLD CUP FINAL

SUNDAY 30 JUNE
64. WINNER 61 v WINNER 62 (Yokohama, 12:00)

TOURNAMENT RULES

The World Cup comprises 32 teams for the second time after the tournament was expanded from the 24 teams that took part in USA '94 to 32 teams for the first time at France '98. The finalists are split into eight qualifying sections of four, with the top two progressing to the knockout second round. If two or more teams finish equal on points after all the group matches have been played, the following criteria shall be applied to determine the ranking:

A) goal difference in all the group matches

B) greater number of goals scored in all the group matches

C) if two or more teams are equal on the basis of (a) and (b) above, their place in the final standings will be determined as follows:

D) greater number of points obtained in the group matches between the teams concerned

E) goal difference resulting from the group matches between the teams concerned

F) greater number of goals scored in the group matches between the teams concerned

G) drawing lots by the World Cup Organising Committee

THE WINNERS AND RUNNERS-UP IN EACH GROUP THEN PLAY THE SECOND ROUND OVER ONE MATCH AS FOLLOWS:

1. 1st Group E v 2nd Group B   Seogwipo June 15
2. 1st Group A v 2nd Group F   Niigata June 15
3. 1st Group F v 2nd Group A   Oita June 16
4. 1st Group B v 2nd Group E   Suwon June 16
5. 1st Group G v 2nd Group D   Jeonju June 17
6. 1st Group C v 2nd Group H   Kobe June 17
7. 1st Group H v 2nd Group C   Miyagi June 18
8. 1st Group D v 2nd Group G   Daejeon June 18

THE QUARTER-FINALS:

A. Winners 2 v Winners 6   Shizuoka June 21
B. Winners 1 v Winners 5   Ulsan June 21
C. Winners 4 v Winners 8   Gwangju June 22
D. Winners 3 v Winners 7   Osaka June 22

THE SEMI-FINALS:

Winners B v Winners C   Seoul June 25
Winners A v Winners D   Saitama June 26

THIRD PLACE PLAY-OFF   Daegu June 29
WORLD CUP FINAL   Yokohama June 30

EXTRA TIME, GOLDEN GOAL AND PENALTIES:

If any match from the second round to the final is level after the end of 90 minutes then extra time will be played – decided by a Golden Goal if it is scored within the extra 30 minutes of playing time. If no Golden Goal produces a winner then matches will be decided on penalties.

SUBSTITUTES:

For the first time at this World Cup, all the squad players – 23 per team – can be named on the starting line-up for every match, so the starting line-up will comprise 11 selected players and 12 substitutes. FIFA have ruled that up to a maximum of three of the 12 substitutes can be used during the match in the usual way.

BETTING GUIDE

by angus loughran

Bookmakers were unanimous that this year's Grand National was the biggest they have ever experienced in the shops. This summer sees the first World Cup of the tax-free era and it also promises to eclipse all previous records.

The kick-off times are not as bad as layers first feared, with the majority of big matches starting at lunchtime rather than 7.30am. This will mean more television viewers and, of course, more bets. It also means UK bookmakers will have the chance to revise their outright prices in the afternoon in response to the morning's results.

There is not going to be the same explosion as there will be in Germany in 2006 when the kick-off times will be primetime, but this World Cup still offers the football punter more choice than he has ever had before.

As well as traditional high-street bookmakers such as Coral, fixed odds punters can also look to burgeoning telephone and internet-based operations such as Victor Chandler and Bet Direct.

Furthermore, the advent of spread betting and, more recently internet betting exchanges, gives the punter the chance to either back or lay.

PREVIEW

BETTING EXCHANGES

This will be the first major football tournament for exchanges like Betfair and Betdaq and they are expecting a huge amount of business, particularly as they will offer in-running person-to-person betting on all matches.

Exchanges have revolutionised fixed odds betting as you can now act as the bookmaker as well as the punter.

The Premiership match between Derby County and Manchester United in March saw Betfair's record amount exchanged on football with £814,796 worth of matched bets. This 2-2 draw was a particularly thrilling encounter which demonstrates the correlation between excitement and turnover.

But prestige of the occasion also plays a factor and the company's biggest-ever international game so far was Holland versus England in February where around £682,000 was staked on the game. Such records are almost certain to be eclipsed during the World Cup and it is odds-on that the tournament will witness a game with more than a million pounds of matched bets at Betfair.

The exchanges offer a wide range of markets – not just the outright result but others such as number of corners, next goal and correct score – and they are open 24 hours a day.

SPREAD BETTING

Spread betting has been around for a lot longer than the exchanges and is similar in so far as you can be for or against an outcome.

With markets based on the principles of the stock market rather than fractional odds, firms like Cantor Sport offer potentially huge returns if your instincts are correct.

For example, England winning a match by four or five goals would hit the spread firms hard as patriotic punters would win more money every time England scored.

Spread firms also offer more quirky markets on such things as the number of bookings in a match. These are likely to see heavy activity during the summer with punters constantly scrutinising the idiosyncrasies of referees.

But a word of warning, going the wrong way on a spread can leave you seriously out of pocket, so consider your bets carefully.

OUTRIGHT

Despite all the recent innovations in the gambling industry, straightforward fixed-odds betting with bookmakers remains the most popular medium.

The arrival of several new players on the scene in the last few years has greatly increased competition among bookmakers which in turn is great news for punters.

For whatever bet you choose to make, be sure to shop around for the best value in the market place. Odds comparison websites like easyodds.com should be your first port of call as they do the legwork by showing you where to find the best prices.

For this World Cup, the two obvious favourites are France and Argentina. However, the way in which the draw has panned out means the value could lie elsewhere.

PREVIEW

Argentina are saddled with the demanding Group F and they are by no means guaranteed to finish in top spot. Second place would mean a last-16 meeting with France who are shoe-ins for Group A. I would rather take the likely 5-2 on the winner of that game than the 9-2 available on either beforehand.

The next hurdle for France, or whoever comes through that part of the draw, would probably be an eye-catching quarter-final with Brazil. Don't underestimate the 1994 winners who struggled in qualifying but can still boast stars like Rivaldo and Ronaldo.

From the remainder, Italy must be considered particularly given their favourable route through to the quarter-finals, although anyone following the Azzurri must be praying they avoid a penalty shoot-out as spot-kicks have been their downfall in the past three World Cups. However, Roberto Baggio, who missed the vital penalty in the 1994 final, has not been included in their squad.

Of the other Europeans, Germany should never be discounted in major tournaments and look good each-way value. Portugal and Spain are perennial under-achievers in World Cups so for a dark horse I will be backing Poland who qualified impressively and have a respectable draw despite their poor showing in friendlies so far this year.

England have drifted due to injury concerns over captain David Beckham, but in my view their chances hinge almost entirely on the opening group game against Sweden. If England triumph, and go on to finish top of the group, then I believe they have a superb opportunity of winning the World Cup.

Second place, however, would mean France in the last 16 and they would be second favourites for that heavyweight clash. For this reason Sven-Göran Eriksson's side have a larger carrot than most dangling over them in the first round.

The Republic of Ireland's crunch game is against Cameroon, a match which will almost certainly decide who joins Germany as second-round qualifiers from Group E. The Lions will be no pushovers for Mick McCarthy's men as they look by far the best African qualifiers.

The top Asian team by some way looks like being Japan. The co-hosts are a neat, well-organised side for whom a semi-final place is by no means impossible. Their recent friendly victory in Poland finally made a few experts sit up and take notice. Hidetoshi Nakata is a key player and he will have a football-mad nation's expectations resting heavily on his shoulders.

Don't be afraid of backing outsiders at big prices. Most bookmakers offer each-way terms of half odds for reaching the final, but if you hunt around some layers will offer a fifth of the odds for a semi-final place. Croatia, who reached the semi-finals in 1998 at massive pre-tournament odds, and Bulgaria, who managed the same feat four years earlier, would have rewarded each-way bandits taking such terms.

All the ingredients are in place for this to be a World Cup of shocks so do not discount the chances of teams like Japan, Cameroon and Poland making a serious impression on some of the more established footballing nations.

There are, however, some countries whose long odds genuinely reflect their prospects. Tunisia, for example, look to have little chance on improving on their poor record in World Cup finals and are one of four teams to oppose in first-round matches. The others are China, Nigeria and South Africa.

PREVIEW

TOP GOALSCORER

Poland's Nigerian-born striker Emmanuel Olisadebe has already been backed in from 80-1 to 40-1 to be the tournament's top goalscorer which remains a big price in my view.

The speedy Panathinaikos forward caught the eye with some outstanding displays in this season's Champions League.

Of the more fancied hotshots, France's David Trezeguet, the hero of their Euro 2000 triumph, at 12-1 looks a better bet than strike partner Thierry Henry to win the Golden Boot. Brazil's Ronaldo is finally returning to form after his injury nightmare and looks tremendous value at 16-1 to win the Golden Boot, while Sweden's prolific Henrik Larsson looks over-priced at 66-1 with Victor Chandler.

WORLD CUP TRENDS

The opening game of the World Cup has been a source of upsets in the past. Bulgaria held Italy to a 1-1 draw in 1986 and who can forget Cameroon's magnificent defeat of Argentina in 1990.

This year France kick off the defence of their crown against Senegal in what will be the biggest game in the African side's history. It is possible that the former colony will field a side filled entirely with players who ply their trade in the French league. They will not go short on motivation or perspiration and a draw is not totally out of the question.

Indeed draws are the order of the day in the early stages of the World Cup as fear of losing the first match often dictates tactics. Fans of course want see to goals but there is a danger in betting with your heart rather than your head in the first round. History shows that the fear factor often prevails with low-scoring, tight matches featuring far more frequently than you would expect on an average Premiership weekend.

England winning the World Cup would be a disaster for bookmakers but a good run from Sven-Göran Eriksson's side could reap its own rewards.

Italia 90 was a gold mine for layers despite England's relative success in reaching the semi-finals. In setting up their epic showdown with Germany, England only won one game in 90 minutes and that was their group game against Egypt with the other two group games against Holland and Ireland ending in draws. Once they had progressed to the knock-out stage all their matches went to extra-time (Belgium – last 16, Cameroon – quarter-final and Germany – semi-final) with those who backed the draw cleaning up every time.

It's no wonder the layers look forward to the World Cup as so many of the big matches seem to go to extra time. Famous examples include the 1998 semi-final between Holland and Brazil and 1994 final when Brazil met Italy. Both games were settled by penalty shoot-outs.

However, the number of penalty shoot-outs is diminishing due to the advent of the "golden goal" in 1998 which means only one goal can be scored in extra time, so be wary of this when considering penalty specials.

PREVIEW

It would nevertheless be a mistake to assume that only the prestigious matches attract significant betting interest at World Cups.

In 1994 there was a colossal gamble on Cameroon to beat Russia. It started on the morning of the game and continued right up until kick-off time. It was one of the first times that bookmakers could be found running for cover in football betting as the size and scale of the bets taken were far greater than anything they had seen before.

Russia had started the match as favourites but before long Cameroon's price had collapsed and they were odds-on. Spread firms turned around two goals from their original match supremacy quotes. There was no let-up in the flood of money for the Africans as punters assumed the Russians, with nothing to play for, would lose the game.

It was the biggest plunge in the history of world football with much of the money coming from the Far East.

By some strange quirk I was the commentator for the only live coverage of the game – on Eurosport – and was well aware of the betting implications. It turned out to be the mother of all bloodbaths for punters as Oleg Salenko grabbed five goals in a 6-1 win for Russia.

Had Cameroon won the match, there is no doubt the cries of fix would have been made through the bookmakers' grapevines, but as the result was such a massive one for them there was very little said about it. In general, layers tend to keep very quiet when they clean up, you only hear them scream when they lose.

The same 1994 tournament saw gambling associated with one of the lowest moments in World Cup history, the murder of Andres Escobar. The defender's death was linked to Colombian gamblers who had lost their money following his own goal against the United States.

Mercifully, this was a one-off and, although Escobar will never be forgotten, it would be folly to suggest that it was anything more than a freak incident.

The players perhaps do not realise the sheer weight of money that is resting on their performances which is probably just as well. But the bookmakers are fully aware of the financial implications and are preparing for a betting bonanza at the first Asian World Cup.

Victor Chandler International are likely to see more business than most on the Asian side. Their Gibraltar-based telephone operation has always had a separate Asian facility and the company has been meticulously planning for this event ever since the venue was first announced.

British punters have missed Victor Chandler himself at UK racecourses, but football gamblers, particularly in Asia, will regard his firm as one of the leading players.

The World Cup takes place once every four years. It is a special event with unique global appeal and the 2002 tournament will undoubtedly take football betting to new levels. The bookmakers are ready, the punters are ready, so let the games begin.

HENRY WINTER

A personal view on the prospects for England and the Republic of Ireland from Henry Winter, Daily Telegraph Football Correspondent

ENGLAND

The Three Lions have proved more domesticated tabby-cats than feared predators in recent tournaments but that may be about to change. England possess a golden generation of young players, good enough to win a World Cup or European Championship in the next five years. Just cast your eye down the team-sheet, look at the celebrated names and revel in the qualities of class acts like the smooth interceptor Rio Ferdinand, the all-action Steven Gerrard, the deft Paul Scholes and darting Kieron Dyer – all their productive ball-work focused on freeing the flying Michael Owen.

If Sven-Göran Eriksson, England's alchemist-in-chief, has his main men fit, and particularly the recuperating David Beckham, then the national side could escape the most perilous-looking group at the World Cup. Sweden seem a hard-fought, Derby-style draw while against Argentina anything can happen and probably will (from diving to dismissals and sensational goals, all set against a deafening backdrop). Nigeria, though, are definitely beatable. Eriksson's unflappability will soothe any fevered brows in the dressing-room. So will his ability to respond cannily to a game's shifting currents with tactical switches or substitutions. England's 4-4-2 against Sweden will change into 4-3-3 with a more compact central midfield against Juan Sebastian Veron and Argentina. Eriksson has the nous, the players have the talent and belief, but this World Cup may eventually prove only a useful learning experience for a real tilt at 2006. The Three Lions' claws will be fully sharpened for a World Cup on German soil.

REPUBLIC OF IRELAND

The Irish love taking a punt on promising thoroughbreds and more than a few Guinness-stained Euros will be laid on the green-liveried dark horses of the World Cup. Inspired by one of football's good guys, Mick McCarthy's talented young Republic of Ireland side are overflowing with confidence, having humiliated the star-studded Dutch in qualifying, done well against Luis Figo and the technical wizards of Portugal and survived a potentially awkward play-off in Iran. Any team captained by Roy Keane, the most influential footballer in the Premiership, has to be respected. Ireland will be driven on by the experience of Keane and the enthusiasm of a crop of lively tyros. Damien Duff could prove one of the stars of Korea and Japan; defenders unfamiliar with Blackburn Rovers' exciting winger could get caught out by his skill and high-speed sense of adventure. Because of his pace and control, Duff may be best used through the middle, running at centre-halves like Michael Owen did so spectacularly at France '98.

Jason McAteer, Matt Holland and Robbie Keane are all nimble internationals while in Shay Given Ireland have one of the most agile and capable goalkeepers in the world. Given may be small but he leaps around like Fabien Barthez, who has a World Cup to his name. The jolly green army of Irish fans will make friends and drinking partners wherever they travel. Long may they stay in the Orient.

WORLD CUP OUTRIGHT

	Eurobet	Victor Chandler	Littlewoods	William Hill	Ladbrokes	totalbet
ARGENTINA	9/2	9/2	9/2	4/1	7/2	4/1
FRANCE	4/1	4/1	4/1	4/1	4/1	7/2
ITALY	6/1	6/1	11/2	5/1	6/1	11/2
BRAZIL	6/1	13/2	7/1	13/2	13/2	15/2
SPAIN	10/1	8/1	10/1	6/1	9/1	9/1
ENGLAND	10/1	9/1	9/1	10/1	9/1	10/1
PORTUGAL	12/1	11/1	12/1	12/1	12/1	12/1
GERMANY	14/1	14/1	12/1	12/1	14/1	16/1
CAMEROON	40/1	50/1	50/1	40/1	40/1	50/1
POLAND	33/1	40/1	66/1	66/1	80/1	40/1
RUSSIA	40/1	50/1	50/1	66/1	33/1	50/1
CROATIA	40/1	40/1	66/1	80/1	50/1	50/1
PARAGUAY	33/1	50/1	66/1	80/1	66/1	50/1
REPUBLIC OF IRELAND	66/1	80/1	66/1	80/1	66/1	66/1
SWEDEN	80/1	50/1	66/1	80/1	50/1	66/1
BELGIUM	66/1	66/1	80/1	100/1	80/1	66/1
JAPAN	66/1	50/1	66/1	80/1	66/1	80/1
NIGERIA	66/1	50/1	100/1	100/1	50/1	100/1
TURKEY	66/1	66/1	50/1	80/1	50/1	66/1
URUGUAY	66/1	50/1	80/1	100/1	50/1	66/1
DENMARK	80/1	66/1	80/1	125/1	80/1	100/1
ECUADOR	66/1	100/1	150/1	100/1	100/1	125/1
MEXICO	125/1	80/1	125/1	150/1	100/1	100/1
KOREA	150/1	100/1	200/1	150/1	125/1	150/1
COSTA RICA	125/1	150/1	300/1	300/1	200/1	175/1
SENEGAL	200/1	250/1	150/1	150/1	100/1	150/1
SLOVENIA	80/1	100/1	150/1	300/1	100/1	125/1
USA	125/1	100/1	300/1	300/1	150/1	150/1
SOUTH AFRICA	100/1	150/1	250/1	500/1	200/1	200/1
TUNISIA	150/1	125/1	300/1	500/1	200/1	200/1
CHINA	200/1	300/1	300/1	750/1	350/1	350/1
SAUDI ARABIA	200/1	250/1	250/1	750/1	250/1	350/1

BETTING GUIDE

EACH-WAY 1,2 1/2 ODDS
PRICES CORRECT AS OF MAY 2.

Sporting Odds	Sportingbet	UKbetting	Blue Square	Betabet	sports.com	bet365	bet internet
7/2	4/1	9/2	4/1	4/1	7/2	4/1	4/1
4/1	4/1	4/1	4/1	4/1	4/1	4/1	4/1
6/1	6/1	11/2	6/1	6/1	6/1	6/1	6/1
6/1	13/2	13/2	7/1	7/1	15/2	9/2	13/2
10/1	8/1	7/1	8/1	9/1	9/1	10/1	10/1
12/1	12/1	10/1	10/1	11/1	12/1	10/1	12/1
12/1	10/1	12/1	12/1	12/1	12/1	14/1	12/1
14/1	14/1	16/1	14/1	12/1	14/1	16/1	16/1
66/1	40/1	50/1	40/1	50/1	50/1	40/1	50/1
66/1	50/1	40/1	50/1	50/1	66/1	66/1	66/1
66/1	50/1	66/1	66/1	50/1	50/1	40/1	66/1
80/1	40/1	66/1	66/1	66/1	50/1	66/1	66/1
66/1	40/1	50/1	66/1	66/1	50/1	50/1	66/1
80/1	66/1	80/1	66/1	80/1	80/1	66/1	80/1
80/1	80/1	80/1	50/1	66/1	50/1	66/1	80/1
100/1	66/1	100/1	80/1	80/1	100/1	80/1	100/1
66/1	66/1	50/1	50/1	66/1	100/1	66/1	66/1
100/1	80/1	80/1	100/1	66/1	66/1	80/1	66/1
100/1	50/1	100/1	80/1	66/1	100/1	80/1	80/1
66/1	66/1	50/1	50/1	66/1	66/1	66/1	50/1
100/1	80/1	80/1	80/1	100/1	80/1	100/1	100/1
100/1	100/1	100/1	100/1	100/1	100/1	100/1	100/1
150/1	125/1	125/1	100/1	125/1	125/1	100/1	125/1
150/1	125/1	100/1	200/1	125/1	150/1	125/1	125/1
300/1	150/1	250/1	200/1	200/1	300/1	250/1	200/1
250/1	150/1	300/1	125/1	250/1	200/1	100/1	125/1
150/1	125/1	200/1	125/1	150/1	150/1	250/1	150/1
200/1	125/1	200/1	125/1	150/1	166/1	250/1	200/1
250/1	150/1	200/1	250/1	150/1	125/1	250/1	200/1
300/1	200/1	150/1	300/1	200/1	300/1	500/1	250/1
500/1	300/1	250/1	500/1	300/1	500/1	500/1	350/1
500/1	300/1	200/1	500/1	300/1	500/1	500/1	250/1

TOP SCORER

PRICES CORRECT AS OF MAY 2

	Eurobet	Victor Chandler	William Hill	Sporting Odds	Betabet	sports.com	bet365	netbet
T. HENRY	10/1	10/1	10/1	10/1	10/1	11/1	9/1	9/1
C. VIERI	11/1	10/1	9/1	12/1	12/1	12/1	11/1	12/1
D. TREZEGUET	9/1	9/1	10/1	10/1	12/1	11/1	12/1	10/1
H. CRESPO	12/1	10/1	12/1	8/1	11/1	12/1	12/1	10/1
RAUL	12/1	12/1	12/1	10/1	12/1	12/1	14/1	10/1
M. OWEN	12/1	16/1	10/1	14/1	12/1	16/1	11/1	12/1
RONALDO	16/1	12/1	16/1	14/1	14/1	16/1	10/1	14/1
F. MORIENTES	20/1	12/1	14/1	14/1	20/1	20/1	16/1	16/1
G. BATISTUTA	16/1	20/1	16/1	10/1	14/1	12/1	16/1	16/1
RIVALDO	20/1	16/1	14/1	12/1	14/1	16/1	14/1	14/1
C. LOPEZ	25/1	-	-	18/1	-	20/1	16/1	16/1
A. DEL PIERO	28/1	-	28/1	25/1	-	25/1	20/1	22/1
D. TRISTAN	20/1	-	-	28/1	-	33/1	28/1	-
F. INZAGHI	22/1	25/1	33/1	18/1	25/1	25/1	16/1	25/1
F. TOTTI	33/1	33/1	33/1	25/1	28/1	33/1	28/1	25/1
G. ELBER	25/1	25/1	33/1	16/1	20/1	25/1	20/1	25/1
V. MONTELLA	-	-	33/1	16/1	-	-	20/1	25/1
J. SAVIOLA	33/1	40/1	28/1	25/1	25/1	40/1	40/1	28/1
M. BALLACK	-	-	40/1	-	50/1	-	-	-
N. ANELKA	-	-	40/1	-	33/1	-	-	33/1
N. GOMES	40/1	40/1	20/1	25/1	25/1	33/1	25/1	20/1
PAULETA	28/1	40/1	20/1	33/1	28/1	25/1	25/1	-
RONALDINHO	-	-	40/1	-	-	-	-	-
A. ORTEGA	-	-	50/1	50/1	40/1	-	40/1	-
E. OLISADEBE	40/1	40/1	40/1	50/1	40/1	40/1	40/1	40/1
J. MORENO	-	-	50/1	-	-	-	-	-
O. NEUVILLE	40/1	40/1	40/1	40/1	40/1	50/1	40/1	33/1
ROMARIO	-	-	-	33/1	40/1	50/1	-	40/1
EDILSON	-	-	33/1	33/1	50/1	-	-	50/1
H. LARSSON	50/1	66/1	40/1	40/1	50/1	-	66/1	50/1
O. BIERHOFF	-	-	50/1	40/1	40/1	66/1	40/1	50/1
P. WANCHOPE	-	-	50/1	-	-	66/1	50/1	-
R. FOWLER	-	50/1	66/1	-	-	-	-	-
Z. ZIDANE	-	33/1	33/1	33/1	50/1	66/1	-	50/1
A. RECOBA	-	-	66/1	40/1	33/1	33/1	-	25/1
C. JANCKER	-	-	66/1	66/1	66/1	80/1	-	-
D. BECKHAM	-	-	50/1	50/1	40/1	80/1	50/1	-
H. SUKUR	50/1	-	-	66/1	-	80/1	66/1	50/1

GROUP BETTING

GROUP A

	Eurobet	Bet Direct	Victor Chandler	William Hill	Ladbrokes	totalbet	Sporting Odds	Sportingbet	UK Bet	Blue Square	betabet	sports.com	bet365	betinternet
FRANCE	1/3	1/4	2/9	2/7	1/4	1/4	1/4	2/9	3/10	2/7	1/5	3/10	1/3	1/4
URUGUAY	9/2	6/1	13/2	13/2	13/2	11/2	6/1	13/2	4/1	5/1	6/1	6/1	5/1	6/1
DENMARK	13/2	7/1	7/1	7/1	7/1	13/2	6/1	15/2	8/1	8/1	8/1	13/2	7/1	7/1
SENEGAL	16/1	20/1	20/1	10/1	20/1	20/1	20/1	22/1	25/1	14/1	25/1	22/1	12/1	25/1

Even without injured playmaker Robert Pires, World Cup co-favourites France should win this group at a canter. Senegal has strong historical and cultural links with France and the emotion surrounding the opening game could make for a surprising result. But the French have too much class for Denmark – a pale shadow of the side that won the 1992 European Championships – and Uruguay, who needed to beat Australia in a play-off to qualify. They are likely to fight out second spot.

GROUP B

	Eurobet	Bet Direct	Victor Chandler	William Hill	Ladbrokes	totalbet	Sporting Odds	Sportingbet	UK Bet	Blue Square	betabet	sports.com	bet365	betinternet
SPAIN	8/15	4/9	4/9	2/5	1/2	8/15	8/15	4/9	8/15	4/9	4/11	1/2	4/9	2/5
PARAGUAY	4/1	4/1	4/1	7/2	4/1	7/2	4/1	4/1	7/2	4/1	4/1	9/2	7/2	4/1
SLOVENIA	15/2	13/2	7/1	9/1	6/1	11/2	6/1	13/2	8/1	13/2	9/1	7/1	8/1	8/1
S. AFRICA	8/1	10/1	8/1	10/1	10/1	8/1	13/2	10/1	10/1	9/1	10/1	8/1	8/1	10/1

At every World Cup, Spain always seem to be everyone's dark horse and at every World Cup the same happens, bitter disappointment. This year however they have a fantastic draw and there will be no excuses for not cruising through this group. Slovenia are just happy to have reached their first finals, Paraguay are not a side to fear if their 4-0 defeat by England in April is anything to go by and South Africa lack flair and make little appeal and look a good bet to prop up the group.

GROUP C

	Eurobet	Bet Direct	Victor Chandler	William Hill	Ladbrokes	totalbet	Sporting Odds	Sportingbet	UK Bet	Blue Square	betabet	sports.com	bet365	betinternet
BRAZIL	1/2	2/7	4/11	3/10	4/11	4/11	3/10	2/7	1/4	1/3	1/4	4/11	1/4	2/7
TURKEY	9/2	4/1	7/2	7/2	7/2	4/1	4/1	9/2	9/2	7/2	4/1	4/1	9/2	9/2
COSTA RICA	10/1	9/1	13/2	11/1	7/1	6/1	8/1	8/1	10/1	9/1	9/1	8/1	10/1	9/1
CHINA	20/1	25/1	25/1	20/1	22/1	16/1	20/1	20/1	20/1	20/1	33/1	22/1	16/1	20/1

It would be unwise to write off Brazil despite the fact that they lost six matches in qualifying. Rivaldo of Barcelona is the key, but a settled side from those that make the final squad is even more important. Costa Rica, inspired by the maverick skills of Paolo Wanchope, could pose a few problems, but are unlikely to have the consistency to win the group. Turkey are likely to prove the main danger although their club sides have not been in great form in Europe this season. China will just be happy to win one match. It's Brazil with either Turkey or Costa Rica for the last 16.

GROUP D

	Eurobet	Bet Direct	Victor Chandler	William Hill	Ladbrokes	totalbet	Sporting Odds	Sportingbet	UK Bet	Blue Square	betabet	sports.com	bet365	betinternet
PORTUGAL	4/7	1/2	4/7	8/15	8/15	8/15	1/2	8/15	8/15	1/2	1/2	4/7	8/15	1/2
POLAND	5/2	10/3	11/4	3/1	11/4	3/1	7/2	11/4	7/2	3/1	3/1	3/1	7/2	10/3
KOREA	9/1	15/2	7/1	6/1	13/2	8/1	7/1	8/1	7/1	8/1	7/1	7/1	6/1	15/2
USA	9/1	9/1	9/1	11/1	8/1	8/1	8/1	10/1	11/1	9/1	11/1	10/1	9/1	10/1

This looks like a two-horse race between Portugal and Poland with Korea and the United States battling it out to avoid the wooden spoon. The Portuguese come into the tournament with a big reputation following their bold showing in Euro 2000, yet they have disappointed in past World Cups and are no value at 4-7. Poland look a decent alternative. They qualified with ease and in striker Emmanuel Olisadebe and goalkeeper Jerzy Dudek they could have two of the stars of the tournament.

BETTING GUIDE

GROUP E

	Eurobet	Bet Direct	Victor Chandler	William Hill	Ladbrokes	totalbet	Sporting Odds	Sportingbet	UK Bet	Blue Square	betabet	sports.com	bet365	betinternet
GERMANY	8/13	8/11	4/6	4/5	4/5	8/11	8/11	8/11	8/13	4/5	4/6	8/11	8/13	4/6
CAMEROON	10/3	3/1	10/3	12/5	11/4	3/1	11/4	3/1	7/2	11/4	3/1	3/1	10/3	10/3
REP. IRELAND	4/1	7/2	7/2	7/2	7/2	3/1	7/2	7/2	3/1	10/3	10/3	4/1	7/2	7/2
S. ARABIA	14/1	16/1	12/1	18/1	12/1	20/1	14/1	14/1	20/1	14/1	20/1	16/1	16/1	20/1

A formidable World Cup record makes Germany the obvious group favourites, yet in home defeats by England and more recently Argentina they have shown uncharacteristic signs of weakness. Both Cameroon and Ireland look well-placed to take advantage. The Lions won the African Nations Cup and could be their continent's best hope of real progress. Mick McCarthy'side are responsible for Holland's absence from the finals and, provided Roy Keane is fit, are the narrow selection simply because they are the better price.

GROUP F

	Eurobet	Bet Direct	Victor Chandler	William Hill	Ladbrokes	totalbet	Sporting Odds	Sportingbet	UK Bet	Blue Square	betabet	sports.com	bet365	betinternet
ARGENTINA	8/11	4/5	4/5	8/11	8/11	8/11	8/11	7/10	4/6	4/5	8/11	8/11	4/6	3/4
ENGLAND	2/1	9/4	2/1	5/2	9/4	5/2	5/2	5/2	5/2	9/4	9/4	13/5	5/2	9/4
NIGERIA	8/1	8/1	13/2	7/1	8/1	6/1	7/1	8/1	17/2	15/2	8/1	15/2	8/1	8/1
SWEDEN	9/1	6/1	17/2	13/2	7/1	15/2	13/2	7/1	6/1	6/1	7/1	15/2	7/1	15/2

With an array of stars plying their trade at top European clubs, Argentina will be hard to beat and should go far. For England everything hinges on the first game against Sweden and it may be best to wait for that result before betting. If England win, I can see them going on to take the group thereby avoiding France in the last 16. Defeat and the section is Argentina's leaving Sven Goran Eriksson's men hoping for Swedish slip-ups to help them qualify. The Nigerian squad is in disarray and they look bankers for an early exit but how the other three will fare is anyone's bet.

BETTING GUIDE

GROUP G

	Eurobet	Bet Direct	Victor Chandler	William Hill	Ladbrokes	totalbet	Sporting Odds	Sportingbet	UK Bet	Blue Square	betabet	sports.com	bet365	betinternet
ITALY	4/9	2/5	4/11	4/9	4/11	1/2	2/5	4/11	1/2	4/9	2/5	4/9	4/7	2/5
CROATIA	9/2	5/1	11/2	5/1	9/2	7/2	4/1	9/2	11/2	9/2	5/1	5/1	4/1	5/1
MEXICO	8/1	8/1	13/2	7/1	8/1	13/2	8/1	8/1	7/1	7/1	15/2	7/1	9/2	7/1
ECUADOR	13/2	7/1	9/1	6/1	9/1	8/1	10/1	10/1	13/2	7/1	7/1	8/1	8/1	9/1

Italy are looking for their fourth World Cup and will never have a better chance. The Azzurri are notoriously slow starters in major tournaments but even they will struggle to avoid a flyer with this group. Croatia are a team of veterans who lack the staying power to emulate their superb semi-final place four years ago. Mexico were lucky to qualify and pose little threat. Ecuador could be the best of the rest as they finished second in the ten-team South American qualifying group.

GROUP H

	Eurobet	Bet Direct	Victor Chandler	William Hill	Ladbrokes	totalbet	Sporting Odds	Sportingbet	UK Bet	Blue Square	betabet	sports.com	bet365	betinternet
RUSSIA	7/4	13/8	2/1	15/8	2/1	7/4	2/1	15/8	2/1	2/1	9/5	2/1	13/8	15/8
JAPAN	11/5	2/1	2/1	2/1	11/5	5/2	7/4	2/1	2/1	7/4	2/1	2/1	7/4	2/1
BELGIUM	11/5	5/2	9/4	2/1	9/4	9/4	9/4	9/4	11/5	9/4	9/4	5/2	11/4	9/4
TUNISIA	7/1	15/2	11/2	8/1	5/1	5/1	8/1	7/1	7/1	7/1	7/1	6/1	15/2	7/1

The most open betting heat of the lot. If you discount outsiders Tunisia, a case can be made for each of the remaining three sides. Japan recorded a highly impressive victory over Poland in March and, roared on by fanatical support, certainly have players capable of causing a few upsets. Belgium are a steady, unadventurous side who will nevertheless prove difficult to beat. However, the vote goes to Russia who don't lose many and could go a lot further than their pre-tournament odds suggest.

BETTING GUIDE

FIRST ROUND MATCHES

PRICES CORRECT AS OF MAY 2

| TO WIN | | | | TO DRAW | | | | TO WIN | | |
Coral	Bet Direct	Victor Chandler		Coral	Bet Direct	Victor Chandler		Coral	Bet Direct	Victor Chandler
			FRIDAY 31ST MAY 2002							
2-9	2-9	1-4	FRANCE	4-1	7-2	4-1	SENEGAL	8-1	15-2	7-1
			SATURDAY 1ST JUNE 2002							
13-8	11-8	13-8	REP OF IRE	15-8	15-8	15-8	CAMEROON	6-4	15-8	6-4
6-5	13-8	5-4	URUGUAY	2-1	15-8	15-8	DENMARK	2-1	15-8	2-1
2-7	2-9	3-10	GERMANY	10-3	7-2	3-1	SAUDI ARABIA	15-2	15-2	17-2
			SUNDAY 2ND JUNE 2002							
4-9	1-2	8-15	ARGENTINA	5-2	9-4	12-5	NIGERIA	11-2	11-2	9-2
4-5	4-5	5-6	PARAGUAY	2-1	2-1	2-1	SOUTH AFRICA	10-3	10-3	3-1
10-11	EV	EV	ENGLAND	11-5	15-8	15-8	SWEDEN	5-2	11-4	13-5
2-5	2-5	4-9	SPAIN	11-4	5-2	13-5	SLOVENIA	6-1	13-2	11-2
			MONDAY 3RD JUNE 2002							
EV	6-5	11-10	CROATIA	2-1	7-4	2-1	MEXICO	12-5	11-5	11-5
4-9	4-7	1-2	BRAZIL	5-2	11-5	9-4	TURKEY	11-2	5-1	11-2
2-5	1-2	4-9	ITALY	11-4	11-4	12-5	ECUADOR	6-1	6-1	6-1
			TUESDAY 4TH JUNE 2002							
11-5	11-5	12-5	CHINA	11-5	2-1	2-1	COSTA RICA	EV	11-10	EV
8-5	8-5	6-4	JAPAN	9-5	9-5	15-8	BELGIUM	8-5	9-5	13-8
12-5	2-1	11-10	SOUTH KOREA	9-4	3-1	2-1	POLAND	11-10	6-5	11-5
			WEDNESDAY 5TH JUNE 2002							
8-13	8-13	8-13	RUSSIA	9-4	11-5	9-4	TUNISIA	4-1	7-2	4-1
11-2	6-1	13-2	USA	5-2	5-2	13-5	PORTUGAL	4-9	1-2	2-5
4-6	-	8-11	GERMANY	9-4	-	11-5	REP OF IRELAND	7-2	-	10-3
			THURSDAY 6TH JUNE 2002							
10-11	-	EV	DENMARK	11-5	-	2-1	SENEGAL	5-2	-	12-5
8-15	-	4-7	CAMEROON	12-5	-	9-4	SAUDI ARABIA	9-2	-	9-2
4-9	-	1-2	FRANCE	5-2	-	9-4	URUGUAY	11-2	-	11-2

BETTING GUIDE

TO WIN				TO DRAW				TO WIN		
Coral	Bet Direct	Victor Chandler		Coral	Bet Direct	Victor Chandler		Coral	Bet Direct	Victor Chandler
FRIDAY 7TH JUNE 2002										
6-4	-	6-4	SWEDEN	15-8	-	15-8	NIGERIA	13-8	-	13-8
4-6	-	4-6	SPAIN	9-4	-	9-4	PARAGUAY	7-2	-	7-2
4-5	-	EV	ARGENTINA	11-5	-	15-8	ENGLAND	3-1	-	13-5
SATURDAY 8TH JUNE 2002										
7-4	-	13-8	SOUTH AFRICA	2-1	-	15-8	SLOVENIA	11-8	-	6-4
8-13	-	8-11	ITALY	9-4	-	15-8	CROATIA	4-1	-	4-1
1-6	-	1-6	BRAZIL	9-2	-	9-2	CHINA	11-1	-	11-1
SUNDAY 9TH JUNE 2002										
2-1	-	6-4	MEXICO	2-1	-	15-8	ECUADOR	6-5	-	13-8
12-5	-	11-4	COSTA RICA	2-1	-	2-1	TURKEY	EV	-	10-11
13-8	-	8-5	JAPAN	15-8	-	9-5	RUSSIA	6-4	-	8-5
MONDAY 10TH JUNE 2002										
6-5	-	6-5	SOUTH KOREA	2-1	-	2-1	USA	2-1	-	2-1
10-3	-	10-3	TUNISIA	11-5	-	2-1	BELGIUM	8-11	-	4-5
4-5	-	4-5	PORTUGAL	11-5	-	2-1	POLAND	3-1	-	10-3
TUESDAY 11TH JUNE 2002										
11-2	-	11-2	DENMARK	3-1	-	13-5	FRANCE	2-5	-	4-9
10-3	-	10-3	SENEGAL	11-5	-	2-1	URUGUAY	8-11	-	4-5
3-1	-	3-1	CAMEROON	11-5	-	11-5	GERMANY	4-5	-	4-5
4-1	-	4-1	SAUDI ARABIA	9-4	-	9-4	REP OF IRELAND	8-13	-	8-13
WEDNESDAY 12TH JUNE 2002										
7-2	-	10-3	NIGERIA	5-2	-	11-5	ENGLAND	8-13	-	8-11
9-2	-	9-2	SWEDEN	12-5	-	9-4	ARGENTINA	8-15	-	4-7
6-1	-	11-2	SOUTH AFRICA	3-1	-	13-5	SPAIN	4-11	-	4-9
11-4	-	11-4	SLOVENIA	11-5	-	2-1	PARAGUAY	5-6	-	10-11
THURSDAY 13TH JUNE 2002										
7-1	-	6-1	COSTA RICA	3-1	-	3-1	BRAZIL	1-3	-	4-11
4-7	-	8-15	TURKEY	9-4	-	12-5	CHINA	9-2	-	9-2
15-8	-	11-5	ECUADOR	2-1	-	2-1	CROATIA	5-4	-	11-10
11-2	-	6-1	MEXICO	3-1	-	12-5	ITALY	2-5	-	4-9
FRIDAY 14TH JUNE 2002										
15-8	-	7-4	BELGIUM	2-1	-	15-8	RUSSIA	5-4	-	7-5
10-3	-	10-3	TUNISIA	11-5	-	11-5	JAPAN	8-11	-	8-11
4-6	-	4-6	POLAND	9-4	-	9-4	USA	7-2	-	7-2
4-7	-	1-2	PORTUGAL	5-2	-	11-4	SOUTH KOREA	4-1	-	4-1

CORALS WORLD CUP ELIMINATION STAGE

by angus loughran

Corals have set a brainteaser for the punters by pricing every country to be eliminated at every possible stage. Remember this is the first tax free betting on the World Cup so you can understand their caution by quoting 1/33 on so-called no hopers China, Saudi Arabia and Senegal. However, it is interesting to note Japan, one of the co-hosts, who failed to score a goal in their only previous World Cup Final appearance in France four years ago, are a shorter price at 11/10 to be knocked out in the last sixteen than the 5/4 on them to be eliminated in the Group Stage. I actually fancy Japan to do really well in this World Cup and rate the 6/1 for a quarter-final knockout to be the value.

France are joint favourites with Argentina with top price 9/2 but it is entirely possible these two heavyweights could clash in the last 16 if France, as expected, win their group and Argentina are runners up in theirs. If it is not Argentina who France face in the last 16 then the odds favour England and either way it will be a massive match for the defending champions. My maths would make France v Argentina 5/6 the pair and France 2/5 and England 7/4 to qualify for the last eight if they meet in the last 16. This would mean Corals' offer of 13/5 France to be eliminated in the first knockout section – the last 16 – to be over the odds and well worth a bet.

The lopsided nature of the draw is clearly illustrated by these prices with France 4/1 favourites to win the tournament yet 8/1 to be runner up. Backers should surely prefer this option than an each way bet where you would only receive 2/1 the place odds as in the final you would be guaranteed a no risk double return place bet rather than sweat on the 90 minutes. Brazil are also a bigger price to be runner up than win the tournament and they are 7/4 to be eliminated at the quarter final stage where, if they as expected win their group, they would face Argentina, France or England.

All credit to Corals for offering such great variety on the World Cup betting this year and France, the holders, at 13/5 to be eliminated during the last 16 is my pick of these prices.

BETTING GUIDE

HOW FAR WILL THEY GO?

	GROUP	LAST 16	QUARTER FINAL	SEMI FINAL	RUNNERS UP	WINNERS
FRANCE	6-1	13-5	3-1	4-1	8-1	4-1
ARGENTINA	11-4	11-4	13-2	4-1	13-2	9-2
ITALY	10-3	10-3	3-1	9-2	6-1	6-1
BRAZIL	5-1	7-2	7-4	9-2	8-1	6-1
SPAIN	7-2	11-4	12-5	4-1	8-1	10-1
ENGLAND	9-4	7-4	9-2	7-1	9-1	10-1
PORTUGAL	10-3	15-8	13-5	11-2	9-1	12-1
GERMANY	5-2	9-4	12-5	6-1	11-1	14-1
POLAND	7-4	EV	9-2	14-1	22-1	33-1
PARAGUAY	11-10	11-8	13-2	11-1	22-1	33-1
CAMEROON	11-10	6-4	11-2	10-1	22-1	40-1
CROATIA	11-10	6-4	11-2	10-1	22-1	40-1
RUSSIA	13-8	11-8	10-3	11-1	22-1	40-1
REP OF IRELAND	EV	11-8	6-1	12-1	33-1	66-1
NIGERIA	4-11	11-4	11-1	18-1	33-1	66-1
URUGUAY	4-7	15-8	9-1	16-1	33-1	66-1
ECUADOR	4-11	11-4	11-1	18-1	33-1	66-1
BELGIUM	EV	7-4	11-2	7-1	33-1	66-1
TURKEY	EV	7-4	11-2	7-1	33-1	66-1
JAPAN	5-4	11-10	6-1	12-1	33-1	66-1
SWEDEN	4-11	13-5	11-1	16-1	40-1	80-1
DENMARK	4-11	13-5	11-1	16-1	40-1	80-1
SLOVENIA	3-10	3-1	11-1	22-1	40-1	80-1
SOUTH AFRICA	1-5	7-2	14-1	28-1	50-1	100-1
COSTA RICA	1-9	5-1	16-1	25-1	60-1	125-1
MEXICO	1-7	9-2	14-1	25-1	60-1	125-1
USA	1-12	11-2	18-1	33-1	60-1	125-1
TUNISIA	1-14	11-2	18-1	40-1	75-1	150-1
KOREA	1-9	9-2	16-1	40-1	75-1	150-1
CHINA	1-33	7-1	20-1	50-1	100-1	200-1
SAUDI ARABIA	1-33	7-1	20-1	50-1	100-1	200-1
SENEGAL	1-33	7-1	20-1	50-1	100-1	200-1

BETTING GUIDE

CANTOR SPORT WORLD CUP 100 INDEX

- 1ST: 100 pts
- 2ND: 75 pts
- LOSING SEMI FINALISTS: 50 pts
- LOSING QUARTER FINALISTS: 25 pts
- LOSING LAST 16: 10 pts
- OTHERS: 0 pts

FRANCE	43-46	CAMEROON	12-15	NIGERIA	5-7
ARGENTINA	38-41	POLAND	11-14	ECUADOR	5-7
ITALY	38-41	REP. OF IRELAND	12-15	COSTA RICA	5-7
BRAZIL	34-37	TURKEY	12-15	SOUTH KOREA	5-7
PORTUGAL	29-32	CROATIA	10-13	SOUTH AFRICA	3-5
SPAIN	29-32	BELGIUM	10-13	SENEGAL	3-5
GERMANY	22-25	URUGUAY	7-9	TUNISIA	3-5
ENGLAND	17-20	SWEDEN	7-9	USA	2-4
PARAGUAY	13-16	MEXICO	6-8	CHINA	1-3
JAPAN	12-15	DENMARK	6-8	SAUDI ARABIA	1-3
RUSSIA	12-15	SLOVENIA	6-8		

GROUP INDICES

- FIRST: 25 - SECOND: 10 - THIRD: 5 - FOURTH: 0

GROUP A
FRANCE	20-21.5
URUGUAY	6.5-8
DENMARK	6-7.5
SENEGAL	4.5-6

GROUP B
SPAIN	17.5-19
PARAGUAY	9.5-11
SLOVENIA	6-7.5
SOUTH AFRICA	4-5.5

GROUP C
BRAZIL	19.5-21
TURKEY	9-10.5
COSTA RICA	6-7.5
CHINA	2.5-4

GROUP D
PORTUGAL	17-18.5
POLAND	9.5-11
SOUTH KOREA	6-7.5
USA	4.5-6

GROUP E
GERMANY	14.5-16
CAMEROON	10-11.5
REP. OF IRELAND	10-11.5
SAUDI ARABIA	2.5-4

GROUP F
ARGENTINA	16-17.5
ENGLAND	10-11.5
SWEDEN	6-7.5
NIGERIA	5-6.5

GROUP G
ITALY	18-19.5
CROATIA	8-9.5
MEXICO	6-7.5
ECUADOR	5-6.5

GROUP H
RUSSIA	11-12.5
JAPAN	11-12.5
BELGIUM	10-11.5
TUNISIA	5-6.5

PRICES CORRECT AS OF MAY 2

*ANGUS LOUGHRAN'S TIP
sell South Africa at 4:
little downside if they scrape 3rd*

31

GROUP A

Maybe, just maybe, one of the great games of the 2002 World Cup Finals will be the opening match when reigning champions France play Senegal in Seoul on May 31. Twelve years ago Cameroon caused a sensation when, down to nine men, they defeated the then champions Argentina in Italia '90.

Senegal lost to Cameroon on penalties in this year's African Nations' Cup but by reaching the final they underlined the progress they have made in the past two years.

Ironically, while most of France's players play abroad, virtually all the Senegal side are with French clubs. "This match will set the tone for the whole competition," says France coach Roger Lemerre. "Senegal is very close to our culture and the fact they have qualified is remarkable. The opening game is always difficult to negotiate whether it's against a champion or a beginner."

Patrick Vieira, the Arsenal midfielder, was born in Dakar, the capital of Senegal. "This is massively emotional for me," he says. "In Senegal it will be an enormous event. I really don't know what to think about the game. Senegal is my country and I know the people there are going crazy about the game. There is an overwhelming feeling of joy that they are playing France."

Bruno Metsu, the Senegal coach, was trained in France and against the odds led the Africans to their first ever World Cup Finals.

"It is a real pleasure to play France in the opening game," says Rennes midfielder Makhtar Ndiaye. "France are the best team in the world and this is an opportunity to find out how good we really are.

"They may not take us seriously which would give us a chance. But we have a good group of players. It is an occasion everyone in the team – in fact everyone in Senegal – is looking forward to."

For the third Finals in succession France will meet Denmark. They beat the Danes 2-1 at France '98 and 3-0 in Euro 2000 and the meeting of the countries will bring together many players familiar with each other from the English Premiership. In fact, the two have been drawn together four times in the past 18 years and each time one has gone on to win the Finals. In 1984 France won the European Championship, in 1992 Denmark shocked Europe with their success while the 1998 World Cup and the 2000 European Championship went to France.

Denmark have Sunderland goalkeeper Thomas Sorensen, midfielders Per Frandsen of Bolton, Charlton's Claus Jensen and Thomas Gravesen of Everton, while striker Jon Dahl Tomasson had a brief and not particularly happy spell with Newcastle.

Four years ago, Denmark lost to Brazil in the quarter-finals and though the Danes qualified with an unbeaten record, a similar achievement this time seems unlikely.

Uruguay qualified after beating Australia in the play-offs so the two-times winners of the World Cup are back in the Finals for the first time since 1990.

"They are an enigma," says Lemerre. "They play a different type of game to Senegal or Denmark."

It would be a surprise if Uruguay made a significant impact on the Finals though in goalkeeper Fabian Carini – a Juventus reserve – captain Paolo Montero and midfielder Alvaro Recoba the South Americans have three outstanding individuals.

Recoba is back from a ban imposed because of passport irregularities and the Inter Milan forward is keen to make up for lost time on the world stage.

Coach Victor Pua is known for his safety-first approach, bringing on defensive players at the expense of attackers when Uruguay take the lead and 22 goals in 20 South American qualifiers, which included two own goals, suggest they may be as difficult to play against as to watch.

FRANCE

"We know how well African teams can play and as this is Senegal's first appearance in the Finals it will mean even more to them. Also, many of their players are from the French league. Denmark are experienced and Uruguay will be out to make their mark after a long time in the shadows." **Zinedine Zidane**, France midfielder.

DENMARK

"I'm not too sure how happy I am with the draw. I'm not impressed by Uruguay but Senegal are a fantastic team technically-speaking and we must give them every respect. We have to try to spoil the play with France. I'd say it is between ourselves and Senegal for second place." **Morten Olsen**, Denmark coach.

URUGUAY

"The most important thing was getting to the World Cup. Now I hope the players and the Uruguayan people enjoy it. We play two teams from Europe and one from Africa so we must prepare for each tie differently but effectively. They are all tough sides. France need no introduction but even Senegal, who might look easy, will be difficult as many of their team play in French football." **Victor Pua**, Uruguay coach.

SENEGAL

"I left Senegal when I was six and I know the streets of Paris better than the streets of Dakar. But I will be doing my best to help Senegal beat France. When we meet they will see what Senegal are made of." **Khalilou Fadiga**, Auxerre and Senegal.

FRANCE

Four years on since winning the World Cup, two years on since their triumph in the 2000 European Championships, a question hangs over France. Has this team reached its peak as some doubters suspect, or are they about to become the first country for 40 years to win successive World Cups?

The last team to retain the trophy was Brazil who followed up their 1958 success in Sweden by holding on to the Jules Rimet trophy in Chile four years later. France are rated as joint-favourites with Argentina to win this year and in one respect whoever wins this summer's tournament will emulate Brazil's 1958 achievement.

To date it is the only World Cup won by a team from another continent. Unless one of the Asian countries upset the odds and somehow lift the trophy in Yokohama in June, either a European or South American team will match Brazil's achievement in Stockholm. You have to wonder if there is any reason why that team won't be France. Almost a year ago France went to South Korea and Japan and won the Confederations Cup, which they used as a World Cup rehearsal tournament. Winning the competition itself may not rate highly in the general scheme of things, but what was important about the competition was that it gave France's players first-hand exposure to living, training and travelling in the Far East for three weeks.

Although some of the senior players were exempted, younger ones like Steve Marlet and Eric Carriere thrived there as did the likes of Patrick Vieira who scored his first ever goals for France during the campaign.

France were vastly superior to Japan in the final and could have won far more convincingly than the 1-0 scoreline suggests – and 12 months on, it is hard to detect much deterioration among the players individually or in the squad at large.

If there are any doubts about France they concern the defence which in the 1998 World Cup finals conceded just two goals in seven matches – and one of them was a penalty.

Since the international retirement of Laurent Blanc two years ago, the centre of the defence has not looked quite as solid as before as former Chelsea centre-back Frank Lebouef, who replaced the suspended Blanc in the 1998 final, is looking far less assured since his move back to France with Marseille last summer.

Mickael Silvestre, Blanc's Manchester United team mate, looks his most likely replacement and has had a good season in England, while United goalkeeper Fabien Barthez, Chelsea's Marcel Desailly and fullbacks Lilian Thuram and Bixente Lizarazu are still in place and likely to be just as impenetrable as they were in 1998 and 2000.

Another motivating factor for the French is that the 2002 tournament is likely to be the last for most of the established players. The average age of the squad is already around 32, and by the time Euro 2004 rolls around in Portugal, most of them will be gone. This, then is likely to be their last hurrah, but Emmanuel Petit, who scored the third and final goal in France's 3-0 win over Brazil in the 1998 final at the Stade de France believes that their experience is far more important than the dates on their birth certificates.

"We are not too old," insists the pony-tailed Chelsea midfielder. "We are experienced. We have been professionals for 10 or 12 years and every one of us knows himself perfectly well. It can be a great advantage in an international event."

Even if there are any doubts about the defence, there is very little wrong with the midfield or attack where France are spoilt for choice.

FRANCE

France won the World Cup without an orthodox on-form striker in 1998, but that situation has now changed. The Arsenal duo of Thierry Henry and Sylvain Wiltord are capable of regularly scoring goals, often of the highest pedigree. David Trezeguet of Juventus, scorer of the Golden Goal winner against Italy in 2000, has also proved himself at the highest level, with Auxerre's dynamic 20-year-old striker Djibril Cisse being hailed as the leading candidate of the youngsters coming through. And if the attack is as good as ever, the midfield is still awesome.

Patrick Vieira has given a series of stunning performances throughout the season for Arsenal and has been courted throughout the winter by continental clubs, most notably Real Madrid. The star though remains the incomparable playmaker Zinedine Zidane, who moved from Juventus to Real Madrid last summer for a world record transfer fee of £47.2 million. Zidane, who scored twice in the 1998 final against Brazil, celebrates his 30th birthday during the tournament on June 23 and could easily be celebrating a week later if he raises the trophy for France in Yokohama.

France, as defending champions, open the tournament against Senegal in Seoul on May 31 and if they go on to win the group as expected, are likely to meet either England or Argentina in the second round. It could all end then and there for the French – especially if they have to face Argentina – but if they get through that match unscathed, the route to the final could well open up nicely for them.

SQUAD

NICOLAS ANELKA (PARIS SG) BORN: 14.03.79 CAPS: 28 GLS: 6
Joined Liverpool on-loan from PSG in December 2001. Transfer story of summer 1999 – moving to Real from Arsenal for £22.9 million with Davor Suker coming the other way for £1.3 million – and then transferred again in summer 2000 moving back to original club PSG for £22 million. Dropped by PSG. Won European Cup medal in 2000 after ban by Real Madrid. Wembley hero v England in February 1999 – two goals and a third disallowed. Not selected in final 22 for 1998 World Cup. Three seasons at Arsenal – played with increasing confidence and scored a fine 19 goals in all competitions in 1998-99 and was club top scorer. Began with PSG – played just ten league games – Arsenal bought him for £500,000 so PSG lost over £21 million to get him back. League debut for PSG at 16, the season he was in the team that won the European U16 Championship along with Henry, Trezeguet and co.

FABIEN BARTHEZ (MANCHESTER UNITED) BORN: 28.06.71 CAPS: 47 GLS: 0
Man Utd bought him for £7.8 million on a six-year contract, British record for keeper World Cup winner's medal 1998 – played all seven games, conceded two goals. Euro 2000 medal. Championship medal 1997 and 2000 with Monaco. He and Pascal Olmeta were the first to wear the short-sleeved keeper's jersey when both were at Marseille. Began career at Toulouse, then was signed by Marseille, where he played from 1992-95, moving to Monaco in summer 1995. Won a 1993 European Cup medal with Marseille, and actually stayed for a season when they were relegated after the Tapie affair. Shaven-headed and keen scuba-diver.

FRANCE

ALAIN BOGHOSSIAN (PARMA) BORN: 27.10.70 CAPS: 25 GLS: 2
Injured knee ligaments in early 2000 – had to drop out of the Euro 2000 set up for the eventual winners, would have been a cert in the squad. But coach Lemerre values his versatility for the squad. A World Cup winner and was the sub for the French midfield stars during the Finals including the final – and joined Parma from Sampdoria in summer 1998 for £5.5 million. Played for Marseille in the sad season of 1994 when they were relegated over the Tapie affair, and he was signed by Napoli. Has been in Italy since 1994 with Napoli. Added to honours in 1999 with club wins in UEFA Cup and Italian Cup – but injuries have struck since.

VINCENT CANDELA (AS ROMA) BORN: 24.10.73 CAPS: 35 GLS: 2
Missed just one game in the Roma 2001 title win (33 of 34 games). One of the French World Cup and Euro 2000 heroes and played odd games in both events – he is back up to Bixente Lizarazu (one game at WC, two at Euro 2000). Rags to riches for this one – he was a full-back in the small Brittany team Guingamp (pop: 20,000), who reached Div One in 1995 as an amateur outfit. They stayed up and Candela went into the national squad after Euro '96 as a rock in the defence, and attracted the attention of the Roma scouts who bought him in the midwinter break in 1996-97.

ERIC CARRIERE (LYON) BORN: 24.05.73 CAPS: 7 GLS: 2
Outstanding season 2000-01 with the French champions Nantes and French Footballer of the Year (April 2001). Then moved for £10 million to Lyon in summer 2001. Played in Div Three in his early career for Muret and Auch in rugby country – joined Nantes in 1995. Six seasons with Nantes with dramatic improvement at the end of his time there.

DJIBRIL CISSE (AUXERRE) BORN: 12.08.81 CAPS: 0 GLS: 0
Leader of the next wave of young French stars – has been outstanding with the club side this season under the guidance of Guy Roux. Is the top scorer for the national U21 side, and was French top scorer at the 2002 World Junior Cup. From the club's juniors and made top flight debut in March 1999.

GREGORY COUPET (LYON) BORN: 31.12.72 CAPS: 1 GLS: 0
First choice keeper at Lyon – played for France A in 2000-1, and was a former U21 international, and who has now won full honours. Excellent 2000-1 seasons with the famous St Etienne club (some 40km away) and the other half of the central France derby. Played some 80 games in Division One for St Etienne and was in their first team at 18 years of age.

PHILIPPE CHRISTINVAL (BARCELONA) BORN: 31.08.78 CAPS: 4 GLS: 0
Was strongly linked with Bayern Munich in summer 2000 – to go with Willy Sagnol – but the deal fell away and he moved to Barca in summer 2001. First cap vs S.Africa in October 2000, replaced Frank Leboeuf and was in the training squad for Euro 2000 though only for experience. First choice in 2000 title win Monaco. Was in the famous U18 French team that won the European title in 1996, with Anelka, Henry, Trezeguet etc.

FRANCE

OLIVIER DACOURT (LEEDS UTD) BORN: 25.09.74 CAPS: 3 GLS: 0
Former U21 international who has joined the squad off the back of Leeds run to the 2000-1 UCL semis and improving form. Made debut in French league with Strasbourg in 1993, and was at that club until a move to Everton in 1998. Didn't settle at Everton, returned to France in 1999 with Lens, then returned to England in summer 2000 with Leeds for £7.2 million.

MARCEL DESAILLY (CHELSEA) BORN: 07.09.68 CAPS:92 GLS:3
Only player to play every game in 1998 World Cup and Euro 2000 success – and on field virtually throughout both competitions – missed last twenty minutes of World Cup final after being sent off. Current national captain since retirement of Deschamps. FA Cup medal 2000. Re-signed a new four-year contract for Chelsea in summer 2000. Moved from AC Milan to Chelsea in summer 1998 for £4.5 million. Won European Cup with two different clubs – Marseille in 1993 and Milan in 1994 and 1996 (first to do so in consecutive seasons), and was in a third consecutive final in 1995. Serie A title in 1996, extended his contract to 1999 but moved instead. Played the Rijkaard role at Milan, after impressing against them in 1993 European Cup final. Born in Accra, Ghana, he began his career with Nantes from 1986-92, then had two seasons at Marseille until a Nov 1994 move to AC Milan in their transfer week.

YOURI DJORKAEFF (BOLTON WANDERERS) BORN: 09.03.68 CAPS: 78 GLS: 28
Joined Bolton Wanderers on a free transfer in February 2002 after his contract at Kaiserslautern was terminated. His contract at Bolton was until the summer of 2002. Is now third equal on the French national all time scoring lists with Papin (28), with only Fontaine (30) and Platini (41) ahead – and top of the current crop. Appeared in all seven games in 1998 World Cup win. Euro 2000 success. Cost Inter Milan £3.2 million in May 1996 from PSG on a three-year contract. Won 1998 UEFA Cup and with Inter. Cost just £1.4 million in summer 1999 from Serie A to the Bundesliga. 1995 French Footballer of the Year. Father played in 1966 World Cup in England (right back) and won 48 caps in a rare father and son double for the French. Was with Monaco from 1990-95 and was top scorer in the last three seasons. French League top scorer in 1993-94.

CHRISTOPHE DUGARRY (BORDEAUX) BORN: 24.03.72 CAPS: 50 GLS: 7
Victim of horror tackle by Kevin Muscat in friendly v Australia in November 2001 but has made full recovery. Moved in January 2000 winterbreak back to first club Bordeaux (born in city) from Marseille for £3.2 million. Seems to have charmed life in national team as club form is poor. Played for Bordeaux from 1988-96, then moved to AC Milan in summer 1996 for £3 million. Then joined Barca in summer 1997 for £3 million but did not fit into plans and left for Marseille on a four-year contract after just seven Primera Liga games in Dec 1997. Too often a sub at Marseille, even after the World Cup heroics – where he played three games (one start and two on the bench, including sub in final).

FRANCE

THIERRY HENRY (ARSENAL) BORN: 17.08.77 CAPS: 35 GLS: 12
Moved to Juventus from Monaco for a season and thence to Arsenal in summer '99 for
£10 million. Switched to central striker by Arsene Wenger. World Cup medal 1998 –
played five games in Finals – and Euro 2000. Monaco debut aged 17y 14d in 1994, but
often sub behind Anderson/Ikpeba tandem. Captain and star player in France's UEFA
U18 triumph in 1996 with Anelka, Trezeguet etc – then was caught in a legal battle with
Real Madrid over transfer. His agent signed a five-year deal with Real, and Henry was
fined £40,000 as he had signed a four-year deal with Monaco. French champion in '97.

CHRISTIAN KAREMBEU (OLYMPIAKOS) BORN: 03.12.70 CAPS: 53 GLS: 1
Joined Olympiakos from Middlesbrough for £3.5 million in the summer of 2001.
Previously joined Middlesbrough for £2.5million from Real Madrid in summer 2000.
Won 1998 World Cup and European Cup medal, and resurrected his career which
appeared to be going nowhere. But he did not see eye-to-eye with John Toshack at
Real, and was brought back by Del Bosque and was on the bench for the 2000
European Cup success. Member of the famous young Nantes team that won the
1995 title, he went to Sampdoria for £4 million but never really settled and was on
the sidelines after a dispute. Comes from New Caledonia, just off the Australian
coast in the Pacific.

MIKAEL LANDREAU (NANTES) BORN: 14.05.79 CAPS: 1 GLS: 0
2001 Championship medal with Nantes – was made the club captain at just 22. Young
'keeper who joined the youth section at the age of 12, and made his first team debut
at 17 in 1996 – and has been in goal ever since. Is also the current French U21
international keeper and captain. Groomed to take over from Barthez in national side.
He took over in 1996 from the 1995 champions' 'keeper Dominique Casagrande, and
has hardly missed a game since. Is only 5'9" tall – has a fine record saving penalties.

FRANK LEBOEUF (MARSEILLE) BORN: 22.01.68 CAPS: 46 GLS: 3
Joined Marseille from Chelsea for £1.2 million in the summer of 2001. Has taken
over full-time from Laurent Blanc as No 1 central defender. Played in World Cup
final when Blanc was suspended – only other game in Finals was vs Denmark
after they won group. Cost Chelsea £2.5 million from Strasbourg in summer
1996. Man of match in 1997 FA Cup final and won 2000 FA Cup medal. Added
Cup Winners Cup and Coca Cola Cup to honours in 1998. Made his name in the
French league with Laval, then had a highly productive spell with Strasbourg from
1991-96 when he became an international and scored over 50 league goals.

BIXENTE LIZARAZU (BAYERN MUNICH) BORN: 09.12.69 CAPS: 73 GLS: 2
In Bayern's 2000 double win. In 2001 Bayern retained the title and won the European
Cup. Played six of seven games (rested for other) in World Cup win. Euro 2000 winner.
Former Bordeaux captain and played at the club between 1988-96, leaving after the
1996 UEFA Cup final for a season with Athletic Bilbao – he is a Basque – then after one
season went to Bayern. Owns his own vineyard. Subject of ETA threats.

FRANCE

CLAUDE MAKELELE (REAL MADRID) BORN: 18.02.73 CAPS: 14 GLS: 0
Joined Real summer 2000 from Celta Vigo for £9 million, after hawking himself around Premiership clubs for £11 million – had fine seasons though for Real in a superb side. Played for France in the pre-World Cup warm up games, but just failed to make the final 22. Not considered internationally until Deschamps retired in autumn 2000, but now back in the national set up. Moved in summer 1998 from Marseille to Celta for £1 million, he spent just one season with Marseille in 1997-98. He first made his name as captain of the French national U21 side and a key player in the Nantes team that won the 1995 title with Loko, Ouedec, Karembeu, Pedros and co. Zaire-born, first club was Brest then Nantes 1992-97.

STEVE MARLET (FULHAM) BORN: 10.01.74 CAPS: 8 GLS: 2
Joined Fulham for a club record £11.5 million from Lyon in the summer of 2001. Joined Lyon from Auxerre in summer 2000. Gained his first cap in France's last game of 2000, as sub v Turkey in November. In the Lyon team which finished second in the 2001 French league and was second top scorer with 14 goals behind Sonny Anderson, and had impressive UCL campaign. Follows the line of previous players whom Auxerre pick up from the Second Division and train to become top class. Marlet arrived at Auxerre in summer 1996 on a four-year contract from Red Star of Paris where he scored 16 goals in 1995-96 and became a national U21 striker. Has American parentage.

EMMANUEL PETIT (CHELSEA) BORN: 22.09.70 CAPS: 56 GLS: 6
Joined Chelsea for £7.5 million from Barcelona in the summer of 2001. Missed Euro 2000 final with illness, and then moved from Arsenal to Barcelona in summer 2000 for around £7 million. Back to England after one season. Played six of seven games in 1998 World Cup win (rested for other) and scored two goals – including the last one in the final. Moved to Arsenal in summer 1997 from Monaco for £3.5 million to re-establish himself with former Monaco coach Arsene Wenger. Was with Monaco's 1997 Championship winning team – and in 1998 with Arsenal's double win. Developed by Monaco – first team debut at 19 in 1989, and won 1997 Championship medal, 1991 Cup medal, and reached 1992 ECWC final with club. Comes from Dieppe and chose Monaco because it was furthest away from home! First capped aged 19 in 1990 in same era as Blanc and Deschamps. Temperament was initially suspect according to French coaches.

ROBERT PIRES (ARSENAL) BORN: 29.01.73 CAPS: 54 GLS: 10
Almost certainly out with knee damage. Joined Arsenal for £7 million after Lens and Lyon tabled £6.6 million and Real Madrid also bid, his mother is Spanish, so an achievement to get him. Missed out on the jackpot twice in two seasons in the French League – runners-up with Metz in 1998 and with Marseille in 1999. Was the big French domestic transfer of the 1998 summer – moved to Marseille in summer 1998 for £7.2 million on a seven-year contract. Is a fine player in the domestic league. Had six seasons at Metz, joined from the famous old Stade Reims when they folded after going into Div Three in 1992.

FRANCE

ULRICH RAME (BORDEAUX) BORN: 19.09.72 CAPS: 10 GLS: 0
Understudy to Barthez since winning the championship with Bordeaux in 1999. First cap vs Andorra in Euro 2000 qualifiers in June 1999. Was impressive in UCL some three seasons ago. Fifth season with Bordeaux, improved rapidly despite shoulder problems last season – and was bought from Division Three club Angers.

LAURENT ROBERT (NEWCASTLE UNITED) BORN: 21.05.75 CAPS: 9 GLS: 1
Joined Newcastle from Paris SG for £10 million in the summer of 2001. Is an orthodox left winger in superb form for Newcastle, and who joined PSG from Montpellier for £2.2 million in summer 1999. Like Anelka, he failed to blossom fully at PSG. Born in French dependancy of Reunion, in the Indian ocean.

WILLY SAGNOL (BAYERN MUNICH) BORN: 18.03.77 CAPS: 8 GLS: 0
Capped in Nov 2000 as sub for Lilian Thuram – been in squad since. Won title in first season with Bayern in 2001 after Monaco in 2000 – also European Cup final 2001. Bayern Munich were always favourites to sign this very promising full-back – and Fiorentina and Lazio were also interested – he arrived in summer 2000 from Monaco for £5million to fill the boots of the Liverpool-bound Markus Babbel. Bayern's full-backs are both French with Lizarazu down the left. Championship medal in 2000 with Monaco. He arrived at Monaco in summer 1997 from St Etienne – the former European Cup finalists from 1976 – he was one of their locally-born players of huge promise who had been offloaded to make ends meet.

MICKAEL SILVESTRE (MANCHESTER UTD) BORN: 09.08.77 CAPS: 10 GLS: 1
Championship medals in 2000 and 2001. Bought by United for £4.5 million from Inter Milan in September 1999. First club was Rennes, he was in the team that won the UEFA junior title with Anelka, Henry and co, and moved into the national U21 side before Inter came in for him. Adjusting problems at Old Trafford now over – can play full-back – France play him in centre defence.

LILIAN THURAM (JUVENTUS) BORN: 01.01.72 CAPS: 72 GLS: 2
Joined Juventus from Parma for £22million in the summer of 2001. Outstanding and currently one of the top defenders in Europe – won 1999 UEFA Cup and Italian Cup medals, but Man Utd are still known admirers. Played six of seven games in 1998 World Cup win (rested for other), and scored both goals in semi-final win vs Croatia, his only international strikes so far. Won Euro 2000. Can play anywhere in back four – France use him as right back. From Guadeloupe, joined Monaco in 1991 and came through the national U21 side to full honours. Moved to Parma in 1996.

DAVID TREZEGUET (JUVENTUS) BORN: 15.10.77 CAPS: 35 GLS: 19
National hero after winning golden-goal at Euro 2000, and that earned a £15million move to Juventus in summer 2000. Second top scorer in the French League with 22 goals as Monaco won the 2000 title – had been back mainly in the U21 set up since the World Cup. World Cup medal in first full season – played five games in World Cup.

FRANCE

His goal at Old Trafford also ended Manchester United's 1998 European Cup hopes. Member of the France team that won the UEFA U18 Cup in 1996 with Henry. Father Jorge was a pro in the French league with Rouen, where David was born, but they moved back home when he was two. However, he has played in Argentina for Platense on an exchange, and after Paris SG turned him down. International debut in 1998 vs S.Africa.

PATRICK VIEIRA (ARSENAL) BORN: 23.06.76 CAPS: 51 GLS: 3
Moved to AC Milan in Nov 1995 for two Serie A games, and then came to Arsenal for £3million in July 1996. Leading role in Arsenal's 1998 League and Cup double win – wanted to stay at Highbury for ten years. Played in World Cup final (sub) – also played vs Danes after French had won the group. Born in Senegal, he was originally with Cannes in Division One, making debut in 1993 aged just 17 and playing 49 league games as a teenager.

SYLVAIN WILTORD (ARSENAL) BORN: 10.05.74 CAPS: 37 GLS: 12
Arsenal bought him for an undislosed club record. Bordeaux wanted £13million as they had to give money to previous club Deportivo. Links with Henry. Goalscorer in 94th minute of Euro 2000 final to bring extra time. He finished a superb 1998-99 season with 22 goals which placed him as top of the French League scorers and has won all his caps from 1999. Fell away in 2000 after internal disputes. Born in the Paris suburbs, he played for Rennes 1991-97 and for Bordeaux from 1997, but was actually signed by Spanish club Deportivo in 1996 and loaned back to Rennes without playing in Spain.

ZINEDINE ZIDANE (REAL MADRID) BORN: 23.06.72 CAPS: 73 GLS: 19
Joined Real Madrid for a world record fee of £47.2 million from Juventus in the summer of 2001. World Player of Year 1998 and 2000 off the back of World Cup and Euro 2000 wins. Carried a lingering ankle injury into the 1998 World Cup – but was outstanding and scored two goals in the final. Scored the first ever international goal at the new Stade de France in January 1998 vs Spain (1-0). Joined Juventus in summer 1996 on a three-year contract. 1997 and 1998 Serie A title wins. This is the same player whom Blackburn once bid £9 million along with Dugarry in their Bordeaux days. It was Zidane's emergence that persuaded coach Jacquet that he could do without Cantona. Began his career with Cannes from 1989 (first team at 17) then played at Bordeaux from 1992-96, leaving after the UEFA final of 1996.

COACH

ROGER LEMERRE BORN: 18.06.41
He's the one on a hiding to nothing after France's '98 World Cup success! But so far, so good, having won Euro 2000. Former international midfielder, six caps from 1968-71 including vs England. He played for Sedan, Nantes, Nancy and Lens from 1961-75, and is a former French Footballer of the Year. Coached Lens, Paris FC, Strasbourg, Esperence Tunis and Red Star Paris. Has been with the French FA since 1986 – was No 2 to Aime Jacquet from Jan 1998.

DENMARK

Exit Peter Schmeichel, Brian Laudrup, Michael Laudrup. Enter – lots of new faces determined to do just as well as them individually – and even better as a team. Denmark's approach to the Finals saw them unbeaten in ten qualifiers which produced six wins and four draws and a healthy goal tally of 22-6 and brought them home in Group Three two points clear of the Czech Republic. They now face France, Senegal and Uruguay in a tough group based in the South Korean half of the Finals but have enough potential to qualify for the last 16.

Coach Morten Olsen shed off the robe of gloom that enshrouded the squad after their dismal showing in Euro 2000 which produced three defeats and a goal tally of 0-8, and now has a squad raring to go. Former coach Bo Johansson of Sweden resigned after that debacle and Olsen, a central pillar of the great side of the 1980's and early 1990's and who went on to win 102 caps, was the automatic choice as his successor. Although Schmeichel played the first three matches of the qualifying campaign before announcing his international retirement after winning 126 caps, Olsen's first job was to build the basis of a new team.

He had no trouble in finding the man to replace Schmeichel – his long-term understudy Thomas Sorensen. The Sunderland 'keeper, who turns 26 the day after Denmark play France in their final group match in Incheon on June 11, has since made the position his own and should be a safe pair of hands at the back.

While Sorensen has settled down well as Schemichel's successor, so others too have made an accomplished step up. The best illustration of this came last June, in a match regarded as the high point of the qualifying campaign, Denmark beat the Czechs 2-1 in Copenhagen with goals from Schalke striker Ebbe Sand and Feyenoord forward Jon Dahl Tomasson.

If ever a match reflected the changing fortunes that a player can experience in a career this was it. Sand has overcome testicular cancer to return to the highest levels, while Tomasson's career has gone from strength to strength in Holland after a disastrous season with Newcastle a few years back when he scored just three goals. Between them Sand (9) and Tomasson (4) scored 13 of Denmark's 22 goals in the qualifiers and that sort of form could prove lethal for their opponents in the Finals. And naturally enough those opponents include France.

Draws for major championships often have a habit of throwing two opponents together time and again as fans of England and Poland do not need reminding. It is also the same for France and Denmark.

Before the draw for the Finals was made in Pusan in December, French and Danish journalists were convinced they would be drawn against each other again – and they were not to be disappointed. The two countries will now meet for the fifth time in a major Finals in 18 years – but there is an odd quirk to their meetings. Each time they have met, one of them has gone on to win the tournament.

The run began at Euro '84 when France beat Denmark 1-0 in Paris with a Michel Platini goal in a group match and went on to win the tournament. At Euro '92 Denmark beat France 1-0 with a Lars Elstrup goal and ended as champions.

In the 1998 World Cup, France beat Denmark 2-1 in a group match and won the World Cup for the first time. Astonishingly the pattern continued in Euro 2000. Another

DENMARK

group match, another French victory – this time 3-0 – and France again lifted the trophy at the end of the championship. It could of course happen again this time. France, as reigning champions and the No 1 ranked side in the world, should qualify for the second round – but will their meeting in Incheon on June 11 prove the real clue as to the eventual outcome of the competition?

One thing France will find when they meet Denmark this time around is that Olsen has replaced Johansson's workman-like 4-4-2 system with a 4-3-3 designed to attack. He is relying on fast, tricky wingers such as Martin Jorgensen of Udinese and Jesper Gronkjaer of Chelsea to make it work. Gronkjaer, who was injured soon after arriving at Chelsea last autumn and missed the bulk of the season, returned to the side in March and immediately began to impress with his pace and crossing. He's an ace up Olsen's sleeve who could yet emerge as one of the new stars of the tournament. Denmark reached the second round on their first World Cup appearance in 1986 and made it to the quarter-finals in 1998 where they narrowly lost 3-2 to Brazil in a memorable match in Nantes.

Olsen appears to have the foundation of a side that could yet better anything Denmark achieved in either of their previous World Cups. If they were to do that and go on and win it, the new faces would become just as lauded as their famous predecessors.

SQUAD

MIKKEL BECK (LILLE) BORN: 12.05.73 CAPS: 19 GLS: 3
Back in squad after withdrawals. Since his Middlesbrough days he played 14 games in all comps for Derby (two goals), five games for Nottingham Forest (one goal) and 11 games for QPR (four goals). He had faded away after Euro '96 in both club and country teams but has regained his appetite since playing in the UCL for Lille last season. Signed by Boro for £400,000 from Fortuna Cologne in 1996.

MORTEN BISGAARD (FC COPENHAGEN) BORN: 24.06.74 CAPS: 8 GLS: 1
Now back home after a spell with Udinese. Joined the Serie A club in Jan 1999 from Odense – played alongside Jorgensen in the club side. Had played for the Olympic team (where he gained his two caps, and on tour with national team in uncapped internationals). Five seasons in Odense's first team before move to Italy.

KASPER BOGELUND (PSV EINDHOVEN) BORN: 08.10.80 CAPS: 2 GLS: 0
Into the Danish national squad for the first time in Feb 2002 for the game in Saudi Arabia. Joined PSV in summer 1999 from Danish junior club Obbelund. Had played five games in the two championship winning seasons of 2000 and 2001. Into PSV's UCL squad for 2001-2 for the first time and claimed regular first team place at club.

SOREN COLDING (VFL BOCHUM) BORN: 08.09.72 CAPS: 26 GLS: 0
Introduced during the 1998 World Cup qualifiers. Was first choice in 1998 World Cup as right-back. Right-sided defender from the 1996 and 1997 champions and 1998 double winners, Brondby, he is now in the German Second Division and joined Bochum in 2001.

DENMARK

THOMAS GRAVESEN (EVERTON) BORN:11.03.78 CAPS: 21 GLS: 2
Joined Everton for £2.5 million from Hamburg in August 2000. He was previously with Vejle in Denmark before moving to Hamburg. In line for a place in the World Cup squad for France and was selected for warm-up squads, but had to withdraw injured. Gained his first caps immediately after the World Cup which suggests that only injury kept him away from France. Noted as somewhat unruly and injury prone (recurring knee problems), but 100 per cent committed. Was the utility man at Hamburg.

JESPER GRONKJAER (CHELSEA) BORN: 12.08.77 CAPS: 24 GLS: 1
Joined Chelsea in December 2000 for £7.8 million from Ajax and now recovered from the dreaded knee ligament damage. A hat-trick for Ajax v MVV in the league in March 1999 clinched his first call-up. Had been playing regularly for Ajax when Jari Litmanen and Shota Arveladze suffered long-term injuries and his progress allowed Litmanen to move without rancour. He previously played three seasons in the first team at Aalborg in the Superliga – nearly 100 games.

JAN HEINTZE (PSV EINDHOVEN) BORN: 17.08.63 CAPS: 82 GLS: 4
Oldest in squad and a playing compatriot of coach Morten Olsen. After a fine season in 1999 with Bayer Leverkusen (second) he left to join former club PSV in the summer 1999 on a free transfer – PSV won the 2000 and 2001 titles. Was out of favour with previous coach Richard Moller-Nielsen after refusing to play at Euro '92, which backfired because the Danes won! He first made his name in the late 1980's with the fine PSV Eindhoven side in Holland. Won five Dutch titles in total (incl. two under Bobby Robson) as well as winning the 1988 European Cup. Played at Euro '88.

THOMAS HELVEG (AC MILAN) BORN: 24.06.71 CAPS: 66 GLS: 2
When Alberto Zacherroni left Udinese to join Milan as coach in summer 1998, he immediately went back to his old club for Oliver Bierhoff and more surprisingly, for Helveg. Helveg cost £5.5 million after a fine 1999 World Cup. The gamble paid off as Helveg won a 1999 Serie A championship medal. 1994 Danish Footballer of the Year. In 1995 he helped Udinese into Serie A after £500,000 move from Odense. Was at Odense 1989-94 and at Udinese 1994-98.

RENE HENRIKSEN (PANATHINAIKOS) BORN: 27.08.69 CAPS: 38 GLS: 0
Danish Footballer of the Year 2000. Currently at Panathinaikos, after 11 seasons with AB Copenhagen. Played over 250 games, and is known as 'Horse' for his charges upfield. Into the squad from spring 1998. International debut at 28. In 1998 World Cup squad as cover defender, did not play in Finals – now first choice.

CLAUS JENSEN (CHARLTON ATHLETIC) BORN: 29.04.77 CAPS: 12 GLS: 1
Central midfielder with a more attacking instinct than Tofting and Gravesen. Charlton's top signing of £4 million from Bolton in summer 2000, he had two seasons with Bolton. Formerly with Naestved and Lyngby, it was Lyngby who sold him to Bolton for £1.6 million. Established in the national squad from 2000.

DENMARK

NICLAS JENSEN (FC COPENHAGEN) BORN: 17.08.74 CAPS: 8 GLS: 0
Cover down the left side for Jan Heintze. Played for Lyngby from 1992-97, then switched to FC Copenhagen, where he won a 2001 title medal. Another who can play in both defence and midfield and would be useful for a tournament.

MARTIN JORGENSEN (UDINESE) BORN: 06.10.75 CAPS: 31 GLS: 4
Into the squad from spring 1998. Joined the Serie A club in summer 1997 from Aarhus. Was the national U21 team's captain and went forward to the full national team and has hardly missed a game — played all five games at the 1998 World Cup, scoring v Brazil. Prefers the left side.

MADS JORGENSEN (BRONDBY) BORN: 10.02.79 CAPS: 1 GLS: 0
One of half a dozen young prospects who might make the final group for the World Cup. He is the younger brother of Martin Jorgensen. Developing in the Brondby set up, and made national debut in the last of the World Cup qualifiers. Two years in the club first team.

PETER KJAER (ABERDEEN) BORN: 05.11.65 CAPS: 4 GLS: 0
Veteran keeper who recently moved from Silkeborg to Aberdeen. Third choice 'keeper at the last two European championships and last two World Cups. Had been with Silkeborg virtually throughout career and was often voted the best in the domestic league. Began career with Vejle in 1983 and has ten years at that club, then moved to Silkeborg in 1993 and won 1994 title with Silkeborg.

MARTIN LAURSEN (AC MILAN) BORN: 26.07.77 CAPS: 15 GLS: 0
Not to be confused with Jacob Laursen of Leicester and Derby – this one is a younger defender with excellent pedigree via the national U21 set up. Jacob Laursen retired after a barracking at the Euro 2000 play-off games v Israel. Joined AC Milan from Verona in summer 2001. Two seasons with Verona, he joined from Silkeborg where he played for three seasons of improvement from his late teens. And was in the Verona team that was promoted to Serie A in 1999.

PETER LOVEKRANDS (GLASGOW RANGERS) BORN: 29.01.80 CAPS: 3 GLS: 0
Made the first team with Rangers in 2000-1 season and has been looked at in 2002 by the national selectors. Originally from the AB Copenhagen club, he played for them as a teenager in 1998, and was in the national U21 squad when spotted by Rangers who bought him for £1.5 million.

STEVEN LUSTU (AB COPENHAGEN) BORN: 13.04.71 CAPS: 3 GLS: 0
Came to the fore after the surprise success of little Herfolge in the 2000 championship win – in the team masterminded by former Arsenal star John Jensen. Switched to AB as the Herfolge team gradually disbanded. Was with Naestved from 1991-93, then had seven years at Herfolge.

DENMARK

PETER MADSEN (BRONDBY) BORN: 26.04.78 CAPS: 4 GLS: 0
Another of the Brondby prospects, he has recently made the national set up, though mainly as substitute. Has come through to the top this season with some impressive forward displays. Has been in the Brondby first team squad since 1996.

JAN MICHAELSEN (PANATHINAIKOS) BORN: 28.11.70 CAPS: 10 GLS: 1
Danish international midfielder who joined the Greeks in summer 2001 from AB Copenhagen. Born in France at Nantes, when father was playing for Nantes, father was an international also. Career spent with AB Copenhagen before move to Greece. Recommended to his club by central defender Henriksen who was also at AB. Quarter-finals of the UCL in 2001-02.

BRIAN STEEN NIELSEN (MALMO) BORN: 25.10.68 CAPS: 64 GLS: 3
Still in the squad and had a useful 1998 World Cup, and is the utility man who can cover defensive and midfield roles. Had an almost unbroken run in the national team from just after the Euro '92, success through to Euro '96 and just afterwards – he spent most of that period with Fenerbahce, with whom he won a championship medal. Defensive midfielder or defender, who has also played in the J-league for Urawa Red Diamonds which may stand him in good stead. Now playing in Sweden after leaving AB Copenhagen.

ALLAN NIELSEN (WATFORD) BORN: 13.03.71 CAPS: 44 GLS: 7
Joined Watford from Tottenham for a club record £2.5 million in August 2000. Winning goal in 90th minute in 1999 Worthington Cup final. Joined Tottenham in summer 1996 from Brondby for £1.65 million after being captain of the 1996 championship winning team at Brondby. Was the hero at Brondby, and very much the fans' favourite. He began his career as a 17-year-old at Bayern Munich but it didn't work out, so he returned to Brondby. George Graham rescued his career that went backwards under Francis and Gross.

JIMMY NIELSEN (AALBORG) BORN: 06.08.77 CAPS: 0 GLS: 0
Probable No 3 keeper in the squad. Had a spell with Millwall in 1994-95 (two games). From Aalborg, he made their first team in 1995 and has been first choice at the club since. Championship medal with club in 1999.

MARK NYGAARD (RODA JC) BORN: 01.09.76 CAPS: 6 GLS: 0
Forward who plies his trade in Holland. Has played all his senior football in Holland – he was a junior FC Copenhagen, then went to Heerenveen, MVV and now to Roda, where he has been since 1998. Roda are playing him more in midfield these days.

CHRISTIAN POULSEN (SCHALKE) BORN: 28.02.80 CAPS: 3 GLS: 0
Another fine prospect, he joined a leading Bundesliga club in winter break in January 2002 for £4million from FC Copenhagen. Broke into FC Copenhagen's first team during their 2001 title success.

DENMARK

DENNIS ROMMEDAHL (PSV EINDHOVEN) BORN: 22.07.78 CAPS: 18 GLS: 5
Played in all the last year's internationals. Bought by PSV from Lyngby as a teenager.

THOMAS RYTTER (FC COPENHAGEN) BORN: 06.01.74 CAPS: 3 GLS: 0
From the 2001 champions and another cover defender. Capped early in his career in the mid-1990s when at Lyngby and that earned him a ticket to Spain with Seville where he played from 1995-97. Returned home to play with curent club in 1997.

EBBE SAND (SCHALKE) BORN: 19.07.72 CAPS: 44 GLS: 17
Was the 2000-1 equal top scorer in the Bundfesliga with 22 goals – and scored nine goals in ten games in the 2002 World Cup qualifiers after recovering from cancer treatment. Moved to Schalke in 1999 in the Bundesliga for £3.5 million after wanting to go to, and then turning down, Premiership clubs. International since being top scorer in the 1998 Danish Superleague with the top club, Brondby, won the double in 1998. Scored 28 goals in the Danish league in 1997-98 – and had a run of 18 goals in eight games!

THOMAS SORENSEN (SUNDERLAND) BORN: 12.06.76 CAPS: 13 GLS: 0
First capped v Israel in Nov 1999 (sub). Call up to national squad since March '99 in place of the ageing Ole Kjaer and Mogens Krogh and has been in the squad set up since, and now taken over from Peter Schmeichel. Joined Sunderland in Jan 1998 from Odense for £500,000 – was the Danish national U21 keeper (25 caps).

STIG TOFTING (BOLTON WANDERERS) BORN: 14.08.69 CAPS: 35 GLS: 2
Currently on loan at Bolton from Hamburg, where he had been since summer 2000 after Hamburg took him from Duisburg. Recalled to midfield after squad injuries - but has played consistently well in the Bundesliga this season despite his side being bottom of the table. Played once at Euro '96 (sub). Known as the Danish Vinnie Jones.

JON DAHL TOMASSON (FEYENOORD) BORN: 29.08.75 CAPS: 37 GLS: 14
Moved back to Holland for £2.2 million to Feyenoord – and immediately forced his way back into the squad after Feyenoord's fine season culminated in the winning of the 1999 title. Was a £2.2 million summer 1997 signing for Newcastle as back up to Shearer and Asprilla, and can also play midfield. He scored 16 and 18 goals in his last two seasons 1995-96, 96-97 in the Dutch Premier Division which persuaded Kenny Dalglish to bid for him. It didn't work out though – he scored just four goals.

COACH

MORTEN OLSEN 14.08.49
The first Dane to reach 100 caps, he is now in the hot seat and has picked up the country from their Euro 2000 slump to a place at the 2002 World Cup. Former player with Cercle Bruges, RWD Molenbeek, then three titles with Anderlecht and then to Cologne. Coach of Brondby, Cologne and Ajax (one championship) before moving to the national job after Euro 2000 with Michael Laudrup as his assistant.

URUGUAY

From Manchester United's substitutes bench into the World Cup against holders France, African surprise package Senegal and the solid Danes – that could be the prize waiting for Diego Forlan.

There were those who said the long-haired young striker would have been better off playing for his place with Independiente but that is not taking into account the frosty relationship between coach Victor Pua and his leading striker Dario Silva of Malaga.

This much troubled squad, who surprised a great many worldwide experts by overcoming messrs Mark Viduka, Harry Kewell and company when they beat Australia in the play-offs to take their place in South Korea after finishing fifth in the qualifying group. It was only their sound defence – they conceded just 13 goals in their 18 games – which squeezed them through with one goal better goal difference than sixth-placed Colombia.

It was a fraught affair from the moment they edged past Bolivia 1-0 in their opening game, made worse when Argentinian World Cup winner Daniel Passarella quit in the middle of the programme after weeks of whinging and moaning. While the fans were of the mind that it was good riddance, the players felt somewhat differently and as a result, the coach Pua has not enjoyed a comfortable ride.

His biggest problem was over striker Silva who was accused of unbecoming conduct from the faintly amusing late night fishing trips to renting a house and filling it with good time girls, a story which did not go down too well with his wife in Malaga.

Silva's somewhat spurious complaint was that his coach did not support him and, worse, that he was the source of the story. The second part of the gripe was proved to be completely unfounded but it has not helped to heal the rift and Forlan has been hastily promoted into the senior squad.

But Silva, with his half dozen goals from his 15 games, is vital as he can be left to forage on his own up field and hold the ball while the Italian-based pair Alvaro Recoba and Federico Magallanes break from their deep positions.

But Pua knows Forlan well having picked him for both the South American Under-20 Championships and the World Youth Cup. However, he is not yet convinced that the youngster is the finished product in front of goal and he is desperately hoping that Manchester United and Sir Alex Ferguson will help him solve that problem before the World Cup rolls around.

Pua has brought in several of those youngsters from the teams he managed in the youth competitions and, if nothing else, Uruguay will once again be the target for the agents and scouts in South Korea.

Apart from the youngsters he experimented with in the Copa America, Pua also changed Passarella's tactics, strengthening the midfield with more defence-minded players and experimenting with three centre backs, with Roma's versatile Gianni Guigou able to move smoothly into a midfield role if the system needs changing mid-match.

Known as one of the great exporters of football talent to clubs around the globe, Uruguay will rely heavily on the Italian influence to carry them through their tough group from Juventus goalkeeper Fabian Carini, through his club mate Paolo Montero, a rock at the back, Gonzalo Sorondo of Inter, Pablo Garcia of Venezia, Guillermo

URUGUAY

Giacomazzi from Lecce, Roma's Guigou, Javier Ernesto Chevanton of Lecce, Federico Magallanes from Venezia and Recoba of Inter. Add to that half a dozen Spanish-based players and it can easily be seen that Uruguay have quality in depth. But can Victor Pua overcome the dressing room whispers and the louder mumblings in the press to make an impact in 2002?

SQUAD

SEBASTIAN ABREU (CRUZ AZUL) BORN: 17.10.76 CAPS: 8 GLS: 4
Now plying his trade in Mexico after a spell with Deportivo la Coruna in 1997-98 that was not successful. Has played now for seven clubs in five countries which says it all. Played in Uruguay, Argentina, Brazil, Spain and Mexico. Known as 'El Loco' (The Madman) and is a gangling 6'5" forward.

DIEGO ALONSO (ATLETICO MADRID) BORN: 16.04.75 CAPS: 8 GLS: 0
First season with Atletico and club top scorer – arrived from Valencia in summer 2001. Signed by Valencia in summer 2000 from Gymnasia of the Argentine first division – he came for an undisclosed fee. Born in Montevideo, played for Bella Vista in their top league for two seasons. Fringe player in 2001 European Cup Final team.

ADRIAN BERBIA (PENAROL) BORN: 12.10.77 CAPS: 2 GLS: 0
Vies with Munua for the reserve 'keeper's role behind Carini. Plays for Penarol and joined from fellow Division One club Bella Vista. Five seasons in the top flight.

JOE BIZERA (PENAROL) BORN: 17.05.80 CAPS: 8 GLS: 1
Has been in the club team for the past couple of seasons and recently made international debut in defence. Will probably be a reserve but is looked on as one for the future.

FABIEN CARINI (JUVENTUS) BORN: 26.12.79 CAPS: 32 GLS: 0
Played both legs of the World Cup games with Australia which qualified Uruguay for the World Cup. Played all 20 matches to get to the World Cup Finals, the only Uruguayan to do so. Reserve at Juventus to Gianluigi Buffon. Two seasons with club, but had been signed earlier and returned to his club Danubio. Won FIFA World Youth Championship with Uruguay.

JAVIER CHEVANTON (LECCE) BORN: 12.08.80 CAPS: 5 GLS: 1
First season in Italy, he joined Lecce in summer 2001 from Danubio of Montevideo for £7 million. Prolific scorer with Danubio – played for them for five seasons and scored 49 goals in five games from 1999-2001 including 32 goals in 30 games in 2000.

DIEGO FORLAN (MANCHESTER UNITED) BORN: 19.05.79 CAPS: 3 GLS: 0
Registered by Manchester United in January 2002 when he signed for £7.5 million from Argentine club Independiente, the 2000 runners-up. Scored 37 goals in 77 games for Independiente after joining as an 18-year-old from Penarol. Father played in the 1974 World Cup together with Montero's father but Diego nearly chose tennis.

URUGUAY

PABLO GARCIA (VENEZIA) BORN: 11.05.77 CAPS: 32 GLS: 1
Plays for relegated Venezia, so will probably be away in summer 2002. Best Uruguayan player in the World Cup qualifiers. Joined Venezia (Venice) in summer 2001 from AC Milan, who signed from Atletico Madrid in Jan 2001 after training with them since the start of last season. Suggested problems with passport. Was in Atletico's B team in 2000 – yet played for Uruguay in World Cup qualifiers. Joined Atletico in 1997 aged 20 from Wanderers of Montevideo, but was loaned back to Penarol and in Spain to Valladolid where he had a full season in the first team in La Liga.

GUILLERMO GIACOMAZZI (LECCE) BORN: 21.11.77 CAPS: 6 GLS: 0
The midfield ball winner cost Lecce £2.6 million from Penarol in summer 2001. Previously had two seasons in the top flight each with both Bella Vista in 1998 and 1999 and Penarol in 2000 and 2001.

GIANNI GUIGOU (ROMA) BORN: 22.02.75 CAPS: 28 GLS: 0
Signed for Roma in summer 2000 from Nacional of Montevideo for £1.75m. One of the heroes of the World Cup qualifying success against Australia, and was a regular part of the side that qualified for the Finals. Played 19 of the 20 games to get the side to the World Cup. Was in the Nacional team for four seasons, and won championship medals in all four seasons. Won Serie A championship medal in 2001. Can play on either flank, scored against Hamburg and Liverpool in last season's UEFA Cup. Is the cover for Cafu and Candela.

ALEJANDRO LEMBO (NACIONAL) BORN: 15.02.78 CAPS: 29 GLS: 1
Is probably the back up to the Sorondo-Montero combination in central defence though worth a place in his own right. Developed by the Bella Vista club since 1997, he recently switched to the bigger Nacional.

PABLO LIMA (DANUBIO) BORN: 26.03.81 CAPS: 5 GLS: 1
Another promising defender from the domestic league – and usually plays down the left side.

GERARDO MAGALLANES (VENEZIA) BORN: 22.08.76 CAPS: 22 GLS: 6
Free kick and penalty expert but suffered successive relegations with his club sides. Now back in Italy since 2001 with his second Italian club – he played for Atalanta from1996-98 after leaving Penarol's title winning team. Moved in 1998 to Real Madrid where he didn't play a first team game but found a home at Racing Santander from 1998 to 2001 before relegation.

PAOLO MONTERO (JUVENTUS) BORN: 03.09.71 CAPS: 45 GLS: 3
Played against Australia in both legs of the World Cup play-offs, and played in 12 of the 18 qualifying matches. Team captain. Was only the second Uruguayan to join Juve and first for 55 years. Summer 1996 free-transfer signing as an out of contract player with his previous club Atalanta, and was formerly with Penarol. His father was in the 1966 World Cup Final squad – didn't play though. Sent-off vs Holland in '74 World Cup. Dreadful disciplinary record.

URUGUAY

RICHARD MORALES (NACIONAL) BORN: 21.02.75 CAPS: 10 GLS: 3
May qualify as the tallest outfielder at the Cup at just over 6'5" tall! Play-off hero with two goals vs Australia to gain entry to World Cup Finals. Has always played for Nacional.

GUSTAVO MUNUA (NACIONAL) BORN: 27.01.78 CAPS: 7 GLS:0
Goalkeeper with the Nacional club of Montevideo, Manua has been their first choice since making his debut in 1997.

NICOLAS OLIVERA (FC SEVILLE) BORN: 30.05.78 CAPS: 22 GLS: 8
Was top scorer in the Seville team that won the Div Two championship, scoring 16 goals. Bought to Spain by Valencia for £2million from Defensor of Montvideo, this tiny (5'5") forward was outstanding in the 1997 World Junior Cup – where he was voted as one of the Players of the Tournament. Was brought along quietly by Valencia, just two Primera Liga games in 1997-98 in his debut season and moved to Seville in 1998-99 season where he has stayed.

FABIEN O'NEILL (PERUGIA) BORN: 14.10.73 CAPS: 14 GLS: 2
Moved to Perugia from Juventus in Jan 2002 and was signed by Juve in summer 2000 from Cagliari for £5.8 million. Just ten games in 2000-01 for Juve. Joined Cagliari in Nov 1995, and had five seasons with them including promotion and relegation.

DIEGO PEREZ (DEFENSOR) BORN: 18.05.80 CAPS: 8 GLS: 0
Another youngster from the domestic league given a chance at the 2001 Copa America. Always been with Defensor as a central midfielder.

GUSTAVO POYET (TOTTENHAM) BORN: 15.11.67 CAPS: 26 GLS: 3
Could well make the squad again after impressive performances in the Premiership. Joined Spurs from Chelsea in summer 2001 after four years at Stamford Bridge and was previously with Primera Liga club Zaragoza through most of the early 1990's.

ALVARO RECOBA (INTER MILAN) BORN: 17.03.76 CAPS: 41 GLS: 8
Had his one year ban for a false passport reduced to four months last year – and is reputedly Italy's best paid player. Has been outstanding in the last South American championships and World Cup qualifiers. Signed by Inter in summer 1997 from Nacional of Montevideo on a four-year contract for around £3.5 million.

MARIO IGNACIO REGUEIRO (RACING SANTANDER) BORN: 14.09.78 CAPS: 11 GLS: 0
A winger who stretched the Australians in the World Cup play-off, but spent 2001-2 in Division Two of La Liga following Racing's demise. Joined Racing in 2000 for their drop, and previously played three seasons for Penarol's first team.

MARCELO ROMERO (MALAGA) BORN: 04.07.76 CAPS: 20 GLS: 0
Joined Malaga in late summer 2001 from the Penarol club. Midfielder with five seasons experience with Penarol and another who plays in front of the back four.

URUGUAY

DARIO RODRIQUEZ (PENAROL) BORN: 17.06.74 CAPS: 18 GLS: 1
This left-sided, 6'3" tall, wing back can also play central defence. Spent time in the mid-1990's with Tolca in the Mexican league, now back in the domestic league.

GONZALO DE LOS SANTOS (VALENCIA) BORN: 19.07.76 CAPS: 27 GLS: 1
The defensive midfielder arrived at Valencia in summer 2001 along with Fransisco Rufete from Malaga, where he also made his name in the team that was promoted to the Primera Liga in 1999. Originally thought to be taking Gaizka Mendieta's place. Formerly with Penarol.

DARIO SILVA (MALAGA) BORN: 02.11.72 CAPS: 36 GLS: 13
Experienced striker who has played three seasons with Malaga, who bought him from Espanyol. Playing in his second European country as he was with Cagliari in Serie A from 1995-99 and originally played for Penarol. Copa America winner in 1995.

GONZALO SORONDO (INTER MILAN) BORN: 09.10.79 CAPS: 16 GLS: 0
Autumn 2001 signing by Inter from Defensor of Montevideo with whom he had played for the previous four seasons. In the Inter line up in 2002. Commanding presence and is often the national captain when Montero is not around, and, though still young he was the captain at the 2001 Copa America.

WASHINGTON TAIS (BETIS SEVILLE) BORN: 21.12.72 CAPS: 20 GLS: 0
Joined Betis in summer 2001 from relegated Racing Santander. Experienced international right back who played for Uruguay from 1995 and has played in Copa America and World Cup qualifiers since. Recalled during this qualifying campaign.

GUSTAVO VARELA (NACIONAL) BORN: 14.05.78 CAPS: 5 GLS: 0
Can play in the back four and up front! Made the Nacional first team in 1998 and has been a regular ever since.

MARCELO ZALAYETA (JUVENTUS) BORN: 05.12.78 CAPS: 11 GLS: 2
Big forward, and back under the Juve wing, he was with the club from 1997-99 as a youngster having signed from Penarol, the Uruguayan champions, but has been allowed away on loan. On loan at Empoli in 1999 then went to FC Seville in Spain from 1999-2001 where he impressed sufficiently in the Primera Liga for Juve to bring him back in summer 2001. Was a star at the 1997 World Junior Cup final and the 1999 Copa America final – both lost.

COACH

VICTOR PUA BORN: 31.03.56
Local top division footballer for seven clubs including Liverpool and River Plate, both of Montevideo. Played in the national Olympic team. Coached the River Plate club (Montevideo version) from 1993 and included lower category national team from 1997 – took over from Daniel Passarella as coach in November 2000 and brought the team to the World Cup.

SENEGAL

To properly understand Senegal's extraordinary path to the World Cup, you have to take yourself back to a Parisian bar last August. The Barrio Latino in the Bastille does a mean cuba libre, but a group of Senegal's most experienced players weren't there to salsa.

There were stirrings of discontent in a squad which had started the World Cup qualifying campaign decidedly sluggishly, and the likes of the captain Aliou Cisse felt that the air needed to be cleared. The renewed spirit that resulted within the group, allied to the replacing of the coach Peter Schnittger with the Frenchman Bruno Metsu, started the Lions of Teranga on their way.

An unlucky draw in Morocco followed, and then a tremendous run of form which allowed the unfancied West Africans to edge out the North African giants Morocco, Egypt and Algeria to win Group C. A Nations Cup final appearance followed in January, and suddenly Senegal seem to have usurped Nigeria as the number two African team behind Cameroon.

Whether they are good enough to progress to the second round in June is quite another matter. But the two teams' familiarity and defensive frailties will surely dictate that it'll be close in that dream opening game. For all their prowess at the back, though, Senegal may struggle to score goals: they rely heavily on El Hadji Diouf of Lens – a terrific player, but also a frustrating one who drifts out wide and doesn't always deliver.

And after him, there is next to nothing, with Henri Camara and Pape Thiaw far too inconsistent. If Diouf can grab a goal or two, though, their extremely sound defence, marshalled by Aliou Cisse, could just be enough for a second round place.

And whatever happens, they'll enjoy the experience of their first World Cup and revel in the fact that this relatively young squad will be one of the forces of African football for years to come.

SQUAD

ISSA BA (LAVAL)
Born in Dakar, and has played for two seasons now in the French Second Division. His return of one goal in 36 games in that period, including none in 31 in this campaign, hardly bodes well for World Cup selection. An outside chance of a place in the squad.

HABIB BEYE (STRASBOURG) BORN: 19/10/77 CAPS: 6 GLS: 0
Born in France, although the son of a former Senegalese international. Was playing in the Fifth Division in France when spotted by PSG. Moved to Strasbourg with the PSG coach Claude Le Roy. Plays at right back, and is the quickest player in the Senegal squad.

SOULEYMANE CAMARA (MONACO) BORN: 22/12/82 CAPS: 8 GLS: 1
Made his debut at 17, two years ago. Has been one of the few Monaco players to flourish this season under Didier Deschamps. Came on as sub and scored the late winner against Zambia in this years Nations Cup.

SENEGAL

HENRI CAMARA (SEDAN) BORN: 10/5/77 CAPS: 34 GLS: 8
Very quick right winger who can also play as a striker but is an inconsistent finisher. Has a Swiss League winners medal with Grasshopper, and came to prominence with his brilliant performances at the Nations Cup in 2000. Was something of a disappointment this year in Mali. Hit the crossbar after four minutes of the Nations Cup final. Had spells at Grasshoppers Zurich and Strasbourg.

ALIOU CISSE (MONTPELLIER) BORN: 24/3/76 CAPS: 19 GLS: 0
The captain of Senegal, and the man who missed the deciding penalty in the Nations Cup Final shoot-out. Left PSG after a row with the then coach Phillippe Bergeroo, but now a first team regular at Montpellier.

FERDINAND COLY (LENS) BORN: 10/9/73 CAPS: 29 GLS: 4
Born in Senegal but brought up in France. In his third season at Lens, during which time he has played in a UEFA Cup semi-final against Arsenal. Infrequent goalscorer, but got a crucial one at Sedan in Lens title run in.

OMAR DAF (SOCHAUX) BORN: 12/2/77 CAPS: 23 GLS: 0
Played at the last two Nations Cups. His move from relegated St Etienne to newly promoted Sochaux has paid off as his new club finished in the top half of Le Championnat.

EL HADJI DIOUF (LENS) BORN: 15/1/81 CAPS: 20 GLS: 13
Describes himself rather unfortunately as 'The Serial Killer', but Diouf has bags of class on the field. His eight goals in nine World Cup qualifiers, which included two consecutive hat-tricks, were one of the major factors in ensuring Senegal's qualification. Shortlisted for this year's African Footballer of the Year award. Consistently brilliant performances this season for Lens in their quest for the title, he often plays wide on the right and still needs more consistency in front of goal.

OUMAR DIALLO (OLYMPIQUE KHOURIGBA) BORN: 28/09/72 CAPS: 42 GLS: 0
Likely to be the only African-based player in the World Cup squad. Saved a penalty against Tunisia in his one appearance in Mali. The former number one showed that he's still a capable replacement for Sylva.

LAMINE DIATTA (RENNES) BORN: 2/7/75 CAPS: 18 GLS: 1
Central defender who can switch to central midfield if required. Started with the Parisian club Red Star, and arrived at Rennes via Troyes.

SALIF DIAO (SEDAN) BORN: 10/2/77 CAPS: 19 GLS: 2
Emerged as a real star at the Nations Cup after strong performances in the centre of midfield and two goals, including the extra-time winner against Nigeria in the semi-final. Ex-Monaco and Bordeaux player who was in the international wilderness for four years before being invited back by Metsu last year.

SENEGAL

PAPE BOUBA DIOP (LENS) BORN: 28/1/78 CAPS: 11 GLS: 2
A recent arrival at Lens after his transfer from Grasshoppers in Switzerland. Huge presence in the centre of midfield.

PAPE MALICK DIOP (NEUCHATEL XAMAX) BORN: 29/12/74 CAPS: 26 GLS: 2
Former captain of the national side, and still takes over on occasion. Had an excellent spell at Strasbourg in 1999/2000. Senegal's Player of the Year in 1998.

KHALILOU FADIGA (AUXERRE) BORN: 30/12/74 CAPS: 24 GLS: 3
A well-travelled player who was born in Paris but played in Belgium for six years, and approached the Belgian national side to offer his services (he qualifies through marriage). Was not required and has since starred for Senegal and Auxerre. His left foot is Senegal's most potent weapon, and switches regularly between the left and right wings. Had serious disciplinary problems in Belgium, but seems to have put those behind him. Only made his international debut two years ago.

AMDY FAYE (AUXERRE) BORN: 12/3/77 CAPS: 5 GLS: 0
Educated under Guy Roux at the Auxerre youth academy. Missed his penalty in the Nations Cup Final shoot-out. Scored just one goal in four seasons at Auxerre.

FARY FAYE (BEIRA MAR) BORN: 24/12/74
After starting at the lower division club Montemor, Faye has now spent six years in Portugal, four of them at Beira Mar. Was left out of Metsu's final cut for Mali, but has just passed the 15 goal mark for his first time in Portugal's top flight, and is very close to a World Cup ticket. Scored twice in Beira Mar's shock 3-2 win in Porto.

CHEIKH GADIAGA (LIERSE) BORN: 30/11/79
Initially went to Belgium with Molenbeek, but now spent two seasons at Lierse, where he is a first team regular. Earlier in his career he spent a month's trial at Barcelona. His lanky running style is reminiscent of Nwankwo Kanu.

IBRE KEBE (SPARTAK MOSCOW)
Plays with the Cameroonian international Jerry Tchuisse in Russia, but has made only eight appearances in two seasons. Formerly with Jeanne D'Arc in Senegal.

FREDERIC MENDY (ST ETIENNE) BORN: 6/11/81 CAPS: 3 GLS: 0
Two caps in friendly matches, regarded as a talent for the future, and may well be included on the basis of that.

SAMUEL MONIN (RAITH ROVERS) BORN: 3/11/79
Was a reserve at Monaco with Sylva. Signed for the Scottish First Division side Raith in March and has played in every game since. Early in his Scottish career he famously saved an injury-time penalty to earn Raith a point against Falkirk. Can be erratic, and enjoys dribbling outside his area.

SENEGAL

ASSANE N'DIAYE (SHAKHTAR DONETSK) BORN: 1/8/74 CAPS: 11 GLS: 0
Played in the Nations Cup in 2000, but has since faded to the fringes of the squad.
Formerly played for the Senegalese club Jeanne D'Arc.

MAKHTAR N'DIAYE (RENNES) BORN: 31/12/81 CAPS: 10 GLS: 0
Has played now for three seasons in the Rennes side, and is surely destined for bigger
things than a Championnat relegation battle. Very quick, an excellent crosser, could
have a major role to play from out wide.

MOUSSA N'DIAYE (SEDAN) BORN: 20/2/79 CAPS: 37 GLS: 5
Spent six years at Monaco from the age of 15, but has flourished with regular first team
football at Sedan. Scored the first goal of Senegal's World Cup qualifying campaign.

SYLVAIN N'DIAYE (LILLE) BORN: 25/6/76 CAPS:5 GLS: 0
Was persuaded by Metsu to join up with the squad late last year. His Senegalese
grandfather qualifies him. Was born in Paris, and proved that he could mix it with the best
after his Champions League performance for Lille against Manchester United. Reportedly
not the most popular player in the squad. Visited Senegal for the first time at Christmas.

ALASSANE N'DOUR (ST ETIENNE) BORN: 12/12/81 CAPS: 6 GLS: 0
Just one appearance at the Nations Cup finals, but a regular run in the first team at St
Etienne will help his cause for more regular international inclusion.

ADAMA SARR (AC MILAN) BORN: 23/12/83
Was on loan at Milan from Treviso when he helped the Italian giants win the prestigious
Viareggio youth tournament. Franco Baresi recommended him, Milan paid a million for
him, and although he isn't a first team fixture, he has contributed a UEFA Cup goal this
season. Was left out of Metsu's final Nations Cup 22. After first moving to Italy, his main
complaint was "frozen feet".

PAPE SARR (LENS) BORN: 7/12/77 CAPS: 30 GLS: 4
Missed the Nations Cup Final after his sending off in the semi against Nigeria for an
elbow. Arrived at Lens in the summer after being relegated with St Etienne. Nearly
moved to Lyon, but that switch was vetoed by the St Etienne directors.

TONY SYLVA (MONACO) BORN: 17/05/75 CAPS: 14 GLS: 0
Voted best goalkeeper at the Nations Cup finals in Mali and has proved a real find.
Seven seasons at Monaco but just six league appearances in that time, and none this
season. Fabien Barthez and now Stephane Porato have kept him out of the first team.
Played over 30 games last season for Ajaccio in the Second Division.

PAPE THIAW (LAUSANNE) BORN: 5/2/81 CAPS:12 GLS: 5
A raw talent who needs to add guile to his considerable pace and power. There's a lot
he could learn from his teammate Diouf. Scored on his debut against Uganda, and got

SENEGAL

the hat-trick in Namibia which made sure of Senegal's win in their final qualifying match. Was the subject of legal action after breaking the nose of Sebastian Fournier in the tunnel after an argument in a Swiss League game.

AMARA TRAORE (GUEUGNON) BORN: 25/9/65 CAPS: 11 GLS: 2
The old man of the squad. Has the respect of the rest of the players and for that alone, is worth his place in the squad. Onto his fifth French club: proudest moment was when he lifted the French League Cup as the captain of Gueugnon after the Second Division side had beaten PSG in the final. Has spent most of his club career in the lower divisions in France, with just two seasons in the top flight, from 1996-98 with Metz.

COACH

BRUNO METSU
Metsu will charm many a television camera this summer. Charismatic and fluent, he has embraced Senegalese culture, and the players and public have welcomed him with open arms. He sets great store by the unity in his squad, but is aware that team spirit alone will not get them out of Group A. He was formerly the man in charge of the Guinean national side, having previously managed the French clubs Beauvais, Lille and Sedan. Didn't have a particularly auspicious playing career, although he had a spell at Anderlecht. He married a Senegalese woman earlier this year, and, whether he leads the Lions to a successful World Cup or not, he looks likely to be the man to lead the Lions for a while to come.

WORLD CUP FACTS

Jozef Barmos 'scored' for England against Czechoslovakia in 1982. It is the only World Cup own goal England have benefited from and they won the match 2-0.

Three of the England World Cup managers were also World Cup players – Sir Alf Ramsey, Bobby Robson and Glenn Hoddle. Sir Walter Winterbottom and Ron Greenwood will be joined in the non-playing list this summer by Sven-Göran Eriksson.

In 1954, only 17 England players went to the finals in Switzerland. The remaining five, who included Johnny Haynes, stayed at home on stand-by. They weren't called up.

Pele and Uwe Seeler are the only players to have scored in four tournaments.

GROUP B

It has become something of a World Cup tradition to tip Spain as a dark horse only for the talented under-achievers to disappoint yet again. While the success of Spanish clubs in Europe owes much to overseas stars, Spain has always boasted a solid backbone of home-grown players, yet somehow when they pull on the national shirt they fail to live up to expectations. This may again be the case this summer but Spain could hardly have hoped for a more gentle group to start their latest World Cup bid. With respect to debutants Slovenia, Paraguay and South Africa it could have been a lot worse for Jose Camacho's team. Spain cantered through their qualifying group undefeated and finishing five points ahead of Austria. In Raul of Real Madrid Spain have the all-time leading goalscorer in the Champions League and a striker as technically gifted as any in the world.

"Realistically only six or seven teams can win the World Cup," says Raul. "I like to think Spain are one of them. With a bit of luck we can go a long way. The side is a mixture of experience and youth and Camacho is taking us in the right direction."

Raul's captain at Real, Fernando Hierro, is the most experienced and he remains a huge influence even if the sands of time are catching up with the defender.

A worry for Camacho is the torrid season endured by Gaizka Mendieta following his transfer from Valencia to Lazio. The midfielder has looked a pale shadow of the outstanding player he was in Spanish football.

Ivan Helguera will provide the midfield steel while the evergreen Luis Enrique of Barcelona, Deportivo La Coruna's tricky Diego Tristan, and Juan Carlos Valeron provide attacking alternatives. Spain open against Slovenia who have followed their Euro 2000 qualification with a place on the world stage for the first time – a magnificent achievement for a country which gained independence in 1990. Five wins and five draws saw Slovenia, like Spain, unbeaten on the road to the Finals. In the European Championship two years ago Spain beat Slovenia 2-1 and now Srecko Katanec's 'unknowns' have the chance to show how much they have progressed. Katanec has moulded a side whose sum total is greater than the individual parts though on his day Zlatko Zahavic, the golden boy of Slovenian football, can damage even the tightest of defences.

Paraguay's best-known player is goalkeeper Jose Chilavert. The penalty-taking free-kick specialist – he scored four goals in the qualifying campaign - is, however, suspended from the first two ties and the South Americans will miss his presence. In France '98 Paraguay lost 1-0 to France in the second round when Laurent Blanc's golden goal in extra-time saw the hosts squeeze through. Expect Paraguay to be solid in defence, industrious in midfield, but the lack of a cutting edge in attack could be their downfall. South Africa were eliminated in the first round of France '98, their first appearance in the Finals and the suspicion is it will be the same-again for the team known as Bafana Bafana.

Club-versus-country confrontations plus the March resignation of coach Carlos Queiroz who guided them to the Finals, have affected their build-up while the long-term injury to Leeds' defender Lucas Radebe has robbed them of their most experienced player. Queiroz was unhappy about having to report to technical director Jomo Sono who was appointed in February. Sono was drafted in after South Africa's disappointing displays in the African Nations Cup when they were eliminated by hosts Mali, ranked 108th in the world.

Sono will lead South Africa in the Finals, effectively becoming the ninth coach they have had since their re-entry into international competitions almost a decade ago. A new coach but there are likely to be some familiar Premiership faces, such as Manchester United's Quinton Fortune and Shaun Bartlett of Charlton, but it will be difficult for the country determined to host the 2010 World Cup to make a significant impact in 2002.

SPAIN

"It is about time Spain did well in the World Cup. Bad luck at certain moments have not helped us but we must develop the knack of winning when we play badly. The current side enjoy playing together and we travel with optimism. We know Slovenia from Euro 2000, Paraguay have beaten Brazil recently and have established themselves as a force in South America, while South Africa will be better for the experience of playing at France '98." **Raul**, Spain striker.

PARAGUAY

"This is a great challenge. It is important we are correct tactically especially against a team as experienced as Spain. If Paraguay can go one better than in France '98 and reach the quarter-finals it would be a dream." **Cesare Maldini**, Paraguay coach.

SLOVENIA

"We rode our luck a little in the qualifiers but now we are here we hope to show people how far Slovenian football has come. We lost narrowly to Spain at Euro 2000 though we gained confidence from the performance. If we play to our capabilities we could get to the second stage which would be an incredible achievement." **Srecko Katanac**, Slovenia coach.

SOUTH AFRICA

"There has to be much improvement this time if we are to build on 1998. That means a lot of hard work and producing a better team. All three opponents play different types of football and it will not be easy. But I hope this can be the start of a good future for us." **Carlos Queiroz**, South Africa coach, who was in charge of the qualifying campaign.

SPAIN

For just over half-an-hour on the afternoon of July 9, 1950, Spain were, theoretically at least, the second best team in the world. They have never reached such heights again.

As most students of the world game are only too aware, Spain's national side are the greatest under-achievers in World Cup history. While Real Madrid have won the European Cup more times than any other team, and while Barcelona and Real have trophy rooms the size of some other clubs' grandstands, the national team have disappointed time and again at the World Cup finals.

Only briefly, on that July afternoon more than half-a-century ago, have Spain ever come close to realising their vast potential. And even then the vision of success proved to be utterly illusory.

There were no semi-finals or final in 1950 – but a final league of four teams comprising Brazil, Spain, Uruguay and Sweden from which the world champion would emerge after each team had played the others once.

In the opening pool match Brazil had crushed Sweden 7-1 and so topped the group. Spain met Uruguay next and were leading 2-1 from the 40th minute of the game until the 73rd. For those glorious 33 minutes, Spain were sitting in second place. Uruguay, the eventual champions, salvaged a 2-2 draw with 17 minutes to play and Spain eventually finished bottom of the final pool following a 6-1 defeat to Brazil and a 3-1 loss to Sweden.

But that fourth-placed finish remains Spain's best-ever showing at the World Cup. As Spanish skipper Fernando Hierro says: "In reality we have never done anything at the World Cup, now perhaps we have the players who can put that right."

Spain have never had a shortage of great players and that is still the case. As usual, they qualified for the Finals easily, finishing five points clear at the top of European Group Seven having won six and drawn two of their eight games with a goal tally of 21-4.

Players like Raul, Hierro, Gaizka Mendieta, Ivan Helguera, Luis Enrique, Diego Tristan – the list goes on and on – were simply too powerful, clever and skilful for the defenders of Austria, Israel, Bosnia and Liechtenstein, and Spain swept imperiously through with matches to spare.

But that is normally where the hard part starts. Spain usually qualify for everything effortlessly. It's when they get down to the real business of winning trophies that the problems begin. They never even got close when they hosted the World Cup in 1982.

Still, Jose Antonio Camacho's side should make it through the first round in Korea having been drawn against Paraguay, South Africa and Slovenia in Group B. But they will be taking nothing for granted. In France four years ago they were drawn against Nigeria, Bulgaria and Paraguay again – and failed to make it into round two.

This time the Spanish players are being understandably humble about their hopes and ambitions. As Real, Valencia and Deportivo Coruna have all proved in European competition in the last few years they can take on and beat the best in the world in the Champions League, but translating the success their clubs have enjoyed without the help of foreign imports has proved elusive.

"Everyone talks about winning the World Cup even before the first qualifying game," Camacho told Don Balon recently. "It seems we have an obligation to win

SPAIN

the competition but how many times have we won the World Cup in the past?"
Exactly. Never.

Although this is their seventh successive World Cup appearance they have only
reached the quarter-finals twice: in Mexico in 1986 and the United States in 1994. Can
they do better this summer?

On paper, there is no reason why not. There are a number of talented youngsters
coming through like Barcelona's Xavi and Carles Puyol and Dani of Real Betis, while
Real Madrid will provide the backbone of the side with Hierro in defence, Helguera in
midfield and Raul looking to overtake Hierro (of all people) as Spain's all-time highest
scorer – if he has not achieved that already in the pre-tournament friendlies.

Familiar faces are still there including Barca defenders Abelardo and Sergi, their ex-
club mate Miguel Angel Nadal, Valencia's keeper Santiago Canizares, and Victor and
Juan Carlos Valeron of Deportivo. Comacho has a problem because Mendieta has
struggled all season to even get into the Lazio team while Pep Guardiola has been
sidelined because of a drugs ban.

Camacho has a fine balancing act to negotiate. He most certainly has enough talent
available, and he himself is a good enough coach to make a real mark on this
tournament. But do the Spanish players believe in themselves enough? Do they honestly
believe they can win the World Cup?

The irony is, most of them probably would answer "yes" to both those questions.
Going out and doing it of course is something else. But just getting to the semi-finals
and at least equalling what their predecessors did in 1950 would be a start.

SQUAD

AGUSTIN ARANZABAL (REAL SOCIEDAD) BORN: 15.03.73 CAPS: 24 GLS: 0
An integral part of the Sociedad line up, but struggling in 2001 and 2002 with a poor
run from his club team. Taken a national place while Sergi has been on Barca's bench
and injured. Interest from Barca and Real Madrid but was born in San Sebastian and
has a contract with the local side until summer 2002. Not in the squad for Euro '96 –
Clemente preferred him in the U21 and Olympic teams, but back in the squad from the
1998 World Cup and for Euro 2000 qualifiers.

JOSE SANTIAGO CANIZARES (VALENCIA) BORN: 18.12.68 CAPS: 35 GLS: 0
First choice keeper for Spain after World Cup – played in 11 internationals on the
trot before a broken leg in autumn 1999 and only returned at the start of 2000. But
lost place after Euro 2000 to young Casillas. European Cup final 2000 and again in
2001. Lost out in the penalty shoot-out in 2001. Winner as sub in 1998 for Real.
Joined Valencia in summer 1998 from Real Madrid when out of contract, to replace
Andoni Zubizarreta who retired after the World Cup – Canizares was his No 2 in
France '98, USA '94 and Euro '96. Valencia finished fourth and won the Cup final in
1999. Only had a spell at the start of 1997-98 as Real No 1 when Bodo Illgner was
injured. He was with Real's juniors since 1986, but returned in 1994 after loan spells
at Elche and Merida and two seasons (1992-94) at Celta Vigo.

SPAIN

CAPI (REAL BETIS SEVILLE) BORN: 26.03.77 CAPS: 1 GLS: 0
Full name Jesus 'Capi' Capitan. Newcomer to squad in March 2002 after fine midfield performances with Betis. From the Seville region. One of the home grown products for the future. Joined the Betis B team in 1998, then loaned out to Granada. Back to claim first team place in the 2000-1 promotion team from D2 and continued excellence in the Primera Liga this season.

IKER CASILLAS (REAL MADRID) BORN: 20.05.81 CAPS: 13 GLS: 0
First national call up was for Euro 2000 squad – first cap as sub v Sweden on 03.06.00 just before the Finals. Born in Madrid – aged 19 just four days before 2000 European Cup win. Won championship medal in 2001. Keeper in the Spanish team that won the European U16 title and in the national U17 and U20 side. First team debut in 1999 after Illgner's injury and Bizzarri's loss of form.

CESAR (DEPORTIVO LA CORUNA) BORN: 02.04.77 CAPS: 4 GLS: 0
Three seasons at Depor 1999-2002 have been ravaged by injury. However his fine form in the UCL has warranted inclusion in national squad. From Oviedo, and formerly the best young defender in the country – had three seasons in their first team before a summer 1999 move to Deportivo. Moved into national team in autumn 1999.

LUIS ENRIQUE (BARCELONA) BORN: 08.05.70 CAPS: 59 GLS: 12
At the end of 2001 he was out with thigh muscle injury suffered at Anfield in the UCL but returned in Feb 2002. Had several outstanding seasons from 1996-99 before injury double-blow when he played in every position bar central defence and keeper – yet managed 17 goals – and again in 1997-98 when he improved to 18 goals in the title win, again playing virtually everywhere. Eleven goals last season. Crossed the great divide between Barca and Real Madrid. He had been at Real from 1991 until the summer 1996 move to Barca. Has won titles with both Real (1995) and Barca (1998 and 1999). Began career with Sporting Gijon 1989-91. Has an Olympic gold medal from 1992 and played at 1994 and 1998 World Cup and at Euro '96.

JOSEP GUARDIOLA (BRESCIA) BORN: 18.01.71 CAPS: 47 GLS: 5
Now playing in Italy since September 2001 after being out of contract at Barcelona – Tottenham thought his wage demands were too much. Then fell foul of the drug testers. First teamer at Barcelona from 1991-2001 and was the club captain, he won six championship medals, two Spanish Cup medals, the 1992 European Cup and 1997 ECWC medals. One year contract at Brescia.

IVAN HELGUERA (REAL MADRID) BORN: 28.03.75 CAPS: 22 GLS: 2
Four seasons at Real as their utility man and cost £3 million from Espanyol. Wound up with 2000 European Cup medal, filling in for injured Fernando Hierro. Former Albacete midfielder, whom Roma took a shine to, and had him at the Olympic stadium in 1997-98. Returned to Spain after a brief stay and joined Espanyol. Back in the full national squad after a superb 1998-99 season. Cost Espanyol just £300,000 from Roma.

SPAIN

FERNANDO HIERRO (REAL MADRID) BORN: 23.03.68 CAPS: 86 GLS: 28
Although a defender, he is the all-time top scorer for Spain! Has won four titles with the Real club, and the European Cups of 1998 and 2000. Club captain at Real for the past five seasons. Joined Real Madrid in 1989 and was signed by John Toshack from Valladolid. Was moved up by the club from central defence to striker and is now back in central defence – moved back by Fabio Capello. With 21 goals he was runner up in the league scoring charts back in 1991-92. Played in all games for Spain at the 1994 and 1998 World Cup and Euro '96, and was captain at Euro 2000 before injury. Hierro means 'Iron' in Spanish, and has his own brand of boots called the Lokomotive. Brother was a pro with Valladolid.

JOAQUIN (BETIS SEVILLE) BORN: 21.07.81 CAPS: 3 GLS: 0
This is the jewel in the Betis youth crown. Another of the young players hoping to take the club to the top. In the Betis B team two seasons ago, then played a full part in the first team last season (2000-1) and continues to show rapid improvement in the league.

JUANFRAN (CELTA) BORN: 15.07.76 CAPS: 7 GLS: 0
Full-back, mainly left side, who has benefitted internationally from Sergi's recent injuries. Moved to Celta from Valencia in summer 1999 with international striker Juan Sanchez going the other way. Improved enormously in the north of Spain. Had joined Valencia in summer 1997 from Division Two club Levante (for whom Johan Cruyff once played). He cost Valencia just £175,000, and had a four-year contract so the move was a surprise though in the end it was beneficial. Won Spanish cub in '99 with Valencia.

GAIZKA MENDIETA (LAZIO, ITALY) BORN: 17.03.74 CAPS: 32 GLS: 7
Valencia's captain in the 2000 and 2001 European Cup finals, moved to Lazio for £27 million in summer 2001. Not settled in Italy though. Has made the national team since 1999 – hardly missed a game. Escaped the Bilbao net (he's a Basque) and was taken by Valencia in 1992 from Castellon. Brought through the system at Valencia since 1992 and has blossomed since being converted from very ordinary right back into midfield.

FERNANDO MORIENTES (REAL MADRID) BORN: 05.04.76 CAPS: 20 GLS: 14
Camacho, the national coach admitted that he was wrong to leave him out of his Euro 2000 line-up. But comeback stalled through injury. Back in national team autumn 2001. Has fine record in internationals. Scorer of first goal in European Cup final win in 2000. Was the major summer signing for Real in 1997 from Zaragoza for £4.2 million, after two seasons at Zaragoza where he scored 15 goals each season and was the first choice striker for the national U21 side. An English style striker, nearly 6'3" tall, and he was originally with Albacete in his younger days. Won 2001 title with Real.

PEDRO MUNITIS (REAL MADRID) BORN: 19.06.75 CAPS: 21 GLS: 2
Recent member of the national team – played at Euro 2000 and signed from home town Racing Santander for £6.5 million in summer 2000. Had come right through the ranks at Racing since a teenager in the lower leagues in 1993 and has been part of national coach Jose Camacho's plans for the national team since 1999 Busy little player.

SPAIN

MIGUEL ANGEL NADAL (MALLORCA) BORN: 28.07.66 CAPS: 60 GLS: 3
In third season back with his first club – played for Mallorca from 1986 until 1991, then moved to Barcelona. His excellence last season earned a recall to the national team – played in the Sept 2001 World Cup games and helped put Spain through to the World Cup finals with the clinching goal in 2-0 win in Liechtenstein, his third international goal. Was with Barcelona as one of Europe's best defenders from 1991-99 winning five titles, two Cups, a European Cup medal in 1992 (non-playing sub) and a Cup Winners' Cup medal in 1997. Missed crucial penalty vs England at Euro '96 – but Manchester Utd and Leeds both bid for him – and was an international throughout the 1990s.

JAVI DE PEDRO (REAL SOCIEDAD) BORN: 04.08.73 CAPS: 5 GLS: 0
Recalled in March 2002 to the national squad after four years following fine performances from Sociedad's climb out of the relegation zone this season. Played in Camacho's first three games in charge of Spain in 1998-99 season but Bilbao's Joseba Echeverria was preferred. Another from the Sanse set up at Sociedad, he progressed to the first team squad in 1991, he's well past 200 PL games but many sub appearances in early days hindered his progress. Usually operates down the flanks.

CARLES PUYOL (BARCELONA) BORN: 13.04.78 CAPS: 8 GLS: 1
First cap v Holland – Nov 2000 – and has been there or thereabouts since. Was the only Barcelona player in the original squad for Holland in March 2002 (there were more Barca players in the Dutch squad). Selected for Olympics in Sept/Oct 2000 where Spain won the silver medal and an U21 international of recent vintage so his national credentials are well known. From the Barca B team into the first team pool in summer 1999 after three years in the B team. Was one of the youngsters brought on by Louis van Gaal.

RAUL (REAL MADRID) BORN: 27.06.77 CAPS: 51 GLS: 25
All-time top scorer in the UCL. Was the youngest in Spain to 100 Primera Liga goals. Primera Liga top scorer in 1999 and 2001. Also won a 1998 World Club Cup medal (winning goals), 1998 and 2000 European Cup medals and 1997 and 2001 championship medal. He was a first teamer at 17 when introduced by Jorge Valdano, and was the only player to play in all 42 games in the 1997 title win (21 goals).

RICARDO (VALLADOLID) BORN: 30.12.71 CAPS: 1 GLS: 0
Either Ricardo or Deportivo keeper Fransisco Molina should be the No 3 at the World Cup. Former reserve keeper at Atletico Madrid from 1993-98, he then moved to Valladolid where he became one of the best in the league, over the past few seasons. First cap as sub against Mexico in November 2001.

MICHEL SALGADO (REAL MADRID) BORN: 22.10.75 CAPS: 18 GLS: 0
£8 million signing from Celta in summer1999 and settled in as Spain's first choice right back at Euro 2000 though currently overtaken. European Cup medal 2000. Won 2001 title with Real. Eventful 1998 - started badly with blame for the foul that broke Juninho's

ankle and he worsened the incident by saying that he should have been sent off – then amazingly he suffered exactly the same injury a month later. Followed by the good news – was in the team that won the 1998 Euro U21 championship, then Man Utd sniffed around with a £4 million fee, and after the World Cup he moved in to the full national squad for his first caps in autumn 1998. A former Celta junior, but moved straight into the Celta first team on a regular basis in 1997.

SERGI (BARCELONA) BORN: 28.12.71 CAPS: 58 GLS: 1
Has a reputation as one of the very best left wing backs in Europe at present, but top players are finding the odd flaw. Is beginning to slow down. The big find back in the 1993-94 season, when he moved from Barcelona B to the World Cup in six months. Johan Cruyff converted him from a left winger. Born in Barcelona. At Euro 2000 but Aranzabal of Real Sociedad played most of the games, Sergi is back for the World Cup games from autumn 2000.

SERGIO (DEPORTIVO LA CORUNA) BORN:10.10.76 CAPS: 5 GLS: 0
Scorer at Old Trafford in the UCL and part of the excellent Deportivo midfield. Moved from Espanyol to Deportivo in mid-August 2001 for $14.92 million on an eight-year contract. Was happy at Espanyol but club were $26 million in debt. From the Espanyol youth set up.

TIKO (ATHLETIC BILBAO) BORN:15.09.76 CAPS: 1 GLS: 0
Full name Roberto 'Tiko' Martinez. First called up in 2002 after some spectacular long range efforts for Bilbao this season and has bedded into the Bilbao team. Midfielder, who joined Bilbao in summer 1999 from Osasuna and played in Bilbao's first team squad for the last three seasons 1999-2002. Improving. Previously played for Osasuna for three seasons in Division Two as a first choice in their side.

CHRISTOBAL CURRO TORRES (VALENCIA) BORN 27.12.76 CAPS: 4 GLS: 0
Gained his first cap v Mexico in November 2001 at Huelva, which was his hometown and he was the local lad chosen. Played for the Valencia B team in 1997 to 1999, then was loaned back to Recreativo Huelva (D2) and Tenerife for the past two seasons. Returned to his first senior club, after being in Tenerife's promotion side to the PL in 2001, and playing under new coach Benitez. Taken over from the 36-year-old Jocelyn Angloma at full-back for Valencia but can play central positions.

DIEGO TRISTAN (DEPORTIVO LA CORUNA) BORN: 05.01.76 CAPS: 7 GLS: 2
Fine form in the UCL this season spoiled by that late tackle on David Beckham. Cost £10 million from Mallorca in summer 2000, though certain reports suggest £13 million. Almost joined Real Madrid in summer 2000, but Real changed presidents and the transfer talk was done with Real's now former chief Lorenzo Sanz. Has really had only three seasons of top class football – starting with the 1999-2000 season with Mallorca where he scored 12 goals and impressed everyone. Prior to that he was released after two seasons with Betis B team from 1976-98, and spent 1998-99 in Mallorca's B team.

SPAIN

ISMAEL URZAIZ (ATHLETIC BILBAO) BORN: 07.10.71 CAPS: 25 GLS: 8
Recalled under Camacho to national squad after fine start to 1998-99 – and has been around the fringes ever since – appeared in all four games at Euro 2000. A former Real Madrid junior prospect, he arrived at Bilbao in summer 1996 to play for his seventh club (a current players' record) and immediately found his way into the national squad, and gained his first cap in the World Cup qualifiers against the Czechs in Oct 1996. Arrived at Bilbao from Espanyol – and now sixth season with Bilbao.

JUAN CARLOS VALERON (DEPORTIVO LA CORUNA) BORN: 17.06.75 CAPS: 22 GLS: 0
Another who has been in superb form vs Man Utd and Arsenal this past season in the UCL – he scored at Highbury and was superb at Old Trafford. Signed by Atletico Madrid from Mallorca in summer 1998 for £4 million – but as a current international squad player he was sold on to Depor in summer 2000 when Atletico went down for £5 million. Was not far short of a 1998 World Cup squad place, instead Javier Clemente played him in the team that won the 1998 European U21 championship – and played the first two games of Euro 2000. He gained his first caps though in 98-99 in a fine season with Atletico. Born in the Canaries.

VICENTE (VALENCIA) BORN: 16.07.81 CAPS: 5 GLS: 0
First call up into national squad for March 2001 friendly v France – and stayed in squad after fine UCL performances through to the final. Very promising young midfielder who joined Valencia from the Levante club who play in D2 and who has come through really well with Valencia from autumn 2000 to stake a place. Took over at the club from Fransisco Farinos (Inter) and the injured Didier Deschamps. Had already played three seasons for Levante, and debut aged 16, before his move to Valencia. Former Junior and U21 international.

XAVI (BARCELONA) BORN: 25.01.80 CAPS: 3 GLS: 0
Selected for Olympics in Sept/Oct 2000 where Spain won silver medal (lost to Cameroon on pens in final) and an U21 international – then won first cap in friendly v Holland in November 2000. Revelation of early part of 1998-99 season – thrown into first team and retained place. In Spain team that won the 1999 World Junior Cup in Nigeria – now in national U21 side. Scored on club debut in final game of 1997-98 season after Barca had won championship.

COACH

JOSE ANTONIO CAMACHO BORN: 08.06.55
Fourth season in charge after Javier Clemente's poor 1998 World Cup campaign and the loss to Cyprus in the following game. Second choice for job after walking out of Real Madrid after just 22 days. Former Spanish cap record holder (81 caps), and former Real Madrid full-back for 16 seasons winning nine championships, five cups and two UEFA Cup medals as a left back. Coached Rayo Vallecano, Espanyol (twice) and Seville, main honour was Division Two title with Espanyol.

Fabien Barthez will be bidding to help France defend the World Cup

Hidetoshi Nakata carries much of the burden for host nation Japan

PARAGUAY

For a while it looked as though Paraguay would be the surprise package out of South America as they beat Brazil and embarked on a seven-match unbeaten run which also saw them draw in Argentina, win in Colombia and Uruguay, and crush Peru 5-1.

But they failed to win their last three games of the qualifying competition and coach Sergio Markarian, who had upset both press and officials, had provided the ready made excuse for the order of the boot.

This was the man who had taken Paraguay to the Olympics in 1992 with the same players and who had picked up the threads with many of the same players and began to look a serious threat to Argentina. But the 4-0 defeat at home to Colombia was enough for the Association to kick their feisty coach into touch and instead brought in the dour former Italian coach, the 70-year-old Cesare Maldini.

The choice of Paulo's father was an odd one to say the least for he had no experience of Paraguayan football and his time in charge of the Italian team with much, much better players available to him was hardly what one would describe as distinguished.

The South Americans qualified for the 2002 Finals using a basic, strong 4-4-2 system but Maldini has already shown that he is more in favour of playing five at the back to make life difficult for his opponents rather than using the new found fire power dredged up by his predecessor. Maldini does not have an easy task for there is little depth in the international squad and that is further diminished with the suspensions of his experienced goalkeeper Jose Luis Chilavert for the opening two games against South Africa and Spain, and by the time he returns against Slovenia for the final game progress may already be out of the team's reach. There will certainly be a heavy work load on Roberto 'El Toro' Acuna, the 30-year-old Real Zaragoza midfield player, and leading goal scorer Jose Cardoza, the 31-year-old who plays in Mexico for Toluca where his strength and power has made him a big favourite. His partner up front is likely to be the tall, rangy youngster Roque Santa Cruz of Bayern Munich who will command a lot of attention with his pace and mature finishing.

Very disappointing in friendly against England at Anfield in April.

SQUAD

ROBERTO ACUNA (ZARAGOZA) BORN: 25.03.72 CAPS: 79 GLS: 5
First name on the midfield team list and closing in on the national caps record. Joined Zaragoza in summer 1997 from Independiente of Argentina, and has been outstanding in Spain. Known as The Bull – El Toro, and played well at France '98.

GUIDO ALVARENGA (LEON) BORN: 24.08.73 CAPS: GLS: 2
Small, left-sided midfielder who plays in Mexico. Was the idol of the fans at Cerro Porteno before moving to Mexico recently.

CELSO AYALA (RIVER PLATE) BORN: 20.08.70 CAPS: 73 GLS: 7
Plays for the Argentinian champions – three times champions in 1997, 1998 and 2000 – and 1996 Libertadores Cup winners. Another quality defender and one of the top players in the Argentinian league. Been with River Plate for some eight seasons. Ten years in national team.

PARAGUAY

FRANSISCO ARCE (PALMEIRAS) BORN: 02.04.71 CAPS: 51 GLS: 6
Usually parades up the right flank – full-back or midfield. Experts say he is the best right back in Brazilian football at present. Also played for Gremio, where he won the 1995 Libertadores Cup. Pre-World Cup problems because he was not released by his club side.

MIGUEL ANGEL BENITEZ (OLIMPIA ASUNCION) BORN: 11.05.70 CAPS: 47 GLS: 14
Now back home after two years out through injury, and has returned from Spanish club Espanyol to try for the World Cup. Top scorer in the 1998 qualifiers with four goals and Paraguay's best forward at the Finals. Went to Spain in 1993 to play for Atletico Madrid, was loaned to Merida in 1994, and joined Espanyol in 1995. Played under Spain coach Jose Antonio Camacho at Espanyol.

ALDO ANTONIO BOBADILLA (CERRO PORTENO) BORN: 20.04.76 CAPS: 3 GLS: 0
Played in the final two World Cup qualifiers.

HUGO BRIZUELA (PACHUCA) BORN: 17.03.71 CAPS: 22 GLS: 3
Has played all over the continent and was in the 1998 World Cup squad. Played in Argentina for the side that developed Maradona – Argentinos Juniors – in 1998-99 and has played for four top clubs in Chile as well. Has played games in both recent qualifying campaigns, but is not first choice.

JUAN CACERES (CERRO PORTENO) BORN: 06.10.73 CAPS: 15 GLS: 1
From the domestic league, he is the club captain. Back up internationally for Ayala and Gamarra. 1998 World Cup squad.

JORGE CAMPOS (UNIVERSIDAD) BORN: 11.08.70 CAPS: 29 GLS: 3
Formerly with the top domestic side Olimpia Asuncion. Now playing in Chile after a spell at Chinese club Beijing Guouan – so a real wanderer. From the 1998 World Cup squad.

DENIS CANIZA (SANTOS LAGUNA) BORN: 20.08.74 CAPS: 48 GLS: 1
Formerly with the Paraguayan champions Olimpia, he was one of the best midfielders in the domestic league. Moved to Mexico around 18 months ago.

JOSE LUIS CHILAVERT (STRASBOURG) BORN: 27.05.65 CAPS: 68 GLS: 8
Extraordinary keeper, good enough to be the 1994 South American Footballer of the Year, but quite eccentric! Has scored no less than 51 goals in his senior career, of which 43 have come during the pressure of the Argentine and South American club cups, and internationals – eight goals have come for Paraguay – shoot-outs NOT included. Forever walking out of national team (1993-95), and suspended (four games in 1998 qualifiers – and will miss first two games of 2002 Finals), is outspoken and free with his fists on and off the field. First hit the headlines with San Lorenzo from 1985-88, then moved to Zaragoza from 1989-91, and then to Velez, where the highlights have been the 1994 World Club Cup win and Libertadores Cup, and three domestic titles. Has been at Strasbourg for 18 months.

PARAGUAY

JOSE CARDOSO (TOLUCA, MEXICO) BORN: 19.03.71 CAPS: 55 GLS: 11
Is equal top scorer in the country's international history. Plays for the recent Mexican champions, which has kept him in favour. From the 1998 World Cup squad, he was top scorer for Paraguay in the qualifiers with six goals. Late developer, playing well internationally from the age of 30.

JULIO CESAR ENCISO (OLIMPIA ASUNCION) BORN: 05.08.74 CAPS: 61 GLS: 2
Midfielder recalled in 1998 to the World Cup squad. Now back with the champions, and was formerly with Cerro Poteno from 1994-95. At the last World Cup he was with Internacional of Porto Alegre, one of Brazil's top clubs.

VIRGILIO FERREIRA (CERRO PORTENO) BORN: 28.01.73 CAPS: 18 GLS: 6
Now back in the domestic league after a spell with Spanish club Extramadura. Midfielder who has a decent goals per game ratio.

CARLOS ALBERTO GAMARRA (AEK ATHENS) BORN: 17.07.71 CAPS: 75 GLS: 3
Now on third spell in Europe and also played well in Brazil. Created fine impression in Portugal a few years ago after joining Benfica from Inter Porto Alegre in summer 1997 but was on the way home when Graeme Souness arrived – the club could not afford his wages. National team for ten years.

DIEGO GAVILAN (GUADALAJARA) BORN: 01.03.80 CAPS: 18 GLS: 0
Now loaned out but Newcastle are believed to still have his contract. Had a fine game against Brazil in the qualifiers, but had little chance to shine in England. Newcastle bought him from Cerro Porteno in February 2000 for £2 million.

PABLO GIMINEZ (GUARANI) BORN: 29.06.81 CAPS: 2 GLS: 0
Brought through with much praise by previous coach Sergio Markarian. Right winger who has been a star of recent youth tournaments.

JULIO GONZALEZ (HURUCAN) BORN: 26.08.81 CAPS: 4 GLS: 0
Plays for Ossie Ardiles club, and is new into the squad. Star of the national youth team and has ben in the full squad for around a year.

GUSTAVO MORINGO (LIBERTAD) BORN: 23.01.77 CAPS: 9 GLS: 1
Forward from the domestic league. Left-sided player, who came through well in the later stages of the World Cup qualifiers.

CARLOS PAREDES (FC PORTO) BORN: 16.07.76 CAPS: 36 GLS: 6
Midfielder who joined Porto in summer 2000 from Paraguay's top club Olimpia of Ascuncion, where he won three national titles from 1997-1999. 1998 World Cup squad and second top scorer in the 2002 qualifiers with five goals. First choice for Porto and played in the UCL in 2001-2.

PARAGUAY

VICTOR QUINTANA (OLIMPIA ASUNCION) BORN: 17.04.76 CAPS: 19 GLS: 0
Moved in summer 2001 to FC Porto for $4 million from Olimpia of Asuncion in the Paraguayan capital. However, he failed to settle and was home again within months. Won a hat-trick of domestic titles with Olimpia from 1998-2000 so time to venture to Europe. Has come onto the international scene since the 1998 World Cup.

CESAR RAMIREZ (CERRO PORTENO) BORN: 24.03.77 CAPS: 10 GLS: 0
Back home with his first club after a spell in Europe with Sporting Portugal of Lisbon. Played in the 1997-98 Champions League, but returned to Cerro Porteno in 1999.

CLAUDIO MOREL RODRIGUEZ (SAN LORENZO) BORN: 02.02.78 CAPS: 5 GLS: 0
Father was Paraguayan international star. Recently joined the national squad, and has been with his Argentinian club for four seasons, since the age of 19.

ROQUE SANTA CRUZ (BAYERN MUNICH) BORN: 16.08.81 CAPS: 22 GLS: 7
Many people thought Bayern were not up to speed when they signed him from Paraguayan champions Olimpia in summer 1999. However his three goals for the host nation in the 1999 Copa America quickly turned the deal into a real bargain. First team player for Olimpia at 15, capped at 17 – he's quite a large forward at nearing 6'2" already so should be okay physically. Fine start to Bundesliga and UCL career – with two championships and a European Cup medal.

PEDRO SARABIA (RIVER PLATE) BORN: 05.07.75 CAPS: 41 GLS: 0
Excellent form in 1998 World Cup finals. Another quality player with the 1998 and 2000 Argentinian champions and 1996 Libertadores Cup holders, he has been with them for around five years. Left-sided defender or midfield.

ESTANISLAO STRUWAY (LIBERTAD) BORN: 25.06.67 CAPS: 41 GLS: 0
Will be 35 at the Finals, but hopes to make the squad to make up for 1998 when he played in the qualifiers but was dropped for France '98. Played extensively on the South American continent for Cerro at home from 1988-94 then for Racing Club (Argentina), Sporting cristal (Peru) and the top Brazilian clubs Portuguesa and Coritiba.

RICARDO TAVARELLI (OLIMPIA ASUNCION) BORN: 02.08.70 CAPS: 18 GLS: 0
Reserve to Chilavert, and picks up several caps in his own right. Plays for the team that has won the last five domestic championships.

COACH

CESARE MALDINI BORN: 05.02.32
Replaced Sergio Markarian who qualified Paraguay for the Finals and who is now at Panathinaikos. Father of the Italian captain, and was an international in his own right Was No 2 to Enzo Bearzot in the 1982 World Cup win. Was then coach of the Italian national U21 side, and was in charge of Italy at France '98.

SLOVENIA

One player cannot make a team but one coach can – and Srecko Katanec has done just that for Slovenia. Working with limited playing resources, a low-level domestic league and also a real lack of finance, Katanec has performed what many once believed impossible. Not only did he steer Slovenia into the finals of Euro 2000, but two years on he did even better. Slovenia qualified for their first-ever World Cup finals with an unbeaten record of six wins and six draws through 12 qualifiers and play-offs – even seeing off the far more fancied Romanians in the two-legged decider between group runners-up last November. Katanec, who played 31 times for the old Yugoslavia and five times for the newly-independent state of Slovenia in the early 1990s, was only 36 when Slovenia's football chiefs asked him to take control of the national team in 1998.

The situation could not have been much bleaker. Slovenia had failed miserably in their first attempt to reach the World Cup finals as an independent side, their eight qualifying matches before the Finals in France producing one draw and seven defeats.

But Katanec did have one ace up his sleeve – Slovenia's only real world class player, Zlatko Zahovic. So he did what any intelligent coach would do. He proceeded to build a team around him. Except, of course, that is far easier said than done.

But as Kaiserslautern defender Aleksander Knavs recalls now: "He totally changed the team's way of thinking which was a significant step for us. He told us to go out and play to win and to look for goals. His attitude was, and still is: "Don't worry about the opposition, just go for goal, you can win this." We had some very good players who responded to his attitude, to his optimism. We now believe we can go out and win when it matters. We have lost the inferiority complex we might have had before."

Katanec's mantra quickly produced results which saw them qualify for Euro 2000 – a huge achievement for the small central-European country where skiing in the Alps, and the indoor pursuits of ice-hockey, basketball and water-polo traditionally took precedence over football.

Although they were eliminated after the first round of Euro 2000, they won many new admirers for the way they played. Only inexperience saw them lose a 3-0 lead against Yugoslavia who fought back for a 3-3 draw in their opening match. A 2-1 defeat to Spain and a 0-0 draw with Norway saw them go out – but they were far from disgraced. They made a slow start to their World Cup qualifying campaign in September 2000 with a 2-2 draw against the Faroe Islands before a narrow 2-1 win over Luxembourg in their second match. A second 2-2 draw, this time against Switzerland did not augur well, but gradually the team regained its composure, starting with an impressive 1-1 draw in Russia.

A 2-1 win over Russia in the return last September followed by a second 1-1 draw with Yugoslavia and a one-sided 3-0 win over the Faroe Islands secured second place in the group and a tough two-legged play-off against Romania. A 2-1 home win followed by a 1-1 draw in Bucharest sent Slovenia wild with delight. They had reached the World Cup finals for the first time – less than ten years after playing their first-ever international as an independent nation. They now face Spain, South Africa and Paraguay in group B in Korea and have a realistic chance of making the second round. Katanec, though has been quick to keep the fans' hopes grounded in some kind of reality. "We played well in the qualifiers overall and have done magnificently to reach the Finals. But as a team and as individuals we still have much to learn. We have proved we are no longer anyone's pushover as we may have been before, but we can still improve to reach our full potential in the World Cup."

His real achievement has been to create a team with a great spirit, whose whole is far greater than the sum of their parts. Only eight of the expected final squad of 23 play in Slovenia's low-level domestic championship, but Katanec also has another problem with those considered good enough to play abroad, as most of them do not actually play regularly for their club sides. They are often on the bench, or left out for weeks on end. Even Zahovic has had his problems at Benfica and both injury and suspension limited him to eight of Slovenia's 12 preliminary matches.

Still, Slovenia are not just a one-man team. Milan Osterc caught the attention during the season with some outstanding displays up front for Hapoel Tel Aviv of Israel, the surprise package in this season's UEFA Cup, while Red Star Belgrade midfielder Milenko Acimovic and Nastja Ceh of Club Bruges -- who scored twice on his debut against the Faroe Islands – have impressed. Ceh, 24, could make a name for himself if he gets the chance to play for long enough in the Finals.

The one prerequisite for every player in the side – apart from Zahovic – is that whatever their primary function in the team – be it striker or creative midfielder, they also have to come back and defend whenever danger threatens. This gives Slovenia a fluidity and movement not seen in other teams – but Katanec is still honing this aspect of their game. They did not look too impressive in their early friendlies after qualifying – but when resources are as stretched as Slovenia's perhaps that is understandable.

Slovenia are unlikely to win the World Cup and in fact they will do well to get past the second round, but in most respects, just being there represents success.

SQUAD

MILENKO ACIMOVIC (RED STAR BELGRADE) BORN: 15.02.77 CAPS: 36 GLS: 9
Plays in Yugoslavia for the famous Red Star Belgrade side, whose youth system has produced so many fine players and who were the 2000 and 2001 Yugoslav champions. Is filling the role at Red Star that was vacated by Dejan Stankovic's move to Lazio – he's married to Stankovic's sister. Scored goal in first leg of Euro 2000 play-off vs Ukraine.

SPASOJE BULAJIC (COLOGNE) BORN: 24.11.75 CAPS: 15 GLS: 1
Is with Cologne, who were disastrously relegated from the Bundesliga in 2002, and is their first team as right-sided central defender. Joined Cologne in summer 1998 for £250,000 after helping Maribor to the 1997 and 1998 Slovenian titles.

ALES CEH (GRAZ AK, AUSTRIA) BORN: 07.04.68 CAPS: 70 GLS: 1
Another who is playing over the border, at another Graz club in the Austrian Premier Division – he is a midfielder who played in Slovenia's first international back in 1992 vs Estonia. Team captain and most capped player. With fine timing, he was the first Slovenian to 50 caps in the opener at Euro 2000. He was in Olympia Ljubljana's first

SLOVENIA

title win in 1992 and played in the old Yugoslav Division One, then switched to Graz in summer 1992. Plays in the holding role just in front of defence.

NASTJA CEH (FC BRUGES) BORN: 26.01.78 CAPS: 4 GLS: 2
Is with the top Belgian club since summer 2001, and doing well alongside teammate Nemec. Was with Olimpia Ljubliana from 1990 as a youngster until 1996, then moved to Maribor form 1996-2001.

SEBASTJAN CIMEROTIC (LECCE) BORN: 14.09.74 CAPS: 11 GLS: 1
First season in Serie A. He was the Olimpia club top scorer and has been recently recalled to the squad. First capped v Poland in 1998, then against Finland in a pre-Euro 2000 qualifier – now played also the last few games in a row.

MLADEN DABANOVIC (LOKEREN) BORN: 13.09.71 CAPS: 19 GLS: 0
6'5" tall keeper, who played in all three games at Euro 2000. Joined the top flight Belgian club in summer 1999 after five years with Maribor and four years with Rudar in the local leagues. Created good impression in Belgium. On debut he came on as a sub for his first game in the warm-up game against Hungary in Sept 1998 and was sent off!

SASO GAJSER (GHENT) BORN: 11.02.74 CAPS: 19 GLS: 1
Plays in Belgium for Ghent who had an excellent season. He plays on the left side of midfield. Three seasons in Belgium, he joined after three seasons with Rudar, and started his career with Maribor. Breakthrough in 2000 and covers for Novak.

MARINKO GALIC (UNATTCHED) BORN: 22.04.70 CAPS: 64 GLS: 0
Won a League and Cup double medal with Maribor in 1997 and then moved to the stronger Croatian league to play for Dinamo Zagreb. Now back home after a move to Sturm Graz fell through. Won title again again in 2000 and 2001 with Maribor, he is the sweeper for club and country. Played for FIFA v Bosnia in April 2000.

AMIR KARIC (MARIBOR) BORN: 31.12.73 CAPS: 42 GLS: 1
From the 1999 and 2000 champions, and experience in the UCL, he then went to Ipswich but is now back home. Had also been playing for Gamba Osaka in the J-League in 1997 and 1998 and earned the nickname Tyson for his aggression before returning to his former club. Also played in Yugoslavia early in his career for Zeleznicar Sarajevo, in their old Superleague.

ALEXANDR KNAVS (KAISERSLAUTERN) BORN: 05.12.75 CAPS: 37 GLS: 2
Joined Kaiserslautern in summer 2001 from Tirol Innsbruck for £900,000. Tirol won the Austrian title in 2000 for the first time in ten years and retained the title in 2001 Summer 1997 signing by the Tirol club from Olimpia Ljubliana – he had a three-year contract with Tirol which has been extended, and is a first choice defender with their side. Looks like being a key defender in the future due to the retirement of the old guard after Euro 2000.

SLOVENIA

ZELJKO MILINOVIC (JEF UNITED) BORN: 12.10.69 CAPS: 32 GLS: 3
Moved at the end of his career to Japan from Austrian Premier Division club Linz ASK in time for the start of the 2001 J-League. Had three seasons with LASK, and has been in the national team for around the same time. Arrived from Maribor, the 1997 and 1998 champions, where he was a key defender in their title wins and was selected in the Slovenian league 'Team of the Season' at left back. A Yugoslav, who has gained Slovenian nationality, hence his late arrival in the squad.

DEJAN NEMEC (FC BRUGES) BORN: 01.03.77 CAPS: 0 GLS: 0
No 3 keeper at Euro 2000. Signed a three-year contract with Belgian runners-up FC Bruges to replace their long serving keeper Dany Verlinden after the Euro finals. Called up 1998 to national squad, yet to gain a cap before 2002.

DZONI NOVAK (UNTERHACHING) BORN: 04.09.69 CAPS: 67 GLS: 2
Another quality player hiding in a quiet backwater – like Milanic, he was in the Yugoslav team that won through to the Euro '92 finals only to be banned because of the War. He won four caps for the old Yugoslavia. He was then with Partizan Belgrade – the army team – and initially got out to Fenerbahce. He then came to Olympia Ljubliana, his home town team in 1993, and won three titles before moving in summer 1997 to Le Havre in the French First Division, and then on loan with Sedan. Moved to the Bundesliga with Unterhaching in summer 2000.

MILAN OSTERC (HAPOEL TEL AVIV) BORN: 04.07.75 CAPS: 40 GLS: 8
Now playing his football in Israel, where he moved after Euro 2000. Originally from the 1996 champions HIT Gorica, and one of the players to have come through the recent national U21 system. Last season he played for Olimpia Ljubliana. Also had a two-year stint with Spanish D2 club Hercules Alicante. Scored four goals vs Oman in 1999 Oman Cup game, which inflates his stats. Scored winning goal vs Chelsea and Parma in 2002 UEFA Cup. Scorer of great goal in first leg of play-off vs Romania.

MIRAN PAVLIN (FC PORTO) BORN: 08.10.71 CAPS: 44 GLS: 6
National hero with the goal in Ukraine that took them to the Euro 2000 finals – then only his second goal in internationals. Moved to FC Porto in summer 2000, now in first team after injury. Played in the Bundesliga in the top flight for Freiburg, also on loan at Karlsruhe. Pavlin joined Freiburg in summer 1997 and was part of the promotion team back to the Bundesliga. He was originally with Olimpia Ljubliana, where he won four league titles in the mid-1990s, and then moved to Dynamo Dredsen.

ZORAN PAVLOVIC (UNATTACHED) BORN: 27.06.76 CAPS: 19 GLS: 0
A Croat who was born in Bosnia and moved to Slovenia with family aged two months. Has played for Dinamo (ex-Croatia) Zagreb where he won the 2000 Croatian title but a subsequent move to FK Austria Vienna did not work out. Home club was Rudar Velenje First capped in 1998, mainly a squad member.

SLOVENIA

DAMIR PEKIC (CELJE) BORN: CAPS: 0 GLS: 0
Top scorer in the 2000-1 championship with 23 goals. In the national U21 squad, and only his second season in the top flight. A target for bigger clubs.

ERMIN RAKOVIC (MARIBOR) BORN: 07.09.77 CAPS: 1 GLS: 0
Busy little winger who has played for Boavistya (Portugal) and Hapoel Petach Tikva in Israel. Recent addition to the national squad after good form at home.

ELVIS RIBARIC (GORICA) BORN: 21.05.72 CAPS: 1 GLS: 0
Lively midfielder on the fringes of the squad for some time but not expected to make the final 23.

MLADEN RUDONJA (PORTSMOUTH) BORN: 26.07.71 CAPS: 56 GLS: 1
Winger, who has yet to score at full level. Very quick but not always sure where goal is. His first goal for country after 53 games took them to the World Cup! Moved after Euro 2000 from Belgian club St-Truiden to English D1 club Portsmouth in summer 2000 for £200,000. Had joined the Belgian premier Division club half way through the 1997-98 season. Former championship winner with Olimpia, he then went into the Croatian league with Marsala, and returned to the Primorje club for the first part of the 1997-98 season before going to Belgium. Portsmouth is his 11th club.

GORAN SANKOVIC (SLAVIA PRAGUE) BORN: 18.06.79 CAPS: 4 GLS: 0
Now playing in the Czech league but being given few chances. Reserve defender who can fill all back-four roles. Home club was Publikum Celje where he played for ten years from 1991-2001.

ERMIN SILJAK (MARIBOR) BORN: 11.05.73 CAPS: 24 GLS: 5
Joined Bradford City from Servette of Geneva but found the Premiership too hard - was released from contract and now back home. Been out for a long time with achilles injury – not certain as to whether he has fully recovered. A lively forward, he had three seasons with the 1999 Swiss champions Servette after two seasons with Bastia in the French top flight, the first of which was being spoilt by a protracted transfer wrangle with Olympia Ljubliana. He played in the 1993, 1994 and 1995 title wins for Olympia, then was Slovenian league top scorer in 1996 with 28 goals which made everyone sit up.

MARKO SIMEUNOVIC (NK MARIBOR) BORN: 06.12.67 CAPS: 42 GLS: 0
Back with first club and regained place for final four UCL games 1999-2000 which was the reason for return. Won 2000 and 2001 championships with Martbor. One of the survivors from the first ever match of Slovenia against Estonia in June 1992. Played for the Olimpia club and Red Star Belgrade in the old Yugoslav superleague and was highly regarded, and also had a spell in Turkey in their D1 with Sekerspor.

SLOVENIA

ANTE SIMUDZA (MARIBOR) BORN: 29.09.71 CAPS: 3 GLS: 0
Has been based with the Maribor club and played for them in the UCL in 1999. First capped in 1996. Was with Zeleznicar Sarajevo (Yugoslav superleague), Young Boys of Berne (Switzerland) and Malmo (Seden) but always seems to return to Maribor.

NATEH SNOFL (GORICA) BORN: 21.02.77 CAPS: 1 GLS: 0
Has been on the fringes of the squad since 2001 and plays in the domestic league. First capped vs Uruguay in Feb 2001

RAJKO TAVCAR (NURNBERG, GERMANY) BORN: 21.07.74 CAPS: 45 GLS: 0
Is in midfield in Nurnberg's runaway win in D2 of the Bundesliga in 2001, and is now sampling Bundesliga life. Has come through via German football, never played at home, and joined Nurnberg on a free in summer 2000 from D2 club Fortuna Cologne.

SENAD TIGANJ (OLIMPIA LJUBLIANA) BORN: 28.08.75 CAPS: 2 GLS: 1
Back from abroad, he has played with Lommel in Belgium and in Israel for Kfar Saba.

MUAMER VUGDALIC (NK MARIBOR) BORN: 25.08.77 CAPS: 12 GLS: 0
Played once in a pre-Euro 2000 warm-up, then has played in several internationals as Slovenia seek to replace the ageing defenders from Euro 2000. 6'3" tall defender, who joined Maribor in summer 1998 from rivals Olimpia Ljubliana, and was a reserve in 1999 title win. Had two seasons in Olimpia's first team.

ZLATKO ZAHOVIC (BENFICA) BORN: 01.12.71 CAPS: 63 GLS: 30
Moved from Olympiakos to Valenica for £4 million in summer 2000 but was not a first choice so moved back to Portugal in summer 2001 with Benfica. Top class player, joined Olympiakos in summer 1999 for £4 million from FC Porto and immediately won the 2000 title – but had a spell when he refused to play under coach Alberto Bigon after being banned for swearing at him, so they fired the coach. Slovenia's record scorer, and scored ten goals in Euro 2000 qualifiers and three times in the Finals. He was originally with the top Yugoslav club Partizan Belgrade until the War broke out.

ANTON TONCI ZLOGAR (OLIMPIA LJUBLIANA) BORN: 24.11.77 CAPS: 3 GLS:0
Late call up for Euro 2000. First capped as sub in the spring '98 friendly with Poland. From the national U21 team and home-based originally with HIT Gorica, now with Olimpia.

COACH

SREKO KATANEC BORN: 17.07.63
Youngest coach at the Euro 2000 finals. Probably Slovenia's finest player. Played for Olimpia Ljubliana, Dynamo Zagreb and Partizan Belgrade in the old Yugoslav league, then moved to Stuttgart and then to Sampdoria from 1989-94. He played 31 times for the former Yugoslavia including the 1990 World Cup finals. In his fourth season as national coach, after being coach of national U21 side 1996-98.

SOUTH AFRICA

When South Africa appointed Carlos Quieroz as their coach in August 2000, the SAFA seemed to have pulled off a masterstroke. Quieroz came with real credentials after his time in Portugal but was ultimately undone by his inability to provide a quick fix to an undeniably long-term problem. Having burst back onto the international stage with their Nations Cup win in 1996, South Africa are paying the price for that success. The majority of their experienced internationals play overseas, and there aren't domestic players of sufficient quality to provide a regularly available backbone. The club versus country debate rages here as much as anywhere, and each squad, with its inevitable withdrawals, has a disjointed look to it.

Quieroz never got on top of this problem, and never successfully walked the tightrope between winning games and entertaining crowds. Attendances are down, and unless Jomo Sono can work a miracle, home interest in the World Cup could be very short-lived. Although South Africa are potentially the weakest team at this World Cup, their faint chances of a positive outcome rest with their defence. If Mark Fish and Lucas Radebe return, Sono could even have a selection dilemma, so good has been the form of Mokoena and Issa. It's in front of that where the problems really start for Sono. John Moshoeou has never really been replaced as playmaker, and there's even been talk of a recall for the veteran, and up front Benni McCarthy has never matched his form of the '98 Nations Cup.

Shaun Bartlett is a potential goalscorer, but South Africa's hopes may lie with their wingers. Nomvete and Zuma have pace and the ability to beat players: if Sono is brave enough to play them both, and they come into form, there could yet be something to cheer for the Bafana Bafana.

SQUAD

ANDRE ARENDSE (SANTOS) BORN: 27/6/67 CAPS: 48 GLS: 0
Former number one, who has been in Vonk's shadow since France '98. Played in England for three years for Oxford, and for Fulham. Won the South African Cup with Santos of Cape Town last season. Was in the side which won the '96 Nations Cup.

BRADLEY AUGUST (SANTOS) BORN: 24/9/78 CAPS: 15 GLS: 2
Looked cumbersome in Mali. Left Lyngby for Santos after the Danish club went bankrupt. Has scored twice for his country.

BRIAN BALOYI (KAIZER CHIEFS) BORN: 6/3/74 CAPS: 17 GLS:0
Has played badly in the League, and his place in the squad could be in danger as a result. Former national number one who captained the Chiefs to the Cup Winners' Cup late last year. The first South African side to do so. Goes by the unusual nickname of 'Spiderman' and his middle name is 'Bafana'.

SOUTH AFRICA

SHAUN BARTLETT (CHARLTON) BORN: 31/10/72 CAPS: 60 GLS: 24
Captain who rowed with former coach Quieroz after his selection for the Nations Cup. He wanted to concentrate on his Premiership career and come back for the World Cup. Formerly with the New York Metrostars. Scored twice against Manchester United on his full debut for Charlton. After seven goals in his first Premiership season, has struggled this time round, only scoring once in ten games. One of the three survivors from the squad which won the Nations cup in '96. South Africa's record goalscorer. One of the great moments of his life off the field was when Nelson Mandela attended his wedding.

MATTHEW BOOTH (MAMELODI SUNDOWNS) BORN: 14/3/77 CAPS: 10 GLS: 1
Captained the U20 side at the '97 World Youth Cup and the Olympic team in Sydney. Captain of the Sundowns who touches the pitch with his right hand every time he runs on, a childhood superstition.

DELRON BUCKLEY (BOCHUM) BORN: 7/12/77 CAPS: 30 GLS: 6
Left-sided midfield player whose form can allow Fortune to move into the centre. Too erratic to be relied upon, although he was first choice at the start of the Nations Cup. Scored three goals for Bochum this season in Bundesliga B, and his lively performances have helped them to the brink of promotion. Played in World Cup '98.

BRADLEY CARNELL (STUTTGART) BORN: 21/1/77 CAPS: 19 GLS: 0
Very compact left back. The first player to represent South Africa at all levels, from U17 through to the senior team. Made his debut as a 20-year-old in '97. Ex-Kaizer Chiefs player who is now an international fixture at left back.

MARK FISH (CHARLTON) BORN: 14/3/74 CAPS: 61 GLS:2
Had retired from the international scene but has been in contact with the national side about a possible return for the World Cup. Formerly with Jomo Cosmos and Orlando Pirates before a move to Lazio, where he played just 15 times. Then went to Bolton, before his arrival in South London. Played over 20 games this season for Charlton.

QUINTON FORTUNE (MANCHESTER UTD) BORN: 21/5/77 CAPS: 39 GLS: 0
Far from a regular at Old Trafford, but as the 'big name' player, was held responsible in much of the South African media for the poor Nations Cup showing. Owns FC Fortune, a team which plays in the South African Second Division. Formerly an apprentice at Spurs under Terry Venables.

PIERRE ISSA (WATFORD) BORN: 11/9/75 CAPS: 41 GLS: 0
Played in Marseille before linking up with Gianluca Vialli in the English First Division. Was born in Johannesburg to Lebanese parents. Had a brief spell at Chelsea without making a first team appearance. Scored two own goals against France in the last World Cup.

SOUTH AFRICA

DAVID KANNEMEYER (KAIZER CHIEFS) BORN: 8/7/77 CAPS: 8 GLS: 0
Another left-sided player. Had spells at Cape Town Spurs and Ajax Cape Town. Signed for the Chiefs for the considerable sum (in South African terms) of 50,000 pounds. A member of the Sydney Olympic squad and a late Nations Cup replacement for the injured Lekgetho.

JACOB LEKGETHO (LOKOMOTIV MOSCOW) BORN: 24/3/77 CAPS: 14 GLS: 0
Played in the Champions League for Lokomotiv. Former Moraka Swallows player who missed the Nations Cup through injury. Reportedly a transfer target for Roma, although his injury problems this season have restricted him to just three appearances.

MBULELO MABIZELA (ORLANDO PIRATES) BORN: 16/9/80 CAPS: 7 GLS: 0
Wears his nickname 'Oldjohn' on the back of his shirt. The right back has been fast- tracked into the national team after playing amateur football for Maritzburg City only a year ago. Made his debut against Egypt in November. Was one of the players held responsible for the Nations Cup quarter-final defeat by Mali.

BENNI MCCARTHY (PORTO) BORN: 12/11/77 CAPS: 42 GLS: 18
Only player to have scored a hat-trick for South Africa but has proved a massive disappointment since he emerged onto the scene in the '98 Nations Cup. Was never a regular at Celta Vigo, and is now trying to make his name all over again at Porto. Missed Nations Cup in 2000, and disappointed in Mali.

MACDONALD MUKANSI (CHERNOMORETS BOURGAS)
Very fast striker who was one of the stars of South African youth football. Formerly with Jomo Cosmos and Paralimni in Cyprus.

HELMAN MKHALELE (GOZTEPE) BORN: 20/10/69 CAPS: 67 GLS: 8
Very pacy winger who is also his country's most capped player. In squad for '96 Nations Cup win, and won the Champions League the year before with Orlando Pirates.

THABO MNGOMENI (ORLANDO PIRATES) BORN: 24/6/69 CAPS: 35 GLS: 5
Occasionally inspirational midfielder who is also a late developer after winning his first cap at 29. Was banned from the League for six months after attacking a referee. Poised to make an impact from the substitute's bench. Former captain of the Bafana Bafana.

BENNETT MNGUNI (LOKOMOTIV MOSCOW) BORN: 18/3/74 CAPS: 7GLS: 0
Candidate for a starting place despite a poor Nations Cup. Was the Sundowns Player of the Year last year. Brilliant long range shooter when he finds his range. Has recently signed for Lokomotiv.

AARON MOKOENA (GERMINAL BEERSCHOT) BORN: 25/11/80 CAPS: 19 GLS: 0
Easily his country's best player in Mali. Was the youngest player to appear for South Africa when he made his debut just after his 18th birthday. Moved to Ajax Amsterdam, but didn't work out for him. Member of the Sydney Olympic team.

SOUTH AFRICA

DUMISA NGOBE (UNATTACHED) BORN: 5/3/73 CAPS: 32 GLS: 2
Without a club after he was released from Ankaragucu in Turkey. Formerly with Genclerbirligi as well. Previously with the Orlando Pirates where he enjoyed such hero status that women would ask him to sign their underwear. Ngobe was quoted as saying: "I'll do it in public, but not in my private room."

SIYABONGA NOMVETE (UDINESE) BORN: 2/12/77 CAPS: 21 GLS: 2
2000 Footballer of the Year and an outstanding creative talent. Needs to be given his head and not used as an impact substitute, like he was for the most part in Mali. Has been given his chance in the Udinese first team after the departure of Roy Hodgson.

CYRIL NZAMA (KAIZER CHIEFS) BORN: 26/6/74 CAPS: 15 GLS: 0
Versatile defender who can play all across the back four. Had an off the field scare earlier this year when he was hijacked, robbed, stripped and left in the middle of the veld by a group of robbers in Johannesburg. He was rescued by his sister, but says the event has scarred him for life.

LUCAS RADEBE (LEEDS UNITED) BORN: CAPS: 63 GLS: 1
A former captain of both club and country who has missed the whole season with injury, but is now fit and hoping to make a late case for inclusion. Lifted the Nations Cup in '96, and captained Bafana Bafana at the last World Cup.

GLEN SALMON (NAC BREDA) BORN: 24/12/77
Has made a late run for the squad with some good performances in Holland. In his fourth season with NAC. His best so far was in 99/00 when he scored 16 goals in 26 games. Formerly with Supersport United in South Africa.

FRANK SCHOEMAN (UNATTACHED) BORN: 30/7/75 CAPS: 13 GLS: 0
On the lookout for a club after Lyngby reverted to the Danish amateur ranks. Formerly at Mamelodi Sundowns where he won a League title. Solid defensive replacement when required.

DILLON SHEPPARD (AJAX CAPE TOWN) BORN: 27/2/79 CAPS: 11 GLS: 0
Has been on trial at clubs in Spain and in Holland but has yet to have been offered a contract. Has played everywhere from left back to centre forward for his club. Seen as a future international captain after starring in that role at Under-20 level.

MACBETH SIBAYA (AJAX CAPE TOWN) BORN: 25/11/77
Inexperienced midfielder and another of the South African domestic players who has been fast-tracked into the senior squad. Used as a substitute in Mali, and won't have more significant involvement this summer.

ERIC TINKLER (BARNSLEY) BORN: 30/7/70 CAPS: 46 GLS: 1
Captained the team in Mali after the injury to Bartlett. Missed last season with Barnsley

because of injury. Played in Portugal and Italy before arriving in Yorkshire. Part of the '96 Nations Cup winning squad. Missed '98 World Cup through injury. Was Barnsley's record signing when he joined them for £650,000 in '97. Injury has restricted him to less than 20 appearances this season.

HANS VONK (HEERENVEEN) BORN: 30/1/70 CAPS: 26 GLS: 0
Born in Johannesburg, raised in Holland by his Dutch parents. Was number one at World Cup '98 and was recently made captain of his country by the former coach Querioz. Great in the air where his height (6'5") helps. In his sixth season with Heerenveen.

SIBUSISO ZUMA (FC COPENHAGEN) BORN: 23/6/75 CAPS: 21 GLS: 3
Player of the Season in Denmark last year. Quick, most effective as a right winger, and believed to be the target of a number of Europe's top clubs. His title winning bicycle kick against Brondby was last season's Danish goal of the season. Formerly played at Africa Wanderers, where Nomvete was his strike partner, and then Orlando Pirates.

COACH

JOMO SONO

Jomo Sono must have differing World Cup emotions: weeks before the 1998 tournament he was replaced by Phillippe Troussier, and this time it's Sono himself who takes over in the final stages of preparation, brought in after the sacking of Carlos Quieroz. There are worries among fans, though, that Sono, rather like Troussier, has not had enough time with the players, and the Bafana Bafana will fail like they did last time. He coached South Africa to silver in the '98 Nations Cup, and has been deeply involved at all levels of the South African game for years: as a result of that, he has the support, but will he have time to make a difference? High points of an extraordinary career include playing alongside Pele for the New York Cosmos team in 1980 and taking over the Highlands Park club in 1982, and renaming it the 'Jomo Cosmos'.

WORLD CUP FACTS

Viv Anderson (1982 & 86), George Eastham (62 & 66) and Chris Woods (86 & 90) all went to two World Cups without playing a game.

Gary Lineker has scored twice as many World Cup goals as any other Englishman. He has 10 from 1986 & 1990; next best is Sir Geoff Hurst (1966 & 70).

Dave Watson won 65 England caps between 1974 and 1982 but never went to a World Cup. No player has more caps and not played in a World Cup.

GROUP C

The old masters and the new boys make Group C fascinating, if seemingly predictable, but after stumbling over the finishing line in uncertain manner four-times winners Brazil will be taking nothing for granted.

For a while there was a chance Brazil would not make it to the Finals. Four coaches were used in the qualifying tournament and Brazil's third-place finish behind Argentina and Ecuador was further proof that their history is greater than the present.

Brazil have been in every Finals, Turkey one (1954), Costa Rica one (1990) while China are making their debut. It should be easy for Brazil but of all the South American countries who qualified the Brazilians had the worst away record. The famous exporters of players do not travel well.

How can a team with Rivaldo, Roberto Carlos, Cafu and Romario struggle? As Brazil were losing 3-1 to Bolivia coach Luiz Felipe Scolari was heard to say: "They've got five little dwarfs up front yet they're tearing our defence to bits."

Many blame the rough and tough Brazilian league whose schedule makes the Premiership seem a doddle. Scolari's ultra-defensive tactics – three central defenders, two full-backs and two 'destroying' midfielders – are hardly the beautiful game Pele had in mind.

Others claim the riches Brazilian players have found in Europe makes them less motivated when they play for the national team with Rivaldo a particular target. Constant stories of corruption do not help the Brazilian cause either.

So Turkey, China and Costa Rica may sense a surprise is in store – even a shock defeat for Brazil who have lost just 13 of 80 final ties while winning 53.

Turkey are one of Europe's most improved nations over the past decade. Some of their players are with Italian clubs – Umit, Okan, Hakan Sukur and Emre – while the consistent impact Galatasaray have made in Europe is testament to the youth academies set up in Turkey.

However, coach Senol Gunes has been a target for criticism and he said upon qualifying: "I am happy to have done my job but I am not filled with joy. Much of what has been said went beyond fair comment."

Some feel he lacks charisma and that Turkey should not have needed to qualify via the playoffs. However, Turkey have a strong, experienced side and could inflict Brazil's 14th defeat in their opening tie.

China, with the world's largest population, have qualified at the seventh attempt. Their coach, Bora Milutinovic will make World Cup history by becoming the first man to coach five different nations at five different finals.

Mexico (1986), Costa Rica (1990), USA (1994) and Nigeria (1998) have all reached the second round at least under the Serbian–born coach who is nicknamed "the miracle worker".

A television audience of 500 million saw China defeat Oman to clinch qualification though even miracle man Milutinovic may struggle to maintain his second-round record.

The professional league set up nine years ago has seen the Chinese FA pump millions of pounds into football and some players, such as Fan Zhiyi who joined Crystal Palace before moving to Dundee and, more recently, Manchester City, have made a career in the west. Milutinovic has made the squad fitter, better organised and more confident and playing Costa Rica represents a chance for China to mark their debut with a historic victory.

The Central Americans have other ideas, though. Despite being a late call-up, Costa Rica did well in last year's Copa America by reaching the quarter-finals when Paulo Wanchope scored some spectacular goals.

The Manchester City striker can look the best and worst player in the world in the same game but his unpredictable style will no doubt give us some memorable moments this summer.

BRAZIL

"Brazil are expected to win every World Cup. Brazil are expected to win every match. It is an enormous pressure but I hope we can oblige." **Luiz Felipe Scolari**, Brazil coach.

TURKEY

"The World Cup is a marvellous opportunity for the world to unite. Football brings together the rich and the poor. It is a game to have fun. I hope Turkey can have fun and success. It will be a great test to play Brazil." **Senol Gunes**, Turkey coach.

REPUBLIC OF CHINA

"I am happy for the people of China that we have made history by qualifying but I just hope everyone stays realistic about the team's chances." **Bora Milutinovic**, China coach.

COSTA RICA

"Our football has improved no end because we have skilful players. We have learned a lot and now that the administration is on the right track we are all pulling together. That can only help us in the Finals." **Hernan Medford**, Costa Rica striker and most-capped player.

BRAZIL

Brazil still conjure thoughts of the beautiful game; of Pele; Garincha; of the four- times winners; twice runners-up; the darlings of South America. But, following an agonising qualifying campaign that saw them scrape home above non-qualifiers Colombia by a meagre three points, the money is going elsewhere in 2002.

The beautiful game, indeed, belongs elsewhere. Football in Brazil is lawless and largely unattractive with defenders who kick and midfield players who destroy rather than create. No wonder controversial coach Luiz Phillipe Scolari is desperate to rush the incomparable Ronaldo back from serious injury of both body and mind, even though his Inter Milan coach Hector Cupar is pleading, no begging, for more time for his striker who has the oldest knees in football after the battering they have taken.

It is with some feeling that the sad Inter President Massimo Moratti says: "We now entrust him to Brazil with whom we have a memory that is not good to say the least. We can only pray that all goes well this time."

How Scolari needs a fit and healthy Ronaldo. It might deflect attention from his row with the laid back but still brilliant Romario who, despite close on a goal a game for his country, is at total loggerheads with his coach.

Certainly on paper Brazil seem to have the quality to challenge the world once again but players like Rivaldo, Jardel, Denilson and Elber fail to produce the form for their country that they display week after week in Europe.

What makes it worse is that there is little chance of the coach gathering together his preferred squad until just before the World Championships as he constructs his squad from all over Europe.

Those from Europe will be stunned by the attitude of the home-based players where violence goes almost unchecked in the domestic game while the rest of the world – and FIFA in particular – are forever closing in on the bandits of the game.

The brutal game began to nose its way into the national team under the guidance of previous coach Vanderlei Luxemburgo and there is little or no sign of Scolari changing that, although once qualification was achieved with that crucial 3-0 win over Venezuela he promised that the Brazilians game will be a touch more adventurous from now on.

He may have been helped by the draw and with Turkey, China and Costa Rica forming the opposition in the first group it at least gives him time to blend a team together ready for the second stage when, again, the opposition will not be so tough against probably either Belgium or Russia.

The draw could not have been kinder to Brazil – especially when compared with Argentina's draw – and failure in the first or second round would make it unlikely for Scolari or any of his squad to head straight for home.

All he has to do now is answer a few questions: is Ronaldo really ready to return? Can Rivaldo prove that he can play for someone else other than Barcelona? Is Denilson really good enough at this level? Does Romario even make the trip at 36? And will the likes of Belletti, Lucio and Cris survive the strict referees in Japan and Korea?

Scolari, who ditched Romario after his first game in charge, said pointedly during the build up: "Now we have a harmonious group without stars and with friendship, the atmosphere is much better than when I took over."

There are so many questions to be asked and, sadly, so few real answers and we can only hope that Ronaldo rediscovers that sublime form that made him the world's undisputed number one player.

SQUAD

ALEX (PALMEIRAS) (24) CAPS: 26 GLS: 9
Lightening quick player who looks like he is dancing with the ball when it is at his feet. A football phenomenon when he hit the papers playing for Palmeiras in the late 1990s. The rumours were flying for a move to Europe, but it never panned out. Played in the 2000 Olympics scoring two times, but was unable to lead the Brazilians to their first football Gold Medal. Expert free-kick taker, has a chance to make this squad as he also played for Scolari. He helped win the 1999 Copa America. Played at Cruzeiro for one season before returning to Palmeiras the club that brought him fame.

BELLITTI (SAO PAULO) (25) CAPS: 10 GLS: 1
First capped in qualifying for the World Cup, and the wing back proved Scolari right with good attacking ability and strong defensive skills. He started his career with Cruzeiro then on to Sao Paulo, to Atletico Mineiro, and now back with Sao Paulo. Good cover for either wing back although prefers the left side. Will join the attack when needed, and has excellent pace.

ANTONIO CARLOS (AS ROMA) (31) CAPS: 37 GLS: 3
A long standing member of the national team, who has travelled a lot of the world playing football. Zago is an old fashioned tough tackling centre back whose defensive work is better than his distribution. Started his career at Sao Paulo, he moved to Spain with Albacete. From there he moved back to Brazil with Palmeiras where he played with Cafu in the mid 1990s. Zago then went to Japan, back to Brazil and then to Italy with AS Roma, again with Cafu.

ROBERTO CARLOS (REAL MADRID) (29) CAPS: 88 GLS: 5
One of the best attacking left wing backs ever. What he lacks defensively he clearly makes up with his ability going forward. A master of free-kicks and has one of the best left feet in the game. He does struggle in the air as he is not tall, and can be exploited defensively. Scored one of the greatest goals ever versus France in "Le Tournoi de France," in 1997 – a curling 40 yard free-kick. Shoots from just about anywhere. Started his career with Uniao San Joao before moving to Palmeiras where he played for Scolari. Then moved to Europe with Inter Milan, but became a superstar with his current club Real Madrid.

CAFU (AS ROMA) (31) CAPS: 107 GLS: 5
The captain is an attacking right wing back – one of the best in the world. Has good speed, and the ability to send in a good cross to set up attackers. Cafu is a leader by his actions, not very vocal but very influential. He is constantly overlapping which makes him hard to mark. Started in Sao Paulo, before moving to Zaragoza in Spain for a miserable year. Moved back to Palmeiras for a couple of trophies before moving to AS Roma. Was inspirational last year in helping Roma win the Scudetto.

BRAZIL

ROGERIO CENI (SAO PAULO) (28) CAPS: 13 GLS: 0
Rogerio Ceni has long been in the mix for the national team, but had been stuck behind Taffarel for years. Unfortunately for him Dida and Marcos have now moved ahead of him in the pecking order. Has spent all of his career with Sao Paulo in Brazil. Good in the air, but like most Brazilian keepers has tendency to make the odd howler.

DENILSON (REAL BETIS) (24) CAPS: 54 GLS:8
Another player who does not always live up to his billing. He is an unbelievable dribbler with the ability to make defenders look silly. Brazilian fans love him because he reminds them of yesteryear. Can play either wing, and has the ability to play as the withdrawn forward, however, he is not a prolific goal scorer. Started his career with Sao Paulo, and was signed by Real Betis as the next Ronaldo for a world record fee at the time. Struggled for two seasons before returning to Brazil with Flamengo where he regained his form. Helped Betis get promoted last season, and is helping them even more this year as they make a run at a Champions League spot.

DIDA (CORINTHIANS) (28) CAPS: 48 GLS: 0
By far the best all-around goalkeeper in Brazil but the new coach Scolari has gone with keepers he is more comfortable with. Dida started his career at Vitoria in Brazil, before claiming fame with Cruzeiro in the mid '90s. He moved to AC Milan in 2000, and was doing quite well before a horrible error in a Champions League match against Leeds sent his career stumbling. Then a passport scandal led to Dida moving back home to Corinthians. Good shot blocker, and strong in the air but sometimes lets in soft goals.

DJALMINHA (DEPORTIVO LA CORUNA) (31) CAPS: 31 GLS: 5
A favourite of the coach. Most of the last five Brazilian managers have left this talented player out of the squad, as they felt his temperament was not right for the team. However, Scolari who likes the battling types, loves this player. Djalminha started his career with Flamengo in 1990, then went to Guarani, before one year in Japan. He moved back to Brazil with Palmeiras, where he played for Scolari. Moved to Deportivo in 1997, where he was brought in to help replace Rivaldo. Did a nice job scoring eight times in his first year. He helped bring the La Liga Primera title to Deportivo in 2000.

EDILSON (PALMEIRAS) (30) CAPS: 17 GLS: 5
Comes from a poor area in Salvador in the north-east of Brazil. He worked at a local hospital when he was very young just to help his family out. Finally he got his chance to play soccer when the coach of Espirito Santo discovered him. He is a very good friend of Vampeta, and former national teamer Amaral. He is strong in the air. Played for Scolari at Palmeiras earlier in his career.

EDMILSON (LYON) (25) CAPS: 13 GLS: 0
Physically strong key cover man on the left side of defence or in the middle. Edmilson started his career with Sao Paulo, but moved to Olympique Lyon, which proved to be a good switch. He is rarely beaten in the air and is fast and powerful.

BRAZIL

EMERSON (AS ROMA) (26) CAPS: 44 GLS: 5
Made his national debut against Ecuador in September 1997, when he scored. Was a member of the group that conquered the Confederations Cup in 1997. He played twice in the World Cup in France, in games against Denmark and Holland. Copa America champion and Confederations Cup runner-up, both in 1999. He started his career in 1993 at Grêmio of Porto Alegre, who went on to be Rio Grande do Sul champions in the same year. Moved in 1997 to Bayern Leverkusen and was runner-up in the German league. Is considered one of the best midfielders in the world, and Leverkusen sold him for US$20 million to AS Roma, where he helped them to the Serie A title last season.

JUAN (FLAMENGO) (23) CAPS: 10 GLS: 0
A strong tackling defender he is still raw at international level, but has been very strong for his club Flamengo since his debut in 1996. Good in the air, seems set to be a substitute for the World Cup.

JUNIOR (PARMA) (28) CAPS: 12 GLS: 0
A defensive player who plays on the left side most often. Very quick and good with the ball. Junior started his career at Vitoria in Brazil, before moving to Palmeiras to play under Scolari. Is now at Parma, where he struggled in his first year, but has been much more involved over the last two seasons.

JUNINHO (VASCO DE GAMA)
A sweet dribbler, who sometimes struggles to come to terms with the strength and defensive part of football. Juninho first came to prominence in the 1990s when playing for Middlesbrough of England. The diminutive midfielder can energize a team by beating players with the dribble, or by finding the wide open player. When Middlebrough were relegated he stayed on until Atletico Madrid stepped in and bought him. He can change the pace of a match and run defenders wild, however, at 5'5" he can be leaned on and taken out of the match. He likes to work in the middle and drift outside to receive the ball. Currently in Brazil with Vasco da Gama, but might be on his way back to Spain after the World Cup.

KAKA (SAO PAULO) (20) CAPS: 2 GLS: 1
An attacking midfielder at club level, but Scolari likes to use the soon to be 20-year-old as an out and out attacker. Was a key member of the U21 squad that made it to the quarter-finals in Argentina last year. Good in the air, and has found the ability to cause problems at full international level. He has a chance to make the squad as a substitute.

KLEBERSON (ATLETICO PARANAENSE) (22) CAPS: 5 GLS: 2
A new member of the national squad. A right-footed player who plays in Brazil with Atletico Paranaense and has excelled at being an all round player. He can defend, join the attack and score the occasional goal. Has notched two goals in his first three games for the national team.

BRAZIL

LUCIO (BAYER LEVERKUSEN) (23) CAPS: 15 GLS: 0
Lucio was first capped during qualifying, and his ability in the air and with the ball makes him a prime candidate for the centre back position at the World Cup. Lucio plays in Germany for Bayer Leverkusen and has shown his worth immediately. He is a tough defender who can man mark, and he can come forward and help out on set plays and corner kicks. Lucio is a terrific header of the ball from a defensive position or attacking. Started his career with Guara in Brazil before moving to Internacional and then to Germany. Can move out to the right side if needed.

LUIZAO (GREMIO) (27) CAPS: 10 GLS: 4
Another former Palmeiras player who has found his way into the World Cup mix. Started his career with Guarani, but did not become a strong scorer until he joined Palmeiras. He moved onto a year with Deportivo with Djalminha, but it did not work out. Is now with Gremio after a few years with the Corinthians. Hard working winger who covers a lot of the field, he will be an excellent substitute with the pace and ability to open defences. Scored two goals in the last qualifier to help Brazil make it to the World Cup.

MARCOS (PALMEIRAS) (31) CAPS: 15 GLS: 0
Coach Luis Felipe Scolari has known Marcos for a long time as he managed him at Palmeiras during their great title runs in the 1990s. He is good with the ball and has good vision for a keeper. Has won many big matches, and Scolari feels very comfortable with him. Should be the No 1 keeper at the World Cup.

ANDERSON POLGO (GREMIO) (23) CAPS: 5 GLS:3
Came out of nowhere this year, and the centre back has been a good addition by Scolari. He is excellent in the air, and always makes sure that an attacker pays for trying to get into Brazil's box. The 22-year-old has spent his short career at Gremio, but many European teams are looking to bring him over. Scored three times in his first three 'A' internationals.

RIVALDO (BARCELONA) (30) CAPS: 63 GLS: 31
One of the best players in the world. A left-footed scheemer, who drifts all over the midfield. Has the ability to get back and help in defence, but is best going forward. He constantly gets harassed by the Brazilian fans because he sometimes is less than spectacular for Brazil. However, Rivaldo is truly amazing. He can beat players in the air and with the ball at his feet or even on set plays. He is slightly built, but still very strong with the ball. Rivaldo scored eight goals in qualifying, but the former World Player of the Year needs to be more aggressive when playing for his country. Has the ability to score when receiving the ball with his back to the net or going straight at it. Rivaldo was found while playing at Palmeiras, then moved onto Deportivo before finding a home in Barcelona. He is constantly rumoured to be going to Italy.

ROQUE JUNIOR (AC MILAN) (25) CAPS: 17 GLS: 2
A talented centre back who is tough as well as having the Brazilian flair that every player

BRAZIL

dreams of. Roque Junior started his career with San Jose in Sao Paulo, but it was his time at Palmeiras under current national coach Felipe Scolari that was his most successful. He has now moved onto Italy with AC Milan, and has been just as good there. He compliments Lucio perfectly at the back.

ROMARIO (FLAMENGO) (36) CAPS: 77 GLS: 62
The hero of Brazil's 1994 World Cup triumph in the United States. In 1998, he took part in the Gold Cup in the US. An injury would lead to his being dismissed from the squad only days away from the '98 World Cup, when the team was already training in France. He returned to the national team in a friendly against Barcelona in April 1999. In 1997 he was in the winning sides in the Confederations Cup and Copa America (where he was named in the tournament's all-stars). He was Brazil's top scorer in the 1994 World Cup, with five goals. Scored the clincher against Sweden in the semi-final, as well as his spot kick in the penalty shoot-out in the final against Italy. Named FIFA Player of the Year in 1994, Romario had already played in the 1990 World Cup in Italy, in the match against Scotland. He scored the winning goal over Uruguay in the 1989 Copa America final. He was part of the silver medal team in the 1988 Seoul Olympic Games. His international debut was in a May 1987 friendly against Ireland. With 64 goals, Romario is number three among Brazil's all-time scorers, behind only Pele and Zico. Romario has scored over 600 goals in his career. Played for PSV Eindhoven of Holland and Barcelona in Spain. After a brief stay at Valencia of Spain in 1996-97, Romario returned to Flamengo. Helped Brazil qualify with eight goals in five qualifiers.

RONALDINHO (PARIS ST GERMAIN) (22) CAPS: 24 GLS:11
Under-17 South American and World champion in 1997, Ronaldinho had his first big chance in the senior side when he replaced Edílson in Brazil´s Copa América winning squad in 1999. He was top goal scorer in the Confederations Cup in which the Brazilian team was runner-up. In the Olympic preliminaries in Londrina, Ronaldinho once again showed his class, scoring goals that were vital to Brazil winning the competition and a place in the Sydney Olympic Games. Quick off the mark and has extraordinary ball control. Competed in the Under-20 team in the South American and World Championships in 1999. Football runs in the family, as he and his brother, de Assis, both played for Gremio. His brother later transferred to Sporting Lisbon and then Fluminense, as well as having played for Brazil in several youth teams. Ronaldinho moved to Europe after a long drawn out transfer with PSG of France.

RONALDO (INTER MILAN) (25) CAPS: 60 GLS:37
Truly one of the best players in the world when fit, however, since the last World Cup there has been injury problem after injury problem. In fact, he played for the national team in late March for the first time since 1999. Ronaldo first came to fame in 1993 with Cruzeiro where he scored 58 goals in 60 matches. He was in the 1994 World Cup squad at the age of 17, but did not play. Moved onto PSV Eindhoven like one of his idols, Romario, had done years before. The move worked out well for Ronaldo as he scored 30 goals in 33 matches, and 12 more the year after before a knee injury. He scored 34

89

BRAZIL

goals in 37 matches and scored the winning penalty kick in the 1997 European Cup Winners' Cup. Won the 1996 European and World Player of the Year, as well as winning the World Player of the Year award again in 1997, the first player to win the award back to back. Ronaldo was bought for £19 million by Inter Milan in 1997 and scored 25 goals. He went to the 1998 World Cup with lots of pressure on his shoulders, and scored four goals, but before the final had a seizure and did not look like he was going to play. Somehow he did, with allegations that Nike forced him to play.

SERGINHO (AC MILAN) (30) CAPS: 10 GLS: 1
Wing back who sometimes slots into the left side of defence, but has found a home with AC Milan on the left of midfield. Serginho can make long darting runs without the ball to find space, but is even better with the ball, screaming down the left side with all his speed. Initially struggled in Italy, but as he has settled in has become a much more dangerous player. Started his career with Itaperuna in Brazil, then Bahia and Cruzeiro. It was with Sao Paulo that he was spotted by Milan.

GILBERTO SILVA (ATLETICO MINEIRO) (25) CAPS: 6 GLS: 3
A new member of the squad, with his first cap coming late last year. Scolari loves this midfielder's game. A strong defensive midfielder who also can get up and join the attack as witnessed by three goals in his first four international appearances. Started his career with America-MG in Brazil, and currently plays for Atletico Mineiro.

VAMPETA (CORINTHIANS) (28) CAPS: 37 GLS: 2
Technically-gifted player, who can play both in midfield and as a right winger. A versatile player, who has struggled to win favour under Scolari. Made his debut in a friendly against Yugoslavia in September 1998. Started his career with Vitória da Bahia in 1992. Joined PSV Eindhoven in 1994. In 1996 he played for Fluminense. In 1997 he returned to PSV, becoming Dutch champion and champion of the Dutch Super Cup. At the suggestion of coach Luxemburgo, he joined Corinthians in 1998. Started this year with Inter Milan, but returned to Corinthians after being stuck on the bench in Italy.

COACH

LUIS FELIPE SCOLARI (BRAZIL)
Scolari is one of the meanest managers in the world. He freely tells his players to foul whenever, and whoever when possible. This being said Scolari is a winner. He took over the Brazilian squad in the middle of June, and struggled but got the Samba's through to the World Cup. He played in Brazil as a defender for Caxias, Juventude and Club Sportivo Alagoano (CSA) of Maceió. He moved into managing in 1982 with CSA, then to Juventude, went to Saudi Arbia with Al Shabab-Arabia, Gremio, where he won a Copa Libertadores in 1995, also went on to Japan with Jubilo, then to Palmeiras where he won another Copa Libertadores championship and found most of his national team players. Scolari, who won 14 Brazilian titles, was with Cruzeiro before coming to the aid of Brazil.

TURKEY

There is something a little bizarre about Turkey's very short entry in the World Cup Hall of Fame. The only three matches they appeared in produced no less than 21 goals, with Turkey scoring ten and conceding 11.

Admittedly the games took place in the devil-may-care high-scoring Finals of 1954, but even so, that kind of defensive profligacy was crazy even by the standards of the mid-1950s. After a 4-1 defeat by eventual champions West Germany in their opening match in Berne, Switzerland, Turkey crushed Korea 7-0 three days later in Geneva.

That, somewhat strangely, meant the Turks had to play-off against the Germans three days later for a place in the second phase. This time Turkey got hammered 7-2 and after handshakes all round and a quick shower then home. And that was that for the next 48 years.

It is doubtful whether their next three World Cup matches -- against Brazil in Ulsan, Korea on June 3, Costa Rica in Incheon on June 9, or China in Seoul on June 13 will produce quite as many goals as 1954 – but with the Turks anything is possible – even a place in the second round.

In fact, a place in the second round looks a real possibility for a Turkey side that has long since ceased to be the laughing stock of international soccer. A huge investment programme at both club and international level over the last decade and a half has paid handsome dividends for the sport in Turkey.

Where once leading European clubs and international teams played Turkish sides expecting to win every time, now a victory over Turkish opposition is a hard-won prize.

The year 2000 saw modern Turkish soccer come of age with Galatasaray becoming the first Turkish club ever to win a European tournament with a penalty shoot-out win over Arsenal in the UEFA Cup Final and the national side making the quarter-finals of Euro 2000.

The first inkling that Turkey were making important strides in international terms came when they qualified for the Finals of Euro '96 – their first appearance in a major tournament since the 1954 World Cup. Although they lost all three first round matches without scoring, they have steadily improved since then and their 6-0 aggregate victory over Austria in the play-offs for this year's World Cup finals surprised no-one.

In fact the real surprise in the qualifying tournament had come two months previously when they let almost-certain automatic qualification slip out of their grasp by losing 2-1 at home to Sweden in Istanbul after leading until two minutes from the end of the match.

Going into that game, Turkey were unbeaten in eight qualifiers and a victory over Sweden, with a final match over Moldova to come, would have all-but ensured Turkey's long absence from the Finals was over.

Coach Senol Gunes, who saw off his critics after the play-off victory, has predicted in the run-up to the Finals that Turkey could reach the last eight of the competition. And he could be right. If they come through the opening round, Turkey could face Belgium, Russia, co-hosts Japan or even Tunisia in the second round – all of whom are beatable.

TURKEY

"My priority is to qualify from the group and reach the quarter-finals," Gunes said shortly after Turkey qualified. "Despite our occasional slips, I think we are capable of proving we are among the top eight teams in the world."

Turkish players now have the technical ability to compete at the highest level – whether they have the mental stamina and collective belief they can reach the later stages of the competition remain to be seen. The one thing not open to doubt is that none of their opponents will under-estimate them for a second.

Former and present Galatasaray players are likely to make up the bulk of the squad of which almost half now play overseas.

Hakan Sukur led the Turkish exodus and after difficult stints with Torino and Inter Milan, appears to have re-discovered his best form at Parma. Others like Tugay Kerimoglu and Hakan Unsal at Blackburn, and Alpay Ozalan at Aston Villa have added new dimensions to their games, while Yildiray Basturk, 23, of Bayer Leverkusen looks set to maintain the improvement shown by the national side for a while to come.

Gunes' belief that Turkey can reach the last eight may be an optimistic one but, in Turkey at least, they believe they can do just that. They have waited a very long time to return to the top table of international soccer and while their opening three matches are unlikely to produce 21 goals again – those three matches could provide Turkey a launchpad for a very successful competition.

SQUAD

ABDULLAH (FENERBAHCE) BORN: 08.12.71 CAPS: 69 GLS: 0
Another of Fenerbahce's international buys from Trabzonspor in summer 1999 as they sought to break Galatasaray's dominance successfully in 2001. Left-sided midfielder who has previous coach Fatih Terim to thank for his progress – he played in all three games at Euro '96 and in all the World Cup qualifiers , after another coach Sepp Piontek first selected him and then discarded him. Also would have known present coach Senol Gunes from his Trabzonspor days. Is the left side midfielder or wing back, and easily recognisable by being one of the few Turks with blond hair. Has been a first choice for the last six seasons.

ALPAY (ASTON VILLA) BORN: 29.05.73 CAPS: 61 GLS: 4
Signed by Villa from Fenerbahce for £6 million in summer 2000. Hat-trick vs Macedonia in qualifiers – and good job too after Turkey looked like losing. First hat-trick of career. Switched the great Istanbul divide from Besiktas to Fenerbahce in summer 1999 but just played the one season with Fener. Central defender who won a 1995 title with Besiktas – can play stopper or sweeper. Played for Besiktas 1993-99 (first capped in 1995) when he arrived from Div One club Altay of Izmir. Played all three games at Euro '96.

METIN AKTAS (TRABZONSPOR) BORN: 01.08.77 CAPS: 2 GLS: 0
Like his national coach, he is an international from Trabzonspor. First capped in last game before the Euro 2000 finals. First choice in goal for the club since 1997.

TURKEY

ARIF ERDEM (GALATASARAY) BORN: 02.01.72 CAPS: 49 GLS: 8
Signed summer 2000 for Spanish club Real Sociedad for £2.4 million on a three-year contract, but returned after just five games to Galatasaray. '93, '94 and 1997-2000 Championship medals with Galatasaray – his 14 goals in 1999 being particularly helpful. Remembered at Old Trafford as player who scored fine opening goal in the 3-3 Champions League game a few years ago. Also scored three goals in 3-0 win in Belfast in Sept '99 Euro 2000 qualifiers. Prefers to be an old fashioned right winger. Now plays more central role. Played all three games at Euro '96 and all four at Euro 2000.

AYHAN (GALATASARAY) BORN: 23.02.77 CAPS: 6 GLS: 0
Joined Galatasaray in summer 2001 from Besiktas. Highly promising midfielder who was in the squad for Euro 2000. Has been capped since 1998, but is still awaiting a regular place in the national team. Three seasons with Besiktas, arrived from Gazientepspor – another D1 club in Istanbul, and is easily recognisable with blond hair.

YILDIRAY BASTURK (BAYER LEVERKUSEN) BORN: 24.12.78 CAPS: 12 GLS: 1
Joined Leverkusen in summer 2001 from relegated Bochum under the Bosman ruling. Was at Bochum playing well for four years – arrived in 1997 from Wattenscheid, a former Bundesliga club in the Bochum area. Capped in Euro 2000 warm-up game – and now has his big move into the UCL. Another of the German-based and developed Turks.

BULENT KORKMAZ (GALATASARAY) BORN: 24.11.68 CAPS: 67 GLS:1
Won his sixth championship medal in 2000 with Galatasaray, and is the club captain. He has been with his club since schooldays and has come through the ranks to be a full international of considerable standing. Had a virtually unchallenged run in the national side – May 1990 until 1998. Now back after injury.

UMIT DAVALA (AC MILAN) BORN: 30.07.73 CAPS: 23 GLS: 1
Signed by AC Milan from Galatasaray in 2001 – his goal after 90 minutes for Gala put AC Milan out of the 1999-2000 European Cup and was in the fine club team that won the 2000 treble. Another of the increasing band who were trained in Germany – his first club was Waldhof Mannheim (now Div Two). Five seasons with the '98 '99 and 2000 Turkish champions, capped at Dyakirspor, hence the bigger club's interest. Back into squad in 1999 on the back of title successes – can play right side defence or midfield, and back after injury.

EMRE BELOZOGLU (INTER MILAN) BORN: 07.09.80 CAPS: 11 GLS: 1
Left Galatasaray for Inter in summer 2001 for £1.6 million along with Okan. Outstanding as a junior – he is a recent junior and youth international, who has gone through to his first cap from 1999-2000 and was in the training squad for Euro 2000. Moved into the national team after Euro 2000 – left wing back, and midfield. In the Galatasaray squad for 1998 title win in first full season. Also played in 1999 and 2000 triumphs and in the UCL.

TURKEY

EMRE ASIK (GALATASARAY) BORN: 13.12.73 CAPS: 14 GLS: 2
Signed by Gala from Istanbulspor in summer 2000 and has made dramatic improvement and played in the World Cup play-offs v Austria. Was a former international defender with Fenerbahce, and left for Istanbulspor after Fenerbahce's title win of 1996. Capped from 1993-1995 just before the Euro '96 group and came through the national U21 system. Not to be confused with the other Galatasaray Emre who went to Inter Milan.

ERGUN PENBE (GALATASARAY) BORN: 17.05.72 CAPS: 19 GLS: 0
First capped in 1994, but recalled in 2000 and played at Euro 2000 in three of the four games in midfield. Part of the recent triple success by the club side, in his seventh season with them, including four titles. Wears No 67 in the Champions League – sponsored by local radio station (wavelength).

FATIH (MALLORCA) BORN: 26.12.77 CAPS: 35 GLS: 0
Joined Mallorca in summer 2001 from Galatasaray to play in the UCL. Joined the national team some five years ago and has settled into a starting role almost immediately on right side of defence. Would remember his international debut: Turkey 6 Wales 4. Had been in the Galatasaray team that won four domestic championships including the 2000 treble. Was developed in the Gala club youth team – and was in the first team for five seasons.

FATIH TEKKE (GAZIENTEPSPOR) BORN: 09.09.77 CAPS: 2 GLS: 0
Forward and club top scorer. Fringe member of the squad, though looking in fine form in the domestic league.

ILHAN MANSIZ (BESIKTAS) BORN: 10.08.75 CAPS: 4 GLS: 2
Breakthrough season with Besiktas for whom he is top scorer. Joined Besiktas from Samsunspor in 2001 and moved into national squad. Born in Munich (Germany).

UMIT KARAN (GALATASARAY) BORN: 10.04.76 CAPS: 6 GLS: 0
Signed in summer 2001 from Genclerbirligi, who won the Turkish Cup last season, and where he developed his game. He scored 14 league goals for them last season and interested bigger clubs, after 18 goals the previous season. Fringe international, brought in to fill the gaps left by departed players. Crucial goals in the qualifying rounds, and is their top scorer this season.

KEREM INAN (GALATASARAY) BORN: 25.03.80 CAPS: 0 GLS: 0
Is the national U21 keeper, but is still struggling to break into the club first team with the performances of the Colombian Faryd Mondragon. Born in Istanbul and always been with the Gla club. Highly rated among Turkish keepers, as the coach is a former national keeper. Played in the UCL but still has limited club chances.

TURKEY

MUZZY IZZET (LEICESTER CITY) BORN: 24.10.74 CAPS: 6 GLS: 0
Worthington Cup medal 2000. Was at Chelsea for three seasons 1993-1996 before a deadline day transfer in March 1996 for £650,000 and has proved a snip. London-born, with a Turkish Cypriot father born in Turkey, who gained a place in the squad at the third invitation, after giving up hope of an England place. Took language lessons in order to understand his teammates!

MEHMET POLAT (GAZIENTEPSPOR) BORN: 06.08.78 CAPS: 4 GLS: 0
From the national U21 side at the European U21 champs in May 2000. First full national call up in 2001. Plays for a team who are down by the Syrian border.

NIHAT KAHVECI (REAL SOCIEDAD) BORN: 23.11.79 CAPS: 10 GLS: 0
Moved from Besiktas to Spain in January 2002 transfer window. Has come through the junior system at the club – and internationally has been in the Turkish teams that won both the UEFA U16 and U18 titles. In summer 2000 was at the European U21 championships where Turkey qualified for final stages – moved into national squad afterwards. One to keep an eye on.

OGUN (FENERBAHCE) BORN: 06.10.69 CAPS: 76 GLS: 5
Club captain. Is Turkey's most capped player in history – he has played for Turkey through the 1990s and beat Oguz record of 70 caps in March 2001. Boosted by championship medal in 2001 with Fenerbahce. He is like several other Turkish players in that he learned the game in Germany when his parents were working in the car works. Had been with Trabzonspor through his senior career until 1999 mainly under national coach Senol Gunes when he came to the capital. Played at Euro '96 and Euro 2000.

OKAN (INTER MILAN) BORN: 19.10.73 CAPS: 25 GLS: 4
Moved to Inter in summer 2001 for £1.4 million and is the third ex-Gala player at that club. A 5'5" tall midfielder, busy and industrious. Played for the Galatasaray side through the last four championship wins in '97, '98 and '99 and then the 2000 treble, and like club mate Fatih, he came through their youth system. Fatih has also left. Has been in the national squad for eight years but limited chances. Hardly missed a Champions League game either.

OMER CATKIC (GAZIENTEPSPOR) BORN: 13.04.74 CAPS: 5 GLS: 0
No 2 keeper, who has displaced Engin and the younger Fevzi of Besiktas after fine performances in the domestic league. Come through in the last couple of seasons with the club side who have challenged the big three clubs. Looks like Fabien Barthez.

UMIT OZAT (FENERBAHCE) BORN: 30.10.76 CAPS: 13 GLS: 0
From the 2001 champions, he joined them in summer 2001 from Bursaspor where he had been on loan after a fall out with previous club Genclerbirligi. Rated as the new strong man in defence.

TURKEY

RUSTU RECBER (FENERBAHCE) BORN: 10.05.73 CAPS: 63 GLS: 0
Won championship with Fenerbahce in 2001. Played in all three games at Euro '96, after also being in Fenerbahce's 1996 championship win the same year. Played all four games at Euro 2000. Is considered by far the best of the recent crop of Turkish keepers, and has been first choice since 1995, the year he joined Fenerbahce from Antalyaspor, a provincial Division One side. Took over from Engin at club and country level, after Engin broke leg in 1996.

HASAN SAS (GALATASARAY) BORN: 01.08.76 CAPS: 14 GLS: 0
Six seasons with the club, joined from the top team in the capital Akaragucu in summer 1995. Fringe first teamer in 1997-2000 title wins but took over as first choice in the club team in 2000 following the departure of Arif (Real Sociedad) and Hakan Sukur (Inter Milan) – though Arif has since come back. Four UCL games in 1999-2000 and first choice in 1999-2000 and 2000-1.

HAKAN SUKUR (PARMA) BORN: 01.09.71 CAPS:72 GLS: 36
Moved from Galatasaray to Inter Milan for £5.5 million in summer 2000 for a second spell in Italy and seemed not overkeen on the idea. Now moved onto Parma in January 2002. He then showed equal form with four goals in the 1997 World Cup qualifier with Wales and is now the all-time Turkish international goalscoring record holder. In his last five seasons with Galatasaray he scored 180 goals in just 211 games. Returned to Galatasaray after just five games in Serie A with Torino (one goal) in 1995-96 and a failed marriage. Cost Torino £2 million. Joined Galatasaray from Bursaspor in 1992 and scored 54 goals in three seasons with the 1993 and 1994 champions. Was seriously looked at by Manchester Utd as he is an English-style centre forward. Has the nickname the Bull of the Bosphorus.

SUAT (GALATASARAY) BORN: 26.08.67 CAPS: 15 GLS: 1
Was a regular first team player back in Galatasaray's 1994 side and won his first caps around that time. Recalled for Euro 2000. Ball winner in midfield. From the club's juniors he has been heavily involved in the five recent title wins in '93, '94 and 1997-99, though more of a squad member in the last two wins. Look out for the wig!

TAYFUR (BESIKTAS) BORN: 23.04.70 CAPS: 37 GLS: 6
Not to be confused with Tayfun – this is the player who scored the penalty from which Turkey came through against Ireland in the play-offs for Euro 2000 and was the Turks top scorer in the qualifiers. John Toshack, his former coach at Besiktas, called him the Icebox for his cool approach. Learnt his early football with Darmstadt in the Bundesliga Div Two. Was released by Fenerbahce (1993-95) and quickly snapped up by Besiktas from Kocaelispor (1995-97 where he was first capped in 1994). International for six seasons.

TAYFUN (REAL SOCIEDAD) BORN: 02.04.74 CAPS: 37 GLS:1
Came through to national prominence from the Championship medal winning Fenerbahce team of 1996. Moved to Spain in summer 2000. Was a summer 1993

signing by Fenerbahce from the Bundesliga Div Two club Stuttgart Kickers (with whom he played as a teenager in the Bundesliga). Parents worked in Germany – Stuttgart is the car centre (Porsche, Mercedes). First capped in 1995.

TUGAY (BLACKBURN ROVERS) BORN: 24.08.70 CAPS: 70 GLS: 2
Joined Blackburn Rovers for £1.3m from Rangers in the summer of 2001, joining up with former Galatasaray boss, Graeme Souness. Moved from Galatasaray to Rangers for £1 million in early 2000 – won double with Rangers – but was not a first team fixture. Became fifth Turkish player to reach 50 caps. Member of the 1997-99 Championship winning teams with Galatasaray and played in first part of their historic 2000 treble for his sixth title with the champions. Scored first international goal vs Ukraine in May 1996. With Galatasaray since a 1988 move from Trabzonspor. He is a bit of a night owl which doesn't please coaches but talent evident since his international debut in 1992.

HAKAN UNSAL (BLACKBURN) BORN: 14.05.73 CAPS: 23 GLS: 0
Fallen out with Gala and away in spring 2002 if he can find club. Not to be confused with the international striker from the same club – no relation. Known as Little Hakan to the other Big Hakan. This one is a left-sided defender who joined in summer 1996 from Karabukspor where he promptly gained a first team spot in Galatasaray's 1997 championship win. He moved into the national squad as a result. Key central defender in the 1997-99 Championship wins and now the historic 2000 treble.

COACH

SENOL GUNES BORN: 01.06.52
Former first choice national keeper from 1975-82 winning 31 caps, and holds the record of 1,140 minutes without conceding a goal in the Turkish championship. Best keeper in the country for a decade. Played for Trabzonspor, whom he later coached. Won six championships. Took over from Mustafa Denizli after Euro 2000, after previously coaching Trabzonspor (1988-89 and 1992-97), Boluspor (1989-92) and Antalyaspor (1997-98) and Sakarayaspor (1998-2002). Contracted until 2004.

WORLD CUP FACTS

Zaire was the first black African country to reach the World Cup finals in Germany in 1974. Every member of the squad was promised a house, a car and a holiday for their families but the offer was withdrawn when they lost all three games against Scotland, Yugoslavia and Brazil, conceding 14 goals.

Teofilio Cubillas is the only player to have scored five goals or more in a tournament on two occasions.

REPUBLIC OF CHINA

For years dubbed the sleeping giant of Asian football, it took the coaching talents of Bora Milutinovic and the automatic qualification of regional powerhouses Japan and Korea to finally see China make their debut on the world stage.

For 44 years the Chinese have been gamely battling for a place at the top table and now, finally, they have overcome their inferiority complex to achieve that long-held goal.

Prior to their run to this year's Finals, China's previous best had seen them fall at the last hurdle in 1982, when they missed out on a place in Spain in a play-off against New Zealand in Singapore.

The pain and anguish felt by that narrow failure was magnified in 1998 when the Chinese missed out again, winning vital matches against Saudi Arabia and Kuwait but losing equally important clashes with Iran and Qatar.

Missing out on France '98 prompted a public apology by the Chinese Football Association and the team, and a change of attitude. Out went Chinese coach Qi Wusheng, felt by many to be tactically inept, and in came Englishman Bob Houghton, who proved a huge gap existed between the talents and experience of Chinese and European coaches.

While Houghton was to eventually lose his job after China missed out on the Sydney Olympics, the dye was cast and, in January 2000 Milutinovic was brought in to lead the charge for Korea/Japan.

With the two co-hosts – both of whom were among Asia's four qualifiers for France – qualifying automatically, China's task was immediately made easier. After a straightforward first round, when the Chinese eliminated Cambodia, the Maldives and Indonesia, they were given an additional boost in the draw for the second phase.

The seeding system decided on by the Asian Football Confederation bizarrely rated the United Arab Emirates ahead of Iran and, as a result, the Persians were lumped in with Saudi Arabia while China were drawn to face a weak UAE.

From there on China's path seemed assured. Opening wins against the Emirates and Uzbekistan made sure nerves were never a factor and China strolled home, winning the group easily and only losing to Uzbekistan in Tashkent when qualification had been assured the week before with a 1-0 win over Oman in Shenyang.

Now that China have qualified for the World Cup, the question is: how will they cope with the huge gap in standard between Asian and world football? Milutinovic's experience will obviously stand the team in good stead as, too, will time spent playing in Europe by the likes of Fan Zhiyi, Sun Jihai and Yang Chen.

But expectations should be kept to a modest level for a team which will enter a transitional phase after the Finals. Many of the team's key players are set to retire or enter the twilight of their careers after this World Cup and Milutinovic is expected to take the opportunity to give some up-and-coming youngsters a chance to earn some much-needed experience.

The coach has also privately admitted that his team have no chance of conquering the group, which is no surprise given China have been drawn to face Brazil. Turkey and Costa Rica will not be easy prospects either and victory for China could well be making sure they don't embarrass themselves in their first foray onto the world stage.

REPUBLIC OF CHINA

SQUAD
***

QU BO BORN: 15/07/81 (QINGDAO)
Like An Qi, Qu Bo came to the fore playing for China's youth team last year and was quickly promoted to the first team by Bora Milutinovic. His performances at the tournament in Argentina alerted Boca Juniors to his talents but, despite much discussion, a move never materialised. Unlikely to start at the World Cup but definitely one to watch in the future.

YANG CHEN BORN: 17/01/74 (EINTRACHT FRANKFURT)
Became the first Chinese player to move to Germany when he joined Eintracht Frankfurt, initially on-loan, from Beijing Guoan. The little-known forward quickly came to the fore in Germany, scoring the goals that kept his new club in the First Division. His impressive displays earned him a full-time contract but since then his form has dipped and Eintracht are now in the second flight of German football. His displays, however, earned him a call-up to the Chinese side and, after initially failing to impress, has forced his way into Bora Milutinovic's team.

WU CHENGYING BORN: 21/04/75 (SHANGHAI SHENHUA)
China's first-choice left back. Solid defensively while in attack he adds another dimension to the team. One of many Chinese first team players who attracted the attentions of European scouts during the World Cup qualifiers.

OU CHULIANG BORN: 26/08/68 (GUANGDONG)
Formerly China's regular goalkeeper and had, until the qualifying tournament, still been seen as Jiang Jin's stand-in. That all changed when An Qi took on the roll with admirable aplomb following Jiang's injury and Ou, once considered to be among Asia's finest goalkeepers, looks set to remain on the bench.

ZHANG ENHUA BORN: 11/05/74 (DALIAN SHIDE)
Solid and reliable centre half who also enjoys stepping into midfield. Zhang has been a stalwart for both China and Dalian over the last five years but missed out on most of the qualifying tournament due to injury. Upon his return was unable to win his place in the team back from Li Weifeng but is still likely to form the defensive partnership in the middle with Fan Zhiyi.

CHEN GANG BORN: 07/11/74 (DALIAN SHIDE)
Another goalkeeper benefiting from the experience and coaching of former Arsenal, Aston Villa and Manchester United custodian Jimmy Rimmer at Dalian Shide. Chen is the club's No 1 keeper but lost out to team mate An Qi during the qualifying tournament.

REPUBLIC OF CHINA

YU GENWEI BORN: 19/08/76 (TIANJIN)
Made his debut for the Chinese national team back in 1997 against South Korea and has been in and out of the team since. Made several appearances during the qualifying tournament, mainly as a substitute.

HAO HAIDONG BORN: 25/08/70 (DALIAN SHIDE)
One of Asia's finest natural goalscorers, the career of Hao Haidong has been blighted by controversy. The 31-year-old was banned from all footballing activities for a year by the Asian Football Confederation after spitting at an official at the Asian Games in Bangkok in December 1998. Shortly after his return he was again in hot water after an altercation during a league match with Dalian. His fiery temperament aside, though, Hao is a major asset to the Chinese. After ending a long-running feud with coach Bora Mllutinovic, Hao has proven that the spark which alerted Uruguay's Penarol to his talents in the mid-1990s remains undiminished.

QI HONG BORN: 03/06/76 (SHANGHAI SHENHUA)
The creative fulcrum of the team, Qi Hong's goals and passing were vital to China's progression to their first-ever finals. Reaching his peak after several years on the periphery of the team, without him China's chances of making an impact in attack are lessened considerably.

SHAO JIAYI BORN: 10/04/80 (BEIJING GUOAN)
Young defender called into the squad at the end of 2001. Like many in the squad, he has been brought into the team with one eye firmly on creating an experienced core of players for the future.

SUN JIHAI BORN: 30/09/77 (MANCHESTER CITY)
One of the brightest hopes and talents in Chinese football, the time is coming for Sun Jihai to fulfill his promise. Joined Crystal Palace in 1998 with Fan Zhiyi after impressing at Dalian Wanda, helping the club win successive Chinese titles. After less than a year in London, though, Sun returned to the club to help them with their fight against relegation, a battle that was eventually won. The turnaround was such that Dalian went on to win the title again the following season, with Sun in his usually right back berth. Sun captained China's Olympic team which missed out on qualifying for Sydney during which he picked up a one-year international ban from the Asian Football Confederation for assaulting an official. He returned to the team after China's run to the semi-finals of the Asian Cup in Lebanon in 2000 and has since signed for English First Division champions Manchester City.

JIANG JIN BORN: 07/10/69 (TIANJIN)
Tall and commanding goalkeeper who took over as the nation's number one during the reign of Englishman Bobby Houghton. Played in the squad that won the bronze medal at the Asian Games in Bangkok in 1998. Has been linked in the past with a move to Dundee to join compatriot Fan Zhiyi but remains in China with Tianjin.

REPUBLIC OF CHINA

SU MAOZHEN BORN: 30/07/72 (SHANDONG)
Su Maozhen's aerial ability has seen him become one of China's most potent attacking threats at Asian level. His aerial prowess has seen him score on average of almost a goal in every other game although whether his unsophisticated approach works against the world's best remains to be seen.

LI MING BORN: 26/09/72 (DALIAN SHIDE)
Another stalwart of the successful Dalian Shide side that have won the league title on six occasions in the eight years of professional football in China. Li missed most of the qualifying tournament due to injury but returned towards the end to make several appearances as a substitute. Had a brief trial at Stockport County and was also linked in 2000 with a move to Crystal Palace.

MA MINGYU BORN: 10/08/72 (SICHUAN)
Became first Chinese player to join a Serie A side when he signed for Perugia in September 2000. Rather than following in the footsteps of Japan's Hidetoshi Nakata, Ma struggled at the Umbrian side and left after seven months without having broken into the first team. Ma is still considered one of China's key performers. The left-sided midfielder says he plans to retire from football at the end of the year.

YANG PU BORN: 30/03/78 (BEIJING GUOAN)
Reserve left back who filled in during the qualifying tournament after Wu Chengying picked up a suspension. Lacks Wu's penetration down the flank and is unlikely to win a place in the starting line-up if Wu is fit.

AN QI BORN: 21/06/81 (DALIAN SHIDE)
Milutinovic made the surprise decision to turn to youngster An Qi during the qualifying tournament following a hand injury to regular starting goalkeeper Jiang Jin and, after a nervous start, the Dalian custodian did not disappoint. Despite having no international experience and having never played in the starting line-up for his club, An performed admirably. The 20-year-old kept goal for China's youth team at the World championships in Argentina last August, when they lost in the second phase to the hosts and eventual champions.

SHEN SI BORN: 12/10/74 (SHANGHAI SHENHUA)
Midfielder who has long been part of China's national set up but never built on the promise he showed while a member of the nation's Olympic team in 1996. A useful squad member, however, and could be called into the line-up as a replacement for Qi Hong.

LI TIE BORN: 18/09/77 (LIAONING)
The reigning Chinese Player of the Year, Li, like Sun Jihai, has attracted much attention from foreign shores. Plays in front of the defence and has matured greatly since his occasionally faltering displays during the failed attempt to qualify for France '98. Li dictates the pace of China's play and will be one to watch this summer.

REPUBLIC OF CHINA

DU WEI BORN: 09/02/82 (SHANGHAI CABLE)
Already being hailed as the new Fan Zhiyi. Like the veteran centre half, Du Wei started his career in Shanghai and is also another one of China's youth team to be promoted to the full national side. Strong and commanding in the air, like Qu Bo and An Qi, Du Wei is likely to form the backbone of China's team of the future.

LI WEIFENG BORN: 26/01/78 (SHENZHEN)
The qualifying tournament for Korea/Japan 2002 proved to be an awakening for Li Weifeng. With Fan Zhiyi's regular defensive partner, Zhang Enhua, out due to injury, Li stepped in with impressive ease to fill the breach. The Shenzhen centre half did so in such style that, when Zhang returned from injury, coach Bora Milutinovic kept faith in Li, who not only kept the opposition at bay but scored several vital goals during the qualifiers.

LI XIAOPENG BORN: 05/11/76 (SHANDONG)
Filled in well for Li Ming when the Dalian Shide player missed the qualifying tournament due to injury. Despite playing on the right, Li is prepared to hold his position in front of the back four to allow full-back Sun Jihai to burst forward.

WEI XIN BORN: 18/04/77 (CHONGQING)
Played a key part in Chongqing's Chinese FA Cup win in 2000, form that earned him a call up to the national team. Made his debut against North Korea in August last year but been unable to hold down a regular place in the team.

GAO YAO BORN: 13/07/78 (SHANDONG)
Peripheral figure who most recently impressed during China's warm-up with Slovenia in Hong Kong in February. However, at best he will secure a place on the bench.

LI YI DOB: 20/06/79 (BEIJING GUOAN)
Yet another youngster given a trial run by Bora Milutinovic in the early stages of the competition, making his debut against Cambodia in the preliminary rounds. Lacks composure in front of goal, however, and needs to gain more experience.

ZHANG YUNING BORN: 25/05/77 (LIAONING)
Showed much promise as a youngster but has struggled to dislodge China's most experienced attackers from the starting line-up. May be used as a substitute if Milutinovic fancies a change of tactics.

XU YUNLONG BORN: 17/02/79 (BEIJING GUOAN)
Another young defender who made his debut for the national team prior to the Asian Cup in Lebanon in 2000. Scored three times for the team but is unlikely to make it into the starting line-up and will travel to the World Cup, if selected, primarily for experience.

REPUBLIC OF CHINA

FAN ZHIYI BORN: 22/01/70 (DUNDEE)

Fan is the heart and soul of the Chinese team and, after leading the side for the best part of a decade, has finally achieved his life-long ambition of qualifying for the World Cup. Became the first Chinese player to sign for an English club when, along with Sun Jihai, he joined Crystal Palace in September 1998. Proved popular with the fans at Selhurst Park but left the club after a fall-out with then-coach Steve Bruce over his appearances for China. Dundee's Ivan Bonetti stepped in and took Fan to Scotland, where he was sent off in his first match, against local rivals Dundee United. The two-time Chinese Player of the Year is expected to move into coaching when his playing career ends and has already been tipped to lead the Chinese national team in the future.

COACH

BORA MILUTINOVIC

Famed for having taken four teams to the second round of the World Cup finals, Bora Milutinovic was handed the unenviable task of trying to take perennial underachievers China to their first-ever World Cup finals in January 2000. Having been dubbed a Miracle Worker while in the United States, who he coached at the 1994 World Cup finals, Milutinovic's greatest achievement could well be qualifying China for this summer's tournament. With a squad made up largely of players who had failed four years earlier, the wily Serb fashioned a team that lost just once in the qualifying tournament, and that defeat came after their place in the Finals had been assured. Milutinovic's place is now guaranteed in world football history with China the fifth side he will take to the Finals. However, the Serb has not been responsible for taking any of the previous four to the World Cup. In 1986, when he coached Mexico, the team qualified as hosts. Four years later Costa Rica had already made it to the Finals when he was appointed just months before Italia '90. As in 1986, Milutinovic was trusted with the hopes of the hosts in 1994 when he was the US coach and, in 1998, Nigeria had already been taken to the Finals by Philippe Troussier before the Frenchman lost his job, again less than six months before the World Cup. Milutinovic has taken a team successfully through the qualifying phase in the past, however, successfully negotiating the CONCACAF phase in 1997 with Mexico before a fall-out with the federation resulted in Bora losing his job.

WORLD CUP FACTS

The first player to be banned for taking drugs in a World Cup final was Ernest Jean-Joseph in 1974 of Haiti. He was extradited by his country's security men and never played again.

The first sub to score in a World Cup was Juan Basaguren of Mexico in 1970.

COSTA RICA

osta Rica are hoping that their second visit to the World Cup will be as eventful and exciting as their first one. In 1990, Costa Rica surprised everyone by getting out of a group with Brazil, Scotland and Sweden. They beat Sweden in a winner takes all match in the first phase, to get into the knockout stages. This team will be less likely to sneak up on opponents as they won the CONCACAF qualifying group and even became the first team ever to beat Mexico in Mexico in qualifying. However, none of this would have happened if not for the managerial change before a one match play-off versus Guatemala after the first round. Alexander Guimaraes took over from Gilson Nunes and turned the team around. Guimaraes, a Brazilian-born Costa Rican played in the 1990 World Cup for the 'Ticos' and is now guiding them to their second World Cup. His team plays either a 3-5-2 or 4-4-2 system depending on who they are playing. If they need to defend then Guimaraes goes with a flat back four, but will shift to three if he wants a more attacking system.

The experienced Erick Lonnis plays in goal and he was in great form in qualifying. Captain Reynaldo Parks leads the defence. In midfield Wilmer Lopez runs the show. Attacking midfielder Rolando Fonseca has been the best player in CONCACAF over the last year. Up front Hernan Medford and Paulo Wanchope are the key men.

SQUAD

ROBERT ARIAS (HEREDIANO) (21)
Has played with Gilberto Martinez at the U23 level, but unlike his centre back partner, Arias has not become an integral part of the full National team. Arias plays for Herediano with Lester Morgan. He received his first cap versus Venezuela in April of 2001, and is likely to be a late substitute for defensive purposes only.

AUSTIN BERRY (HEREDIANO) (31) CAPS: 65 GLS: 6
Outside wing back who has fantastic pace, but has found himself a little out of the mix with the emergence of Castro and Martinez. Berry has also had problems with FIFA, and was suspended with drug problems three years ago. He can also play in the midfield, and can cause defenders all kinds of problems with his speed and ability to make mazy runs.

STEVEN BRYCE (ALAJUELENSE) (24) CAPS: 32 GLS: 4
Winger who played for the youth squad in Malaysia in 1997, and has also played on the Olympic squad. Made his debut with the A team in 1999 during the UNCAF Cup, and scored the winning goal vs Trinidad & Tobago last month. As Bryce is growing stronger and more mature he is starting to play more of a central role.

CARLOS CASTRO (ALAJUELENSE) (23) CAPS: 22 GLS: 0
Castro is a new member of the squad, gaining his first cap in the CONCACAF first round play-off versus Guatemala. A right wing back, who shifts inside when needs be, but likes to patrol the right side. Very fast, not a great distributor, and enjoys getting involved with the play.

COSTA RICA

WALTER CENTENO (SAPRISSA) (27) CAPS: 48 GLS: 6
Started his career with Goicoechea, and Belen, and then moved to Saprissa, one of the
bigger clubs in Costa Rica. Centeno was involved in the 1996 Olympic qualifying
process and the 1998 and 2001 Copa Americas. Normally plays creative midfielder with
Saprissa, and has played well when given a chance at the same spot for the 'Ticos', but
is behind Lopez in the pecking order, and normally is the first midfielder off the bench.

RODRIGO CORDERO (HEREDIANO) (27)
Plays on the left of midfield, but often works his way into the centre to make life hard
for the opposition. He is strong in the air and on the ball, and is slowly becoming a
better distributor. He can play central midfielder, and be the playmaker, but Guimaraes
likes to keep the pressure off him, and let him clog up the middle.

JERVIS DRUMMOND (SAPRISSA) (25) CAPS: 38 GLS: 1
Has been at Saprissa for a lot of his career, but has also played in Brazil for Flamengo.
Drummond came to prominence in the U20s in Qatar '95, and was part of the World
Cup qualifying process in 1998. His brother Gerald has been in and out of the national
team. Drummond is very fast, strong in the air and can move outside if needs be, but
most often a stopper in a back three.

JUAN ESQUIVEL (SANTO) (21) CAPS: 1 GLS: 0
Helped Santo to win the Championship this year. Newly capped midfielder though he
has been in and around the squad for the past year. Full debut against Morocco in
March. Can also play in the back four if needed. Has been with Santos for three years
now. Is quick but has a poor goal-scoring record.

ROLANDO FONSECA (SAPRISSA) (37) CAPS: 78 GLS: 38
A speedy, dangerous attacker with all the tools except height. He is lighting quick, and
his mazy runs give defenders all kinds of problems. Although he is not tall, he is strong
in the air, scoring numerous goals in qualifying with his head. He has great composure,
and a brilliant first touch. Fonseca moved to Saprissa in Costa Rica last year, but is
rumoured to be going to Mexico. Fonseca can also play as the attacking midfielder. The
all-time leading scorer in the Costa Rican national side.

RONALD GOMEZ (OFI CRETE) (27) CAPS: 52 GLS: 17
Has been one of the leaders in showing how good Costa Rican football has become.
Gomez started with Alajuelense, then moved to Spain to Sporting Gijon of Spain in 1996-
97, then to Hercules in the Second Division of Spain. He has now gone to Greece, where
he plays for OFI Crete in the First Division. Gomez biggest problem is that he is rarely
called in because of the releasing hassle. Guimaraes tends to use Gomez as a sub.

RICARDO GONZALEZ (ALLAJUELA) (27) CAPS: 5 GLS: 0
In the squad because the third keeper Lester Morgan hurt his knee before the Copa
America, and has not recovered. Gonzalez is Mesen's deputy at Alajuela.

COSTA RICA

RONALD GONZALEZ (COMMUNICACIONES)
A hard working midfielder with the ability to put the ball in the net at all levels. Gonzalez is playing at Communicaciones in Guatemala, where him and international teammate Rolando Fonseca helped the most successful Guatemalan club to more titles. Has been in the national squad since the early 1990s.

GEOVANNY JARA (HERDIANO) (32) CAPS: 11 GLS: 0
The Herediano defender was brought in as an emergency full-back in the middle of the qualifying campaign, but rarely played. He was in the 1990 World Cup squad, coached by Bora, but never got a chance to play. Then disappeared from the National team scene until 1999 UNCAF Cup where he played once. Guimaraes played him in the lead up to the 1990 World Cup, and he will use Jara as a late defensive substitute if needs be.

ERICK LONNIS (SAPRISSA) (26) CAPS: 74 GLS:0
Has been a member of the National squad since 1990, but did not play in the World Cup of 1990, and did not make his debut until 1992. Had a great run during qualifying, where he took over the starting job from Alvaro Mesen when new manager Alexander Guimaraes took over. He has played in three UNCAF Cups ('97, '99), three Gold Cups ('98 and 2000), and been through two World Cup qualifying tournaments.

WILMER LOPEZ (ALAJUELENSE) (30) CAPS: 67 GLS: 6
Might be most important member of the national squad. He is an excellent dribbler, with good vision and the ability to score. He has become the main distributor of the ball for the Ticos since Guimares took over. Lopez is the key to the team – if you can stop his long passes from the middle, then the team will struggle to create chances.

ALEXANDER MADRIGAL (LA PIEDAD) (29) CAPS: 28 GLS: 2
Was a key component to the first round of 2002 qualifying, but when Guimaraes took over Madrigal was dropped. He has not been back on the squad since, but has been mentioned by many as a player who could really help Costa Rica with his pace and his composure. Good in the air, Madrigal can run the game from his central position.

LUIS MARIN (ALAJUELA) (27) CAPS: 73 GLS: 3
Centre back who has taken Carlos Castro, under his wing at Alajuela. Marin had a good run last year which put him back into the fray of the starting line-up. The 6'0" full-back is good in the air, but some times slow to get back. Has also been used in midfield.

GILBERTO MARTINEZ (SAPRISSA) (23) CAPS: 27 GLS: 0
After playing only one season of Division One football with Saprissa, Martinez quickly made his mark with the national team. His debut for Costa Rica like Castro's was versus Guatemala in the CONCACAF play-off. A central defender at his club, he moves outside left often for his country. He is exceptionally quick and a sure tackler, which has earned him looks from Serie A teams, most recently Brescia.

COSTA RICA

HERNAN MEDFORD (SAPRISSA) (33) CAPS: 87 GLS: 20

Mostly used as a substitute these days, but in his prime he was one of the best all-around strikers from the continent. Was the first Costa Rican to play in Italy, and was the hero of the 1990 World Cup when he scored the winner versus Sweden to put the Ticos into the second round. Still has the ability to score an important goal as he showed with the winner in Mexico City to hand Mexico their first ever qualifying defeat at home.

ALVARO MESEN (ALAJUELENSE) (29) CAPS: 15 GLS: 0

Has become a member of the squad within the last two years. Was the first choice keeper in the first round of qualifying before a knee injury before the United States match last April kept him out. He has played for Alajuela since he was 18 in 1990, and has been a fixture for the last few years. He was even been spectacular at times in qualifying. He helped Alajuela to the title last term. He is good in the air, and on crosses but can be beaten from distance.

REYANLDO PARKS (TECOS) (27) CAPS: 46 GLS: 1

A true outside back who can play on either the right or left side of the field, although more often than not he is on the right. He is very quick, but does not get forward often. Started his career with Limonense, then Herediano, then UAG Tecos in Mexico, and now back in Costa Rica with Saprissa. Parks is the national captain, and played in all 17 qualifiers that the team played.

OSCAR ROJAS (LA PIEDAD) (23) CAPS: 4 GLS: 0

Rojas was involved with the national teams for the last few years, but did not receive a cap until the meaningless last World Cup qualifier versus Jamaica in November. Plays in Mexico for La Piedad, and is a squad member rather than a likely starter.

MAX SANCHEZ (SANTO) (29) CAPS: 5 GLS: 0

Sanchez has been playing in Costa Rica for almost ten years now, but did not receive his first cap until January of this year. Can play on the outside, but is more often used to clog the middle with his defensive capabilities. Guimaraes admires the player's pace and desire to get involved.

MAURICIO SOLIS (HEREDIANO) (29) CAPS: 83 GLS: 5

A creative midfielder with a solid foot and the ability to be very physical. Solis played with countryman Paulo Cesar Wanchope in England at Derby. He has been through a lot with the Costa Rican national team, and was an important member of the 1998 qualifying squad. However, he was not a part of the first round of qualifying as Gilson Nunes was not a fan. Guimaraes brought him back, after Solis played well for Alajuela. For the national side Solis has become a super sub.

JAFET SOTO (TECOS) (26) CAPS: 40 GLS: 8

One of the most skilled players from Costa Rica. However, Guimaraes views Soto as a luxury type player and has found no room for him. Is brilliant with the ball, and can make things happen with his pace and ability to dribble. Has suffered from knee problems, and that slowed him down for a while, but is now at full strength.

COSTA RICA

WILLIAM SUNSING (HEREDIANO) (23) CAPS: 23 GLS: 3
Costa Rica still have high hopes for this talenetd but frustrating player. Shows glimpses of fantastic pace and skill, but then disappears. He played for Herediano before he moved onto the New England Revolution, and moved back to Herediano on the off seasons to play some more. Is very creative, but can often loses possession after making long mazy runs.

HAROLD WALLACE (ALAJUELENSE) (26) CAPS: 53 GLS: 1
A left sided wingback, who has been with the the entire Costa Rican National teams growing up. He is a good crosser of the ball, but he is better at making sure the forward does not get time with the ball. Wallace's strength is his ability to bring the ball forward out of defence. He was supposed to play in Greece this year, but his club Alajuelense's demanded too much money.

PAULO WANCHOPE (MANCHESTER CITY) (35) CAPS: 48 GLS: 34
Has the ability to be the natural scorer that every team searches for. He is sometimes lazy, but can all of a sudden wake up and score a breathtaking goal. He was brilliant in qualifying scoring a seven goals in thirteen matches. He started his career with Herediano in Costa Rica then moved to Derby County of English Premier League. Scored often for Derby, but went through too many times of poor play. West Ham bought him before the 1999-2000 season for five million dollars, and he scored 12 times in 39 matches. He moved onto Manchester City, but could not help the Maine Road Crew from relegation. Last summer Wanchope added to his mystique, scoring five times in Copa America while working hard, and played well in the Gold Cup as Costa Rica finished second.

COACH

ALEXANDER GUIMARAES
One of the best stories of the World Cup would not have happened were it not for the hiring of Alexander Borges Guimaraes. Guimaraes took over Costa Rica from Gilson Nunes for the semifinal playoff match versus Guatemala, the 'Ticos' won 5-2. In fact since Guimaraes has been in charge, the team has lost just one qualifier, away to the United States. Alexandre was born, in the northeast of Brazil, but became a citizen of Costa Rica 1984. In Costa Rica, Guimaraes played 12 seasons with four teams Durpanel San Blas (1979), Puntarenas (1980 to 1981), Saprissa (1982 to 1991) and Turrialba FC (1992), in First Division. With Saprissa Guimaraes won three national championships, in 1982, 1988 and 1989. He played 16 times for the National team, including the 1990 World Cup. In 1994 he became manager at Bethlehem, but gained success with Sport Club Herediano and Saprissa. With Saprissa he won two titles of first division. His teams play in the manner he did: always looking to attack.

PENALTY TAKERS

EXPECTED PENALTY TAKERS FOR THE 32 NATIONS IN THE TOURNAMENT

	1ST CHOICE	2ND CHOICE
BELGIUM	MARC WILMOTS	
CROATIA	ROBERT PROSINECKI	DAVOR SUKER
DENMARK	EBBE SAND	
ENGLAND	MICHAEL OWEN	TEDDY SHERINGHAM
FRANCE	ZINEDINE ZIDANE	
GERMANY	MICHAEL BALLACK	
ITALY	ALESSANDRO DEL PIERO	
POLAND	EMMANUEL OLISADEBE	MICHAEL ZEWLAKOW
PORTUGAL	LUIS FIGO	
REPUBLIC OF IRELAND	IAN HARTE	
RUSSIA	VLADIMIR BESCHASTYNYKH	
SPAIN	HIERRO	RAUL
SLOVENIA	ZLATKO ZAHOVIC	
SWEDEN	HENRIK LARSSON	
TURKEY	HAKAN SUKER	
ARGENTINA	HERNAN CRESPO	BATISTUTA
BRAZIL	RIVALDO	RONALDO
PARAGUAY	CHILAVERT	FRANCISCO ARCE
URUGUAY	FEDERICO MAGALLANES	NICOLAS OLIVERA
COSTA RICA	ROLANDO FONSECA	
ECUADOR	ALEX AGUINAGA	AUSTIN DELGADO
MEXICO	BLANCO	GARCIA ASPE
USA	BRIAN MCBRIDE	
CAMEROON	LAUREN	
NIGERIA	AUSTIN OKOCHA	
SENEGAL	EL HADJ DIOUF	KHALILOU FADIGA
S AFRICA	SHAUN BARTLETT	THABO MNGOMENI
TUNISIA	ZOUBIER BAYA	
CHINA	FAN ZHIYI	
JAPAN	NAKATA	
SAUDI ARABIA	SAMI AL-JABER	
SOUTH KOREA	SUN-HONG HWANG	

GROUP D

Hosts traditionally do well in World Cups. Buoyed by the home support and familiar with conditions, countries staging the competition tend to play above themselves but this time FIFA are faced with the real possibility that South Korea and Japan will both fall at the first hurdle.

In terms of marketing and PR it would be a huge setback and disappointment. However, form and reality suggests Portugal and Poland will advance to the second round, the United States will go home and South Korea will – well, stay where they are.

Portugal are great underachievers of world football. Despite the European successes of their clubs the national side have reached the finals only twice before, in 1966 and 1986. The golden generation of Luis Figo, Rui Costa and Sa Pinto has probably reached a peak and this represents the last chance on the world stage for the bulk of this team.

Individually Portugal stand comparison with most. Their problem has been turning these individuals into an effective unit which can find a cutting edge to the delightful build-up play.

The impression is that sometimes Portugal are hell bent on scoring only great goals. However, nine different players were on the scoresheet during the qualifying programme so perhaps at last Figo and company have both quality and quantity when it comes to finding the back of the net.

Poland, like Portugal, are in the finals for the first time since 1986. The perennial opponents of England are a nightmare for John Motson, Clive Tyldesley and their fellow commentators – they are also likely to be similarly difficult to play against.

Coach Jerzy Engel has transformed the team and he says: "Poland no longer aim to avoid defeat. We go out to win and score twice or more. We play what I call Yes Football which means we are looking for goals and not afraid to lose one."

Twenty one goals in 10 qualifying ties makes Engel as good as his word yet their top scorer Emmanuel Olisadebe was born in Nigeria.

The Panathinaikos striker was discovered by a Polish scout and made an impact playing for Polonia Warsaw. Following a plea from former Polish great Zbigniew Boniek, the FA's chairman, Olisadebe was granted citizenship.

"It was not easy for a young player to come from Africa to Europe," he says. "The football is quite different. I wanted to learn, I was calm and it's worked well."

The most familiar face is Liverpool goalkeeper Jerzy Dudek who has impressed during his first season in English football following his £4.9 million transfer from Feyenoord which made him the most expensive Polish player ever.

Poland open against South Korea in Busan and the joint-hosts' Dutch coach Guus Hiddink will discover whether the meticulous preparation work his squad have put it has paid off.

Only two or three of the Korean players are with European clubs. The team will be fit, motivated and ready for the historic moment. This is the country's sixth appearance in the finals and it looks like they will need to take points off Portugal or Poland to stand a chance of staying in the competition.

Meanwhile, the USA will be playing in their fourth consecutive finals even though qualification was far from easy. The USA beat Jamaica 2-1 in the last game but went through only because Honduras surprisingly lost to Trinidad and Tobago.

"We deserve to be through and I'm proud of my team," says coach Bruce Arena. "I'm optimistic you'll see a better USA team at the World Cup."

Brad Friedel (Blackburn) and Kasey Keller (Spurs) will contest the goalkeeper's jersey with Sunderland's Claudio Reyna pulling the strings in midfield and Joe-Max Moore of Everton in the front line.

But this looks the weakest of the USA's recent sides though they could prove stubborn opponents.

SOUTH KOREA

"I have been preparing the team with a long-term view of the World Cup. I know the expectations of the fans and I am sure if we play as well as we can we'll do ourselves justice. Portugal and Poland are solid, strong European teams but we will be ready." **Guus Hiddink**, South Korea coach.

PORTUGAL

"We want to show the world how good Portugal can be. We must be wary of complacency but I am confident in my players. South Korea will be motivated by being hosts, the USA are experienced and Poland strong." **Antonio Oliveira**, Portugal coach.

POLAND

"I would be delighted to repeat our success of 1974 and 1982 when Poland finished third. I don't feel pressure because football has moved on since then. The games in the first round will be a learning experience and hopefully we can build on that." **Jerzy Engel**, Poland coach.

USA

"Bruce Arena has done a great job with what he had. Our aim is to go through the first round so the draw was crucial. We'll be tested and we know how being hosts can lift a nation." **Dr Bob Contiguglia**, president United States Soccer Federation.

SOUTH KOREA

Tournament co-hosts South Korea may have Asia's best qualifying record at World Cup level but their achievements in the finals have been nothing to boast about. This will be the nation's sixth World Cup – and their fifth in a row – the most of any country in the 44-member Asian Football Confederation but in all those visits to the game's greatest competition, Korea have not won a single game.

The call went out to GuUs Hiddink and after a shaky start, the Koreans have definitely moved forward under the former Real Madrid and Real Betis coach, with the defence in particularly good shape. But there are still problems. The team has found scoring goals tough although there is no lack of confidence in either midfield or attack. Finding a player who is a top class creative influence has also been difficult.

Then there is the added pressure from Japan. Although Hiddink plays it down, the Koreans are mindful of the progress the Japanese have made under Philippe Troussier and are hoping to, at the very least, match the achievements of their neighbours this summer. No host of the World Cup has ever failed to reach at least the second round and the Koreans will be hoping they don't create a tournament first. To make sure they don't they will have to record several firsts of their own. The pressure is most definitely on.

SQUAD

KIM BYUNG-JI (POHANG STEELERS) BORN: 08/04/70 CAPS: 56 GLS: 0
After falling foul of coach Guus Hiddink following a number of errors in the Dutchman's early games at the helm, Kim, known for his ever-changing hair colour, has returned to the fold after an exceptional season with Pohang Steelers. Looking for a place in his third World Cup squad.

CHO BYUNG-KUK (SUWON BLUEWINGS) BORN: 01/07/81 CAPS: 1 GLS: 0
Taken to Europe this spring for the training camp and, at the age of just 20, should expect no more than a place in the squad at best. Tall and strong he is one for the future.

SONG CHONG-GUG (PUSAN I.CONS) BORN: 20/02/79 CAPS: 24 GLS 2
To label Song a defender is something of a misnomer for one of the most versatile and accomplished young players in Asia. Replaced Hong Myung-bo when he was injured as sweeper but is equally adept on the wing or as a play maker, where he is most likely to feature at this, his first World Cup.

LEE CHUN-SOO (ULSAN HYUNDAI) BORN: 09/07/81 CAPS: 18 GLS: 3
One of the young sensations of Korean football, Lee has picked up almost 20 caps for Korea despite his age. Cocky and confident he is sure to be in Hiddink's squad. Joined Ulsan Hyundai after trials at Lille and Brescia.

KIM DO-HOON (CHONBUK HYUNDAI) BORN: 21/07/70 CAPS: 57 GLS: 20
One of the most highly-paid players in Korea after signing for Chonbuk upon his return from the J.League in 2000. Had been in everyone's Hiddink's squads in 2001 but was left out in 2002, suggesting the Dutchman may have no place for him in the squad.

SOUTH KOREA

LEE DONG-GOOK (POHANG STEELERS) BORN: 29/04/79 CAPS: 29 GLS: 9
Finished the Asian Cup as top scorer in Lebanon in 2000 as Korea finished third. Joined Werder Bremen for a loan spell shortly after but failed to impress and returned to Pohang Steelers, where he won the Asian title in 1998.

CHA DU-RI (KOREA UNIVERSITY) BORN: 25/07/80 CAPS: 8 GLS: 0
Son of the most famous footballer in Korean history, two-time UEFA Cup winner Cha Bum-kun. Fast and explosive, Cha is expected to earn a place in the squad and his pace is an asset off the bench.

CHOI EUN-SUNG (DAEJON CITIZEN) BORN: 05/04/7 CAPS: 1 GLS: 0
Experienced K-League campaigner who was picked by Hiddink for the squad that travelled to Europe and North Africa in March. Unlikely to feature, however.

SIM JAE-WON (EINTRACHT FRANKFURT) BORN: 11/03/77 CAPS: 21 GLS: 2
Wingback who struggled in Hiddink's early days but the Dutchman has stuck by him. However, since his move from Busan to Frankfurt, Sim's limited playing opportunities have also reduced his World Cup chances.

PARK JI-SUNG (KYOTO PURPLE SANGA) BORN: 25/02/81 CAPS: 30 GLS: 1
Snubbed the normal Korean route into football and joined J.League side Kyoto Purple Sanga directly from high school. The skilful midfielder is useful from set pieces and could be expected to take on the playmaker's role, although his slight physique could work against him.

CHOI JIN-CHUEL (CHONBUK HYUNDAI) BORN: 26/03/7 CAPS: 10 GLS: 1
Plays on the right side of Korea's three man back line. Solid and reliable, he made the position his own during the European tour, when Korea kept three consecutive clean sheets.

YOON JONG-HWAN (CEREZO OSAKA) BORN: 16/02/73 CAPS: 34 GLS: 2
Despite being one of the older midfielders in the team, Yoon has been restricted to just 34 caps for Korea as a result of his fragility. The talented playmaker picks up injuries often and Hiddink remains unsure over his future in the squad. Impressed at the Asian Cup in Lebanon as Korea reached the semi-finals.

AHN JUNG-HWAN (PERUGIA) BORN: 16/02/76 CAPS: 17 GLS: 2
Became the first Korean to play in Serie A when he joined Perugia from Pusan Icons. Struggled to adapt until the end of his first season, when he scored several vital goals but has again failed to impress this year. Rarely impressed for Korea and is uncertain of a place in the squad.

SEO JUNG-WON (SUWON BLUEWINGS) BORN: 17/12/70 CAPS: 86 GLS: 16
Quick and skilful, Seo has had a renaissance at Suwon since returning to Korea after a difficult period at Strasbourg. Was in the last three World Cup squads.

SOUTH KOREA

SEOL KI-HYUN (ANDERLECHT) BORN: 08/01/79 CAPS: 25 GLS: 7
Jumped to the top of the queue of strikers vying for a place in the starting line up in the middle of last year when he started well with Anderlecht. However, injury this year has caused him problems and, while certain to be in the squad, Seol looks set for a place on the bench.

LEE LIM-SAENG (BUCHEON SK) BORN: 18/11/71 CAPS: 25 GLS: 0
Defender known for his combative style. Was a member of the squad that played in France four years ago.

LEE MIN-SUNG (PUSAN ICONS) BORN: 23/06/73 CAPS: 54 GLS: 2
Usually a regular in the back line, Lee has struggled with injury over the last few months and his position in the squad is questionable. Played in France '98 and is a former winner of the Asian Club Championship with Ilhwa Chunma.

HONG MYUNG-BO (POHANG STEELERS) BORN: 12/02/69 CAPS: 123 GLS: 9
Hong's place at his fourth World Cup finals looked in doubt at the start of 2002 due to injury and the form of his replacement, Song Chong-gug. However, his return during the European and North African tour was a revelation as the Koreans kept three clean sheets with the veteran playing in his usual sweeper's role.

KIM NAM-IL (CHUNNAM DRAGONS) BORN: 14/03/77 CAPS: 17 GLS: 1
Plays in the centre of midfield alongside Yoo Sang-chul. Combative and strong, along with Yoo he can control the pace of the team's play.

YOO SANG-CHUL (KASHIWA REYSOL) BORN: 18/10/71 CAPS: 92 GLS: 16
After initial reservations, coach Hiddink seems set to stick with Yoo in defensive midfield, giving the Kashiwa player his third World Cup appearance. Can score and create from midfield although in his time in Japan, where he has also played for Yokohama F Marinos, he has also played as a striker.

HA SEOK-JU (POHANG STEELERS) BORN: 20/02/68 CAPS: 91 GLS: 23
Scored Korea's opening goal against Mexico in France 98 before being sent off less than a minute later as his side crashed 3-1. Has re-emerged under Hiddink and earned several caps in 2001 although was missing from the squads that travelled to Europe and played at the Gold Cup.

CHOI SUNG-YONG (SUWON BLUEWINGS) BORN: 15/12/75 CAPS: 58 GLS: 1
Wingback who likes to go forward and is a threat when the Koreans are attacking. Plays on the right side. Returned to play in Korea with Suwon Bluewings last season after a brief stint in Austria with LASK Linz.

HWANG SUN-HONG (KASHIWA REYSOL) BORN: 14/07/68 CAPS: 95 GLS: 49
Commanding forward set for his fourth World Cup. Was included in the squad for France

but didn't play after picking up a knee injury just days before the tournament. Has been one of the few strikers in Hiddink's squad to hit form recently.

CHOI TAE-UK (ANYANG CHEETAHS) BORN: 13/03/81 CAPS: 14 GLS: 3
Picked up an ankle injury at the Gold Cup, which mean he missed the friendly against Uruguay in Montevideo and remains doubtful for the World Cup. Plays on the left side and is in competition for the position with Lee Young-pyo.

KIM TAE-YOUNG (CHUNNAM DRAGONS) BORN: 08/11/70 CAPS: 68 GLS: 3
Usually plays at full back but has recently slotted into the back three in the absence of Lee Min-sung and has done so in style. Picked by Hiddink to captain the team in recent months and could retain that honour this summer.

LEE WOON-JAE (SUWON BLUEWINGS) BORN: 26/4/73 CAPS: 29 GLS: 0
Had looked to have made the number one position his own last year when Hiddink arrived but has since been challenged by Kim Byung-ji, with the pair battling it out for the starting place between the posts.

KIM YONG-DAE (PUSAN ICONS) BORN: 11/10/79 CAPS: 12 GLS 0
Formerly with Yonsei University, where he was playing when he made his national team debut. Earned rave reviews while playing for the Olympic team for his impressive shot stopping while he is also strong in the air.

CHOI YONG-SOO (JEF UNITED ICHIHARA) BORN: 10/09/73 CAPS: 56 GLS: 27
Moving to the J.League from Anyang Cheetahs has developed the striker's game after guiding his Korean club to the league title in 2000. Was among the top scorers in Japan last year and has improved since his disappointing showing in France four years ago.

HYUN YOUNG-MIN (HYUNDAI) BORN: 25/12/7 CAPS: 6 GLS: 0
Inexperienced youngster brought in to the squad by Hiddink for the tour of Europe.

LEE YOUNG-PYO (ANYANG CHEETAHS) BORN: 23/04/77 CAPS: 45 GLS: 3
Called into the team by former coach Huh Jung-moo, Lee is one of Korea's most creative players. Tends to play on the left side but can also go through the centre and was instrumental in Anyang lifting the league title in 2000.

COACH

GUUS HIDDINK
Took over at the helm in Korea in January 2001, succeeding former Korean international Huh Jung-moo after his failure at both the Olympic Games in Sydney and at the Asian Cup in Lebanon in 2000. Took the Netherlands to the semi-finals of France '98. First experience of working in Asia.

PORTUGAL

The mantra coming out of Lisbon, Porto, the Algarve and every town and village in between is the same today as it was two years ago except for one crucial difference: this REALLY is the last chance for Portugal's "Golden Generation" to leave a tangible mark on history by winning a major trophy. They came close at Euro 2000 losing 2-1 to France only on a Golden Goal penalty scored by Zinedine Zidane three minutes from the end of extra time. They had done enough in the tournament to suggest they could go all the way, coming from 0-2 down to convincingly beat England 3-2 in their opening group match, before wins over Romania (1-0), Germany (3-0) and Turkey (2-0). In fact that defeat to France is one of only two Portugal have suffered in their last 25 competitive games in the last four years. Their only other reverse was a 1-0 defeat against Romania early in the qualifying competition for Euro 2000. They came through the 10-match qualifying programme for the World Cup finals unbeaten winners of a group which also included Ireland and Holland, winning seven and drawing three with an impressive goal tally of 33-7.

Statistics of course will mean nothing when Portugal play co-hosts South Korea, Poland and the United States in the finals – but they are an indication that Portugal could make a very big impression on the tournament this summer.

Coach Antonio Oliveira, a former international midfielder himself who won 24 caps for Portugal and turns 50 on June 10, the day Portugal face Poland in Jeonju, inherited a fine squad when he took over from Humberto Coelho after Euro 2000. But as he has said repeatedly to the Portuguese papers over the last few months: "The time has come for us to stop just being the best – we must be first instead."

The focal point of the team is Real Madrid's Luis Figo, the current FIFA World Player of the Year, and the most expensive player in soccer history until Zidane joined him at Real from Juventus last summer in a £47.9 million deal.

Figo proved his mettle by coping with the venom of the Barcelona fans following his £37 million move to Real in the summer of 2000. In many ways he is an even better player now than he was two years ago – and that can only be beneficial for Portugal.

Figo is part of Portugal's so-called "Golden Generation", the youngsters who won the World Youth title in both 1989 and 1991 and who now, a decade or so on, provide the backbone of the squad.

Joao Pinto is the sole survivor of the 1989 team, but Nuno Capucho, Jorge Costa, Rui Costa and Figo all figured in the victorious 1991 team which beat Brazil 4-2 on penalties after a 0-0 draw in front of 120,000 people in Lisbon. These players have been living in the spotlight for a very long time.

And they qualified for the finals in some style, with their most important win coming in only their third match when they played superbly to beat the Dutch 2-0 away. In the return leg they had to show some real resilience and did just that by salvaging a 2-2 draw with two goals in the last seven minutes when all seemed lost.

Portugal's team is built around the concept of open, attacking soccer, usually with two wingers and a target man, with Rui Costa providing the ammunition through the middle and Figo's wide play pulling defences out of position towards the flanks. Defenders make mistakes trying to second-guess him. He punishes them with some excellent crosses – and a few goals of his own.

PORTUGAL

Oliviera is also likely to use Pedro Pauleta as the spearhead in the attack with Nuno Gomes having to be content with a place on the bench – even though when he scored four times against Andorra in Portugal's 7-1 win over the minnows last September he became the first Portugal player to do that in an international since Eusebio cracked four past North Korea in the 1966 World Cup finals.

Those finals of course still represent the high-water mark of achievement for Portugal at international level. Benfica, Porto and Sporting Lisbon might all have enjoyed success at European club level over the years, but Portugal have never bettered their third place finish in the 1966 World Cup.

After losing an epic semi-final 2-1 to England at Wembley, Portugal returned a few days later and beat the Soviet Union 2-1 in front of 87,000 fans who had supported them throughout the game. Eusebio had left the field in tears after losing the semi-final but he came back to score in the third place game and left Wembley smiling with the cheers of the fans ringing in his ears. But in reality that was Portugal's last significant contribution to the World Cup.

It might be hard to believe, but their only other World Cup appearance was in Mexico in 1986 where they gained a modicum of revenge over England with a 1-0 win in the group stage – but failed to get past the first round after defeats to Poland and Morocco.

Sixteen years on and a new chapter is waiting to be written. Portugal are already assured of a place in the 2004 European championships as they are hosting the tournament. It is not beyond the bounds of probability that they could do so as World Champions too.

SQUAD

JORGE ANDRADE (FC PORTO) BORN: 09.04.78 CAPS: 5 GLS: 1
Two seasons with the Porto club – he came from club coach Santos' former club Estrela Amadora in summer 2000. Is from the national U21 side and now into the full national squad. Four improving seasons with Estrela in D1.

VITOR BAIA (FC PORTO) BORN: 15.10.69 CAPS: 75 GLS: 0
Four knee operations and 17 months on sidelines. Had a nightmare 1997-98 season with Barcelona. The only senior game he played in was the Champions League return game with Dynamo Kiev, where he let in 4 goals and was dropped again. Went back to Porto in Jan 1999 and promptly won 6th title in 1999. He was certainly one of the best in Europe when previously at Porto. He moved there in 1988 and won five league titles at the club, before moving in summer 1996 to Barcelona for £4.8 million along with Bobby Robson. Won ECWC and Spanish Cup medals with Barca in 1997-98, and runners up in the league – as first choice keeper. But from there it was a disaster.

PEDRO BARBOSA (SPORTING LISBON) BORN: 06.08.70 CAPS: 21 GLS: 5
Experienced international who played back at Euro 96. Sporting captain of the 2000 champions and key midfielder, he has been six seasons with the club, following four seasons with Vitoria Guimaraes – so 10 seasons in top flight and over 250 D1 games.

PORTUGAL

PAULO BENTO (SPORTING LISBON) BORN: 20.06.69 CAPS: 31 GLS: 0
Signed by Sporting in summer 2000 from Primera Liga club Oviedo - after Euro 2000 where he had ban for his part in the punch-up after the semi-final v France. Defensive midfield and grafter. Four seasons in the Primera Liga with Oviedo. Originally with Benfica, he was loaned to Estrela (1989-91) and Guimaraes (1991-4), before Benfica hauled him back for two seasons in their first team, thence to Oviedo. Does the graft in the midfield.

RUI BENTO (BOAVISTA) BORN: 14.01.72 CAPS: 6 GLS: 0
10 seasons at 2001 champions Boavista, who have just won the title for the first time ever, and over 200 games for them. Released by Benfica after one season with them in 1991-92 and swopped as part of the package that took Joao Pinto in the other direction. Intermittent caps – his first four caps were from 1991-95 – and one in September 1999 after a four year gap. One of the stars of the 1991 World Junior Cup win, so surprising Benfica let him go.

LUIS BOA MORTE (FULHAM) BORN: 04.08.77 CAPS: 4 GLS: 1
First time into squad for France game in April 2001 and first cap. 21 goals in Fulham's run to the Premiership (18 in league) though was not always first choice - Barry Hayles kept him out for much of the season as Saha's partner. Originally from Sporting Lisbon where he was an U21 international, he moved to Arsenal in 1997, then on loan to Southampton and initially on loan at Fulham in the 2000-1 season. Move from Southampton completed in summer 2001 for £1.5 million.

NUNO CAPUCHO (FC PORTO) BORN: 21.02.72 CAPS: 29 GLS: 2
Six seasons at Porto, he was from the Vitoria Guimaraes club originally, and was a leading figure in Porto's 1998 and 1999 championship wins. Started against Germany at Euro 2000 after group qualification was assured. Was a member of the 1991 Junior World Cup winning team, whom Sporting amazingly let go after a spell from 1992-95. Rediscovered form with Guimaraes, won his first caps, and moved to Porto.

SERGIO CONCIECAO (INTER MILAN) BORN: 15.11.74 CAPS: 42 GLS: 10
Moved summer 2001 from Parma to Inter for £15 million. The man who blitzed Germany in Euro 2000 with all three goals - more than doubling his international goals tally at the time. Now back after injury. Moved to Lazio in summer 1998 from FC Porto for £3.7 million after Juventus and AC Milan had shown much interest – was in the team that won the 1999 ECWC and finished runners up in the league. Then joined Parma in 2000 with Mathias Almeyda with Hernan Crespo moving the other way.

FERNANDO COUTO (LAZIO) BORN: 02.08.69 CAPS: 82 GLS: 6
National captain, and won double with Lazio in 2000 - but is only a sub at Lazio as they consider him too undisciplined. Was up on a failed drugs test (nandrolone) v Fiorentina in Jan 2001. Played all 5 games at Euro 2000 with Jorge Costa. Moved in summer 1998 for a give-away £2 million from the Spanish champions. From Barcelona to Lazio in Serie A because he was only a reserve also at Barca. That was his first poor spell after

useful career with Porto (three titles), then Parma from 1994-96, and a fine first season at Barca in 1996-97 after a £2 million move. Was one of those players to have come through from the 1989 World Junior Cup winning team.

JORGE COSTA (CHARLTON ATHLETIC) BORN: 14.10.71 CAPS: 46 GLS: 2
Recently left FC Porto to play in the Premiership on a loan deal. Played all five games at Euro 2000 in tandem with Fernando Couto. One of the stars from the 1991 World Junior Cup winning team. He arrived at Porto from Gil Vicente in 1989 and has been a key defender through the 1990's championship successes, and has won 6 Championship medals with the club including the five in a row to 1999. Returned in the 1997 New Year to club and country after missing six league games with a broken nose following the Champions League game with AC Milan and a post match altercation with George Weah.

RUI COSTA (AC MILAN) BORN: 29.03.72 CAPS: 68 GLS: 20
Moved from Fiorentina to AC Milan in summer 2001 for £28 million. Quality midfielder in Serie A – highly regarded. Excellent international scoring ratio for a midfielder. Is the player who fed Batistuta at Fiorentina yet still picked up 10 goals a season himself. He moved from Benfica for £5 million after winning the Portuguese Cup in 1993 and the League in 1994. From the 1991 World Junior Cup winning side.

FRANSISCO DA COSTA (FC PORTO) BORN: 01.12.74 CAPS: 10 GLS: 1
Also known as Costinha. First call up for this midfielder just before Euro 2000, who had four seasons with Monaco before moving to Porto in summer 2001 on a 4-yr contract. Scored winner v Romania as sub at Euro 2000. Joined Monaco in summer 1997 from Nacional of Madeira. Moved into the national squad with Monaco's 2000 title win.

LUIS FIGO (REAL MADRID) BORN: 04.11.72 CAPS: 81 GLS: 27
Current FIFA World Player of Year. The world record man until Zidane – from Barcelona to Real Madrid for a fee of around £38.4 million (Reuters), and scourge of recent defences. 4 seasons at the Nou Camp with increasing authority down the right flank – won ECWC and Spanish Cups in 1997 and the 1998 and 1999 Championships.
From Sporting Lisbon (debut at 17, capped at 19) he might have gone to Juventus or Parma but his transfer dissolved into a real mess as he signed for one club and his agent signed for another, so he went to Barca for only £1.9 million which has to be one of football's bargains. Initially not allowed to play in Italy for 2 seasons. Was under contract at Barca until 2005 and club value was only £20 million, so at least they got a bargain sale!

NUNO FRECHAUT (BOAVISTA) BORN: 29.09.77 CAPS: 9 GLS: 0
Key midfielder in Boavista's 2001 maiden championship win and into the squad for the first time in 2001. Six seasons with Boavista, who signed him in summer 2000 from Vitoria Setubal, and has become an immediate influence. Had four seasons in Setubal's first team from 1996-2000 .

PORTUGAL

NUNO GOMES (FIORENTINA) BORN: 05.07.76 CAPS: 28 GLS: 13
Star at Euro 2000 – winner v England and four goals - but was sent off and banned after the semi-final with France. Moved to Fiorentina from Benfica in summer 2000 for £10.5 million. Joined Benfica in summer 1997 from Boavista as a full international already and the former pride of the national U21 side. Was top scorer at Benfica for three seasons. Made good progress and the country hopes he will eventually solve their scoring problem.

RUI JORGE (SPORTING LISBON) BORN: 27.03.73 CAPS: 19 GLS: 1
Was recalled in 2000 after a four year gap, after fine performances in Sporting's 2000 title win. Now looks as though he may take Dima's long-held place. Played at Euro 2000. Was the domestic Player of the Season 2000. Five seasons with Sporting, he was previously with Porto from 1992-98 and was a bit part player in most of the five title wins that the club won in that time. Moved to Sporting and benefited from first team place – left sided midfield/defender.

LITOS (MALAGA) BORN: 25.02.74 CAPS: 6 GLS: 0
Captain and key defender with the 2001 champions Boavista, who won the title for the first time in their history and the first club outside the 'Big Three' to win the title since 1946. But then moved summer 2001 to the Primera Liga with Malaga to try his luck in a harder league. Joined Boavista back in 1993, but was away on loan with Estoril and Rio Ave until 1995 – since then he has been a first choice in the first team and hardly missed a game. First start for Portugal in March 2001 vs Holland.

FERNANDO MEIRA (STUTTGART) BORN: 05.06.78 CAPS: 7 GLS: 0
Recently moved to the Bundesliga from Benfica. First capped as a sub in autumn 2000, vs Holland and Israel. Recently was the only Benfica player in current squad – arrived at club in summer 2000 from Vitoria Guimaraes. Recent national U21 star midfielder, but can play in defence.

FERNANDO NELSON (FC PORTO) BORN: 05.11.71 CAPS: 7 GLS: 0
Former Aston Villa full back, he arrived back in Portugal in summer 2000 as cover for other defenders but has found himself in the national squad again. Was initially at Sporting Lisbon for seven seasons, then had a couple of seasons at Villa, where he battled to make the first team. Another from the 1991 World Junior Cup winners.

PEDRO PAULETA (BORDEAUX) BORN: 28.04.73 CAPS: 33 GLS: 12
Moved to Bordeaux from Deportivo in summer 2000 for around £5 million to replace Sylvain Wiltord (Arsenal) - and finished up 2nd in the French league scorers in 2000-1 season behind Sonny Anderson of Lyon (22) with 20 goals. Has continued in excellent scoring vein. Was in the Deportivo club team that won its first ever Primera Liga in 2000 – contributed with 8 goals, he played 30 games of which 18 were as sub. 2 seasons at Deportivo. Moved Primera Liga clubs from Salamanca to Deportivo in summer 1998 for £5 million after 15 goals in the 1997-98 season for struggling Salamanca. Had been in Spain for five seasons after Salamanca took a gamble on him from small Portuguese D2 team Estoril.

PORTUGAL

ARMANDO PETIT (BOAVISTA) BORN: 25.09.76 CAPS: 9 GLS: 0
Is with the champions of Portugal for 2001. Joined Boavista in summer 2000 from fellow D1 club Gil Vicente, and has come through well in the past 18 months.

RICARDO PEREIRA (BOAVISTA) BORN: 01.02.76 CAPS: 10 GLS: 0
Keeper and first call up in April 2001. Is with the 2001 champions and first choice in the national team. Six seasons with his only club – this is only his third season as first choice.

JOAO PINTO (SPORTING LISBON) BORN: 19.08.71 CAPS: 77 GLS: 23
The best of the current crop of domestic forwards - he recently turned down a £14 million move to Deportivo. However Benfica couldn't afford his wages at the end of last season, so he moved to champions Sporting. Prefers to play on the wing, and chips in with 12-15 goals a season. Is the only player to have won two World Junior Cup medals (1989 and captain in 1991). That meant a move in 1992 from Boavista to Benfica, who were anxious to get as much for him as they could to ease their debts. Not to be confused with two other international Joao Pinto's – both of whom played for Porto.

RICARDO SA PINTO (SPORTING LISBON) BORN: 10.10.72 CAPS: 44 GLS: 9
Re-joined Sporting in summer 2000 for £1.5 million after a spell at Real Sociedad in the Primera Liga. Missed the entire 1997-98 season, his first with Real Sociedad, after copping a 13-month ban for thumping former Portuguese national coach Artur Jorge and assistant Rui Aguas at a squad session. Sociedad bought him just before the FIFA suspension, so they had to stick with him. Signed from Sporting Lisbon, where he had been from 1994-97, his first club was Salgueiros. Played at Euro 96 and Euro 2000.

'SIMAO' SABROSA (BENFICA) BORN: 30.10.79 CAPS: 13 GLS: 1
Barca invested £10 million in him from Sporting Lisbon in summer 1999 and expected him to replace Figo but now released from his contract and returned home to Portugal in summer 2001. Not in Euro 2000 squad. Scored on national debut Nov 1998 vs Israel, and rated the best young Portuguese forward. Former youth star. Was three seasons in first team at Sporting with increasing influence – normally plays wide on the right.

CARLOS SECRETARIO (FC PORTO) BORN: 12.05.70 CAPS: 35 GLS: 1
Recalled to the national side recently – he was in the team at Euro 96 and made the squad for Euro 2000 and played once. Has been in squad since 1998 recall but Carlos Xavier seems to have taken first choice. Returned to Porto in autumn 1997 from Real Madrid in mid-season after 18 unhappy months when former coach Fabio Capello wouldn't play him and bought Christian Panucci instead. He played for Porto from 1993-96, and won championship medals in 1995, 1996 and again in 1998 and 1999 on his return. His first club was Sporting Braga.

PORTUGAL

'BETO' SEVERO (SPORTING LISBON) BORN: 03.05.76 CAPS: 16 GLS: 1
Key defender with the 2000 champions, who won their first title since 1982 - which must embarrass Benfica who let him go to Campomaiorense, and then on to Sporting because they thought he wouldn't make the grade. Six seasons with Sporting, he has been with Portugal's squad since the national U21 side and was first capped in 1998. Had a couple of games at Euro 2000.

JOAQUIM SILVA 'QUIM' (SPORTING BRAGA) BORN: 13.11.75 CAPS: 12 GLS: 0
Played first choice since Euro 2000 and took over from Vitor Baia. Former reserve to Vitor Baia, and has had a couple of useful seasons with Braga. Has always played for Braga, he made his debut in 1992, and was club first choice from 1997. Played at Euro 2000 as sub in the win against Germany by 3-0.

JOSE VIDIGAL (NAPOLI) BORN: 15.03.73 CAPS: 13 GLS: 0
Moved in summer 2000 from the champions Sporting Lisbon to Napoli for £4 million - one of three Sporting players to move to Napoli. Excellent Euro 2000 in the midfield defensive role. Is unique in that he has a brother Litos that plays for another country - Angola - and who is captain of their national side. Has four brothers, all pros in Africa and Europe. Angolan born, had come through the system at Sporting, and was a key midfielder in the 2000 title win.

HUGO VIANA (SPORTING LISBON) BORN: 15.01.83 CAPS: 4 GLS: 0
The new star of the future and may make the squad – capped in late 2001 after just a couple of months in the Sporting first team. Former youth international, and into U21 squad as well.

ABEL XAVIER (LIVERPOOL) BORN: 30.11.72 CAPS: 18 GLS: 0
Joined Liverpool from neighbours Everton on a free transfer in February 2002. Was to be out of contract at Everton in the summer of 2002. Another to have returned from a ban after the Euro 2000 semi-final dust-up with France. Joined Everton in Sept 99 from PSV Eindhoven for £1.5 million. Slow start with viral infection at beginning of Merseyside career. Is a bit of a wanderer, having played for Bari (Italy), Oviedo (Spain) before PSV (Holland) and Everton (England). Was with Estrela then a couple of seasons with Benfica at home – born in Mozambique. Exotic hairstyles.

COACH

ANTONIO OLIVEIRA BORN: 10.06.52
Back for a second spell in charge after Humberto Coelho's resignation after the semi final loss at Euro 2000. First spell ended with elimination from Euro 96 finals at quarter-final stage. Held post 1994-96. After Euro 96, he took Porto to the 1997 and 1998 titles and was briefly in charge at Betis Seville last season. Played for Porto and Betis also, and Sporting Lisbon. Won 24 caps. Early coaching career with Guimaraes, Gil Vicente and Braga – took over national job for first time after elimination from 1994 World Cup.

POLAND

A Nigerian-born striker playing in Greece could emerge as Poland's star performer in the World Cup finals. Indeed, Emmanuel Olisadebe is already a star in his adopted homeland, a country he was not born in and now no longer even lives in. But the eight goals he scored during Poland's successful qualifying campaign were crucial in seeing Poland through to the World Cup for the first time in 16 years.

Olisadebe made his name at Polonia Warsaw under coach Jerzy Engel – now in charge of Poland. Engel saw Olisadebe's pace and strength were something special and by the summer of 2000 he was established as the best striker in Poland.

Enter Zbigniew Boniek, one of Poland's greatest ever players and now the vice-chairman of the Polish Football Association. Boniek suggested that Olisadebe should apply for Polish citizenship and in August 2000, just a month after being issued with his new Polish passport, Olisadebe made his debut for his new country, scoring Poland's goal in a 1-1 friendly with Romania.

Engel gradually introduced a new crop of talented players, blending them into a new-look national side. Goalkeeper Jerzy Dudek, who last August became the most expensive Polish player when he moved from Feyenoord to Liverpool for £5million, has made the No.1 shirt his own, while the long-established Schalke 04 captain Tomasz Waldoch and Olisadebe provided a solid backbone for Engel to flesh out.

Waldoch's Schalke teammate Tomasz Hajto provides the other half of a solid defensive partnership, at the core of Engel's 4-4-2 system. If there are any criticisms of Poland it concerns the midfield which lacks a little flair and enterprise.

Olisadabe, and his usual striking partner Pawel Kryszalowicz often have to funnel back to support the midfield play – and it's an area Engel needs to work on before the Finals start. Piotr Swierczewski, who had a spell in Japan with Gamba Osaka in 1999 and is now at Olympique Marseille, is the recognised playmaker, but his record of ujust one goal in his first 62 internationals speaks volumes for how he operates.

At worst Poland should at least match their achievement in 1986, the last time they were in the Finals, when they reached the second round. Anything more than that, is likely to be a bonus for Jerzy Engel's men.

SQUAD

ARKADIUSZ BAK (BIRMINGHAM CITY) BORN: 06.10.74 CAPS: 10 GLS: 0
Midfielder with the Polonia club, who were the 2000 champions, and recently in England on loan. Eight seasons with Polonia, and has a useful scoring record of nearly 50 goals in nearly 200 games for the club from midfield. No relation to the other Bak (Bonk).

JACEK BAK (LENS) BORN: 24.03.73 CAPS: 35 GLS: 1
Pronounced Bonk and recently moved French clubs from Lyon to Lens. Defender who was injured for much of his early time at Lyon since joining from Lech Poznan in summer 1995. Had recovered from knee ligament trouble and a couple of broken noses to claim a regular place in the Lyon team last season. Key player when fit for both club and country.

POLAND

JERZY DUDEK (LIVERPOOL) BORN: 23.03.73 CAPS: 21 GLS: 0
Joined Liverpool from Feyenoord for £4.85 million in the summer of 2001. Established as first choice in national side from 2000. Outstanding season in 1999 Dutch title win after club stood by him after poor start. Manchester Utd had a long look at him before deciding on Fabien Barthez. Spent five seasons at Feyenoord after signing from the Polish club Sokol Tychy - he played seven games as back up to Ed de Goey (Chelsea) in 1996-97, then took over from de Goey. Good shot stopper.

RADOSLAV GILEWICZ (TIROL INNSBRUCK) BORN: 08.05.72 CAPS: 10 GLS: 0
Top scorer in the Tirol team that won the 2000 Austrian championship with 18 goals and retained the title in 2001 where he went one better by being top scorer in the Austrian league with 20 goals. Former Bundesliga player with Stuttgart & Karlsruhe, playing 70 games for the two clubs between 1995-98, and then a move to Tirol in 1998. Is now playing in his third foreign country - started with Ruch Chorzow at home, and then went to St Gallen in the Swiss league before the Bundesliga and Austria.

TOMASZ HAJTO (SCHALKE) BORN: 16.10.72 CAPS: 44 GLS: 6
Club Captain of Schalke, he has been in Germany for some six seasons. Former Polish Footballer of the Year. Formerly with the Polish mining team Gornik Zabrze, he was first capped in 1996. Suffered with a whole host of national coaches, all of whom wanted a different angle from him.

TOMASZ 'TOMEK' IWAN (AUSTRIA VIENNA) BORN: 12.06.71 CAPS: 40 GLS: 4
Key member of the PSV side that won the 2000 Dutch title after his career was re-vitalised by Bobby Robson - now moved to Austria. Bit of a surprise £1 million move from Feyenoord in summer 1997 to PSV after being only a fringe player at Feyenoord. Spent four seasons with PSV. In Holland 1994-2001, he spent 1994-95 season with Roda JC then 1995-97 with Feyenoord and then onto PSV. Played at home for Warta Poznan.

ANDREIJ JUSKOWIAK (VFL WOLFSBURG) BORN: 03.11.70 CAPS: 39 GLS:13
Moved in summer 1998 from Borussia Monchengladbach to Wolfsburg for £900,000. Arrived in Germany from Sporting Lisbon in summer 1996. He was always a useful scorer as befits a player who was the tournament top scorer (7) at the 1992 Olympics, and was Polish league top scorer (18) as a teenager when Lech Poznan won the 1990 Championship.

RADOSLAW KALUSZNY (ENERGIE COTTBUS) BORN: 02.02.74 CAPS: 28 GLS: 10
Rewarded with a national recall for an excellent 1999 championship win when Wisla beat Widzew by 17pts in a 30-match league! Now playing in the Bundesliga. Hat-trick in World Cup game vs Belarus in autumn 2000. Originally capped back in 1996-7 season when at Zaglebie Lubin, then moved in early 1998 to Wisla and on to Germany. Had been in previous coach Wojcik's squads but only as cover defender – now called back by Engel and pushed much further forward.

POLAND

BARTOSZ KARWAN (LEGIA WARSAW) BORN: 13.01.76 CAPS: 17 GLS: 3
Has been with Legia for eight seasons now and is one of their experienced, though still youngish, midfielders. Has been on the fringes of international recognition for the past five seasons, but is still more of a squad member for Poland.

TOMASZ KIELBOWICZ (POLONIA WARSAW) BORN: 21.02.76 CAPS: 5 GLS: 0
Left sided midfielder from the 2000 champions who has come into the national team after the club's success. Also won a championship medal with Widzew Lodz, and has been playing in the top division for nine seasons.

TOMASZ KLOS (KAISERSLAUTERN) BORN: 07.03.73 CAPS: 36 GLS: 1
Moved from French club Auxerre to the Bundesliga in summer 2000 First joined the national squad in 1997, and has become since a fixture in the team after the 1998 championship win of his former club LKS Lodz. He moved immediately after the LKS title win to Auxerre in the French League.

MAREK KOZMINSKI (BRESCIA) BORN: 07.02.71 CAPS: 40 GLS: 1
Amost the forgotten man – a star of the 1992 Olympic silver medal team in Barcelona, he played in the early 1990's for Poland and was a competent performer in the tough world of Serie A. But his star faded and Engel has decided to give him another go. Udinese came in for him and he spent six seasons with them, before moving to Brescia on loan in Nov 1997. Settled well at Brescia and helped restore the club into Serie A, and in his 10th season in Italy so has huge experience.

JACEK KRZYNOWEK (FC NURNBERG) BORN: 15.05.76 CAPS: 22 GLS: 2
Will play in the Bundesliga next season after his club – with whom he has finished his second season – were promoted in May 2001 as Div Two champion. One of those favoured by coach Engel, and recalled. First capped with the provincial Belchatow club in Poland, after a fine junior career, but was a bargain for Nurnberg for just £75,000.

MARIUSZ KUKIELKA (AMICA WRONKI) BORN: 07.11.76 CAPS: 6 GLS: 0
Back in Poland with a provincial team in the top flight after a spell with the useful Dutch club Roda JC. D1 debut as a teenager and played for Tarnoberg and Beltachow before the Dutch trip. Mostly capped as sub – defender.

PAWEL KRYSZALOWICZ (EINTRACHT FRANKFURT) BORN: 23.06.74 CAPS: 22 GLS:
Plays in the Bundesliga Division Two and earned a recall to the national team under Engel last autumn. Formerly a useful player with provincial club Amicki Wronki, where he was first capped, he moved in Jan 2001 winter break to Eintracht.

MARCIN MACIEL (LEGIA WARSAW) BORN: 22.12.75
Scored on his debut for Poland, back in 1996 against Cyprus in the Cyprus Cup. Nine seasons in Division One football, he was also with LKS Lodz, and is in second spell with Legia.

POLAND

RADOSLAW MAJDAN (GOZTEPE IZMIR) BORN: 10.05.72 CAPS: 4 GLS: 0
Third choice 'keeper, he made his international debut in Jan 2000 in a friendly against
Spain. The best of the domestic league keepers for the past three seasons until a recent
move to Turkey. Is from the Pogon junior set up, and has passed 200 D1 games.

ADAM MATYSEK (ZAGLEBIE LUBIN) BORN: 19.07.68 CAPS: 33 GLS: 0
Now back home after coming back to Poland in summer 2001 from Bayer Leverkusen.
Recalled to the national squad in spring 1998 for the first time in four years, and was first
choice until 2000 when Dudek took over. Still No 2 in the national set up. Joined Bayer
Leverkusen in the Bundesliga in summer 1998 when out of contract and was usually their
first choice keeper. He has spent some time in Germany from 1993-97 with the Division
Two clubs Fortuna Cologne & Gutersloh, then moved to Leverkusen for £250,000. Won his
first 13 caps between 1992-94 when he was originally with Slask Wroclaw before Fortuna.

EMMANUEL OLISADEBE (PANATHINAIKOS) BORN: 22.12.78 CAPS: 15 GLS: 10
Made a sensational start to international career. Moved in the winter break in Jan 2001
for £1.5 million from champions Polonia Warsaw to Greece. A Nigerian who was with
the Polonia club since Nov 1997, and has now gained Polish nationality since August
2000. Originally joined one of the youth schemes set up in Europe for young Africans
which FIFA/UEFA are monitoring to see whether they are run properly. Played for Jasper
United back in Nigeria. Four seasons with the 2000 champions Polonia.

TOMASZ RZASA (FEYENOORD) BORN: 11.03.73 CAPS: 8 GLS: 1
From Feyenoord's 1999 championship winning team. Then moved to Grasshoppers in
Switzerland from 1995 to 1997 where he was first capped with their champions and also
went on loan to Lugano and Young Boys. Came to Holland in 1997 with de Graafschap,
thence after good performances to Feyenoord in 1999. Made name at home with Sokol
Pniewy from 1991-95 when they came form D3 to D1 in successive seasons.

PIOTR SWIERCZEWSKI (MARSEILLE) BORN: 08.04.72 CAPS: 64 GLS: 1
Moved in May 2001 to Marseille on a Bosman ruling transfer for two years from his French
base at Bastia. Returned to France after a short spell in the J-League with Gamba Osaka.
Had enjoyed excellent previous seasons with Bastia, and was respected in the French First
Division. Was formerly with the famous St Etienne club (1993-95) who sold him to Bastia
when they hit hard times. Usually a first choice midfielder – Polish club was Katowice.

IGOR SYPNIEWSKI (WISLA KRAKOW) BORN: 10.11.74 CAPS: 3 GLS: 0
Moved recently from RKS in ther Polish league to the 2001 champions. Has returned to
Poland after years in Greece with OFI Crete and Panathinaikos. Played Champions
League for Panathinaikos. Two brief appearances for Poland before April 2002.

TOMASZ WALDOCH (SCHALKE) BORN: 10.05.71 CAPS: 71 GLS: 2
He has had superb recent seasons with Schalke. Moved Bundesliga clubs in summer
1999 from relegated Bochum to more secure Schalke – down the Ruhr – for £1.7

million. Probably the key central defender in recent seasons but has been relegated to a sub's role in the previous coach's games – only to re-appear on the side of defence.

MAREK ZAJAC (WISLA KRAKOW) BORN: 17.09.73 CAPS: 2 GLS: 0
Defender who was capped last season, and then recalled in 2001. Seven seasons with Wisla, and over 100 league games. Cover defender in national team.

MICHAL ZEWLAKOW (MOUSCRON) BORN: 22.04.76 CAPS: 23 GLS: 1
One of twins who both play for Mouscron, the other is Marcin Zewlakow – this one is a defender, the other is a forward. Been in Belgium for five seasons, first with Beveren, after coming through Polish national U21 side and both are excellent prospects. Michal has been in the squad since Feb 1999.

MARCIN ZEWLAKOW (MOUSCRON) BORN: 22.04.76 CAPS: 16 GLS: 4
Like his twin he is with Mouscron, the pair have been together through their careers. First stop was Polonia Warsaw, where they both made the first team by 1998 and moved as Poland U21 internationals to Belgium. Played 1998-9 for Beveren in the Belgian League then both moved to Mouscron.

TOMASZ ZDEBEL (GENCLERBIRLIGI) BORN: 25.05.73 CAPS: 10 GLS: 0
Polish born, raised in the USA, and spent his early career in Germany with Rot Weiss Essen in the lower leagues, then joined Cologne until 1997. Then moved to Lierse, who had just won the 1997 Belgian title, and has played for three seasons as playmaker in midfield and in the UCL season of 1997-8. Capped for the first time last season, he has moved to Turkish capital Ankara where he now plays for the Genclerbirligi club.

JACEK ZIELINSKI (LEGIA WARSAW) BORN: 10.10.67 CAPS: 51 GLS: 1
Was a key player in the Legia team that won the 1994 and 1995 Championships, and played in Champions League. 11 years with Legia after joining from Debica, he is approaching 400 games in the domestic league, which is one of the longer serving performances in recent seasons. Key defender in national team, quick and incisive and rarely misses a game.

MACIEJ ZURAWSKI (WISLA KRAKOW) BORN: 12.09.76 CAPS: 10 GLS: 2
Former Lech Poznan winger. League top scorer in first half of last season has earned a recall to the national set up. Has ben in and out of the national squad for four years.

COACH

JERZY ENGEL BORN: 06.10.52
Was appointed in Jan 2000 after the non-qualification for Euro 2000. PE teacher since 1975, and former coach of Legia Warsaw in two spells broken by a trip to Apollon Limassol in Cyprus. Since 1997 he was with Polonia Warsaw as coach and manager, whom he guided to the 2000 championship, and then to the national job.

USA

The United States are hoping to erase the horrible memory of the 1998 World Cup. After the 1994 showing the United States thought that they may be able to become a big player on the world stage but things fell apart quickly in France and the team finished 32nd out of 32 teams. The most successful manager in the United States Bruce Arena took over after that, and slowly and surely the team has improved. He has used over 70 players in his matches in charge giving everybody a chance, and now as the 2002 World Cup approaches the United States seems to be firing on all cylinders. The team won this year's Gold Cup for the first time since 1991, and Arena seems to be pressing all the right buttons.

The team plays a 4-4-2 system, with a diamond shape midfield and a strong defence. The team pressures the ball well, and can counter attack, although more than likely will build slowly. Has some speed on the flanks, and ball winners in the middle. The biggest issue for the USA as they march to Korea is how to mesh the European and home-based players so that they get along, and play as one.

The job of making this team click will fall to Claudio Reyna who struggled in that role in 1998. However, four more years of plying his trade in Scotland and England has made Reyna stronger. Kasey Keller will be asked to be as brilliant on the road as he has been at home as he has conceded one goal in his last 16 matches on American soil. The defence will be run by Jeff Agoos, who has missed out on the last two World Cups. Up top Brian McBride will be asked to win the balls in the air and hold the ball for his teammates to catch up.

The bench will be lined with home-based players like Clint Mathis, Josh Wolff, and Landon Donovan, all of which can score and add much needed speed. If this team is to make some noise at the World Cup it will need to keep its defence error free while finding ways to put the ball in the net.

SQUAD

JEFF AGOOS (SJ EARTHQUAKES) (33) CAPS: 127 GLS: 4
Has been around the United States national side since 1983. He was one of the last players to miss out before the 1990 and 1994 World Cups then made the squad in 1998, but never played. However, he has been one of the soundest fullbacks the USA has seen in awhile, and is getting better with age. He played for DC United during their successful run at the start of MLS. Agoos is now with the San Jose Earthquakes and helped them to their first championship while becoming the MLS defender of the year. Played for Arena at the University of Virginia.

CHRIS ARMAS (CHICAGO FIRE) (29) CAPS: 45 GLS: 2
Was first capped in coach Bruce Arena's first match in charge vs Australia. Armas has rarely missed a game for his country since. He is steady in the defensive midfield role, and rarely gets beaten by the opposing team's attacking midfielder. He has started to attack more now, and has found his ability to get a key pass through to his forwards. He hurt his knee before the 2000 Olympics, missing out on it. Plays for Chicago Fire.

USA

DAMARCUS BEASLEY (CHICAGO FIRE) (19) CAPS: 9 GLS: 1
A young player who burst onto the scene three years ago at the U17 championships in New Zealand. He finished with the Silver Ball there, behind United States teammate Landon Donovan. Beasley, a left sided player has loads of pace, and the ability to shoot well. Covers a lot of ground, and tracks back to help on defence. "Jitterbug," as he is known, plays for the Chicago Fire of MLS.

GREGG BERHALTER (CRYSTAL PALACE) (28) CAPS: 25 GLS: 0
A hard nosed full-back that when healthy is a key addition to the squad. Berhalter has played in Holland and England, and his time in both has made him a better player. He is a tough tackler but not a great distributor.

JEFF CUNNINGHAM (COLUMBUS CREW) (26)
Jamaican born, became a United States citizen last November and joined the US team immediately. He has great pace, but has struggled to find his touch at this level. Cunningham partners with McBride at the Columbus Crew. Adds a sense of urgency when on the pitch, and has good vision.

LANDON DONOVAN (SJ EARTHQUAKES) (19) CAPS: 20 GLS: 4
Looks to be the superstar that the United States has been looking for. He is good on the ball and has vision and touch far beyond his 20 years. Donovan has played as an attacker and also as an attacking midfielder of late. Has become an integral part of the United States attack over the last year. Donovan did a great job in the 1999 U-17 World Cup winning the Golden Ball. Very fast, and likes to roam making him tough to mark. Donovan started his career with Bayer Leverkusen, but went to the San Jose Earthquakes last year and led them to their first championship.

KASEY KELLER (TOTTENHAM HOTSPUR) (32) CAPS: 58 GLS: 0
The best keeper the United States has ever had. He has played in College at Portland University, and then moved onto Milwall, then to Leicester City, then onto Spain with Rayo Vallecano, before returning to England with Tottenham. This has not been an easy club year for Keller, as he has struggled with Scotland International Neil Sullivan in front of him. Was a star in the U20 tournament in 1989 in Saudi Arabia, and was the back-up to Tony Meola in the 1990 World Cup. Keller missed out on the 1994 World Cup due to differences with the coach Bora Milutiniovic. Started in the 1998 World Cup and is the number one keeper. Technically sound, and has only conceded one goal on home soil since February of 1998. He is an impressive 12 wins, four draws, and no losses in that span with 15 clean sheets.

BRAD FRIEDEL (BLACKBURN ROVERS) (30) CAPS: 74 GLS: 0
Friedel has been unlucky to come about when he did. Was a key member of the 1992 Olympic squad in Barcelona. He was the back-up to Meola in the 1994 World Cup, and to Keller in the 1998 World Cup, although he played the last game for the USA in that tournament. Friedel looked to be the number one keeper for the USA before Keller's impressive display at the recent Gold Cup.

USA

TIM HOWARD (NY/NJ METROSTARS) (23) CAPS: 1 GLS: 0
A very athletic keeper, who came into his own in the last year. Howard was the MLS goalkeeper of year with the NY/NJ MetroStars, and finally got his first cap vs Ecuador in March. He was the back-up to Friedel at the 2000 Olympics.

FRANKIE HEJDUK (BAYER LEVERKUSEN) (27) CAPS: 37 GLS: 5
Has good pace and ability to score important goals, but lacks defensive prowess and touch. He did well early in his career in MLS but has found life much more difficult in the Bundesliga for Leverkusen.

COBI JONES (LA GALAXY) (31) CAPS: 153 GLS: 14
The most capped player in US history. Has played in the last two World Cups, and his pace and versatility makes him a strong bench player. At one time a starter, but has lost a step and now is used more for 30 minutes. Jones can play wing on both sides, and up top. He has scored over 50 goals in MLS, and is a star. However, he is weak on the ball, and his unwillingness to shoot can cost the team dear sometimes.

JOVAN KIROVSKI (CRYSTAL PALACE) (26)
Has been full of potential for years, but at age 26 his time might be running out. He played with the Manchester United reserves for a while, then went to Germany, Portugal, and is now playing for Crystal Palace. Is a good linking forward, but has not found his touch or his shot when he plays for the USA. Can score spectacular goals, but does not do enough of the little things to put his influence on a match.

EDDIE LEWIS (FULHAM) (27) CAPS: 38 GLS: 3
A left-sided midfielder that Arena took a liking to when he took over, but since a red card in the Guatemala match in the first round of qualifying Lewis has been in and out of the line-up. He is a good crosser of the ball, and can score sometimes. He would never have made it to England to play for Fulham if it wasn't for Major League Soccer. He was a star at San Jose, before leaving to England.

CARLOS LLAMOSA (NE REVOLUTION) (32) CAPS: 27 GLS: 0
Colombian born – was naturalized after the last World Cup, and has become an important role player for the squad. Llamosa thought his career was over, before DC United discovered him. He is a central defender that will man mark the opposing team's best player. Was with the Miami Fusion last year, and will move onto the New England Revolution.

BRIAN MAISONNEUVE (COLUMBUS CREW) (28) CAPS: 13 GLS: 0
Another Columbus Crew player, and as in 1998 Maisonneuve has appeared from nowhere. Maisonneuve was not in the mix until the last few matches before the World Cup four years ago, but made the squad and played in one match. He again appeared at the start of this year, and looks well on his way to making this squad. He is technically sound, and can play all over the midfield. Sometimes struggles with injuries.

USA

CLINT MATHIS (NY/NJ METROSTARS) (25) CAPS: 19 GLS: 8
Fast becoming a star. A tough competitior, Mathis was a fringe player at the Los Angeles Galaxy, but quickly turned star when he joined the NY/NJ MetroStars two summers ago. He was one of the Major League's top scorers when healthy, and has made it back from a knee injury last June. He is dangerous from free kicks, and combines well with long time friend Josh Wolff.

PABLO MASTROENI (COLORADO RAPIDS) (25) CAPS: 8 GLS: 0
A prime example of the MLS working. He had a good year for the Miami Fusion, and before the United States match in the Korea Republic he was called into the USA squad. He is fast central defender who is good in the air. Had a good Gold Cup, and that has given him a chance to be in the squad for the World Cup.

BRIAN MCBRIDE (COLUMBUS CREW) (29) CAPS: 58 GLS: 18
Has been great over the last three months and is now a definite starter if fit. That is a big if. McBride has been struggling with injuries for over the last two years. He is a force in the air and scored the only goal for the United States in the last World Cup. A tireless worker who plays for the Columbus Crew.

JOE-MAX MOORE (EVERTON) (30) CAPS: 95 GLS: 24
Not the most talented player on the United States team, but his hardworking style and lack of concern for his body makes him a true leader. Was one of the few USA players to do well in the 1998 World Cup. He has a powerful, accurate shotand has scored some great goals from free kicks for the United States. Scored both goals vsJamaica to put the USA into this World Cup. Moore is second on the all-time list of National Team scorers.

RICHARD MULROONEY (SJ EARTHQUAKES) (25) CAPS: 4 GLS: 0
Broke into the national squad in March of this year, but with his pace and ability to get forward he seems to have a serious chance at making the squad. He was a key member of the San Jose Earthquakes last year in helping them to their first title. Can play on the outside right or left midfield position.

JOHN O'BRIEN (AJAX) (24) CAPS: 13 GLS: 1
A left-footed player, with lots of pace and a willingness and ability to take on opposition players. These are qualities that make him a prime candidate to start at the World Cup. Plays for Ajax in Amsterdam and like many of his teammates he is versatile playing left midfielder, defensive midfielder and left full-back. Has had foot injuries in the past.

EDDIE POPE (DC UNITED) (28) CAPS: 48 GLS: 5
One of the most talented defenders in the United States, but suffers from the inability to shake injuries. He is tall, fast, and good going forward. Scored the game winner for DC United in the first ever US Cup final. Normally will play in the centre, but can also shift out to the right.

USA

DAVID REGIS (FC METZ) (33) CAPS: 25 GLS: 0
Became a US citizen months before the World Cup in 1998, and started all three matches at the tournament. He forced out Agoos, but now plays alongside him in the back. Regis, born in Martinique, became an American citizen thanks to his wife. Plays at Metz in France, and is still learning the English language. A fast defender, who likes to push up, but sometimes get caught on the counter attack.

CLAUDIO REYNA (SUNDERLAND) (28) CAPS: 86 GLS: 8
Might very well be the most talented United States player ever. Has a deft touch, and can control the match. He is an accurate passer, and has been known to score every once and awhile. Has seen it all with a number of European clubs - Wolfsburg in Germany, to Rangers in Scotland, to now Sunderland of England. Reyna can get involved in the match with some hard tackles early. Key to the USA attack, played for Bruce Arena at the University of Virginia.

TONY SANNEH (FC NURENBERG) (30) CAPS: 29 GLS: 1
Was found in Minnesota playing A-League, but blossomed under United States Manager Bruce Arena while at DC United. He is big and fast, and will mix it up. Sanneh is versatile, with the ability to play up front or in the back, but more comfortable in the midfield. Played for Hertha Berlin earlier this year, but has moved onto FC Nurenberg.

EARNIE STEWART (NAC BREDA) (32) CAPS: 77 GLS: 15
Has been getting better with age, which is quite an accomplishment since he played in both the 1994 and 1998 World Cups. He scored eight goals in qualifying, and played some inspiring football as he drove the USA to their fourth straight World Cup. He was Dutch born, but his father was a US Citizen, and he thus started playing for the USA in 1992. Stewart plays for NAC Breda as a withdrawn midfielder. He plays left or right midfielder, or forward for the USA. His pace and willingness to shoot makes him a valuable commodity.

GREG VANNEY (FC BASTIA) (27) CAPS: 17 GLS: 0
Vanney is a left footed player who lacks pace, but his accurate powerful foot is worth it. Has been tried at outside left and in the middle, but has not been great. He seems to always have lapses that cost the team. Is now in France at Bastia on loan, after playing for the Los Angeles Galaxy since 1996.

BRIAN WEST (COLUMBUS CREW) (23) CAPS: 7 GLS: 0
A right-sided midfielder was recruited by Bruce Arena to play at Virginia. But Arena left before West did. West is lightening quick, and his pace helped him emerge as a candidate for a bench spot at the World Cup. Has struggled to find his touch in National team matches, but as his nerves settle he is becoming more dangerous. West plays for the Columbus Crew.

USA

RICHIE WILLIAMS (DC UNITED) (31) CAPS: 20 GLS: 0
Another University of Virginia graduate, never seems to impress at this level yet he never embarrasses himself either. Is a defensive midfielder who is the most successful player in USA history. He has won every title possible from youth on up in the USA. He was a key member to DC United's run. Is always going to be a bench player, but can play if needed.

JOSH WOLFF (CHICAGO FIRE) (24) CAPS: 16 GLS: 4
Another up and coming star. Wolff started out in the World Cup qualifying process as well as anyone, scoring the game winner versus Mexico and Costa Rica. He then hurt his foot and missed most of the rest of qualifying. Wolff has plenty of pace and the ability to score. Wolff played in the 2000 Olympic squad. Played with Mathis in college at South Carolina, and now the US national team is enjoying the two's knowledge of each other.

COACH

BRUCE ARENA (USA)
A tough coach who seems to be able to get results out of his players. When he took over the national team after the terrible struggle in the 1998 World Cup, he vowed to use more MLS players, and he has been able to get the right mix between the MLS and European players. The USA finished third in the 1999 Confederations Cup, qualified for their fourth straight World Cup, and won the Gold Cup in 2002. Bruce Arena is the most successful manager in United States' football history. He won the first two MLS championships and the 1996 U.S. Open Cup, and also claimed an impressive victory in the CONCACAF Champions Cup final over Toluca, 1-0, on Aug. 16 in Washington, D.C. The victory crowned D.C. United as the club champion of CONCACAF, an amazing achievement for a team which didn't play its first game until 1996. The triumph put United into the Interamerican Cup, a two-leg battle with Brazil's Vasco da Gama, a 2-1, two-game aggregate victory which crowned D.C. as the champions of the Western Hemisphere. Those titles, combined with his four NCAA titles, one U.S. Open Crown, and two MLS Cup victories, marked Arena's eighth and ninth championships of the 1990s. Arena was capped once for the US National side as a goalkeeper.

WORLD CUP FACTS

Ferenc Puskas appeared for Hungary in the 1954 finals and for Spain in the 1962 competition.

The England squad that went to France four years ago had no previous World Cup finals experience. David Seaman had been selected for the Italia 90 squad but had to withdraw because of injury.

GROUP E

Next to Brazil, Germany boast the best record in world football. World Cup winners in 1954, 1974 and 1990, they could be forgiven for claiming that it is time they won the trophy a fourth time. But German football has been in decline for a decade, witnessed by their failure to progress beyond the quarter-finals in 1994 and 1998.

The descent of German football almost reached an all-time low when they came close to failing to qualify; the 5-1 defeat by England in Munich will, for ever, act as a reminder of, possibly, the country's lowest ebb. Only a two-legged 5-2 play-off win over the Ukraine secured the Germans their place in Asia.

Germany started well enough in their qualifiers, with wins over Greece, twice, England and Albania, but the 2-2 draw in Helsinki, followed by the defeat by England, highlighted the problems and a goalless draw against Finland confirmed how far the Germans had dropped.

One man who carries the hopes of his nation is Michael Ballack, the Bayer Leverkusen striker who has versatility and is showing a maturity that could be vital.

"There was an enormous pressure on us to qualify," admits Ballack. "The disappointment would have been massive if we hadn't made it. But Rudi Voller's tactics worked perfectly and we showed, against the Ukraine, that we can play.

"It's great to be in the finals; there's nothing bigger in football. Now we musn't sit back. Now we must aim to improve still further."

Saudi Arabia endured a disappointing campaign four years earlier, with one point and an early exit. Therefore, their approach to the 2002 finals, their third in succession, has been less enthusiastic. Saudi, Asia's leading light for 20 years, qualified after heading a second round group which included Iran, Bahrain, Iraq and Thailand. Coach Nasser Al-Johar is in his second spell, replacing Yugoslav Slobodan Santrac two games into the final qualifying tournament.

Germany will be more concerned by the presence of the Republic of Ireland and Cameroon, both of whom will expect to qualify for the next stage. Mick McCarthy has carried on the success story started by Jack Charlton and Ireland qualified, via a 2-1 aggregate play-off win over Iran, having remained unbeaten in their group and seeing off Holland.

Yorkshire-born McCarthy has stuck to his task and after narrowly missing out on reaching the last World Cup and Euro 2000, patience has paid off. They did it the hard way, beating Iran over two legs, and now they will turn to the experience of Roy Keane, Matt Holland, Jason McAteer and Niall Quinn, while expecting the youth, players such as Gary Doherty and Ian Harte, to flourish.

Keane, the captain, was outstanding in the qualifying games, and with goalkeeper Shay Given coming to the fore both at international level and with Newcastle, Ireland arrive in Japan in confident mood.

Cameroon complete the group under the leadership of German Winfried Schafer, the African country's fourth coach inside 12 months. The happy-go-lucky approach the likes of Roger Milla offered has gone; Cameroon, the Sydney Olympic gold medal winners, can be formidable and their success in winning the African Nations Cup early this year, beating Senegal on penalties, gives an idea of their strengths.

In that tournament the Indomitable Lions did not concede a goal, in six matches, to become the first country for 37 years to retain the trophy. Most of their players operate in Europe, including Arsenal's Lauren, and Real Mallorca's Samuel Eto'o. Eto'o, now 21, was, at 17, the youngest player in the last finals and has forged a promising partnership with Parma's Patrick Mboma, who spent the latter part of the season at Sunderland.

GERMANY

"Ireland knocked out Holland in qualifying, but I think we can do it. Ireland may not be a top name, but you have to look at their current form and, from what they did in qualifying, they have to be regarded as very dangerous. They have many players in the Premier League and will be extremely tough." **Rudi Voller**, German coach.

REPUBLIC OF IRELAND

"We were supposed to have seen the fall of the German team against England but we have seen since that is complete nonsense when they spanked the Ukraine. But I think we have a chance of getting out of it. Losing 5-1 at home to their greatest rivals was bad but results like that awaken your senses; the England game was a turning point for them." Republic of Ireland manager **Mick McCarthy**.

CAMEROON

"We are again shackled with Rudi Voller who we are going to meet in the same group. We didn't want it but perhaps we can both pass the first round." Cameroon's German coach **Winfried Schafer**.

SAUDI ARABIA

"I have no doubt the Saudi Arabian Football Federation will make sure this endeavour reaches a level the like of which has never been seen before. The foundation of what we have accomplished will be the catalyst for even greater and more gratifying glories." **Nawaf Al-Temyat**, Saudi Arabian midfielder and Asian Player of the Year.

GERMANY

In March last year everything appeared normal as far as Germany and the World Cup were concerned. They had opened their qualifying campaign with four straight wins over Greece (2-0 at home and 4-2 away), England (1-0 at Wembley) and Albania (2-1 at home in Leverkusen).

England, their main rivals for the automatic qualifying spot from Group Nine, had stumbled out of the traps, losing to the Germans and drawing with Finland and had undergone an upheaval with the resignation of Kevin Keegan and the subsequent hiring of Swede Sven-Göran Eriksson.

But despite appearances, not everything in Germany's soccer garden was as rosy as it seemed. True they had beaten both Albania and Greece in four days in March, but they had played fitfully in both matches, and only an 88th minute goal from late substitute Miroslav Klose, making his debut, gave them their 2-1 victory over the Albanians.

Four days later, in Athens, Germany had another real scare when Greece twice fought back to level the scores at 2-2 by half-time. Midway through the second half coach Rudi Voeller threw on Klose again and with 12 minutes left and with the scores still at 2-2 he gambled again by sending on Marco Bode. It was a gamble that paid off. Klose and Bode both scored in the last eight minutes to seal a flattering 4-2 winning margin.

But things did not go quite according to plan after that. Nine weeks later in Helsinki, two goals from Chelsea striker Mikael Forssell gave Finland a 2-0 half-time lead and only second half goals from Michael Ballack (penalty) and Carsten Jancker saved a point. Real questions were now being asked about the quality of the side.

The criticism never really stopped even after their fifth, and what proved to be their final group win over Albania (2-0) in Tirana on June 6.

And the myth of German invincibility and resilience was about to be cruelly exposed proving all the criticism well-founded. In Munich on September 1 Germany crashed to their worst home defeat for 70 years and only their second ever defeat in a World Cup qualifier when England beat them 5-1.

The result has already entered World Cup folklore and while the English hailed the victory as their greatest since beating West Germany in the 1966 World Cup final, the Germans were left totally stunned – especially as they scored first through Jancker and had several chances of doubling or even trebling their lead before England had scored once.

Despite the calamity, Germany, mathematically at least, could still qualify automatically but with Germany drawing 0-0 with Finland in their final game and England drawing 2-2 with Greece, England sealed top spot and Germany had to face Ukraine in the play-offs.

A 5-2 aggregate win over the disappointing Ukrainians ended fears that Germany might miss out on the World Cup for the first time since 1950. The debate now concerns what will happen when they get there. Will Germany flop as they did in Euro 2000 and be eliminated after the first round – or are they good enough to maintain a challenge through to the later stages?

Germany probably will do neither. They should advance with some ease from their first round group which contains Ireland, Saudi Arabia and Cameroon, although both the Irish and Cameroonians cannot be taken lightly. After that Spain, Portugal and Italy are all possible opponents.

Whether Voeller's team has the defensive capability – or even the power in attack to repel ever more dangerous opponents is open to some doubt, but as any student of the game knows, even if they start a tournament slowly, the Germans usually gain in strength and confidence as it goes on. That is why they can never be under-estimated.

However, with a shortage of top class youngsters and with the established stars not quite as good as some of their now-retired greats of recent years, Germany might have to be content with a place in the last eight this time around. A fourth World title following their successes in 1954, 1974 and 1990 does look beyond them.

Still, the team is not without its major talents. Goalkeeper Oliver Kahn is arguably the best goalkeeper in the world – the five he let in against England notwithstanding – and midfielders Sebastian Deisler of Hertha Berlin and Michael Ballack of Bayer Leverkusen – both due to join Kahn at Bayern Munich next season – have the opportunity to display their prodigious talents in a midfield that should also include the irrepressible Jens Jeremies and Mehmet Scholl, both fully fit again after long-term injuries.

Up front there are problems with the international pedigree of Jancker and Oliver Neuville open to debate. Jancker scored just twice in the qualifiers, Neuville once.

Since Germany's shock first-round exit from Euro 2000 – their worst-ever overall performance at a major tournament – they have improved. Voeller, who took over from Erich Ribbeck in the wake of, that failure, has rejuvenated the team but is still faced with the problem of finding top quality replacements for the players who have retired.

SQUAD

GERALD ASAMOAH (SCHALKE) BORN: 03.10.78 CAPS: 9 GLS: 2

A Ghanaian, who received his German papers in early 2001 and has gone straight into national squad. Utility player down right flank – wing back or forward. Arrived at Schalke for £1 million in summer 1999 from Div Two club Hannover 96 (like Kehl), and whose third Bundesliga season this is. Was at Hannover from the age of 14, and parents based in Germany since he was nine years old.

MICHAEL BALLACK (BAYER LEVERKUSEN) BORN: 26.09.76 CAPS: 22 GLS: 6

Best player in the Bundesliga 2001-02. Moved in July 1999 from Kaiserslautern to Leverkusen for £2.9 million. First call up into the national squad was in August 1998 after the World Cup retirements. Cost Kaiserslautern just £35,000 in summer 1997 from the old GDR top club Chemnitz. He was firstly with Karl-Marx-Stadt so is a real product of the new Eastern system. Won Bundesliga title win in first season in 1997-98 with Kaiserslautern. Takes free-kicks and penalties. Scored own goal to cost Leverkusen in 2000. Almost certain to be with Bayern Munich next year, Two goals vs Liverpool in Champions League quarter-final second leg in April.

GERMANY

FRANK BAUMANN (WERDER BREMEN) BORN: 29.10.75 CAPS: 10 GLS: 2
He arrived at Bremen in summer 1999 on the Bosman ruling from Nurnberg, who were relegated. Just missed out on Euro 2000 final squad. Had eight seasons with the Nurnberg club but this season was the third only in the Bundesliga for him. Came from a junior club, FC Grombuhl. Internationally he came through the U21 system.

OLIVER BIERHOFF (MONACO) BORN: 01.05.68 CAPS: 62 GLS0: 33
National captain until Oliver Kahn took over. Hero of Euro '96 with two goals in the final. Top scorer in Serie A with Udinese in 1997-8 with 27 goals in 32 games in superb season – beat Ronaldo, Del Piero and the rest and it was the highest tally since 1961. Then signed a four-year deal to join AC Milan in summer 1998 and won 1999 title and scored 22 goals, but down a little subsequently as Shevchenko took over. Spotted by German selectors while playing in Serie A. Rumour has it that Mrs Vogts told Berti to pick him for Euro '96 when he was dithering over the 22nd player! Former Uerdingen, Hamburg SV and Borussia Monchengladbach forward, he has been abroad since 1990. He went first to Austria Salzburg where his 23 goals in 1990-91 caught the attention of Serie A club Ascoli. Went from Ascoli to Udinese in 1995.

MARCO BODE (WERDER BREMEN) BORN: 23.07.69 CAPS: 32 GLS: 6
One of the fringe members of the squad – first capped in South Africa in Dec 1995 – and recalled in summer 2001 for about the sixth time. Left-sided forward. Former U21 international striker, who is 6'4" tall and now plays left side midfield as a German edition of Ian Ormondroyd! Been at Bremen for ten years and played over 250 Bundesliga games.

JORG BOHME (SCHALKE) BORN: 22.01.74 CAPS: 6 GLS: 1
He moved across to Schalke in summer 2000 from relegated neighbours Arminia Bielefeld for £500,000 after being en route to Div Two. Then he took his chance in the Schalke side. With the Schalke team who lost the 2001 Bundesliga title by just a point to Bayern, but who also won the 2001 German Cup. Scored both goals in the 2001 German Cup final 2-0 win vs Union Berlin. From the former GDR and the Carl Zeiss Jena club, he has had spells with Nurnburg, Eintracht Frankfurt and 1860 Munich in the south, before moving to the Ruhr.

HANS-JORG BUTT (BAYER LEVERKUSEN) BORN: 28.05.74 CAPS: 2 GLS: 0
Keeper who joined Leverkusen in summer 2001 when out of contract at Hamburg. The penalty king – he scored 19 goals in the last three seasons for Hamburg from the spot and missed just one. Added three to his tally with Leverkusen to date. But a little behind Jose Luis Chilavert who now has 62 goals as a free-kick/penalty kicker for the record as a keeper but over a much longer period. He also saved 11 penalties in the last three seasons! Has scored two penalties in open play in UCL –

and both against Juventus for Hamburg and now for Leverkusen. All this activity clouds the fact that he is a fine keeper, capped just before Euro 2000 and was in the squad for the Finals, and in the squad for the World Cup games of autumn 2000. Cost HSV some £100,000 from Div Two club Oldenberg in summer 1997 – and missed just one game for the Hamburg club.

SEBASTIAN DEISLER (HERTHA BERLIN) BORN: 05.01.80 CAPS: 16 GLS: 2
Succumbed to the dreaded knee ligament injury – and out for months from October 2001. Made a fine breakthrough at the start of 1999-2000 following a move to Hertha from then relegated Borussia Monchengladbach, and impressed in Bundesliga and Champions League (vs Chelsea). He cost the Hertha club £1.5 million and after a series of favourable displays at the start of 1999-2000 was called into the national squad for the September 1999 Euro 2000 qualifiers as a teenager. First capped as sub v Holland in February 2000. Had two lengthy breaks recently for injuries, the first was a knee ligament damage, and the second was also knee related. Was at BMG for five seasons, and made debut in 1998-9 aged 18. Set to sign for Bayern next season.

TORSTEN FRINGS (WERDER BREMEN) BORN: 22.11.76 CAPS: 5 GLS: 1
Rumoured to be away to Bayern in summer 2002 for some £6 million. Improved greatly from the 1998-99 season and was picked for Germany A in May 1999 and went on to full caps in spring 2001. Sixth season with the Bremen club, he arrived from regional club Alemenia Aachen in summer 1996. Defensive midfield player and one of the best in the league.

DIETMAR HAMANN (LIVERPOOL) BORN: 27.08.73 CAPS: 38 GLS: 4
Scored Wembley's final goal. Record five Cup successes by Liverpool in 2001 – Worthington, FA, UEFA, Charity Shield, Super Cup. Joined Newcastle from Bayern in 1998 and had a season under Ruud Gullit, before an £8 million move to Liverpool in summer 1999. Was new to the national squad in autumn 1997 after helping Bayern to the 1997 Bundesliga title. Had been with Bayern since the age of 16 and worked his way through the youth and reserve sides.

JORG HEINRICH (BORUSSIA DORTMUND) BORN: 06.12.69 CAPS: 35 GLS: 2
Returned to Dortmund from Fiorentina for £2.3 million just two years after leaving for Fiorentina for £5.7 million – and immediately recalled to the national team since September 2000 for a brief spell. Fiorentina originally won a bidding war with Juventus, Inter Milan and Atletico Madrid. Played in 1998 World Cup finals – one of the better players in a poor side – his left-sided play is appreciated. From the old GDR club Vorwarts Frankfurt, first made name with Freiburg. Won 1996 championships with Dortmund plus 1997 European Cup vs Juventus and World Club Cup in his first spell at the club from Jan 1996 to 1998.

CARSTEN JANCKER (BAYERN MUNICH) BORN: 28.08.74 CAPS: 23 GLS: 6
Has now won 2001 European Cup, the 1996 UEFA Cup, the 1997, 1999, 2000 and
2001 Bundesliga, plus 1998 and 2000 Cups with Bayern. Is 6'3" tall and made his
name in 1995-6 season after being top scorer in Rapid Vienna's 1996 Championship
win and overall top scorer in the 1996 ECWC when Rapid made it to the final (six goals).
Is an East German who played for Hansa Rostock in the GDR but had only six games
for Cologne and was an U21 international before going to Austria. Back to Germany
with Bayern from summer 1996 from Rapid for £1.2 million.

JENS JEREMIES (BAYERN MUNICH) BORN: 05.03.74 CAPS: 30 GLS: 1
Just back in the club side after a long spell out with damaged knee ligaments (seven
months out). Dropped from the squad in April 2000 for a stinging attack in the
media on coach Ribbeck – he said that he knew his role with Bayern but not with
Germany. Then also missed final month of last season after breaking collar bone in
tackle with Anelka in the UCL semi with Real Madrid. Recalled after not playing for
Germany since Euro 2000. Switched Munich clubs after playing in the 1998 World
Cup from 1860 to Bayern – cost just £500,000 as out of contract. Another of the
increasing band from the old GDR, he arrived at 1860 from former Bundesliga club
Dynamo Dresden in summer 1995 for £17,000. He was born in GDR near Polish
border and joined Dresden aged 12. He was in the famous old GDR Sportschool
that produced the athletes and swimmers. Champion's League winner 2001.

OLIVER KAHN (BAYERN MUNICH) BORN: 15.06.69 CAPS: 42 GLS: 0
Has now captured a German record for a keeper beating Hans Tilkowski – the 1966
World Cup final keeper – who captained 16 times. 2000 and 2001 German
Footballer of the Year. Has now won 2001 European Cup (penalty saves), the 1996
UEFA Cup, the 1997, 1999, 2000 and 2001 Bundesliga plus 1998 and 2000 Cups
with Bayern. Still prone to outbursts and eccentrics – which is why neither Vogts or
Ribbeck were entirely happy with him. He twice lost out to Jens Lehmann, until
Bayern's recent success. Was signed by Bayern for £2.2 million around the time of
the 1994 World Cup from Karlsruhe.

SEBASTIAN KEHL (BORUSSIA DORTMUND) BORN: 13.02.80 CAPS: 5 GLS: 1
Moved in the mid-winter break from Freiburg to Dortmund after Bayern thought they
had their man. The young revelation of the 2000-1 season – a defender who joined
the small, well-run Freiburg club in summer 2000 from D2 club Hannover '96 for just
£70,000 and who then went straight into the national U21 side and thence onto the
full national team. Began his career in midfield, but Freiburg coach Finke has moved
him back into defence with immediate results. He seems to play as defensive midfield.
Was outstanding with the national U21 side.

MIROSLAV KLOSE (KAISERSLAUTERN) BORN: 09.06.78 CAPS: 9 GLS: 5
Has been plucked out of the U21 side with no real club form. Has enjoyed a fine

start to his international career. Born at Opole, Poland. Broke into the Kaiserslautern first team in 2000-1 season and claimed a front-role ahead of better known names. Was given a chance by Andy Brehme, the former World Cup winner who is his club coach. Had just two games in 1999-2000, and nine goals in 29 games last season, but an impressive five goals in UEFA Cup. Joined summer 1999 from D2 club Homburg, who are situated close to the Kaiserslautern club.

JENS LEHMANN (BORUSSIA DORTMUND) BORN: 10.11.69 CAPS: 14 GLS: 0
Twice ousted Kahn from the No 1 slot until 2000 – played against Swiss and made absolute howler for Swiss goal in Euro 2000 warm up game. Now back in Germany from midseason 1998-99 after a move to AC Milan ended – Dortmund rescued him from the Milan reserves. Reserve keeper at 1998 World Cup which was a reward for several seasons of graft with first club Schalke – he joined in 1987 and completed 11 seasons and 200 Bundesliga games for them.

THOMAS LINKE (BAYERN MUNICH) BORN: 26.12.69 CAPS: 31 GLS: 0
Recalled to the squad for the 1999 Confederation Cup in Mexico, and stayed in squad since. European Cup win in 2001 plus Bundesliga title. Signed from Schalke in summer 1998 when out of contract on a free transfer on the Bosman ruling – has regained international place since move. 1997 UEFA Cup winners medal with Schalke, then was in the 1999 European Cup final vs Man Utd, and in the Bayern team that won the League and Cup double in 2000. From the former GDR, he left Rot Weiss Erfurt for Schalke in 1992 and had six seasons at Schalke in their first team.

CHRISTOPH METZELDER (BORUSSIA DORTMUND) BORN: 05.11.80 CAPS: 3 GLS: 0
Former Schalke junior, released to Prussia Munster in D2, and joined Dortmund in 2000 on a free transfer. Proved an instant hit, and the free transfer man won his first cap a year later in August 2001 vs Hungary. Has also moved straight into the national U21 side as left back/central defender for the current Euro U21 games.

JENS NOWOTNY (BAYER LEVERKUSEN) BORN: 11.01.74 CAPS: 37 GLS: 0
Club captain at Leverkusen, and will not need knee surgery after good reports on his problems. Was Matthaus' understudy as sweeper, but also central defender. Started all three games at Euro 2000. He has been picked since the 1998 Finals and in coach Ribbeck and Voller's first squads. AC Milan are rumoured to be bidding £10+ million for him. Nowotny joined Leverkusen in summer 1996 from Karlsruhe where he benefited from playing alongside Thomas Hassler.

MARKO REHMER (HERTHA BERLIN) BORN: 29.04.72 CAPS: 27 GLS: 4
Premiership interest – Arsenal and Liverpool in 2001 – but not after Owen skinned him in Munich in the 5-1 game. Joined Hertha in summer 1999 for £2.8 million from Hansa Rostock. Won seven caps in a row in 1998-9 season, but then missed a year before a return after regaining fitness with Hertha from 2000. Brought in by Vogts directly after

GERMANY

the World Cup, and retained by Ribbeck, From the East German side of Berlin, he played Div Two football in the new capital, and was at Rostock for three seasons.

LARS RICKEN (BORUSSIA DORTMUND) BORN: 10.07.76 CAPS: 16 GLS:1
Scored third goal in 1997 European Cup final, just seconds after coming on as sub – but seemed to disappear. Now restored in a wider role. Has come through the club's junior section after joining at the age of 14 from feeder club Eintracht Dortmund. Championship medals in 1995 and 1996 and European success in 1997 all by the age of 21, been fallow since.

CARSTEN RAMELOW (BAYER LEVERKUSEN) BORN: 20.03.74 CAPS: 25 GLS:0
In Euro 2000 squad but did not play – plays in front of back four. Was elevated into the national training squad of 40 for Berti Vogts World Cup seminar and 1998 tour to the Middle East and recalled in Erich Ribbeck's first squad. He moved to Leverkusen from Hertha Berlin in 1995 as an U21 international at the time. Seventh season at club, and developing really well and just past 200 club games. Runners-up in 2000.

MARKO REHMER (HERTHA BERLIN) BORN: 29.04.72 CAPS: 27 GLS: 4
Premiership interest – Arsenal and Liverpool in 2001 – but not after Owen skinned him in Munich in the 5-1 game. Joined Hertha in summer 1999 for £2.8 million from Hansa Rostock. Won seven caps in a row in 1998-9 season, but then missed a year before a return after regaining fitness with Hertha from 2000. Brought in by Vogts directly after the World Cup, and retained by Ribbeck, From the East German side of Berlin, he played Div Two football in the new capital, and was at Rostock for three seasons.

FRANK ROST (WERDER BREMEN) BORN: 30.06.73 CAPS: 1 GLS: 0
Capped v USA in March 2002. First choice for four years at his club following departure of Oliver Reck to Schalke – and tenth season with Bremen. Former amateur keeper who made his first team debut in 1995-96 season and is from the old GDR club VfB Leipzig. At Bremen as an amateur since 1992, now a pro.

BERND SCHNEIDER (BAYER LEVERKUSEN) BORN: 17.11.73 CAPS: 9 GLS: 0
Recalled after two fine seasons with high riding Bayer Leverkusen. Was dropped for Euro 2000 – then played v Ukraine in November 2001 – a gap of 25 months. Joined Leverkusen from Eintracht Frankfurt in summer 1999 for £750,000 and was immediately taken to the 1999 Confederations Cup where he won his first caps.

MEHMET SCHOLL (BAYERN MUNICH) BORN:16.10.70 CAPS: 36 GLS: 8
One of only four players in the German team to start all three games at Euro 2000. Played in the last three games of Euro '96 including the final, and now has a contract at Bayern until 2002. Not considered for 1998 World Cup by Berti Vogts. He is at last beginning to fulfill youthful promise and was another from Karlsruhe, arriving at Bayern in 1992. He had been with Karlsruhe since the age of 13. An

attacking midfielder who is of Turkish extraction but is German as regards football nationality, who cost a then German internal record £2.1 million for his move to Bayern. Championship medals 1994, 1997, 1999, 2000 and 2001. One of the few left footers in the squad. Champion's League winner 2001.

CHRISTIAN WORNS (BORUSSIA DORTMUND) BORN: 10.05.72 CAPS: 39 GLS: 0
Cost Dortmund £4.2 million to bring him back from PSG after one season in France in 1998-9 after the World Cup – PSG paid Leverkusen the same fee to get him in the first place. Had seven seasons with Leverkusen prior to going to PSG for the one season so would be known to Rudi Voller. First capped back in 1992 at barely 20 when he was at Waldhof Mannheim – rated by former coach Franz Beckenbauer but less so by Berti Vogts. Red card in QF vs Croatin in 1998.

ALEXANDER ZICKLER (BAYERN MUNICH) BORN: 28.02.74 CAPS: 10 GLS: 2
Injured after gaining his first three caps in 1998-99 season. Seems to be a sub for both club and country. From the old East Germany, he signed for Bayern back in 1993 from Dynamo Dresden, and cost nearly £1 million. Is nearly 6'3" tall. Was in the national U21 team. Championship medal 1997 and 1999, domestic double in 2000, and Euro/Bundesliga double in 2001.

CHRISTIAN ZIEGE (TOTTENHAM) BORN: 01.02.72 CAPS: 64 GLS: 9
Was on the fringe of Liverpool's Cup successes in 2001, so moved to Spurs in summer 2001 for £4 million. Had moved to Liverpool in summer 2000 for £5 million from Middlesbrough. Won 1997 Championship medal with Bayern – then moved in summer 1997 to AC Milan for £4 million, and then after winning title with Milan in 1998-9, moved to the Riverside for £4 million in summer 99. Hat-trick v N Ireland in Sept 1999. Serious ankle injury ruled him out of 1994 World Cup. Originally a keeper, so may be called on in emergency. Replaced Andy Brehme in national team – he is a left sided midfielder/defender who was with Bayern since the age of 18 in 1990, when he signed from Hertha Zehlendorf, which is a Berlin club and the first club of Pierre Littbarski, the famous former international. Euro '96 winner.

COACH

RUDI VOLLER BORN:13.04.60
90 caps/47 goals. Was interim coach until Christoph Daum was meant to have taken over in July 2001 after working his contract out at Bayer Leverkusen. But Daum fell foul of drugs. This is Voller's first senior coaching job and he has now been confirmed until after the 2002 World Cup finals. Won World Cup medal 1990, runner-up 1986. European Cup 1993. Played also 1994 World Cup and Euros '84, '88, and '92. German Footballer of the Year 1983 and Bundesliga top scorer 1983. Played for 1860 Munich (1980-2), Werder Bremen (1982-7), Roma (1987-92), Marseille (1992-4), Bayer Leverkusen (1994-6). Career league goals 201 in 432 games in all countries.

REPUBLIC OF IRELAND

Republic of Ireland return to the World Cup for the first time in eight years – and could hardly have had a tougher time in doing so. Not only did they have to come through a qualifying group that included Portugal and Holland, they then had to overcome Iran in a tough play-off game. Unlike some European countries who only had to play eight matches to qualify, Ireland played 12.

But it says much for their tenacity, fighting spirit and skill that the only game they lost was the last one – and that to a last minute goal in the second leg of the play-off to Iran in Tehran when qualification was 99.9 per cent assured. One minute after that goal was scored against them, the match was over and Ireland were through.

After their punishing qualifying campaign they deserved at least a little luck when the draw for the Finals was made and they got it – relatively speaking. Grouped with Germany, Saudi Arabia and Cameroon in Japan, Ireland have a reasonable chance of advancing.

To remain unbeaten home and away against both Portugal and Holland took some doing from Mick McCarthy's men – and to beat Holland 1-0 with only ten men to ensure first or second place in the group was a real achievement. Jason McAteer's memorable goal against the Dutch in Dublin on September 1 sent the visitors crashing out of the tournament and ensured the Irish a play-off place at worst.

McCarthy, who captained Ireland in their first World Cup in Italy 1990, has now emulated Jack Charlton, the manager of the side in 1990 and 1994, in taking Ireland to the Finals. Whether he can take them all the way to the quarter-finals as they did 12 years ago is doubtful, but with a world-class midfielder like Roy Keane of Manchester United in the heart of the side, anything is possible. Keane was outstanding for Ireland throughout the qualifying campaign, but the entire squad from goalkeeper Shay Given through to target man striker Niall Quinn seemed to never give less than 100 per cent.

McCarthy adheres to a 4-4-2 formation and with the midfielders and even defenders coming forward in search of goals when possible, Ireland are a difficult side to play against and a harder one to beat. Keane, for example, scored four goals in the qualifiers from midfield, Matt Holland grabbed three, with Robbie Keane, Kevin Kilbane, Mark Kinsella and McAteer all adding to that total. The main worry for McCarthy is that Quinn, Ireland's all-time record scorer, is, at the age of 35, running on a near-empty tank – and there is no natural successor waiting in the wings. Leeds' Robbie Keane is a dangerous finisher but in a different mould to Quinn.

In reality, any goals that Ireland do score will probably come from deeper positions – but as German coach Rudi Voeller said minutes after the draw for the Finals was made, that just makes Ireland very hard to play against.

"They knock the ball around well, and with Roy Keane have one of the best players in the world. So we will not underestimate them. And don't forget – they knocked out the Dutch, and I tell you if the Dutch were here everyone would be treating them as favourites."

Ireland have now qualified for the final stages of the World Cup three times following their appearances in Italy in 1990 and the United States in 1994 and in fact this tournament saw them lay a jinx after they went out in the play-offs, just one step away from Euro '96, France '98 and Euro 2000.

McCarthy took over from Charlton following their elimination by the Dutch in a play-off for Euro '96 at Liverpool – and while some players from Charlton's days are still around – like Steve Staunton, Ireland's most capped player who could become the first from the Republic to win 100 caps this summer – most of the squad have been nurtured by McCarthy. He would like to win the World Cup of course, but would probably settle for matching Ireland's achievements in 1990 when they reached the last eight.

SQUAD

GARY BREEN (COVENTRY CITY) BORN: 12.12.73 CAPS: 43 GLS: 5
Cost Coventry £2.4 million from Birmingham in February 1997. Previously with Maidstone, Gillingham and Peterborough. Capped nine times by the Under-21s. Voted Coventry's 'Player of the Year' for 2000-01. Was relegated from the Premiership with Coventry in 2000-01. Born in Hendon.

LEE CARSLEY (EVERTON) BORN: 28.02.74 CAPS: 19 GLS: 0
Joined Everton from Coventry for £1.9 million in February 2002. Spent only 14 months at Coventry, having joined them from Blackburn for £2.5m in December 2000. Central midfielder. Was Blackburn's top scorer in 1999-00 with 11 goals (ten in league). Eight of these being penalties. Has played in the Premiership for four clubs now – Derby, Blackburn, Coventry and Everton. Was relegated from the Premiership with Coventry in 2000-01. Born in Birmingham.

NICK COLGAN (HIBERNIAN) BORN: 19.09.73 CAPS: 1 GLS: 0
Won his first cap as a sub v Denmark in March 2002. Has been capped at every level for the Republic, including nine U-21 caps. Joined Hibernian on a free from Bournemouth in July 1999. A former Chelsea trainee, made one Premiership appearance.

DAVID CONNOLLY (WIMBLEDON) BORN: 06.06.77 CAPS: 32 GLS: 8
Joined Wimbledon from Feyenoord on a free transfer in the summer of 2001. Made Republic debut v Portugal in May 1996. Scored a hat-trick in 5-0 win vs Liechtenstein in WCQ in May 1997. Joined Feyenoord from Watford in 1996. Came up through youth ranks at Watford. Also had an 18-month loan spell at Dutch Div Two side Excelsior, where he scored 42 goals in 48 games for them. Was sent-off vs Belgium in a World Cup play-off defeat in November 1997 in Brussels.

KENNY CUNNINGHAM (WIMBLEDON) BORN: 28.06.71 CAPS: 37 GLS: 0
Made his international debut v the Czech Republic in April 1996, in 2-0 defeat in Prague. Joined Wimbledon from Millwall in November 1994. Missed most of 2000-01 with a groin injury. Plenty of previous Premiership experience with Wimbledon. Was relegated from the Premiership with Wimbledon in 1999-00.

RORY DELAP (SOUTHAMPTON) BORN: 06.07.76 CAPS: 7 GLS: 0
Joined Southampton for £4 million from Derby in the summer of 2001 – a club record fee. Made his international debut vs the Czech Republic in March 1998.

REPUBLIC OF IRELAND

GARY DOHERTY (TOTTENHAM) BORN: 31.01.80 CAPS: 9 GLS: 1
Made his international debut v Greece in April 2000, as a sub. Centre-back or centre-forward. Has played up front for the Republic. Former Republic of Ireland Under-18 captain. Cost Tottenham £1m from Luton in April 2000. Has missed most of the 2001-02 season with a broken ankle.

DAMIEN DUFF (BLACKBURN) BORN: 02.03.79 CAPS: 25 GLS: 1
Made his international debut v the Czech Republic in March 1998, in 2-1 defeat in Olomouc. Was a member of the Republic's youth side that finished third in the World Youth Championships in Malaysia in 1997. Now in seventh season at Blackburn. Member of their side which won promotion to the Premiership in 2000-01.

RICHARD DUNNE (MAN CITY) BORN: 21.09.79 CAPS: 14 GLS: 3
Named the Republic of Ireland U-23 Player of the Year in November 2000. Scored his first senior international goal in 2-2 draw v Mexico in June 2000 – in only his second start for his country. Won his first cap in 1-0 defeat vs Greece in April 2000. Joined Man City from Everton for £3 million in October 2000. Was sent-off three times in 1999-00 – twice for Everton (at Derby and Leeds) and once for the Rep of Ireland U-21 side (in Croatia). Member of Man City side that have been crowned Div One champions in 2001-02.

GARETH FARRELLY (BOLTON) BORN: 28.08.75 CAPS: 6 GLS: 0
Joined Bolton from Everton for £300,000 in December 1999. Has played in the Premiership for Aston Villa, Everton and Bolton. Born in Dublin and hails from the famous Home Farm club. Member of a Bolton side that was promoted to the Premiership via the play-offs in 2000-01.

STEVE FINNAN (FULHAM) BORN: 20.04.76 CAPS: 14 GLS: 1
Was called into the senior squad for the first time, as late replacement for Duff and Delap, in game v Czech Republic in February 2000. Scored his first international goal v Finland in November 2000. Cost Fulham £600,000 from Notts County in November 1998. Previously played for Welling Utd and Birmingham. Hardly misses a Fulham game. Member of Fulham side that won the Div Two Championship in 1998-99 and Div One Championship in 2000-01.

SHAY GIVEN (NEWCASTLE) BORN: 24.04.76 CAPS: 38 GLS: 0
Made his international debut vs Russia in March 1996. Cost Newcastle £1.5 million from Blackburn in July 1997. Was previously a junior at Celtic. Was also loaned out to Swindon and Sunderland. In superb form with Newcastle in the 2001-02 season.

IAN HARTE (LEEDS) BORN: 31.08.77 CAPS: 39 GLS: 8
Now in seventh season at Leeds. Began his career at Elland Road as a trainee. Turned pro in 1995. Scored over 30 goals for Leeds, including 11 in the 2000-01 season (seven in Premiership and four in Champions League). Is the left-sided version of David Beckham at free-kicks.

REPUBLIC OF IRELAND

COLIN HEALY (COVENTRY – ON-LOAN FROM CELTIC) BORN: 00.00.00 CAPS: 3 GLS: 0
Made his international debut when he started the friendly win v Russia on February 13. Won his second cap, as a sub, in the 3-0 win v Denmark on March 27. Nine Ireland U-21 caps. Joined Coventry on-loan until the end of the 2001-02 season from Celtic in January 2002. Made 11 league apps for Celtic in 2000-01 (making the required nine to win a Championship medal). Started Celtic's 2000-01 League Cup final win vs Kilmarnock.

MATT HOLLAND (IPSWICH) BORN: 11.04.74 CAPS: 18 GLS: 3
Made international debut as sub vs Macedonia in October 1999. Scored his first international goal v Portugal in October 2000, after coming on for Niall Quinn at half-time. Joined Ipswich for £800,000 from Bournemouth in July 1997. Has hardly missed a game for Ipswich since joining. Scored his 50th club career goal v Millwall in the Worthington Cup in September 2000. Started career at West Ham, before joining Bournemouth. Born in Bury.

ROBBIE KEANE (LEEDS) BORN: 08.07.80 CAPS: 32 GLS: 10
Made his international debut vs the Czech Republic in March 1998 (as a sub). Joined Leeds from Inter Milan in December 2000. Was initially on-loan at Leeds, but was then signed permanently for £12 million. Spent only five months or so at Inter Milan, having joined them from Coventry for £13 million in the summer of 2000. Scored 12 Premiership goals for Coventry in 1999-00. Began his career at Wolves. Now spent three seasons in the Premiership – one for Coventry and two for Leeds.

ROY KEANE (MAN UTD) BORN: 10.08.71 CAPS: 57 GLS: 9
Now in his 11th year of international football. Made his debut v Chile in May 1991. Was voted the PFA and Football Writers Player of the Year for 1999-00. Man Utd captain. Has now had nine seasons at the club. Cost them £3.75 million – a British record fee at the time – from Nottingham Forest in July 1993. Was suspended from Man Utd's 1999 Champions League final win. Joined Nottingham Forest from Irish football in June 1990 for £10,000.

ALAN KELLY (BLACKBURN) BORN: 11.08.68 CAPS: 34 GLS: 0
Made Republic debut v Wales in February 1993. Cost Blackburn £675,000 from Sheff Utd in July 1999. Has just completed his 17th season as a pro – has made over 400 career league appearances. Began his career at Preston. Hasn't been a regular in the Blackburn goal since the arrival at Ewood Park of Brad Friedel. Went on-loan to Birmingham in the 2001-02, making six appearances for them.

GARY KELLY (LEEDS) BORN: 09.07.74 CAPS: 45 GLS: 2
Leeds' longest-serving current player, having joined them in September 1991. His first international goal came in 2-0 win vs Germany in Hanover in May 1994. Was sent off in WCQ v Holland on September 1, 2001. Joined Leeds from the famous Home Farm club.

REPUBLIC OF IRELAND

MARK KENNEDY (WOLVES) BORN: 15.05.76 CAPS: 34 GLS: 3
Joined Wolves from Man City for £2 million in the summer of 2001. Spent two years at Maine Road. Cost Man City £1 million from Wimbledon in July 1999. Experienced promotion and then relegation in his two seasons at Man City. Scored once in 30 games for City last season. His only goal came in 4-2 Worthington Cup win at Gillingham on Sept 26, 2000. Began his career at Millwall. Made his League debut for Millwall at the age of 16 in a 1-0 win vs Charlton (April 24, 1993). Joined Liverpool from Millwall for £2.3 million in March 1995 at the age of 18 – a British record for a teenager at the time (still Millwall's record sale).

DEAN KIELY (CHARLTON) BORN: 10.10.70 CAPS: 6 GLS: 0
Kept 19 clean sheets in his 51 games for Charlton in 1999-00, which equalled the club record which was held by Nicky Johns, who also kept 19 clean sheets (18 in League, 1 in FA Cup) in the 1980-81 season. Kiely also kept 19 clean sheets in 51 games for Bury in 1998-99. Former England youth and schoolboy international. Cost Charlton £1 million from Bury in 1999. Has made over 450 league appearances in his career.

KEVIN KILBANE (SUNDERLAND) BORN: 01.02.77 CAPS: 32 GLS: 3
Scored his first senior international goal vs Finland in Nov 2000. Plays left-midfield for the Republic and right-midfield for Sunderland. Cost Sunderland £2.5 million from West Brom in December 1999. Began his career at Preston, his hometown club.

MARK KINSELLA (CHARLTON) BORN: 12.08.72 CAPS: 27 GLS: 3
Joined Charlton from Colchester for £150,000 in September 1996. Was named the Republic of Ireland Player of the Year in November 2000, at a banquet attended by FIFA President Sepp Blatter. Scored his first senior international goal v Estonia in October 2000. Made his international debut vs Czech Republic in March 1998. Signed a new 5-year contract with Charlton in 1999. Previously spent seven years at Colchester.

JASON MCATEER (SUNDERLAND) BORN: 18.06.71 CAPS: 46 GLS: 3
Joined Sunderland from Blackburn for an undisclosed fee in October 2001. Had been dropped by Blackburn manager Graeme Souness on numerous occasions in 2000-01 and 2001-02. Scored 1-0 winner vs Holland in WCQ on September 1, 2001. Cost Blackburn £4 million from Liverpool in January 1999. Began his league career at Bolton before joining Liverpool for £4.5 million in September 1995. Played 139 games for Liverpool in four years.

STEPHEN MCPHAIL (LEEDS) BORN: 09.12.79 CAPS: 4 GLS: 1
Joined Millwall on-loan from Leeds in March 2002. Was sent-off on his Millwall debut, v Sheff Wed on March 16, 2002. Member of the Rep of Ireland U-18 side that won the UEFA U-18 Championship in 1998. Joined Leeds as a trainee ands turned pro in 1996. Talented left-footed midfielder.

REPUBLIC OF IRELAND

CLINTON MORRISON (CRYSTAL PALACE) BORN: 14.05.79 CAPS: 6 GLS: 2
Scored on his Rep of Ireland debut, in a 2-2 draw v Croatia (August 15, 2001). Marked
his first start for Ireland (fifth cap) with a goal in the 3-0 win vs Denmark on March 27.
Signed by Palace from being a trainee in March 1997. Was Palace's top-scorer in 1998-
99 (13 goals), 1999-00 (15 goals) and 2000-01 (19 goals). Scored 19 goals in 2000-01.

ANDY O'BRIEN (NEWCASTLE) BORN: 29.06.79 CAPS: 5 GLS: 0
Joined Newcastle from Bradford for £2 million in March 2001. Scored his first Newcastle goal
in 1-1 derby draw at Sunderland on April 21, 2001. Scored three goals in 150 appearances
for Bradford, the club where he came up through the junior ranks. Signed a new long-term
contract extension in March 2002 which will keep him at St James' Park until 2007. Played
for both England and Rep of Ireland U-21 teams in 1998-99, but eventually opted for Ireland
because he sees his chances of gaining senior honours more of a reality with them.

NIALL QUINN (SUNDERLAND) BORN: 06.10.66 CAPS: 88 GLS: 21
Is the highest Republic scorer of all time. Scored his 21st international goal in WCQ vs
Cyprus on October 6, 2001. The previous record was held by Frank Stapleton, who scored
20 goals in 71 caps. Made full debut v Czechoslovakia in May 1986, in a mini-tournament
in Iceland, playing alongside Mick McCarthy. Cost Sunderland £1.3 million from Man City
in August 1996. Has formed a prolific partnership with Kevin Phillips at the Stadium of
Light. Previously with Arsenal. Has just completed the 19th season of his pro career.

STEVEN REID (MILLWALL) BORN: 10.03.81 CAPS: 4 GLS: 1
Made his international debut in the 2-2 draw vs Croatia (August 15, 2001). Scored his first
goal for Ireland in the 2-0 friendly win vs Russia on February 13, 2002. Sent-off twice in
2000-01, v Wycombe (league) and vs Ipswich (Worth Cup). Has come up through the youth
ranks at Millwall. Former England youth international and Rep of Ireland U-21 international.

STEVE STAUNTON (ASTON VILLA) BORN: 19.01.69 CAPS: 97 GLS: 8
Is the all-time highest appearance maker for the Republic. Received a testimonial, along with
Tony Cascarino, for their services to the Republic, in May 2000 at Lansdowne Rd – a Republic
of Ireland XI beat Liverpool 4-2. Made international debut vs Tunisia in Dublin in October
1988, winning 4-0. Mick McCarthy and Niall Quinn also played that day. Re-joined Aston Villa
in December 2000 after a short spell at Palace. Was released by Liverpool, where he also had
two spells (1986-91 and 1998-00). Has won every domestic major honour in English football
(League title with Liverpool in 1990, FA Cup with Liverpool in 1989, and League Cups with
Aston Villa in 1994 and 1996). Has made over 350 top division appearances in his career.

COACH

MICK MCCARTHY BORN: 07.02.59
Appointed national manager in February 1996. Previously managed Millwall from 1992
to 1996. Played for Barnsley, Manchester City, Milwall, Lyon and Celtic. Won 57 caps
for Rep of Ireland. Played in the 1990 World Cup finals.

CAMEROON

Cameroon's 1990 quarter-final appearance still stands out as Africa's best ever World Cup performance, and the 'Indomitable Lions' remain the continent's best chance this time out. Having deservedly retained their Nations Cup crown in Mali, and tasted Olympic success in Sydney, Schafer's men are winners. The team has a tight defence, bar the occasional lapse in the centre, a hardworking midfield driven by Marc Vivien Foe, and two of the best opportunists around up front in Samuel Eto'o and Patrick Mboma. There's a real solidity about Cameroon, and if they match that with enough commitment, they could go a long way, if not necessarily all the way.

One cautionary note should be sounded about the lack of depth in their squad. A couple of injuries and the profligate Pius N'Diefi and the temperamental Patrick Suffo would move into the first team. Enough said.

If Schafer and his coaching team keep the top men fit, the side which rarely moved out of first gear in Mali might show us just how good they really are. Much will depend on their opening game against a talented Republic of Ireland team. These two nations may end up battling it out for second place, and a win here would put Cameroon in a strong position and give them some much needed momentum. Failure there would leave them needing to get something out of Germany on June 11th.

This Cameroon team showed against France last year they it can tackle the world's best, but, as they showed in '98 against Austria and Chile, the Indomitable Lions can lose their sharpness in the blink of an eye. The best in Africa, but will that be good enough? And if you believe in fate, then any Cameroon fan will tell you that they never play well in a World Cup when they've succeeded in that year's Nations Cup.

SQUAD

BOUKAR ALIOUM (SAMSUNSPOR) BORN: 3/1/72 CAPS: 39 GLS: 0
Replaced Songoo as number one for France '98. Has been the first choice for his club for six years now. Nicknamed 'The Panther' for hopefully obvious reasons.

NICOLAS ALNOUDJI (RIZESPOR) BORN: 9/12/79 CAPS: 15 GLS: 0
Helped Cameroon win Olympic gold and a regular substitute in the national side.

SERGE BRANCO (EINTRACHT FRANKFURT) BORN: 11/10/80 CAPS: 2 GLS: 0
Another with an Olympic gold medal but has played only one minute of senior international football. Started off in the lower leagues in Germany before getting dream move to Eintracht.

JEAN DIKA DIKA (UNIAO DE LAMAS) BORN: CAPS: GLS:
Joined up with the Atletico Madrid youth side as a 19-year-old. Didn't make it there, and had spells at several Spanish lower league clubs before moving to the Portuguese Second Division.

CAMEROON

ERIC DJEMBA (NANTES) BORN: 4/5/81 CAPS: 0 GLS: 0
Most impressive in the Champions League for Nantes in this, his first season since graduating from the famous youth academy.

JOEL EPALLE (PANAHAIKI) BORN: 20/12/78 CAPS: 22 GLS: 2
A midfield worker, a useful squad member, his only two international goals came on his debut, against Gabon. Olympic gold medallist who is expected to move to Aris Salonika this summer.

SAMUEL ETOO (REAL MALLORCA) BORN: 10/3/81 CAPS: 28 GLS: 7
Spent a couple of seasons at Real Madrid where he never really held down a first team place. Flourished during a loan spell at Real Mallorca, and it was no surprise when he moved there permanently for a fee of 4.5 million pounds. Was the youngest player involved at France '98. Carries the burden of being described as Roger Milla's goalscoring heir.

MARC VIVIEN FOE (LYON) BORN: 1/5/75 CAPS: 47 GLS: 6
Won a French title with Lens in '98, and was on the verge of a move to Manchester United and a World Cup debut before breaking his leg. Signed for West Ham in late '98, and is now an outstanding, 'Viera style' midfielder for club and country. Lyon paid £6 million for his services.

GEREMI (REAL MADRID) BORN: 20/12/78 CAPS: 38 GLS: 1
Captained the gold medal team in Sydney and is now a two-time Nations Cup winner. Was taken to Madrid from Turkey by John Toshack. Squad member there for three seasons without ever gaining a regular place. At his best when linking down the right side with Lauren. Scored in this season's Champions league quarter-final against Bayern Munich.

JOSEPH DESIRE JOB (MIDDLESBOROUGH) BORN: 1/12/77 CAPS: 34 GLS: 5
Born in France, and actually rejected a place in the French Under-21 squad to follow the wishes of his father and take his chance with Cameroon. Great start to his professional career with Lyon, but has struggled since at both Lens and Middlesborough. Has been on loan at Metz for the end of the French season.

RAYMOND KALLA (EXTREMADURA) BORN: 22/4/75 CAPS: 47 GLS: 2
Massive figure at the heart of the defence. Spent time with Panahaiki in Greece before going to Spain. Scored on his international debut in '94, and went on to play in all three games in the USA.

IDRISS KAMENI (LE HAVRE) BORN: 18/12/84 CAPS: 1 GLS: 0
Exploded onto the international scene as a 16-year-old in the Sydney Olympics, when his penalty save, and stunning performances helped Cameroon to the gold medal. Wasn't a regular at Le Havre, so spent time training at Juventus, and has now been given a contract by the Italian club. Is one of their six keepers.

CAMEROON

LAUREN (ARSENAL) BORN: 19/10/77 CAPS: 16 GLS: 1
Was brought up near Seville in Spain and made his breakthrough at Real Mallorca. Player of the Tournament at the last Nations Cup, and has proved very adaptable for Arsene Wenger, playing in a variety of roles. Scored the late penalty that beat Spurs in the North London derby at Highbury.

PATRICK MBOMA (PARMA) BORN: 15/11/70 CAPS: 42 GLS: 23
Twice a Nations Cup winner, although injury meant that he missed the latter stages of this year's tournament. An Olympic gold medallist as an over-age player. Started off at PSG in France, but found his feet after a move to Japan with Gamba Osaka. He scored 25 goals in 28 games and scored the J League's first hat-trick. Has been something of a nomad since then, spending time at Cagliari and Parma and on loan at Sunderland.

LUCIEN METTOMO (MANCHESTER CITY) BORN: 19/4/77 CAPS: 18 GLS:0
Out of the squad for a year but brought back for another Nations Cup appearance where he was as reliable as ever when called upon. Joined Manchester City from St Etienne. Would have joined Blackburn but had a problem with a knee injury.

PIUS NDIEFI (SEDAN) BORN: 5/7/75 CAPS: 13 GLS: 3
Started both the semi-finals and final in place of Mboma in Mali, and was his usual blend of dangerous pace and dreadful finishing. Averages ten goals a season for Sedan, it should be plenty more. Was a youth player at Lens before moving to Sedan.

CYRILLE NDO (STRASBOURG) BORN: CAPS: 12 GLS: 0
Has been playing for the national team since prior to the '98 World Cup. Had a spell in Switzerland before settling with Strasbourg.

SALOMON OLEMBE (MARSEILLE) BORN: 8/12/80 CAPS: 39 GLS :3
Missed out on an Olympic gold medal by refusing to travel to Sydney. Pacy and very left footed, he recently moved to Marseille after leaving Nantes. Came through the famous Nantes youth academy. Played in France '98. Scored two goals in this year's Nations Cup semi-final win over the hosts Mali.

JACQUES SONGOO (METZ) BORN: 17/3/64 CAPS: 66 GLS: 0
Spent five years at Deportivo La Coruna in Spain and retired from international football, but has come back into the frame with some brilliant performances in Metz's struggle against relegation. Made his international debut 19 years ago, against Angola. Was an outfield player when he was younger. This would be his fourth World Cup.

RIGOBERT SONG (COLOGNE) BORN: 1/7/76 CAPS: 59 GLS: 2
Captain who scored the winning penalty in the 2000 Nations Cup. Made his World Cup debut at 17, promptly became the youngest player ever to be sent off in a World Cup. Followed up with another red card in '98. Has played for Metz, Salernitana, Liverpool and West Ham. Is nicknamed 'German'. Won African Nations Cup in 2000 and 2002.

CAMEROON

PATRICK SUFFO (SHEFFIELD UNITED) BORN: 17/1/78 CAPS: 18 GLS: 2
Has been told by manager Neil Warnock that he will never again play for Sheffield United after his sending off in the infamous game against West Brom, when United were reduced to six players. Was a controversial figure in his time at Nantes, where he once served a lengthy ban for spitting at a referee. Scored the equaliser in the friendly draw against Argentina.

BILL TCHATO (MONTPELLIER) BORN: 14/5/75 CAPS: 12 GLS: 1
Had an outstanding Nations Cup in the centre of defence. Can also play in either full- back position, and now a likely World Cup starter. Brought up in France, and formerly played in the lower leagues with Caen and Nice.

JERRY CHRISTIAN TCHUISSE (SPARTAK MOSCOW) BORN: 13/1/75 CAPS: 3 GLS: 0
Played in the Russian Third Division and found himself in severe financial trouble after not being paid. Has since arrived at Spartak after a spell with Chernomorets. Was called up to the Russian national team, but illness prevented him from joining the squad and he has now opted to play for the country of his birth.

BERNARD TCHOUTANG (RODA JC) BORN: 2/9/76 CAPS :35 GLS: 6
Right-sided midfielder-winger. Had a spell in Turkey before going to Holland. Will be one of the smallest players on view in Japan and Korea, and also one of the fastest.

PIERRE WOME (BOLOGNA) BORN: 26/3/79 CAPS: 46 GLS: 1
Has been the picture of calm and class since making his international debut at 16. Played in France '98 and scored the winning penalty in the Olympic final. Made his international debut as a 16-year-old. Had a spell at Roma before joining Bologna.

COACH

WINIFRIED SCHAFER
The German only had three months to prepare Cameroon for their Nations Cup defence in Mali after becoming their fourth coach in 12 months. Their victory says a lot about his organisational skills and his team's natural ability. When he took over, his stated objective was to instill some discipline into the team, a trick he appears to have pulled off so far while not hampering the team's natural flair. Schafer was previously at Karlsruhe and Stuttgart in the Bundesliga, and latterly at Tennis Borussia Berlin of the second division.

WORLD CUP FACTS

England have used 128 players in the World Cup. Sir Bobby Charlton (1958-70) is the only one to go to four tournaments although he didn't play in 1958.

SAUDI ARABIA

With their pedigree as one of Asia's most successful nations, it was no surprise that Saudi Arabia qualified for the World Cup finals for a third time in a row. However, for all their dominance on paper, their route to this year's Finals was anything but straight forward.

Yet again the revolving door was in full swing on the head coach's office as Slobodan Santrac was replaced by his assistant Nasser Al Johar following poor performances in the opening games of the second phase of Asian qualifying. Al Johar, with his deep knowledge of the squad, a fact reflected in the respect the players hold for the former Al Nassr defender, turned the team around, much as he had done a year before following Milan Macala's sacking at the Asian Cup. But they still needed a little help from some of their Arab friends and a win for Bahrain against Iran in the final qualifying round saw the Saudis through at the expense of the Persians.

Saudi Arabia's World Cup record is second only to that of Korea in Asia, although the Middle Eastern side have succeeded where the Koreans have failed on five occasions. At their first World Cup in the United States in 1994, a 1-0 win over Belgium, as well as giving the Netherlands a scare, saw the Saudis into the second round, where they lost narrowly to Sweden. That success proved to be a double-edged sword. While it brought attention to Saudi football, it also heightened expectations for France '98. The signing up of Carlos Alberto Parreira, winner of the title with Brazil four years earlier, only increased the delusions of grandeur and the Saudis genuinely believed they had a chance of a place in the last eight.

However, a tough group which saw them drawn to face hosts France, Denmark and South Africa presented the team with too many problems and Parreira was sacked two games into the campaign following the 4-0 loss to the eventual champions.

That failure, though, seems to have had a calming effect on the Saudis and expectations this time around are not so ludicrous. Drawn to face Germany, the Republic of Ireland and Cameroon, this year's group will present a tough test for Al Johar's team. But with experience and youth in the team, a one-off surprise result is not out of the question. A place in the knock-out phase, though, would appear beyond them.

Saudi Arabia have been the most dominant nation in Asia over the last 20 years. Reached the final of the last five Asian Cups, winning the title on three occasions, a record haul they share with the Iranians.

They have also won the hotly-contested Gulf Cup twice, including earlier this year in Riyadh, the first time they have done so since the months following their debut performance at the World Cup in 1994.

This summer also looks like it will be the end of an era for the Saudis with the remaining members of the USA '94 squad looking set to end their careers. Striker Sami Al Jaber and goalkeeper Mohammad Al Daeyea – one of world football's most capped players – have voiced their intentions to quit after the tournament while injuries could well force Mohammad Al Khilaiwi to do the same.

The young talent has been coming through, though, and Saudi Arabia's future at the top of the Asian game is assured. Whether they can make the step up to challenge the world's best remains in doubt.

SAUDI ARABIA

SQUAD

TISIR AL ANTAIF (AL AHLI) BORN: 16/02/074
Rarely had the chance to prove himself at international level due to Al Daeyea's long career at the top of Saudi goalkeeping.

MOHAMMAD BABKR (AL NASSR) BORN: 15/01/73
Replaced Al Daeyea during the qualifying tournament while the regular custodian recovered from a shoulder injury. An able deputy although, like Al Daeyea, suspect on crosses.

MOHAMMAD AL DAEYEA (AL HILAL) BORN: 02/08/72
Saudi Arabia's starting goalkeeper for the last 12 years, Al Daeyea recently said this, his third World Cup, would be his last before retiring from international football. A decent shot-stopper, Al Daeyea's weakness is in the air. Despite this he has been hailed by many as Asia's number one.

ABDULLAH JUMAAN AL DOSSARY (AL HILAL) BORN: 10/11/77
Another powerfully-built midfielder, Jumaan is famed for his powerful shot from long range. At both club level and internationally, Jumaan tends to be used by coaches off the bench, when his strength and pace can change the outcome of a game in the later stages.

AHMED DUKHI AL DOSSARY (AL HILAL) BORN: 25/10/76
Displaced regular right back Mohammad Shliya several years ago after impressive performances at both domestic and Asian level for Al Hilal. Equally strong in defence and attack, Dukhi's crossing provides the Saudis with another creative outlet.

OBEID AL DOSSARY (AL AHLI) BORN: 2/10/75
Skilful striker who has failed to live up to his initial promise. However, featured in the Saudi squad at the last World Cup and has become more involved in the national set up since Al Johar took over. Likely to vie for a place in the starting line-up with Sami Al Jaber.

AHMED KHALIL AL DOSSARY (AL HILAL) BORN: 30/07/70
Solid defender who has impressed at club level but has rarely had the opportunity to perform for the national team as a result of the successful partnership between Khilaiwi and Suleiman.

SAAD AL DOSSARY (AL AHLI) BORN: 03/09/77
Short and stocky, Saad Al Dossary's power and pace surging through from midfield helped steer the side to the World Cup finals. Was brought into the team by Nasser Al Johar following the sacking of Slobodan Santrac and both Al Dossary and the team blossomed.

SAUDI ARABIA

OMAR AL GHAMDI (AL HILAL) BORN: 11/04/79
A tough tackling defensive midfielder, Omar Al Ghamdi has become a key component in the Saudi team. Replaced club mate Khamis Owairan Al Dossary at the Asian Cup after the latter was banned by the Saudi federation and made the position his own.

IBRAHIM MATER AL HARBI (AL NASSR) BORN: 10/07/75
Another nearly man of Saudi football, Ibrahim Mater has been a member of the Saudi national team squad for a number of years but has never been able to hold down a regular place in the starting line-up.

MOHAMMED NOUR HAWSAWI (AL ITTIHAD) BORN: 26/2/78
A key member of the Al Ittihad club that have dominated Saudi league football in recent seasons. Shares the defensive midfield duties with Omar Al Ghamdi. Featured in the squad that reached the final of the Asian Cup in Lebanon in 2000, losing out to Japan.

SAMI AL JABER (AL HILAL) BORN: 11/12/72
Has vowed that this, his third finals, will be his last World Cup. Al Jaber returned to Saudi Arabia in 2001 after an unsuccessful stint at Wolves and since then has taken Al Hilal to success in the Asian Cup Winners' Cup. Usually plays as the second striker and likes to run at defenders.

MOHAMMED SHLIYA AL JAHANI (AL AHLI) BORN: 28/09/75
Was the regular right back for the Saudis until the Asian Cup in Lebanon in 2000 when he lost his place to Ahmed Dukhi. Likes to go forward and has been rated as one of the best in his position in Asia.

MOHAMMAD AL KHILAIWI (AL ITTIHAD) BORN: 21/08/71
Experienced centre half who played at both USA '94 and France '98 and was sent off in Saudi's 4-0 drubbing at the hands of the hosts last time around. Missed out on a number of qualifiers last year due to an ankle injury.

TALAL AL MESHAL (AL AHLI) BORN: 07/06/78
When Saudi Arabia go for the direct route, Talal Al Meshal is usually their weapon of choice. This tall and powerful forward has scored regularly since graduating from the under 20s side and, after missing the qualifying tournament due to injury, returned for the Gulf Cup win in Riyadh at the start of the year.

MARZOUQ AL OTAIBI (AL ITTIHAD) BORN: 07/11/75
Hit a hat-trick against Egypt at the Confederations' Cup in 1999, a feat which took the Saudis to the semi-finals and earned Al Otaibi the title of Saudi Arabia's most expensive player following his transfer from Al Shabab to Al Ittihad. Has failed to show similar form since, however.

SAUDI ARABIA

SALEH AL SAQRI (AL ITTIHAD) BORN: 23/01/79
Defender who fills the same role down the left side as Hussein Abdul Ghani. A young player who has come through the ranks at Al Ittihad as the club have dominated domestic football in Saudi Arabia. Was a member of the Saudi squad that finished as runners-up at the Asian Cup in Lebanon in 2000.

IBRAHIM SWAID SHAHRANI (AL AHLI) BORN: 21/7/74
Like Ibrahim Mater, Swaid has been a member of the Saudi squad for a number of years but has yet to secure a regular place in the starting line-up. Scored the goal that qualified the Saudis for France '98, against Qatar in November 1997.

ABDULLAH BIN SHEEHAN (AL SHABAB) BORN: 10/08/76
With his lightning pace, Abdullah bin Sheehan has been one of the most on-form players in Asian football over the last year with his goals guiding his club, Al Shabab, to the Asian Cup Winners' Cup, and Saudi Arabia to the World Cup. Has a strong claim to a place in Al Johar's side.

MANAF ABU SHGEER (AL ITTIHAD) BORN: 06/02/80
Another youngster who broke into the squad in the run-up to the Asian Cup. Unlikely to feature in Korea/Japan but should travel for the experience.

MOHAMMED AL SHLHOOB (AL HILAL) BORN: 09/12/80
His slight frame and diminutive stature belie the talents of the youngster known as 'Baby Maradona' in Saudi football. The tricky winger has become one of the great hopes of Saudi football, playing on the left side for both club and country, from where he both creates and scores regularly.

HUSSEIN ABDULGHANI SULAIMANI (AL AHLI) BORN: 23/01/77
An experienced campaigner despite his age, Hussein Abdulghani is one of the most versatile players in the Saudi squad. Usually plays at left back but is just as likely to pop up in the centre of midfield and has, occasionally, played up front for his club Al Ahli.

NAWAF AL TEMYAT (AL HILAL) BORN: 28/06/76
Named the Asian Player of the Year for 2000, Nawaf Al Temyat had a dreadful 2001, missing the qualifying tournament due to a knee ligament injury. Returned in early 2002 and has since been linked with a move to Europe.

ABDULLAH AL WAKAD (AL SHABAB) BORN: 29/09/75
Broke into the side during the qualifiers despite being a peripheral figure in the squad in the past. Another player favoured by Al Johar but is unlikely to be in the starting line-up if all of the key men are fit for the World Cup.

SAUDI ARABIA

AL HASSAN AL YAMI (AL ITTIHAD)
Plucked from second division side Nigeriana, Al Yami has become one of Saudi Arabia's late bloomers at league champions Al Ittihad. Picked by Al Johar for the qualifying tournament as a back-up to Al Jaber, the 30-year-old should travel to Japan as a squad member.

ABDULLAH SULEIMAN ZUBROMAWI (AL HILAL) BORN: 15/11/73
Central defender who broke into the national squad during the qualifying tournament for France '98 after several successful outings for the Saudi Olympic squad in 1996. Represented the nation at France '98 and has been the back bone of the team's defence for the last five years.

COACH

NASSER AL JOHAR
A quiet man, Nasser Al Johar has become known as the saviour of Saudi Arabian football in the last two years. Currently in his second stint as national team boss, Al Johar will become the first Saudi coach to take the team to the World Cup finals in this, the country's third World Cup. A player with Al Nassr and a former international himself, Al Johar, originally employed as assistant coach, took over as head coach first time around when Czech Milan Macala was fired during the Asian Cup in Lebanon in October 2000. Al Johar took the team to the final, where they lost 1-0 to the same Japan side that had hammered Macala's team 4-1, and then retained his position during the first phase of qualifying as the Saudis easily disposed of Bangladesh, Mongolia and Vietnam. For the second round, Yugoslavia's Slobodan Santrac took over as Al Johar reverted to his original role as assistant, only to take over the hot seat again following a draw against Bahrain and a loss to Iran in the first two games of Asia's final round of qualifying. Al Johar worked his magic again, inspiring the team to their third finals in a row. His position looked in danger, however, as reports spread that the Saudi Arabian Football Federation were negotiating with Humberto Coelho and Craig Brown but eventually the association decided to stick with Al Johar. Their faith was rewarded with victory in the Gulf Cup regional tournament, the first time the Saudis had won the biennial competition against their Arab neighbours in the Gulf since 1994.

WORLD CUP FACTS

The smallest number of players used by any team in the World Cup was TWELVE by Brazil in 1962 in Chile when only Amarildo replaced the injured Pele after the second game. Brazil went on to beat Czechoslovakia in the final.

Billy Wright captained England in three tournaments (1950-58).

ENGLAND
VS
ARGENTINA

by bob harris

On June 7 Argentina and England clash head on in Sapporo, Japan at 12.30 British Summer Time in a game which will go a long way in deciding who goes forward from the Group of Death to face World Champions France in the second round. It may not, of course, be quite as simple as that but going into the Finals that is what will be on the players' minds of both sides — to win the toughest qualifying group of all and avoid the holders who are favourites to take Group A.

That, of course, will only serve to add the pressure to the powder keg of a first round match which history tells us will have at least one flare up and one sending off.

The Argentinian captain Rattin was dismissed against England at Wembley in 1966 when the hosts went on to win the game 1-0 and the tournament. Four years ago it was the turn of the current England captain David Beckham to be dismissed and for the South Americans to advance at England's expense.

PAST CONTESTS

2 JUNE 1962 – GROUP D
ENGLAND 3 ARGENTINA 1
(half-time 2-0)

RANCAGUA, CHILE
REFEREE: Nicolaj Latyschev (USSR) ATTENDANCE: 10,000
England: Springett, Armfield, Norman, Wilson, Moore, Flowers, Douglas, Greaves,
Peacock, Haynes, Bobby Charlton.
ARGENTINA: Roma, Capp, Navarro, Marzolini, Sachi, Paez, Oleniak, Rattin, Sosa,
Sanfillipo, Belen.
ENGLAND – Flowers (18), Charlton (42), Greaves (65)
Argentina- Sanfillipo (78)

England was not a happy team. With players out of form and a poor training camp,
there was an air of resignation about the affair but after a lack lustre display against
Hungary, England pulled up their sleeves against an aggressive, spoiling team from
Argentina and played their best football of the tournament.

It was all over by half-time with Ron Flowers, who scored in the first match, opening
their account from the penalty spot with Bobby Charlton making it two with a typical
pile driver before the break. Jimmy Greaves made it three mid-way through the second-
half and Argentina's consolation was a gift goal 12 minutes from time.

That was it for England. A dreadful soulless 0-0 with Bulgaria, where the sparse
crowd jeered them, gave them a second round match against Brazil, which the South
Americans won at a canter 3-1.

WORLD CUP FACTS

Arise Sir Michael Owen and Sir David Beckham? If they score this
summer, they will become part of a most exclusive club. Only five players
have previously netted in two different World Cups – and three of them
have since been knighted. The quintet are Gary Lineker, Sir Bobby
Charlton, Sir Geoff Hurst, Martin Peters and Sir Tom Finney.

Manchester United are the only club who have contributed to every
England World Cup squad. Four of their players went to France 98: David
Beckham, Paul Scholes, Teddy Sheringham and Gary Neville.

England's first game in the World Cup finals was on June 25, 1950. They
beat Chile 2-0 in Rio de Janeiro's legendary Maracana Stadium with Stan
Mortensen scoring the opening goal.

23 JULY 1966 – QUARTER-FINAL
ENGLAND 1 ARGENTINA 0
(half-time 0-0)

WEMBLEY STADIUM, LONDON.
REFEREE: Rudolf Kreitlein (West Germany) ATTENDANCE: 90,000
ENGLAND: Banks, Cohen, Jack Charlton, Moore, Wilson, Stiles, Bobby Charlton, Ball, Hurst, Hunt, and Peters.
ARGENTINA: Roma, Ferreiro, Perfumo, Albrecht, Marzolini, Rattin, Gonzalez, Solari, Onega, Artime, Mas.
GOAL: Hurst.

The scene was set. England, starting sluggishly, had drawn 0-0 with Uruguay; beaten Mexico 2-0 and France 2-0 while Argentina, in a much tougher group, had beaten the fancied Spaniards 2-1; drawn with the regimented East Germans and beaten Switzerland 2-0 for the two nations to square up against each other in the quarter-finals.

Even before this game there were deep mutterings from the South Americans about the interpretation of the referees, particularly those from Europe and clearly the Argentinians were unhappy with the appointment of a German with no Spanish to officiate their match against the hosts. Argentina decided to test Herr Kreitlein to the full. None was more provocative than the Argentinian captain Rattin, a large man who towered over the little German referee, arguing, protesting and tormenting until the German's patience ran out and he caution the Argentinian skipper for a foul on Bobby Charlton. But when Rattin was not in the referees face he was proving to be the axis of the South American's defence and their counter attacking measures that caused the alert Gordon Banks some trouble when he saved from the lively Mas.

Suddenly, nine minutes before half-time, the game exploded. The German referee was booking one of the Argentinian players when Rattin, in his role as captain, interfered. He claimed he was asking for an interpreter but the balding referee said that the look on his face was enough to tell him what was going on and he issued a second, devastating yellow card. Rattin refused to go and chaos reigned supreme for ten minutes with the Argentina team threatening to walk off if Rattin was not allowed to play on. It was not until Ken Aston, an Englishman who was head of the World Cup referees, appeared on the sidelines that order was gradually restored, Rattin went off and the game resumed with the South Americans ten men facing the 11 of England.

Argentina settled back to defend with Antonio Roma saving superbly from Hurst and it was not until 13 minutes from the end that Martin Peters' cross from the left was met by his West Ham teammate on the near post and headed into the far corner. The game was an international scandal with Mas adding to the problems when he cuffed a young boy across the head when he ran on to the pitch to celebrate Hurst's goal.

Even after the final whistle the furore did not die down and England's manager, Alf Ramsey, described the opposition as "Animals" to raise another furore. England went on to win the World Cup with Ramsey's wingless wonders, thankfully with no more controversy.

22 JUNE 1986 – QUARTER-FINAL
ENGLAND 1 ARGENTINA 2
(half-time 0-0)

MEXICO CITY, MEXICO
REFEREE: Ali ben Nasser (Tunisia) **ATTENDANCE:** 114,580
ARGENTINA: Pumpido, Ruggeri, Cuciuffo, Olarticoechea, Brown, Giusti, Batista, Burruchaga (Tapia 75), Enrique, Maradona, Valdano.
ENGLAND: Shilton, Stevens, Sansom, Hoddle, Butcher, Fenwick, Steven (Barnes 74), Reid (Waddle 63), Lineker, Beardsley, Hodge.
GOALS: Argentina – Maradona (50, 54) England – Lineker (80)

Just how much did Diego Maradona's infamous 'Hand of God' goal affect the result of England's narrow defeat in the glorious Azteca Stadium?

It is difficult to quantify as Carlos Bilardo had planned carefully, stifling England's attacks by using Ruggeri and Cuciuffo as man-for-man markers on Peter Beardsley and Gary Lineker while using Brown as a sweeper and Enrique to police Glenn Hoddle.

It has to be admitted that Argentina were the better side but neither looked like scoring and, clearly, it was going to be down to which team tired first in the strength sapping Azteca Stadium and who used their substitutes better.

But the first of the world's greatest player, Maradona, changed everything. A sliced clearance from Steve Hodge was gross but Peter Shilton looked a comfortable favourite as Maradona ran in to challenge.

Stunningly Maradona won the race but from my view in the press box it was a clear and blatant handball that saw the England goalkeeper chase inexperienced referee Ben Nasser of Tunisia right up to the half-way line in protest.

But the goal stood and the game changed dramatically. Within minutes the rejuvenated Argentina had increased their lead with one of the goals of the tournament as Maradona picked up the ball on the halfway line and waltzed past a succession of despairing defenders before sliding the ball past Shilton.

But then manager Bobby Robson threw on his jokers and substitutes Chris Waddle and John Barnes suddenly had the South Americans on the retreat. Waddle hit a screamer which goalkeeper Pumpido saved while a Hoddle free kick had him scrambling across his goal.

With ten minutes remaining, and England in full cry, Gary Lineker headed home Barnes' inch perfect cross and seven minutes later it looked certain that the game would go into extra time when Barnes served up an identical cross from the left only for Lineker to inexplicably overrun it.

It was all hands to the pump as the South Americans held on to their place in the semi-finals – but would they have made it without the 'Hand of God' and two officials who were totally out of their depth?

JUNE 30 1998 – SECOND ROUND
ENGLAND 2 ARGENTINA 2
Argentina win 4-3 on penalties (half-time 2-2)

ST. ETIENNE, FRANCE
REFEREE: Kim Milton Nielsen (Denmark) **ATTENDANCE:** 30,600
ARGENTINA: Roa, Vivas, Ayala, Chamot, Zanetti, Almeyda, Simeone (Berti 91), Ortega, Veron, Batistuta (Crespo 68), Lopez (Gallardo 68)
ENGLAND: Seaman, G. Neville, and Adams. Campbell, Anderton (Batty 96), Beckham, Ince, Le Saux (Southgate 70), Scholes (Merson78), Owen, Shearer.
GOALS: Batistuta 6 (pen), Shearer 10 (pen), Owen 16, Zanetti 45
PENALTY SHOOT OUT: Berti score, Shearer score, Crespo save, Ince save, Veron score, Merson score, Gallardo score, Owen score, Ayala score, Batty save.

England, managed by Glenn Hoddle, had an uneven route to the second round as they carefully put aside the unfancied Tunisia; then lost to a last minute Petrescu goal against Romania and finally beat Colombia 2-0 for the right to face Argentina who were 100 per cent in the first round against Japan, Jamaica and Croatia. So, once again Argentina and England were to clash again, this time with the battle over the Falklands still needling the fans who were at each other in the town of St Etienne and in the ground.

Everything revolved around the controversial sending off of England's David Beckham, who, under provocation, lifted a foot as he lay on the ground to Diego Simeone right under the nose of fussy Danish referee Kim Milton Neilson who reacted with an instant red card as Simeone went for the Oscar nomination. A yellow, yes. A red, I don't think so.

It spoiled what was developing into the best game of the entire World Cup, full of drama, full of skill. Argentina went in front when goalkeeper David Seaman brought down that man Simeone for Batistuta to score from the spot. Then Neilson evened up matters by awarding Michael Owen a penalty when he was brought down by Ayala, allowing England skipper Alan Shearer to step up and score from the penalty spot. Six minutes later and England, growing in strength and confidence, were in front through a dazzling goal from Owen as he ran onto a pass from Beckham on the halfway line. England were rampant and favourites to go on to the next round as Ince, Owen and Scholes all wasted chances to extend the lead before Argentina levelled on the stroke of half-time as Zanetti equalised.

But it was just two minutes into the second half when Beckham was sent off and plunged into despair and to become the butt of the blame from the England fans. Argentina were now on top and poured forward with England hitting on the break. Sol Campbell had a goal disallowed for a foul by Shearer on the goalkeeper while Batistuta headed wide from an outstanding position. There were claims by the South Americans when Adams was struck on the elbow but although the penalty claim was waved aside it was penalties that were again to decide England's fate with goalkeeper Roa saving from Paul Ince and David Batty.

It was, without doubt, the best game of the tournament but the victory did Argentina little good as they went out in the next match to Holland while England made their way home convinced that they had deserved better.

GROUP F

When the draw was made for the World Cup finals, England, in the second set of seeds, knew they would face a tough draw. Within minutes of the draw being made it had already attracted the over-used, but in this case, suitable sub-title: The Group of Death. England have been rocked by foot injuries to captain David Beckham and Gary Neville. Understandably, the pairing with Argentina – they play in the roofed Hiroba Stadium in Sapporo on June 7 – evokes memories of their previous World Cup meeting, four years earlier. On that second round occasion Michael Owen came to world prominence with a wonder goal, Beckham was sent off and England went out, losing 4-3 on penalties. Both nations have improved. Argentina dominated the South American qualifiers from the start and arrive in Asia as one of the favourites, alongside holders France. But England, under Sven-Göran Eriksson, have discovered confidence and belief and though they needed an element of fortune to qualify, the 5-1 win over Germany is a result they will never forget.

Argentina led their qualifying group by 12 points, ahead of second-placed Ecuador. They won 13 and drew four of 18 qualifiers, scoring 42 goals and conceding just 15. The decline of Brazil and Uruguay has left Argentina the dominant force in South America but, in coach Marcelo Bielsa, they have a man who has instilled an intelligence to sit alongside their undoubted ability.

Bielsa, whose biggest problem this summer will be his fear of flying, is a student of the game who has been known to sleep with a black board in his bed room in case he comes up with a new tactical ploy in the middle of the night. But Bielsea also has to decide how he can accommodate both Hernan Crespo and Gabriel Batistuta in attack. Of course, both Argentina and England could qualify from Group F. Certainly, the depth of belief in Eriksson's squad is probably stronger than at any time in the last decade. Certainly, if one had suggested such spirit and confidence prior to the finals, back on that fateful night when England said farewell to Wembley with a 1-0 defeat by Germany, followed by the resignation of Kevin Keegan, few would have believed it.

Eriksson became England coach in January 2000 after signing a six-year contract and his first World Cup qualifier was the 2-1 Anfield win over Finland. Victories over Albania and Greece set up England nicely for the visit to Munich; what followed was remarkable. England won 5-1 and Owen scored a hat-trick. Another win over Albania maintained the dream and so to Old Trafford where a win against Greece would have been enough. Germany, playing Finland, could still qualify automatically and when Greece led 2-1, Germany thought their goalless draw was sufficient. Then, up stepped Beckham and his scintillating free kick ensured England were in the finals.

In addition to having to face Argentina, Eriksson faces an emotional conundrum; England also play Sweden, his home nation. Sweden won eight and drew two of their qualifiers while conceding just three goals. They have a reputation for being dour but well organised and pose a massive threat to England's hopes of qualifying.

Nigeria, though, have been beset with problems. Boavista coach Jaime Pacheco rejected an offer to coach the Super Eagles after Shaibu Amodou was sacked in February after they went out of the African Nations Cup to Senegal at the semi-final stage. He was replaced by Adegboye Onigbinde, promoted from technical director to reassume the post he first held in 1984, but there have been constant rumours. suggesting a big-name European coach would be brought in for the World Cup.

ARGENTINA

"I celebrate the fact that we will have matches that are worth playing. Playing England and Nigeria is a challenge and I'm happy. One dreams all one's life of playing in a World Cup and, when it happens, it's better to do it against great teams. My evaluation of the group we were given is that our rivals are apparently the most difficult because, in general, each group has a favourite to win it but, in our group, everyone is a candidate." **Marcelo Bielsa**, Argentina coach.

ENGLAND

"There are no easy games. They are all very good teams. It is difficult, but anything is possible. We have to be prepared and hope we can go on and not have only three games at the World Cup. I think we can beat any team in the world on a good day. If we can go to Munich and win 5-1 why can't we beat Argentina?" England coach **Sven-Göran Eriksson**.

SWEDEN

"If you like to meet tough and great teams we have landed in a group like that. I always try to see things positively and I do it even now. We do not have much experience of South American football and of Argentina, but it must be the same the other way around for Argentina." **Tommy Soderberg**, Sweden's joint coach.

NIGERIA

"Nigeria has come of age in football. We should not be thinking of going back. Our ambition is to see Nigerian football move forward. But we are in an emergency situation at the moment. The players have been on the scene for some time, while I am new in the job and am getting to understand the terrain. We have to plan our strategy on how to put up a credible performance at the World Cup." **Adegboye Onigbinde**, newly-appointed Nigeria coach.

ARGENTINA

The quality of the Argentina World Cup squad bears no resemblance to the parlous state of their country. Their squad, now scattered around the football world, is stylish, rich, poised and play football of huge quality while the country at political, economic and social level struggles hugely and their domestic football along with it, as the scouts from European countries gather to pick the bones of the rapidly depreciating local footballer.

The result is that while there are riots at home, the urbane Argentinean footballers have settled abroad with far more style than many of their fellow South Americans and their football has developed a style that is far removed from Brazil's violent displays.

Amazingly Argentina did not suffer a single red card throughout the entire 18 match programme during which time they lost just the one match, away to Brazil, and scored 42 goals, leaving them with the huge margin of a dozen points ahead of second-placed Ecuador.

Goals came from everywhere with Hernan Crespo of Lazio leading the way with nine in 12 games, followed by Roma's Gabriel Batistuta (5 games), Lazio's Claudio Lopez (16) and Manchester United's Juan Sebastian Veron (16) with five each, and three each from Marcelo Gallardo (6) of Monaco and River Plate's Ariel Ortega (16), the only regular in the team based in Argentina.

The strange thing is, however, that because the players are based abroad the home fans have not been quick to get behind them and that has not been helped by the fact that none of their preparations or pre-World Cup games were played on home soil.

They even complain that coach Marcelo Bielsa has adopted a hard running, hard working European style for his European-based players since taking over from the much loved Daniel Passarella.

That will not worry El Loco, called that because of his obsession to football, and privately he is happy for his players to develop and show their flair while playing within the 3-3-1-3 systems he adopts. The players also sought to capture their public's hearts when they played their final game in Argentina and carried banners and wore shirts proclaiming the importance of education.

But if that helped sway the hearts of their fans, victories in 2002 will win them over even quicker, particularly as they play in the so called 'Group of Death' along with the rapidly growing England, pride of Africa Nigeria and the ever solid Sweden who will knock over any team if they take them too lightly or have an off day.

They know that winning the World Cup – and they are amongst the favourites – will temporarily at least ease the pain of the apparent collapse of their country and bring a halt to the internal strife at least while everyone celebrates.

With friendly victories over Spain and Italy away from home in recent times coach Bielsa was quick to play down the favourites role, saying: "We haven't won anything yet and friendlies in Europe count for nothing compared with actual competition."

If Argentina do have a problem it is in their consistency and with such a strong opening group they are well aware that they will have to be at their very best from match one if they are to have a safe passage through to the knock out competition.

While they are out on their own in South American terms that will not be the case at the Worlds Cup finals and the pressure will be intense from day one.

ARGENTINA

But they are settled almost like a club side having used just 28 players in qualifying compared to Brazil's stunning 63 in the same number of games.

It is clear, however, that Manchester United's Juan Sebastian Veron is a crucial building block and his understudy Juan Roman Riquelme of Boca Juniors is clearly not ready to replace him.

Argentina also missed Crespo and Batistuta when they were absent in Brazil for their only defeat, although the two would not be played together in the narrow system that Bielsa prefers.

But whomever he picks from his adult, mature and much travelled squad, Argentina will start as one of the tournament favourites.

SQUAD

PABLO AIMAR (VALENCIA) BORN: 03.11.79 CAPS: 21 GLS: 2
Probably the best midfielder in the Argentine league in 2000, and certainly the most promising, he was signed in Jan 2001 from River Plate for around £14 million ($20m) on a 7-1/2 year contract, which emphasises his quality. Was Valencia's most expensive purchase – but last minute wranglings over sell-on fees took him to the 31 January deadline for UCL. Had four years in the River Plate first team – who won both the Opening and Closing Championships in 2000. First capped in 1999. Won World Youth Championships in Malaysia in 1997, scoring a great goal against England.

MATIAS ALMEYDA (PARMA) BORN: 22.12.73 CAPS: 34 GLS: 1
Played in all five games in the holding midfield position for Argentina in the 1998 World Cup finals, and continued with excellent seasons in 1998-2000 at Lazio. Now with Parma in the switchback of players between the clubs. He first made the national team for the 1998 World Cup qualifiers and has been first choice in a very competitive midfield since. His first club was River Plate where he spent five seasons winning championship medals in 1994 and 1995. Moved to Spain with Seville then to Italy. His first 12 caps were all in the 1998 World Cup qualifiers after being introduced in the first qualifier.

ROBERTO AYALA (VALENCIA) BORN: 14.04.73 CAPS: 79 GLS: 3
Has been with Valencia since the end of 2000, and played a key role in the 2001 European Cup final run. Capped by former coach Daniel Passarella pencilled into his national squad, having used him in his first game after the 1994 World Cup. Bielsa continued the theme. Was originally with River Plate, where he won a couple of championships while barely out of his teens under Passarella's coaching – he was signed by Parma in 1995, then loaned out to Napoli immediately. AC Milan then bid for him, but has had greater success with Valencia. Silver medal in Atlanta Olympics 1996.

ROBERTO BONANO (BARCELONA) BORN: 24.01.70 CAPS: 12 GLS: 0
Gained the first of his caps in the mid-90s. Moved to Barca in summer 2001 from River Plate for an undisclosed fee. Made the Rosario Central first team in 1994 and was with River Plate from 1996-2001.

ARGENTINA

GABRIEL BATISTUTA (ROMA) BORN: 01.02.69 CAPS: 75 GLS: 55

Argentina's best ever scorer, and first in their history to pass 50 international goals. Is the best modern scorer in Italy and his first season with Roma saw him win his first title in 2001. Hat-tricks at two World Cups 1994 and 1998 Was an integral part of Argentina's 1991 and 1993 South American Championship wins. Known as the 'Angel Gabriel' or 'Batigol'. Formerly with Newells Old Boys, River Plate & Boca Juniors, he came to Fiorentina in 1991 for a bargain £1.5 million and spent nine seasons with the club. Then came his £22 million move to Roma in summer 2000.

GERMAN BURGOS (ATLETICO MADRID) BORN: 16.04.69 CAPS: 36 GLS: 0

Moved from Mallorca to Atletico in summer 2001 after being with Mallorca for two seasons. Ten seasons in the Argentine top flight, with Ferrocarril Oeste (where Pumas play rugby) and then River Plate, where he won three seasonal titles.

CLAUDIO CANIGGIA (GLASGOW RANGERS) BORN: 09.01.67 CAPS: 57 GLS: 18

Has had a new lease of life since joining Dundee, the Scottish club in October 2000. After a fine start he was transferred to Rangers in summer 2001 for £900,000 and has played again for Argentina. He had been playing out his days with Boca Juniors before moving to Scotland. Played in the 1990 and 1994 World Cup finals (banned for 1990 final) and also played for Atalanta, Roma and Benfica in the mid-1990s, but was often ill-disciplined.

PABLO CAVALLERO (CELTA VIGO) BORN: 13.04.74 CAPS: 7 GLS: 0

Argentina's reserve keeper at the 1998 World Cup, he cost Celta £4 million from Espanyol in summer 2000 after one season with the Barcelona-based club in 1999-2000. Injured immediately on joining Celta (broken leg) in 2000 but now restored. At home he played for Velez Sarsfield, but was reserve to Jose Luis Chilavert, so moved in 1998 to Union Santa Fe where he made the national squad.

FABRICIO COLOCCINI (ALAVES) BORN: 22.01.82 CAPS: 0 GLS: 0

Arrived at Alaves in summer 2001 from AC Milan on loan, as part of package that took Javi Moreno and Cosmin Contra in the other direction. What is known is that he is of huge promise and was in the Argentina team that won the 2001 World Junior U20 Cup along with Barca's Saviola. Has been in the Milan youth set up. Played for San Lorenzo - Argentinian champs in 2001. Milan contract runs until 2005.

HERNAN CRESPO (LAZIO) BORN: 05.07.75 CAPS: 36 GLS: 17

Cost a fleeting world record £35 million in summer 2000 when moving to Lazio from Parma before Luis Figo topped it. Broke through in the Olympic silver medal team of 1996 and made fine progress. Critics (including Batistuta) said he was one of Passarella's favourites as he coached him at River Plate as a youngster from 1993. Won two championship medals with River Plate, and the Libertadores Cup in 1996 before coming to Europe – and won 1999 Italian Cup and UEFA Cup with Parma.

ARGENTINA

JULIO RICARDO CRUZ (BOLOGNA, ITALY) BORN:10.10.74 CAPS: 13 GLS: 2
Moved to Italy from Feyenoord in summer 2000 for around £8 million but found Italian defences less accommodating. Top scorer for Feyenoord for three seasons and played for Argentina in 1999 Copa America on recall to international duty – he had previously played in the 1997 Copa America finals. Signed from the Argentine champions River Plate in summer 1997 for US $7.5 million after 17 goals in 29 games in the Argentine league in 1996-7 for River Plate. Was first capped in 1997 but did not make squad for World Cup in France. Won Dutch title with Feyenoord in 1999.

MARCELO GALLARDO (MONACO, FRANCE) BORN: 18.01.76 CAPS: 39 GLS: 14
Joined Monaco in summer 1999 from River Plate for a club record £6.3 million. Played in three River Plate title wins until the 1998-9 domination by Boca Juniors of the domestic scene. Fine player, and voted the French Player of the Year in their 2000 title win, and continues to be outstanding in the French league. Played in '98 finals.

CHRISTIAN 'KILY' GONZALEZ (VALENCIA) BORN: 04.08.74 CAPS: 33 GLS: 4
Appeared in European Cup finals of 2000 and 2001. Joined Valencia in the summer of 1999 from Zaragoza for £2.2 million. A summer 1996 signing for Zaragoza as part of the deal that took Fernando Caceres back to Boca Juniors – Kily is a former Boca forward who was in the Argentine national squad from 1996-7. Blotted the proverbial copybook in his second game for Argentina by being sent off. Olympic finalist in '96.

ANDRES 'GULY' GUGLIELMINPIETRO (INTER MILAN) BORN: 14.04.74 CAPS: 6 GLS: 0
Switched clubs in summer 2001 from AC Milan to Inter Milan for around £6 million. Won first Argentina caps in 1999 on the back of the AC Milan Serie A title win and played at 1999 Copa America. The name on his back is Guly, which will please commentators! Signed by AC Milan from their Div 1 club Gimnasia in summer 1998, he represented a bit of a gamble as he cost £6 million, but has since proved to be well worth it. Has Italian origins so arrived as a Euro Community player.

CLAUDIO HUSAIN (NAPOLI) BORN: 20.11.74 CAPS: 14 GLS: 1
Been in national squads for seven seasons now. Stuck with Napoli in Serie B, after last season's relegation and should be used at the World Cup as cover in midfield.

CLAUDIO LOPEZ (LAZIO) BORN: 17.07.74 CAPS: 53 GLS: 10
Outstanding winger from Argentina's 1998 World Cup team – introduced by Daniel Passarella into the team for the World Cup qualifiers, he played 12 of the qualifiers, after gaining a silver medal at the Atlanta Olympics. Known as 'Piojo Lopez' (the flea), he was a summer 1996 purchase by Valencia from the Argentinian top club Racing Club for £2.6 million. He then switched to Lazio in summer 2000 for around £17 million. Outstanding in Valencia run to European Cup final in 2000. Spanish cup winner '99. Recently struggled with injuries.

ARGENTINA

GUSTAVO LOPEZ (CELTA VIGO) BORN: 13.04.73 CAPS: 30 GLS: 4
Joined Celta from Zaragoza in summer 1999 for around £4 million – played in the 1997
Copa America and now back in the side for the qualifying success and into the 2002
finals. He is from the famous Independiente club and joined Zaragoza for the final few
matches in early 1996. Capped while at Independiente from 1991-5, and in early days
with Zaragoza – but lost out to namesake Claudio Lopez of Valencia in national team,
before 1999 recall. Winger who had four improving seasons at Zaragoza after poor
start and is now settled.

ARIEL ORTEGA (RIVER PLATE) BORN: 04.03.74 CAPS: 80 GLS: 17
Is one of the few first choices from the domestic league, where he has now returned
after spells in Spain and Italy. Capped at 19 with River Plate, with whom he won two
titles, and moved for £5.5 million to Valencia in Jan 1997. Then moved in 1998 to
Sampdoria for £7.8 million and a year later moved to Parma for £9.5 million – but is
happier at home. Usually wears Maradona's No 10 shirt. Olympic finalist in '96.

DIEGO PLACENTE (BAYER LEVERKUSEN) BORN: 27.07.77 CAPS: 6 GLS: 0
Fine long-haired defender from the Argentine club River Plate, who joined Leverkusen
in midwinter 2000-1 for £3 million, and immediately impressed. From the team that
won the 1997 World Junior U20 Cup, but was then a forward. Followed the Maradona
path at home from Argentinos Juniors and had three seasons with River Plate before
coming to Europe.

MAURICIO POCCHETTINO (PARIS ST GERMAIN) BORN: 02.03.72 CAPS: 16 GLS: 3
Is the reserve to Walter Samuel, but does well in his own right. In sixth season at
Espanyol. Plays in France now after six seasons with Espanyol in Spain. Joined Espanyol
in the summer of 1994 from Newells Old Boys where he had spent some of 1993-4
playing alongside one Diego Armando Maradona. Has been in the national squad since
1999 and the Copa America – he was spotted in the brief spell by Bielsa, who coached
Espanyol for two months before being appointed national coach. First Division player
back home with Newells from 1987-94. Won Spanish Cup with Espanyol in 2000.

JUAN ROMAN RIQUELME (BOCA JUNIORS) BORN: 24.06.78 CAPS: 6 GLS: 0
Huge talent from the 1997 FIFA Junior World Cup winning side. Ran the show in the
Boca 1999 title wins in Opening and Closing championships and in subsequent seasons
including the 2000 Liberatores Cup wins. World club cup winner in 2000. First capped
aged 19. One of the hottest properties in the world. Linked with move to Barcelona.

WALTER SAMUEL (ROMA) BORN: 23.03.78 CAPS: 34 GLS: 3
Joined Roma in summer 2000 from Boca Juniors after winning the 2000
Libertadores Cup for around £15 million – and won title with Roma in first season.
Fine defender. Had three seasons with Boca. Introduced internationally against
Venezuela in the first game after France 98 – he is from the Argentine team that won
the 1997 FIFA World Junior Cup.

ARGENTINA

JAVIER SAVIOLA (BARCELONA) BORN: 11.12.81 CAPS: 3 GLS: 0
The world's most expensive teenager – he cost Barca £21.7 million (inc salary) from River Plate in the summer of 2001 – actual fee was £17.86 million. Set a competition record of 11 goals in the summer 2001 win in the FIFA World Junior U20 Cup hence the interest. Was also top scorer in the 2000-1 Argentinian championship with 20 goals and had scored 58 goals in 120 games for River as a teenager. Settled in well at Barcelona in first season.

NESTOR SENSINI (PARMA) BORN: 12.10.66 CAPS: 68 GLS: 0
Arrived at Lazio from Parma in the summer of 1999 for £2.8m to strengthen the defence but has now made the return journey. 13 seasons in Italy, and veteran of the 1990, 1994 and 1998 World Cup finals. He gained what might have been the last of his caps in the 1990 World Cup final, but the move to Parma brought him back into the frame, and he played in the World Cups in both the USA and France. He began his career with Newells Old Boys and was in their first team from 1986-9, before moving to Udinese for what proved to be four years, thence to Parma and Lazio. Been an international since 1986, but has not always been available because of club commitments. Olympic captain in '96. UEFA cup winner '95 and '99. Serie A winner in 2000.

DIEGO SIMEONE (LAZIO) BORN: 28.04.70 CAPS: 104 GLS: 11
Been in national team since 1988 and is the all time caps record holder and the first Argentine to 100 caps. Recovering from knee damage. Moved from Inter to Lazio in summer 1999 in the Vieri package for £5 million – Vieri was valued at £27.5 million in the deal which totalled £32.5 million. Arrived at Inter in summer 1997 from Atletico Madrid for £5.5 million, he is a regular member of the national set up and has been in the 1993 and 1995 Copa America wins, as well as playing in the 1994 and 1998 World Cups. Played in all five games at the 1998 World Cup – involved in the 'Beckham incident'. First made his name in Europe as Maradona's minder at Seville, he did all the great man's donkey work in the side while Maradona had his problems – then moved to Atletico in 1994 for £6 million. He was one of the stars of the 1996 League and Cup double win and after a few disciplinary problems caused mainly by frustration, he moved country to Italy.

JUAN PABLO SORIN (CRUZEIRO) BORN: 05.05.76 CAPS: 38 GLS: 6
Now plying his trade with one of Brazil's top clubs. Had a spell with Juventus as a teenager a few seasons ago, and has a clause he has yet to take up of a return – he was in the team that won the 1995 FIFA World Junior Cup. Originally with Argentinos Juniors, he went to Juve in 1995. First capped aged 20, now more of a first choice in the squad. Won World Cub Cup with Juventus in 1996 as a sub.

SANTIAGO SOLARI (REAL MADRID) BORN: 07.10.76 CAPS: 4 GLS: 0
Switched across the city of Madrid from Atletico when they suffered a shock relegation in 2000 and joined Real for £2.25 million. Created an excellent impression with River Plate, and won two seasonal titles with them before an 18 month stint at Atletico. Played well for Atletico in a sinking ship, and hardly missed a game, then won 2001 title with Real.

ARGENTINA

JUAN SEBASTIAN VERON (MAN UNITED) BORN: 09.03.75 CAPS: 49 GLS: 8
Joined Manchester United in summer 2001 from Lazio for British record £28.1 million.
Outstanding in 1998 World Cup finals. Was a summer 1999 arrival at Lazio from Parma
for £17.5 million – third club in three seasons after Sampdoria (who bought him for £2.6
million from Boca Juniors in 1996) and Parma (who paid £17 million to Samp). Son of
'La Buija' Veron, the winger who scored the winner in the 1968 World Club Cup final

NELSON VIVAS (INTER MILAN) BORN: 18.10.69 CAPS: 36 GLS: 1
Spent three years at Arsenal from 1998 to 2001. Now with Inter but was injured in
October 2001 and is doubtful for the finals. Formerly with Boca Juniors at home in
Argentina. Also played on loan for Lugano (Switzerland) and Celta Vigo (Spain). Played
in Passarella's first team after 1994 World Cup, after just a few earlier caps, and been
part of his squad all through, now still part of Bielsa's squad.

JAVIER ZANETTI (INTER MILAN) BORN: 11.04.73 CAPS: 70 GLS: 4
Summer 1995 signing by Inter from the Argentine first Division club, Banfield, he is the
current right wing-back in their national team, and was a key player in the 1998 World
Cup team. Scored against England in France '98. Cost Inter Milan £1.8 million, which
has turned out to be a bargain. Olympic finalist in '96. Won UEFA Cup in '98.

COACH

MANUEL BIELSA BORN: 21.07.55
Took the Espanyol job in Spain's Primera Liga in summer 1998 but was then wanted by
the Argentine national team just weeks later after Daniel Passarella resigned – the AFA
offered Miguel Angel Brindisi, former midfield star, to Espanyol as coach and Bielsa took
over the national job. Former central defender in the top league with Rosario Central.
Took up coaching aged 27. Former coach at Newells then with America and Atlas in
Mexico. Returned to help Velez to the 1998 Closing title, then to a brief stint with Espanyol.

WORLD CUP FACTS

Geoff Hurst of England is the only player to score a hat trick in the World
Cup Final, with his three against West Germany in 1966.

England came within an ace of being knocked out of the 1966 World Cup
when seven England players left their identity cards behind in the hotel.
Referee Istvan Zsolt from Hungary said no cards, no game and it took a
speeding police motor cyclist to save the day.

Thirty players have scored World Cup goals for England. David Beckham
was the latest addition on the list when when he curled in a free-kick
against Colombia in France 98.

ENGLAND

If England are to win the World Cup they might have to beat Argentina, France and Brazil along the way – and that's even before they get into the final. The euphoria that greeted England's astonishing 5-1 win over Germany in Munich in September last year has since been replaced by a sense of realism regarding England's chances in the finals. A tough first round draw grouped England with World Cup favourites Argentina, unpredictable Nigeria and tough-to-beat Sweden in the opening round. If England do come through that minefield but finish in second place they are likely to face France in the second round. If they overcome that obstacle, Brazil could be their next opponents in the quarter-finals.

The so-called 'Eriksson Effect' may well have galvanised England's qualifying campaign, but even Sven-Göran Eriksson's notable coaching talents will be stretched to the limits to guide England as far as the last four. Eriksson, of course, transformed England's qualifying campaign after he became the country's first foreign coach in January 2001. When he took over England were in some disarray. After losing their opening qualifier 1-0 to Germany in the last match played under Wembley's Twin Towers, coach Kevin Keegan resigned and that miserable defeat was compounded by a bleak 0-0 draw in Finland four days later under caretaker coach Howard Wilkinson. By the evening of October 11 2000, four days into the qualifying campaign, it seemed England's chances of reaching the finals had already gone.

The English FA, not always the most far-sighted organisation, decided that something drastic needed to be done – and in the face of fierce criticism from sections of the press and public alike, appointed Eriksson as boss the following January. He was an inspired choice. Five successive victories over Finland (2-1), Albania (3-1), Greece (2-0), Germany (5-1) and Albania again (2-0) saw England move from bottom to top of European Qualifying Group Nine in six heady months last year. Although automatic qualification was not ensured until almost the very last kick of the competition – David Beckham's equalising free-kick in the last minute of the last qualifier earning a 2-2 draw against Greece at Old Trafford in October – the job was done. Eriksson had steered England into the finals.

Eriksson has experimented widely in an attempt to find the right players to take to Asia, but really only has three world class players to build his team around – skipper Beckham, European Footballer of the Year Michael Owen, and Owen's Liverpool team mate Steven Gerrard.

The latter two are injury prone while Beckham is already a finals doubt after breaking a bone in his left foot. Owen, who scored a hat-trick in the 5-1 demolition of Germany, first announced himself to the world as an 18-year-old with his brilliant goal against Argentina in France '98. But he is often sidelined by hamstring problems and without him up front, England struggle for goals.

However, Eriksson does have a number of options including Owen's Liverpool team mate Emile Heskey and their former Liverpool colleague Robbie Fowler, now at Leeds United. However, neither of them have ever been consistent scorers for England and if Owen is out injured, the next likely source of goals is from midfield where Beckham and his Manchester United colleague Paul Scholes are a threat.

Beckham has blossomed for England as captain. His performance against Greece at

ENGLAND

Old Trafford was exceptional and he appears to have matured hugely since being sent off for a petulant kick at Diego Simeone of Argentina during the 1998 finals.

The English midfield appears to be one settled area of the team, but the defence gives cause for concern. David Seaman is still a fine goalkeeper, but at 38 he is reaching the veteran stage while in front of him centre-backs Rio Ferdinand and Sol Campbell have not appeared the most solid of defensive pairings when played together.

Although in one way the draw was hard on England, in another way it has proved really beneficial to Eriksson and his men. Even the more jingoistic members of the English press have realised that England face an enormously difficult draw – not just in the first round but throughout the tournament if they should progress. England will therefore set off for Asia with a rather more realistic sense of what might be achievable. Of course, England could win the World Cup for the first time since 1966, but the likelihood is that they will not. Without having that millstone of expectation around their necks, and with Eriksson's pragmatic approach obviously having an effect, England may be able to go to Japan and Korea in a far more relaxed frame of mind – play some decent football and come back ready to mount a realistic challenge for the 2004 European Championship. And of course... then go on to win the 2006 World Cup. England expects nothing less.

SQUAD

DARREN ANDERTON (TOTTENHAM) BORN: 03.03.72 CAPS: 30 GLS: 7
Made his international debut v Denmark in March 1994 – Terry Venables' first game in charge. Played in Euro '96 and France '98. Scored v Colombia in France '98. Joined Tottenham for £1.75 million in June 1992. Has had his injury problems since arriving at White Hart Lane. Was a Worthington Cup winner with Tottenham in 1999.

NICK BARMBY (LIVERPOOL) BORN: 11.02.74 CAPS: 23 GLS: 4
Scored the first goal of the Eriksson era, in the friendly win over Spain on February 28, 2001. Missed the final four internationals of the 2000-01 season with an ankle injury. Kevin Keegan recalled him to the national side after a near four-year absence, at the end of the 1999-2000 season and he won a place in the Euro 2000 squad. Scored the first goal of Hoddle's reign in the World Cup qualifying away win in Moldova (September 1996). Joined Liverpool from Everton for £6 million in July 2000.

DAVID BECKHAM (MANCHESTER UTD) BORN: 02.05.75 CAPS: 49 GLS: 6
England's inspirational captain. Faces a race against time to be fit for the finals after breaking a bone in his foot when playing for his club. First named skipper for a friendly v Italy in November 2000 under the management of Peter Taylor. Made his international debut in Glenn Hoddle's first game in charge, in September 1996. Scored in 1998 World Cup v Colombia. Didn't score again for England until in a WCQ v Finland in March 2001. Sent off for kicking out at Argentina's Diego Simeone in the 1998 World Cup second round game. Won his fifth Championship medal with Manchester Utd in 2000-01. Won Champions League in 1999.

ENGLAND

WAYNE BRIDGE (SOUTHAMPTON) BORN: 05.08.80 CAPS: 3 GLS: 0
Southampton-born left-back who made his England senior debut in friendly v Holland on February 13, 2002. Also started the friendly v Italy on March 27. Former England U-21 and youth international. Has hardly missed a game in the past two years. Was a Premiership ever-present in 2000-01.

WES BROWN (MANCHESTER UTD) BORN 13.10.79 CAPS: 4 GLS: 0
Given his England debut by Keegan, aged 19, when he started the friendly against Hungary in Budapest (April 1999). Later that summer he suffered a cruciate knee ligament injury, which kept him out for the whole of the 1999-2000 season. Won Championship honours with Man Utd for the second time in 2000-01. Was selected for the PFA's Premiership team of the year for 2000-01.

NICKY BUTT (MANCHESTER UTD) BORN: 21.01.75 CAPS: 18 GLS: 0
Made his international debut as a sub in friendly v Mexico at Wembley in March 1997. Played over 300 games for Manchester Utd winning his fifth Championship medal in 2000-01. Not always a regular starter at Man Utd – Keane, Scholes and Veron are often preferred. Played in 1999 Champions League final in place of the suspended Keane.

SOL CAMPBELL (ARSENAL) BORN 18.09.74 CAPS: 44 GLS: 0
Made his England debut as a sub in friendly v Hungary in May 1996. Was the most capped player under Hoddle – appeared in 22 of his 28 games in charge (21 starts, 1 as a sub). Former Tottenham captain who joined Arsenal on a Bosman free transfer in July 2001 after his contract at White Hart Lane had expired. Captained Tottenham to 1999 Worthington Cup honours.

JAMIE CARRAGHER (LIVERPOOL) BORN 28.01.78 CAPS: 8 GLS: 0
Made first international start against Holland in August 2001. He was the only England player to play the whole game. Started as the holding midfielder. Given his debut by Keegan as a sub in friendly against Hungary in Budapest, April 1999. England's most capped Under-21 international with 27 appearances. Played in all three of Liverpool's major cup final successes in 2000-01.

ASHLEY COLE (ARSENAL) BORN 20.12.80 CAPS: 7 GLS: 0
Broke into the England Under-21s at start of 2000-01 season, making a scoring debut against Georgia in August 2000. Capped four times at Under-21 level. Made his senior debut in WCQ v Albania in March 2001. Made Arsenal's left-back position his own in the second half of the 2000-01 season ahead of Brazilian international Silvinho.

JOE COLE (WEST HAM) BORN: 08.11.81 CAPS: 4 GLS: 0
Made his international debut as a sub in friendly v Mexico at Pride Park, Derby in May 2001. Has come up through the youth ranks at West Ham. Has played at every level for England. Was a member of West Ham's 1999 FA Youth Cup winning side. Has already played over 100 games for West Ham.

ENGLAND

KIERON DYER (NEWCASTLE) BORN: 29.12.78 CAPS: 9 GLS: 0
Made his international debut in a Euro 2000 qualifier v Luxembourg at Wembley in September 1999. Joined Newcastle from Ipswich for £6 million in July 1999. Has had his injury problems during the last two English seasons – shin splints, a stress fracture of the foot... etc. Ipswich-born midfielder – quick and elusive.

UGO EHIOGU (MIDDLESBROUGH) BORN: 03.11.72 CAPS: 4 GLS: 1
Made his England senior debut under Terry Venables in a Euro '96 warm-up game v China in Beijing in May 1996. Scored in Eriksson's first game in charge, v Spain in February 2001. Joined Middlesbrough from Aston Villa for £8 million in October 2000 after nine years at Villa Park. Began his career at West Brom. Has had his disciplinary problems since arriving at Middlesbrough (has been sent off a few times).

RIO FERDINAND (LEEDS UTD) BORN 07.11.78 CAPS: 20 GLS: 0
Has played under five different England head coaches since being given his senior debut by Hoddle against Cameroon at Wembley in November 1997. One of the six players to be cut from the final Euro 2000 squad. Officially named as Leeds' captain for the start of the 2001-02 season. Began his career at West Ham. Joined Leeds for £18 million in November 2000 – a world record fee for a defender.

ROBBIE FOWLER (LEEDS UTD) BORN: 09.04.75 CAPS: 24 GLS: 5
Made his international debut under Terry Venables as a sub v Bulgaria in March 1996. Joined Leeds from Liverpool for £11m in November 2001. Scored 171 goals in 330 games for Liverpool (120 in 236 in Premiership) since making his debut for them in September 1993. Captained Liverpool to success in all three of their major cup final wins in 2000-01. Scored 17 goals in 48 appearances in all competitions for Liverpool in 2000-01. Has scored over 100 Premiership goals.

STEVEN GERRARD (LIVERPOOL) BORN: 30.05.80 CAPS: 10 GLS: 1
Given debut by Kevin Keegan, against Ukraine at Wembley in May 2000. Has missed quite a lot of internationals since – mostly due to back and groin-related problems. Was voted The PFA Young Player of the Year for 2000-01. Played in all three of Liverpool's major cup final successes in 2000-01.

OWEN HARGREAVES (BAYERN MUNICH, GERMANY) BORN: 20.01.81 CAPS: 4 GLS: 0
Could have chosen to represent England, Canada, Wales, or even Germany (if he chose to become a naturalized citizen there). In the end he chose England. Made his senior England debut when he played the first half of the defeat against Holland in August 2001. Also came on as a sub v Germany in Munich in September 2001. Canadian born with an English father (Colin) and Welsh mother (Margaret). Emerged as a star during the latter stages of Bayern's Champions League success in 2000-01 with outstanding performances in the semi-final second leg against Valencia (when Effenberg was suspended) and then the final win over Valencia in the final (when Jeremies was injured). Also won Bundesliga title honours in 2000-01. Former England U-21

international. Made his England U-21 debut against Georgia in August 2000. Joined Bayern, aged 16, in July 1997 after a German youth team coach spotted him playing for his local Canadian club, Calgary Foothills.

EMILE HESKEY (LIVERPOOL) BORN: 11.01.78 CAPS: 22 GLS: 3
Given England senior debut by Keegan, as a sub against Hungary in Budapest (April 1999). Scored in Eriksson's first game in charge, against Spain on February 28, 2001. Scored his first international goals in a friendly against Malta in June 2000. Played in all three of Liverpool's cup final wins in 2000-01. Scored a career best 22 goals in 56 apps for Liverpool in 2000-01. Club's second top scorer behind Owen. Joined Liverpool from Leicester, his hometown club, for £11 million in March 2000. Won two League Cup winners' medals with Leicester.

DAVID JAMES (WEST HAM) BORN: 01.08.70 CAPS: 7 GLS: 0
Made his international debut in a friendly v Mexico at Wembley in March 1997. Joined West Ham from Aston Villa for £3.5m in the summer of 2001. Missed the start of 2001-02 after suffering a knee injury for England v Holland on August 15, 2001. Former England B, U-21 and youth international. Began his career at Watford. Previously played in Premiership for Liverpool (1992-99) and Aston Villa (1999-01). Now more reliable after suffering some calamities in the past.

MARTIN KEOWN (ARSENAL) BORN: 24.07.66 CAPS: 41 GLS: 2
Made his England senior debut under Graham Taylor in a friendly v France at Wembley in February 1992. Scored on his second cap, in a friendly v Czechoslovakia in Prague in March 1992. Now in his second spell at Arsenal. Was a member of the Gunners' League and FA Cup double winning side of 1997-98. Also played for Brighton, Aston Villa and Everton.

FRANK LAMPARD (CHELSEA) BORN: 20.06.78 CAPS: 5 GLS: 0
Made his senior England debut in friendly win against Belgium at the Stadium of Light in October 1999 (playing alongside his cousin Jamie Redknapp). Father Frank senior won two caps for England, eight years apart. Captained the England U-21s for two seasons (1998-2000). Scored nine goals in 19 apps at that level. Moved to Chelsea from West Ham for £11m in June 2001. Goalscoring midfielder.

STEVE MCMANAMAN (REAL MADRID, SPAIN) BORN: 11.02.72 CAPS: 37 GLS: 3
Made his international debut under Terry Venables in friendly v Nigeria in November 1994. Won Champions League honours with Real Madrid in 2000, scoring in their 3-0 final win over Valencia in Paris. Forced his way back into the first-team reckoning at Real Madrid after the club had wanted to sell him at the start of the 2000-01 season. Made 28 League apps (2 goals) to help Real Madrid win the Primera Liga title in 2000-01. Played for some eight seasons at Liverpool before joining Real Madrid on a free transfer in the summer of 1999.

ENGLAND

NIGEL MARTYN (LEEDS UTD) BORN: 11.08.66 CAPS: 21 GLS: 0
Stands 6ft 2in tall. Graham Taylor gave him his debut as a sub against the CIS in Moscow (April 1992). Played in the Euro 2000 defeat by Romania in Charleroi as an 11th hour replacement for Seaman, who had been injured in the pre-match warm-up. Saved a 79th minute penalty from Javi Moreno in England's win over Spain in February 2001. Spent the majority of his international career in the shadow of Seaman. Began career at Bristol Rovers. Moved to Crystal Palace, then joined Leeds for £2.25 million in July 1996.

DANNY MILLS (LEEDS UTD) BORN 18.05.77 CAPS: 5 GLS: 0
Made senior debut as a 67th minute sub in the friendly win over Mexico in May 2001. Had been a late call-up to the squad as cover for the injured Brown. Capped 14 times at Under-21 level. Made the right-back position his own at Elland Road in the second half of the 2000-01 season, keeping out Gary Kelly. Had had some disciplinary problems in 2001-02. Has been sent off twice for Leeds in 2001-02, v Arsenal and Newcastle. He was also given a two-match ban and a £7,500 fine for being found guilty of using foul and abusive language towards fourth official Andy D'Urso in the tunnel at Arsenal in August 2001, after being sent off. Previously with Norwich and Charlton. Joined Leeds for £4.37 million in July 1999.

DANNY MURPHY (LIVERPOOL) BORN: 18.03.77 CAPS: 3 GLS: 1
Made his senior international debut as a sub in friendly v Sweden in November 2001. Capped by England at U-21 (five caps), youth and schools level. Becomes another product of Dario Gradi's Crewe academy to be capped for England. Others include David Platt, Rob Jones, Geoff Thomas and Seth Johnson. Started the UEFA Cup final and FA Cup final for Liverpool in 2000-01. Made 47 apps (28 starts) for Liverpool in 2000-01, scoring ten goals. Joined Liverpool from Crewe in July 1997 (Roy Evans signing). Forced his way back into Gerard Houllier's plans during the 1999-2000 season, having looked certain to be sold in the summer of 1999.

GARY NEVILLE (MANCHESTER UTD) BORN 18.02.75 CAPS: 52 GLS: 0
Given England debut by Terry Venables, aged 20, against Japan in the Umbro Cup at Wembley, June 1995. Had made only 24 senior starts for Manchester Utd before his England debut. Played in Euro '96, France '98 and Euro 2000. Faces a race against time to make the finals after suffering an identical injury to Beckham.

PHILIP NEVILLE (MANCHESTER UTD) BORN: 21.01.77 CAPS: 37 GLS: 0
Given England debut by Terry Venables, aged 19, in friendly against China in Beijing (May 1996). The joint most capped player (same as Shearer) under Keegan. He appeared in 16 of Keegan's 18 internationals (11 starts, five as sub). Started all three games at left-back during Euro 2000. Was not selected for the France '98 squad. Conceded 89th minute penalty (for foul on Viorel Moldovan) against Romania in Charleroi, which sent England to a 3-2 defeat and eliminated them from Euro 2000. Won his fifth Championship medal with Man Utd in 2000-01.

ENGLAND

MICHAEL OWEN (LIVERPOOL) BORN: 14.12.79 CAPS: 34 GLS: 15

Became the youngest ever England scorer when he netted against Morocco in Casablanca (May 1998), aged 18 years and 164 days. England's youngest cap of the last century, aged 18 years, 59 days, when he made his debut against Chile at Wembley in February 1998. Played in Liverpool's FA Cup final (scored both goals v Arsenal) and UEFA Cup final wins in 2000-01. Sub not used in the Worthington Cup final. Was Liverpool's top scorer in 1997-98 (23 goals), 1998-99 (23 goals), 1999-00 (12 goals) and 2000-01 (24 goals). Voted European Footballer of the Year for 2001 – the first Englishman to win the award since Kevin Keegan in 1979. Has now scored over 100 goals for Liverpool.

DAVID SEAMAN (ARSENAL) BORN: 19.09.63 CAPS: 68 GLS: 0

The third most-capped goalkeeper in England's history. Only Peter Shilton (125) and Gordon Banks (73) have played more times in goal for England. Has played under seven England coaches since his senior international debut, under Bobby Robson, against Saudi Arabia in Riyadh (November 1988). Stands 6ft 4in tall. Has been at Arsenal since 1990. Has made more appearances than any other Arsenal goalkeeper. Member of Arsenal's 1997-98 League and FA Cup double-winning side. Played at Euro '96 (saved a McAllister penalty v Scotland), France '98 and Euro 2000.

PAUL SCHOLES (MANCHESTER UTD) BORN: 16.11.74 CAPS: 42 GLS: 13

Made his international debut v South Africa at Old Trafford in May 1997. Scored a hat-trick in Euro 2000 qualifier v Poland in March 1999 at Wembley – Kevin Keegan's first game in charge. Sent off against Sweden in Euro 2000 qualifier at Wembley (June 1999) becoming the only England player to be dismissed in a home international. Won fifth Championship medal with Manchester Utd in 2000-01. Suspended from the 1999 Champions League final. Scored twice on his Manchester Utd debut in League Cup 2nd round 1st leg v Port Vale in September 1994, and also scored v Ipswich in League three days later. Played in France '98 and Euro 2000. Scored v Tunisia in France '98.

TREVOR SINCLAIR (WEST HAM) BORN: 02.03.73 CAPS: 3 GLS: 0

Made his international debut in friendly v Sweden in November 2001 (started). Now at West Ham after a £2.3 million move from QPR in January 1998. Also played in the Premiership for QPR. Began his career at Blackpool. Is noted for having scored some spectacular goals.

TEDDY SHERINGHAM (TOTTENHAM) BORN: 02.04.66 CAPS: 45 GLS: 11

Made his international debut in a World Cup qualifier in Poland in May 1993. Scored his first international goal v Sweden at Elland Road in June 1995. Now back to Tottenham after rejoining them from Manchester Utd on a free transfer in the summer of 2001. Began his career at Millwall. Had just over a season at Nottingham Forest before joining Tottenham in 1992. Joined Manchester Utd in 1997 where he won three Premiership titles, one FA Cup and one European Cup, scoring in the final v Bayern Munich. Was

Manchester Utd's top scorer in 2000-01 with 21 goals. Has now scored over 100 goals for Tottenham, and has scored over 100 Premiership goals. Formed a formidable partnership with Alan Shearer at Euro '96. Also played at France '98.

GARETH SOUTHGATE (MIDDLESBROUGH) BORN: 03.09.70 CAPS: 47 GLS: 1
Made his international debut as a sub in friendly v Portugal in December 1995. Of course, he had that fateful penalty saved in the Euro '96 semi-final defeat by the Germans. Scored his first international goal away against Luxembourg in European Championship qualifier, October 1998. Joined Middlesbrough for £6 million from Aston Villa in July 2001 after six seasons at Villa Park. Renews his old defensive partnership with Ugo Ehiogu. Began his career at Crystal Palace, where he was their youngest ever captain.

DARIUS VASSELL (ASTON VILLA) BORN: 13.06.80 CAPS: 3 GLS: 2
Made a sensational England debut, scoring in friendly v Holland in Amsterdam on February 13, 2002. Birmingham-born striker who joined Aston Villa as a trainee in 1998. Until the 2001-02 season he had mainly been used as a substitute. Made a sensational impact for Villa against the Norwegians of Stromsgodset in the UEFA Cup 1st rnd, 1st leg at Villa Park on September 15, 1998. Came on as sub with Villa 2-0 down and scored in the 90th and 93rd minutes to inspire the club to a 3-2 win.

RICHARD WRIGHT (ARSENAL) BORN: 05.11.77 CAPS: 2 GLS: 0
Won first cap under Eriksson as a 48th minute sub for the injured James against Holland in August 2001. Made eventful senior debut, under Keegan, in friendly against Malta in Valletta, June 2000. Gave away two penalties, conceded an own goal from the first, and saved the second in the 89th minute. England won 2-1. Keegan chose him ahead of James for the No 3 keeper spot in Euro 2000 squad. Moved from Ipswich to Arsenal in a £6m transfer in July 2001. Told by Wenger that he would start the season as No 2 to Seaman.

COACH

SVEN-GÖRAN ERIKSSON BORN: 05.02.48
A Swede who was appointed England's first foreign head coach on January 11, 2001. He is the 13th different man to take charge of England, and he became the 6th manager/head coach in a five-year period after Venables, Hoddle, Wilkinson, Keegan and Peter Taylor. He has signed a five-year contract, with a two-year option, that will take him through to the 2006 World Cup finals. He guided Gothenburg to 1982 UEFA Cup and Lazio to 1999 Cup-Winners' Cup honours. He also took Benfica to the 1983 UEFA Cup final (lost to Anderlecht) and the 1990 European Cup final (lost to Milan) and Lazio to the 1998 UEFA Cup final (lost to Inter Milan). Won four League Championships in his coaching career, the Portuguese title with Benfica in 1983, 1984 and 1991, and the Italian title with Lazio in 2000. Won 4 Italian cups.

SWEDEN

Before Euro 2000 most pundits were agreed: Sweden wouldn't win the tournament but would be very hard to beat. The pundits were spot on. The problem for Sweden was that while they were hard to beat, they were definitely beatable and first round losses to Belgium and Italy, along with a goalless draw with Turkey meant an early flight home. This time around most pundits are agreed again: Sweden will not win the tournament but will be very hard to beat.

The Swedish side that lines up in their first match against England in Saitama on June 2 will be markedly different from the one that started the qualifying campaign in tepid style with a narrow 1-0 win over Azerbaijan in September 2000. Veterans like Roland Nilsson, Kennet Andersson, Joachim Bjorklund and Stefan Schwarz have all called time on their international careers since then, joint-management team of Tommy Soderberg and Lars Lagerbaeck grooming a younger-looking side with players like Everton's Tobias Linderoth and Aston Villa's Olof Mellberg now established in important midfield and defensive roles respectively.

Still, there is much of the Volvo in the Swedish team. In the same way the car is traditional, safe and predictably reliable, so too the boys in yellow and blue. Trade the old one in for another and the new version will be just like the one before – albeit with a few minor improvements here and there.

Sweden are probably now a better team than they were two years ago and improved as the qualifying competition progressed to finish unbeaten at the top of European Group Four with eight wins and two draws from their ten matches. In Arsenal midfielder Fredrik Ljungberg, Celtic striker Henrik Larsson and Barcelona defender Patrick Andersson – if he is fit – Sweden do have players of genuine world-class ability. But they are too regimented and predictable to really excite the senses and if Ljungberg has an off-day and Larsson is mis-firing in front of goal, Sweden's threat rapidly diminishes.

The main problem they will pose for England in Japan is that the English players hold absolutely no mystery for the Swedes, with possibly as many as seven of the squad playing in the Premiership or first division and at least two more based in Scotland – Johan Mjallby and Larsson who are both at Scottish champions Celtic. The teams drew 1-1 in a friendly at Old Trafford in November and Sweden have now gone ten matches unbeaten against England since their last defeat, at Wembley in 1968. England coach Sven-Göran Eriksson was impressed by his countrymen after the Old Trafford game. "Sweden's strength is that they are very disciplined and aggressive. They don't give you time to play or the space to play in. You can understand why they are in the World Cup," he said afterwards.

What they lack in artistry or flamboyance they more than make up for in team spirit – Sweden pulled out one of the best results in the entire European qualifying campaign in September last year when they scored twice in the last four minutes against Turkey in Istanbul to win 2-1 and clinch their place in the finals – while Soderberg and Lagerback complement each other well in their joint coaching capacity. If Sweden do survive the group stage they could face either defending champions France or Scandinavian rivals Denmark in the second round, but for now just negotiating their way out of the first round is the priority.

SQUAD

NICLAS ALEXANDERSSON (EVERTON) BORN: 29.12.71 CAPS: 57 GLS: 6
Moved to Everton in summer 2000 after previous club Sheffield Wednesday were relegated. First capped in the 1994 World Cup qualifiers, but did not make the final party for the USA. Played for Halmstad in the first Division from 1988 when aged 17 until 1996 and moved to the champions Goteborg for the 1996 season, when he collected a championship medal.

MARCUS ALLBACK (HEERENVEN) BORN: 05.07.73 CAPS: 17 GLS: 8
Swedish League top scorer in 1999 with 15 goals and second in 2000 (summer leagues) with 16 goals – that earned the ticket to Holland. Based at home with Orgryte, he returned after a brief spell in Serie A with Bari (16 games, no goals) and in Denmark with Lyngby. Father and uncle played for Orgryte, father is a director of club.

ANDREAS ANDERSSON (AIK STOCKHOLM) BORN: 10.04.74 CAPS: 31 GLS: 7
Returned to Sweden to join AIK in 1999 and play in the UCL, after an unhappy spell at both AC Milan and Newcastle – his English association being ruined by knee ligament damage. Made his international breakthrough with Goteborg's 1996 championship winning side – missed UCL for Goteborg as he had gone to AC Milan.

CHRISTOFFER ANDERSSON (HELSINGBORGS IF) BORN: 22.01.78 CAPS: 12 GLS: 0
Defender who has been in the squad for a year. Is in his fifth season with the club side. Was the left back in the club's 1999 championship success and earned first caps then. One of eight Anderssons in the Swedish league.

DANIEL ANDERSSON (VENEZIA) BORN: 28.08.77 CAPS: 37 GLS: 0
Brother of Patrik Andersson, the central defender, and father Roy won 20 caps from 1974-8. Joined Bari in summer 1998 from Malmo – he moved for £2.5 million with Yskel Osmanovski. Switched clubs in summer 2001 to Venezia, after Bari's relegation, the cost was £4 million. Had three excellent seasons in Serie A with Bari in a poor team. Was in the Malmo first team for three seasons and made debut at the age of 18. Came through the U21 system with current national coach Soderberg.

PATRIK ANDERSSON (BARCELONA) BORN: 18.08.71 CAPS: 94 GLS: 3
Joined Barcelona in summer 2001 for £5 million from Bayern Munich. Won European Cup with Bayern in 2001 in an increasingly influential role following the departure of Lother Matthaus. Also won 2001 Bundesliga title, and 2000 Bundesliga and Cup. Younger brother Daniel is also in the squad – and father Roy gained 20 caps from 1974-78. Joined Bayern from relegated Borussia Monchengladbach following their relegation – earlier in his career he was with Malmo before moving to Blackburn. He moved from Blackburn to BMG in 1993-4 season and has rapidly become an integral part of their team. Made international debut aged 21 in 1992. Took over the captaincy from Jonas Thern in 1997.

SWEDEN

KARL CORNELIUSSON (AIK STOCKHOLM) BORN: 17.11.76 CAPS: 6 GLS: 1
Home based defender who has been with AIK for three seasons. Originally with Orgryte from 1994 to 1999. Right back with nine years service in the Premier Division. In national squad for past three seasons, previously a junior and U21 international.

ERIK EDMAN (HEERENVEEN) BORN: 11.11.78 CAPS: 4 GLS: 0
In his first season in the Dutch league, he was with Helsingborgs from 1997-1999 and AIK in 2000 and 2001 for some 90 Swedish games. Had unsuccessful spell in 1999-2000 winter season with Torino and Karlsruhe. Defender, who is nominally the left back, and gained first cap in Jan 2000 v Faroes in a friendly.

MAGNUS HEDMAN (COVENTRY CITY) BORN: 19.03.73 CAPS: 43 GLS: 0
The Beckham of Sweden - his wife has had three No 1 hits in the pop charts. Is certainly looking like the best of the recent crop of keepers since Thomas Ravelli (142 caps) – has played in most recent games when available from Coventry and with increasing confidence. Club were relegated in summer 2001 from the Premiership for the first time since 1967. Left AIK in summer 1997 and joined up with fellow Swede Roland Nilsson at Coventry – his fee was £600,000. Came into the national squad in 1996 when Bengt Andersson found it difficult to get a first team game at Tenerife – former trainer Svensson only picked top flight players. Joined AIK in 1990, progressing into the first team in 1993.

ZLATAN IBRAHIMOVIC (AJAX) BORN: 03.10.81 CAPS: 8 GLS: 1
Signed by Ajax in spring 2001 for a then Swedish record £5 million from Swedish Div 2 club Malmo (found themselves relegated) after Juventus, AC Milan, Arsenal and Monaco had shown interest. Is Swedish but of Bosnian parentage – first capped in March 2001 in friendly v Swiss and is current U21 international. Twelve goals in Malmo's 2000 promotion to Premier League. Big and powerful. Reputedly paid £550,000 a year.

ANDREAS ISAKSSON (DJURGAARDENS) BORN: 03.10.81 CAPS: 1 GLS: 0
Could well take the No 3 place from Mattias Asper of Besiktas. First cap as sub against Switzerland in March 2002. National U21 keeper and best prospect in his position in the land.

ANDREAS JAKOBSSON (HANSA ROSTOCK) BORN: 06.10.72 CAPS: 12 GLS: 0
Back up to the Andersson-Bjorklund pairing in defence. Joined Rostock in summer 2000 for £800,000 from Helsingborgs where he had been the key defender in their 1999 title win. Had six seasons at Helsingborgs, and originally from former D1 side Landskrona.

MATTIAS JONSSON (BRONDBY) BORN: 16.01.74 CAPS: 23 GLS: 2
Plies his trade in neighbouring Denmark. Former Helsingborgs midfielder from their 1999 championship winning side. Moved to Brondby before last season's UCL. Won first caps in 1995 when with former club Orebro, then swopped to Helsingborgs in 1996. Also played in 1998 World Cup qualifiers.

SWEDEN

PONTUS KAAMARK (IFK GOTEBORG) BORN: 05.04.69 CAPS: 57 GLS: 0
Recalled recently for his first cap since April 2000 – he had to drop out of Euro 2000
contention with serious knee ligament damage. Now back with his first club after coming
back to Sweden with AIK and the UCL in 1999. Returned in summer 1999 to Sweden
after several seasons with Leicester City in the Premiership. He was happy at the club but
felt that he was missing his kids growing up – they were at school in Sweden. Former
captain of champions IFK Goteborg with whom he won five titles in six seasons – he was
there from 1989-95 before going to Leicester for four seasons (1995-99).

MAGNUS KIHLSTEDT (FC COPENHAGEN, DENMARK) BORN: 29.02.72 CAPS: 12 GLS: 0
Now plays for the 2001 Danish champions after a move from Brann Bergen of the
Norwegian league. Never played for Sweden at any level until full cap – he was first
capped v USA in Jan 1998 in Soderberg's first match in charge. Had been playing in the
Norwegian league for Lillestrom in 1997 and 1998 in a position that was vacated by
Frode Grodas, then moved in 1999 to Brann. Swedish club was Oddevold, in Division 2.

MARCUS LANTZ (HANSA ROSTOCK, GERMANY) BORN: 23.10.75 CAPS: 4 GLS: 0
Joined Rostock for £750,000 in Jan 2000 from Serie A club Torino, where he failed to
settle. Joined Torino in summer 1999 from Helsingborgs for £2 million. Had four seasons
with Helsingborg – and played the first half of the 1999 championship winning season
for them, also twice previously when they were runners up. Close to Sweden's 22 for Euro
2000 but did not make final squad. Has a chance to make amends this summer.

HENRIK LARSSON (CELTIC) BORN: 20.09.71 CAPS: 66 GLS: 21
Retained title with Celtic in 2002. Won Celtic's Player of the Year, and Scottish Footballer
of the Year, after an extraordinary 54 goals in all competitions in the 2000-1 treble success.
Scored 38 goals in 1998-1999, and in 1999-2000 he recovered from a terribly broken leg
to score 12 goals in 13 games that season. Signed new four-year contract with Celtic in
April 1999. Also member of Celtic's 1998 championship winning team – signing in July
1997 from Feyenoord. Made his name as club top scorer for Helsingborg in 1993 with 15
goals before moving to Feyenoord. Formerly a Swedish Ruud Gullit, his mother is from the
Cape Verde Islands off the West African coast.

TOBIAS LINDEROTH (EVERTON) BORN: 21.04.79 CAPS: 18 GLS: 1
Joined Everton from Norwegian club Stabaek for £2.5 million in January 2002. Midfielder,
who gets his caps now as first choice down the left flank. Recent U21 international, he
had been with Stabaek since 1999, after joining them from Elfsborg in the Swedish league.

FREDRIK LJUNGBERG (ARSENAL) BORN: 16.04.77 CAPS: 31 GLS: 2
Signed new contract at Arsenal until 2006 having joined the club for £3 million in Sept
1998. Sweden see him as a successor to Thomas Brolin. Chosen for Soderberg's first
game in charge in Jan 1998 v USA – off the back of some superb performances for
Halmstad, with whom he won the 1997 Championship. Scored the first goal of
Soderberg's reign (v Denmark).

SWEDEN

TEDDY LUCIC (AIK STOCKHOLM) BORN: 15.04.73 CAPS: 40 GLS: 0
Utility player who can play either full back, central defence or midfield. Moved from IFK Goteborg in midwinter 1998-9 to Bologna, where he played eight games in second half of Serie A season. Was rumoured to be on way to Spanish club Zaragoza – but returned to help AIK. Was stand-in for Jan Eriksson in the 1994 World Cup squad though he didn't play and wasn't then capped. Played at Euro 2000. Resurfaced again in the squad for the 1995 Umbro Cup tournament in June in England, and this time gained his first caps. Swedish mother and Croatian father.

OLOF MELLBERG (ASTON VILLA) BORN: 03.09.73 CAPS: 21 GLS: 0
This is an improving player – he joined Villa in summer 2001 from Racing Santander in Spain for £6 million to replace Gareth Southgate. Spent three seasons with Racing in the Primera Liga until their relegation in summer 2001. Arrived at Racing from AIK Solna as an U21 international after two seasons in the AIK first team winning the championship in 1998 before he left. International debut in Feb 2000 v Italy. Cover central defender as well as first choice full back.

HAKAN MILD (WIMBLEDON) BORN: 14.05.71 CAPS: 69 GLS: 8
Moved to the Dons in autumn 2001 from Goteborg, whom he has played for in three spells. Also played in Spain for Real Sociedad. Won championship medals with Goteborg in 1990, 1991, and bit parts in 1993 and 1996. Good ball winner and member of the 1994 World Cup squad. Scored twice v England at 1995 Umbro Cup.

JOHANN MJALLBY (CELTIC) BORN: 09.02.71 CAPS: 69 GLS: 8
Now with Celtic after Liverpool took an interest – cost £1.5 million in Nov 98 after AIK's 1998 title win and a goal v England in start of Euro 2000 qualifiers. Part of Celtic's 2001 and 2002 Scottish title wins. Was at AIK for 14 years from school, missed AIK's 1992 championship win through injury – did not play a match – but was a key player when Tommy Soderberg was the coach at AIK.

YSKEL OSMANOVSKI (TORINO) BORN: 24.02.77 CAPS: 14 GLS: 2
Was at Bordeaux on loan from Torino for 2002. Moved from relegated Bari in summer 2001 for around £3 million to promoted Torino – but still finds goals difficult in Serie A. Scored both goals in 2-1 win v Jamaica back in '99 and caused his coach problems as he was only a stand-in for Kennet Andersson who was playing for Bologna. Arrived at Bari with Daniel Andersson from Malmo – each cost £2.5 million in summer 1998. Swedish-born despite the name – he was first tried out after the Swedes failed to qualify for France '98 under their then new coach Tommy Soderberg.

KLEBER SAARENPAA (AALBORG) BORN: 14.12.75 CAPS: 12 GLS: 0
Recently moved to Denmark from Norrkoping. Defender who formed a useful partnership with Patrick Andersson in the qualifiers. Has had recent injuries but now back to full fitness.

SWEDEN

STEFAN SELAKOVIC (HERENVEEN) BORN: 09.01.77 CAPS: 7 GLS: 3
Key forward in the 2000 championship success of Halmstad – club top scorer. Then
moved to Holland. Played all his football in Sweden – joined Halmstad from a junior club
in 1996. Is of Bosnian origin, born in Bosnia. Has new contract with club to fend off
Premiership bids.

FREDRIK SODERSTROM (FC PORTO) BORN: 30.01.73 CAPS: 5 GLS: 0
Played in the UCL in 2001-2 in Celtic's group. Spent five seasons with Guimaraes and
appears to have spent most of his playing days with Portuguese teams – was with
Sporting Braga from 1993-6, and then Vitoria. Now been with FC Porto since 2001.
Capped by Sweden as recently as August 2001 v S Africa.

ANDERS SVENSSON (SOUTHAMPTON) BORN: 17.07.76 CAPS: 24 GLS: 6
Scored two crucial winners in the World Cup qualifiers. Joined Saints in summer 2001
from Elfsborg for £800,000 – with Sunderland, Fiorentina, Monaco, Celtic and Benfica
all in contention. Spent eight seasons with Elfsborg, and success at last with the 2001
Swedish Cup win.

MAGNUS SVENSSON (BRONDBY) BORN: 10.3.69 CAPS: 25 GLS: 2
Quietly efficient – known as 'Turbo' which explains his style. Played four seasons for
Halmstad in the Swedish league from 1994-7 then went abroad. Spent 1998 and 1999
with Viking Stavanger in Norway, then moved in winter 2000 to the Danish club Brondby.

MICHAEL SVENSSON (TROYES) BORN: 25.11.75 CAPS: 11 GLS: 0
Moved in August 2001 from Halmstad, the 2000 champions, to Troyes in France, and
played in UEFA Cup v Leeds. Five seasons in the Halmstad team, joined from a junior
club. Was the best defender in Swedish football, club gave him a new contract to stop
him going to French club Troyes, but they failed to get to the UCL, so off he went.

COACHES

TOMMY SODERBERG BORN: 19.08.48
PE teacher who played only junior football – took up coaching via the schools system.
Was in charge of four junior teams from 1972-86. Took charge of the two Stockholm
Premier Division clubs Djurgaarden (1986-90) and AIK (1991-3), and took AIK to the
1992 championship. In 1994 he moved to the national U21 job, and took over from
Tommy Svensson in the senior role in October 1997.

LARS LAGERBACK BORN: 16.07.48
Former national assistant to Soderberg, now moved into a co-role as coach, and seems
to be working given the results. Like Soderberg, he was a junior player and from 1977-
90 was a coach in the junior leagues. Was appointed to the Sweden boys and youth
coaching post in 1990, and in 1996 moved to the B team post. From 1998-99 he was
assistant coach to Soderberg, and has been co-national coach since 2000.

NIGERIA

If you want an idea of the problems which face Nigerian football going into this World Cup then look no further than the list of names printed below. We have selected 30 players who we hope will have some involvement in the World Cup, but have done so with little confidence, because after the recent team selections of the new coach Festus Onigbinde anything could happen. With a handful of friendlies to go until he names his 23, Onigbinde has thrown in youngsters from the Nigerian League, and pointedly left out more established stars such as Oliseh and Finidi.

After a lacklustre Nations Cup display something clearly needed to be done, but it's far too late to make wholesale changes, and whether he likes their attitude or not, Onigbinde surely should rely on the likes of Okocha, Kanu and West. There may be places for a couple of youngsters, and Finidi's recent performances for Ipswich haven't exactly merited inclusion, but a team of tyros would be torn apart in the Group Of Death.

The disarray could yet work in Nigeria's favour. They have gone into the two previous World Cups with a reputation, yet have imploded and failed to progress beyond the last 16. Although it's very hard to see at the moment, maybe the monumental lack of expectation will work in their favour, and the likes of Okocha will take responsibility and take Nigeria somewhere. It's a long shot, but it's just about all that the Super Eagles can hope for.

SQUAD

RABIU AFOLABI (STANDARD LIEGE) BORN: 18/4/80 CAPS: 5 GLS: 0
Left out of the Nations Cup squad despite his excellent form in Belgium.

VICTOR AGALI (SCHALKE 04) BORN: 29/12/78 CAPS: 9 GLS: 6
Made his debut last January, but wasted no time in scoring five times and ensuring a starting place. Series of lukewarm performances in Mali mean that his stock has fallen somewhat.

JULIUS AGAHOWA (SHAKHTAR DONETSK) BORN: 12/12/82 CAPS: 10 GLS: 6
The super sub of the 2000 Nations Cup looked much more the finished article in Mali, but even his pace (he does the 100 metres in 10.3 seconds) couldn't save Nigeria. Watch about for his acrobatic goal celebrations. They could provide some of the images of the World Cup. Says that he would like to move to the Premiership. This summer provides him with a window of opportunity.

MURPHY AKANJI (SLIEMA WANDERERS) BORN: 1/12/77 CAPS: 6 GLS: 0
Was rumoured to be on his way to trials with Chievo in Italy after excellent performances in Malta. Has made only one competitive appearance for Nigeria after coming to prominence in Julius Bergers League win in 2000.

BENEDICT AKWUEGBU (GRAZER AK) BORN: 3/11/74 CAPS: 13 GLS: 5
Missed out on a trip to Mali, is one of many fringe players with a chance of making it this summer.

NIGERIA

YAKUBU AYEGBENI (MACCABI HAIFA) BORN: 22/11/82 CAPS: 7 GLS: 3
Started out with Julius Berger and came into the national side as the World Cup qualifiers got underway. Scored two important goals against Sudan.

TIJANI BABANGIDA (VITESSE ARNHEM) BORN: 25/9/73 CAPS: 33 GLS: 5
Olympic Gold medallist in '96, but things haven't gone right for him since leaving Ajax for Turkey. Now back in Holland and may yet be a threat in the summer. Played in WC '98. Scored vs Denmark. Began career with Roda JC. Dutch champion with Ajax in '98.

CELESTINE BABAYARO (CHELSEA) BORN: 29/8/78 CAPS: 23 GLS: 0
If his mind is focused on football rather than the endless disputes he seems to be involved in with the Nigerian FA, will be a crucially experienced member of the squad. Became Chelsea's most expensive teenager when he moved from Anderlecht. Under pressure for his place at left back from Udeze, although there's every chance that they'll both be accommodated. Knows what it's like to win a major tournament with Nigeria after his Olympic gold in Atlanta. Won CWC with Chelsea in '98 and FA Cup in 2000.

ADEMOLA BANKOLE (CREWE ALEXANDRA) BORN: 9/09/69 CAPS: 5 GLS: 0
Started his English career at Crewe before having a spell at QPR and then a loan period at the then Premiership club Bradford. Is now back as the number one at Crewe, where he has just suffered relegation to the Second Division. Nicknamed George by the supporters. Was previously called up by his country in 98, but was dropped from the pre tournament squad after conceding 4 goals in a warm up game against Grasshoppers Zurich.

JUSTICE CHRISTOPHER (ROYAL ANTWERP) BORN: 24/12/81 CAPS: 4 GLS: 0
Made debut in the qualifier against Liberia, and has been subject of interest by Manchester City. Manchester United would have first call on him, though, as he plays for the Red Devils Belgian feeder club.

NDUBUISI EGBO (AL MASRY) BORN: 25/7/73 CAPS: 8 GLS: 0
Was briefly number one after Shorunmuäs injury a couple of years ago, but has been too inconsistent to hold onto top spot. Played in the World Cup qualifier against Liberia and his mistakes then cost him his first team place.

ERIC EJIOFOR (MACCABI HAIFA) BORN: 21/7/79 CAPS: 9 GLS: 0
Helped the 'People's Elephants' of Enzimba to their 2001 League win in Nigeria. A recent arrival in Israel and definitely a back up player in the national squad.

FINIDI GEORGE (IPSWICH TOWN) BORN: 15/4/71 CAPS: 56 GLS: 6
The longest serving player with the national squad, who was first capped 11 years ago. Has now played in two World Cups ('94 and '98) and won the European Cup with Ajax and World Club cup. Had spells with Betis and Mallorca before his move to England.

NIGERIA

LUCKY IDAHOR (DYNAMO KIEV) BORN: 30/08/80 CAPS: 8 GLS: 0
Was wanted by Spartak Moscow but eventually decided to sign for the Ukrainian side.
Scored the goal which qualified Kiev for the Group Stage of the Champions League.

EMEKA IFEJIAGWA (WOLFSBURG) BORN: 30/10/77 CAPS: 11 GLS: 0
Injury has both cost him his place in the last two Nations Cups, and halted his development
as one of the defensive stars of the future. Has been on loan at Wolfsburg after his move
to Osasuna in La Liga failed to work out. Had brief spells at Charlton and Brighton in '98.

PIUS IKEDIA (AJAX) BORN: 11/07/80 CAPS: 22 GLS: 4
The star of the 1999 World Youth Cup. Was awarded the silver ball for the second best player
in the tournament. Formerly with ASEC Mimosas in Nigeria. Played at the 2000 Olympics.

VICTOR IKPEBA (REAL BETIS) BORN: 12/6/73 CAPS: 30 GLS: 7
Has played for Nigeria for ten years now, but after becoming African Player of the Year
has always seemed to struggle for consistency. Had a bad time on and off the field with
Borussia Dortmund, and missed the penalty that should have stood in the infamous
Nations Cup final shootout against Cameroon in 2000. French champion in '97 with
Monaco. Played in USA '94 and France '98 (scored vs Bulgaria).

BLESSING KAKU (GENK) BORN: 5/03/78 CAPS: GLS:
Formerly at Harelbeke where he was very highly rated. Can play as a central defender,
but more comfortable in a holding midfield role.

CHRISTOPHER KANU (ALAVES) BORN: CAPS: 0 GLS: 0
After failing to match his brother's success at Ajax, Christopher has been on a season
long loan at Alaves in La Liga.

NWANKWO KANU (ARSENAL) BORN: 1/8/76 CAPS: 27 GLS:6
Twice African Footballer of the Year, European Cup winner with Ajax , and Olympic gold
medallist. It's a miracle that he is still playing after overcoming a heart condition.
Important squad member at Arsenal. Won UEFA cup with Inter in '98.

GARBA LAWAL (RODA) BORN: 22/5/74 CAPS: 27 GLS: 3
Always seems to appear as Nigeria's classy looking substitute without ever doing quite
enough to earn a starting place. Started as Julius Berger in Nigeria before going to
Esperance of Tunisia. Roda beat off considerable competition to sign him six years ago.
Lawal comes from the same northern Nigerian town as Babangida and Babayaro.

PASCAL OJIGWE (BAYER LEVERKUSEN) BORN: 11/12/76 CAPS: 15 GLS: 1
Has played in the Bundesliga for Cologne and Kaiserslautern after starting his career at
Enyimba. Left both his previous Bundesliga clubs under a cloud, but Leverkusen paid
over a million pounds to sign him at the start of the season. Like Lawal, he is a defensive
midfielder who allows the likes of Okocha to concentrate on flair.

NIGERIA

BARTHOLOMEW OGBECHE (PSG) BORN: 10/01/84
This incredible youngster's childhood hero was Jay Jay Okocha and he says playing his international debut against Paraguay alongside him fulfilled one of his childhood dreams. Another was to play in the World Cup and a great first season with PSG, where he has replaced Nicolas Anelka, has given him every chance of inclusion.

JAY JAY OKOCHA (PSG) BORN: 14/8/73 CAPS: 51 GLS: 12
Clearly Nigeria's most talented player, and up with the best in the world on his day. PSG paid nearly £15million for him from Fenerbahce, and he has been too inconsistent to justify the fee. Has provided some great moments though, notably his equalising goal in the 2000 Nations Cup final. Missed a penalty in PSG's UEFA Cup defeat by Rangers. Described by none other than Michel Platini as "world class". Has played in two previous World Cups.

ISAAC OKORONKWO (SHAKHTAR DONETSK) BORN: 1/5/78 CAPS: 5 GLS: 0
Great prospect but looked occasionally shaky in Mali. Was discovered playing for Sherif Tiraspol in the Moldovan League and moved to the Ukraine. Has developed something of a penchant for own goals in recent seasons, including two for his country and one for his club in a Champions league game this season.

SUNDAY OLISEH (BORUSSIA DORTMUND) BORN: 14/9/74 CAPS: 50 GLS: 7
Was left out of the initial squad of 54 named by the new coach Onigbinde although it would be a major surprise if the former captain was left out of the final squad. Still best known for scoring a wonder goal against Spain in '98. Previously with Ajax.

WILSON ORUMA (SERVETTE) BORN: 30/12/76 CAPS: 8 GLS: 2
Was a last minute replacement in Mali after showing excellent form in Switzerland. Was captain of the national Under 17 team which won gold at the World Championships in 93. Spent four years at Lens, and a season on loan at Second Divison Nimes before his move to Switzerland. Scored four goals in this season,s Swiss league. Missed the extra time penalty in the Nations Cup semi final against Senegal. Scored the last minute goal when Servette put Real Zaragoza out of this season's UEFA Cup. Very strong, and could be the first choice as ball winning midfielder.

IKE SHORUNMU (NO CLUB) BORN: 16/10/67
Missed the last World Cup with a broken arm. A dispute with Besiktas over unpaid wages and international commitments has left him clubless. Has been told that he must find a club to guarantee him a World Cup place. Was in goal for Besiktas when they lost 6-0 to Leeds in the Champions League.

EFE SODJE (CREWE ALEXANDRA) BORN: 5/10/72
Renowned for wearing a bandanna whenver he plays, he started his English career by helping Macclesfield to promotion from the Conference. Also played at Luton and

Colchester, he has made a late run for the World Cup squad after some outstanding performances in the relegated team.

IFEANYI UDEZE (PAOK SALONIKA) BORN: 21/7/80
Lightning fast left back who is set to be a regular in the World Cup. Sent off in the semi-final Nations Cup defeat by Senegal. Was initially called to a training session by the former coach Jo Bonfrere after he was sent a video of Udeze playing in Greece.

TARIBO WEST (KAISERSLAUTERN) BORN: 26/3/74
Played in France '98 but has since become more famous for his passionate religious beliefs than his defending ability. Had an excellent loan spell at Derby last season, learned his trade in the Auxerre double winning side of '96, under Guy Roux. Has played for both Milan clubs, and was sent off in the '98 UEFA Cup Final while playing for Inter. Currently no club. Sacked in April after missing a match to attend a Buddhist Mass.

JOSEPH YOBO (MARSEILLE) BORN: 6/9/80
Has been one of the shining lights for Marseille during their troubled last couple of seasons. Played for Standard Liege in Belgium before moving to France. Formerly a striker in the national youth team and gets forward very stylishly from right back.

COACH

FESTUS ADEGBOYE ONIGBINDE
64-year-old retired schoolteacher who took over in February after the sacking of Amodu Shaibu. He has already attracted strong criticism from big names in Nigerian football. Steven Keshi, who was Onigbinde's captain during his previous spell in charge in 1983-84, says the coach does not have the ability to adapt his tactical ideas to the modern game. Onigbinde has already given debuts to several young players from the Nigerian League, some of whom seemed hopelessly out of their depth. Doesn't seem to have any idea of his best XI. Says that he'll step down after the tournament.

WORLD CUP FACTS

England's Captain Marvel Bryan Robson scored the fastest goal in the World Cup finals when he netted against France in 1982 in Spain in just 27 seconds although the Czechs claim that Vaclav Masek's goal against Mexico in 1962 in Chile was faster, timed on film at just 15 seconds.

Brazil hold the longest unbeaten run in the World Cup between 1958 and 1966 when they won 11 and drew two games before crashing 3-1 to Hungary at Goodison Park in England.

GROUP G

The manner in which Italy qualified has brought a weight of expectation upon the shoulders of the Azurri. Italian club football may be struggling, but at international level, Italy expects. They exited the 1998 finals after holding the hosts and eventual winners France to a goalless quarter-final draw only to lose, once more, on penalties.

To reach Japan and South Korea, Italy won their qualifying group at a canter, winning six and drawing two of their eight games, while conceding only three goals. They also maintained a steady squad and expectations are high.

Hopes, too, are high that Roma captain Francesco Totti can achieve his potential; at the age of 25, he has emerged as the key play in coach Giovanni Trapattoni's attack alongside Filippo Inzaghi, who scored seven of Italy's 18 qualifying goals.

In Ecuador, Italy face something of an unknown quantity. But, having finished ahead of Brazil in the qualifying programme thanks to a 1-0 home win over the former World Champions, they announced their intentions.

Coach Hernan Dario Gomez, a Colombian, former assistant of Matunama, will probably consider facing Italy a doddle after what he has experienced. A year ago, the 44-year-old was sitting in a restaurant in the city of Guayaquil when he was shot in the leg and beaten with the butt of a gun, breaking his nose. The attack was said to be revenge for a former president of Ecuador whose son had been dropped from the under-20 team.

Gomez made a full recovery, but went home to Colombia, vowing never to return. The people of Ecuador demanded otherwise, a song was written in his honour, there were public demonstrations, and eventually Gomez decided to complete the job, helping Ecuador to their first ever appearance in the finals. Gomez, though, is no stranger to the World Cup finals, making his fourth consecutive appearance. In 1990 and 1994, Gomez was an assistant coach with Colombia and in the 1998 World Cup in France, was his nation's head coach.

Croatia must not be underestimated after claiming third place in 1998 in their first ever World Cup finals. They even took the lead against eventual winners France in the semi-final before they succumbed to two goals from Lillian Thuram. Beating Holland for third place was a reasonable consolation. Their qualifying programme was comfortable, with an unbeaten run allowing them to win their group by a point from second-placed Belgium, thanks to a 1-0 last game victory. Croatia switched coaches during the campaign, replacing elder statesman Miroslav Blazevic after the first two games, which were drawn. In came Mirko Jozic, a 62-year-old who coached the Yugoslavian under-20s team which won the 1987 World Youth Cup in Chile.

Key to the campaign will be Alen Boksic, the Middlesbrough striker, though the lack of first team games afforded to Bosko Balaban at Aston Villa, despite the fact that he was top scorer in qualifying with five goals, will be of some concern to Jozic.

Other English-based players, such as Portsmouth's Robert Prosinecki and Chelsea's Mario Stanic, will be vital to their success. Age, though, has caught up with Davor Suker and Robert Jarni and Croatia will not be expected to emulate their success of four years ago.

Mexico complete the group and they will hope Real Valladolid's Cuauhtemoc Blanco can repeat his form in the qualifiers when he scored nine goals despite starting only four matches and coming on at half-time in another three. Mexico also owe their 12th appearance in the finals to coach Javier Aguirre, who replaced Enrique Meza to win 13 out of a possible 15 points. With other talents such as Espanyol's Juan Francisco Palencia and veteran defender Claudio Suarez, the world's most capped international, they might finally live up to their potential.

ITALY

"On paper it looks like it's an easy group for us but I don't think you can say that. Croatia are an excellent team and some of their players have experience of Italian football, which is a big advantage. Mexico has a long football tradition so of course I'm worried about playing them. Ecuador is a new, emerging side and play some nice football. We will have to be extremely careful." **Giovanni Trapattoni**, the Italian coach.

CROATIA

"I wish I could have chosen another group but I cannot. You don't need to waste words describing Italy. Ecuador and Mexico are also dangerous but I still think we can make it to the second round." **Mirko Jozic**, Croatia coach.

MEXICO

"It appears that a surprise could come out of our Group G. I think Croatia could expect to get something out of it, the same as Ecuador and Italy. I think we are the dark horses. Mexico need to open the tournament with a win and then focus on beating Italy in order to qualify for the second round." **Javier Aguirre**, Mexico coach.

ECUADOR

"We are going to the World Cup to learn. It's a difficult group, especially with three-times world champions Italy but it's good to meet the top teams because it gives us a chance to prove ourselves." **Hernan Dario Gomez**, Ecuador coach.

ITALY

Brazil are the only country to have won the World Cup four times. No-one will be surprised if Italy join them on June 30. Two years on since their shattering Golden Goal defeat to France in the final of Euro 2000 in Rotterdam, Italy appear to have gained in strength, experience and confidence, and look set for a glittering tournament with the chance of winning the World Cup itself a real possibility.

Everywhere you look the team exudes skill and class, but there is something there now which may have been lacking two years ago – real self-belief. Italy ground their way into the final of Euro 2000 almost by stealth, but this Italian team demands to be noticed. There is no doubt it will be.

Coach Giovanni Trapattoni steered his side through the qualification tournament unbeaten with Italy romping home four points clear of Romania after chalking up six wins and two draws in an admittedly unremarkable group consisting of Georgia, Hungary and Lithuania as well as the Romanians, a shadow of the side that performed so brightly in the 1990s.

And the luck has stayed with the Italians for their first round group should not exactly tax them too much either.

They will face Croatia, Ecuador and Mexico in Group G in Japan, and if they win that as expected, will face the runner-up from Group D in the second round. Assuming Portugal win Group D as expected, their opponents will be one of South Korea, Poland or the United States. With all due respect to that trio, a place in the last eight is already beckoning the Azzuri.

Italian optimism is based on the fact that a generation of great players have come together as a cohesive, forceful unit at the same time. From goalkeeper Gianluigi Buffon (and his likely deputies Francesco Toldo and Christian Abbiati) right through the team to Francesco Totti and Christian Vieri up front it is hard to find a weak link.

As well as those players, Trapattoni can call on a host of others including Fabio Cannavaro, Alessandro Nesta and the evergreen Paolo Maldini in defence; Totti, Gianluca Zambrotta, Damiano Tommasi in midfield, and Alessandro Del Piero, Filippo Inzaghi as well as Vieiri in attack.

And if Trapattoni has been blessed with a great squad, he has also honed it in his own image since he took over from Dino Zoff after Euro 2000. Trapattoni has added a zest for attack and an ability to entertain to Zoff's team which was solid, successful up to a point, but unspectacular.

The clearest example of this came in Milan in October 2000 when Italy demolished Romania 3-0 with goals from Inzaghi, Marco Delvecchio and Totti – all before half-time. Trapattoni's persistence with Inzaghi was completely justified as the Milan striker ended up top scorer in the qualifiers with seven goals.

There are some worries for the Italians. Over-confidence is one certainly, and Italy have disappointed in the past when the pressure of expectation has been on them. And while the 'first' team as it were, more or less picks itself, there are worries about quality cover for the likes of Maldini and Nesta, if, for any reason, they do not perform at the highest level after a season beset by injury.

Maldini, who could end the summer with more than 130 caps depending on the number of friendlies he plays in and how far Italy progress in the tournament, will be taking part in his fourth World Cup and could, if results fell a certain way, come up against Paraguay, coached by his father Cesare in the quarter-finals.

Cesare Maldini coached the side in 1998 when Italy reached the quarter-finals where they went out to France on penalties after a 0-0 draw in Paris – and despite the fact it was the eventual World Champions who beat them, it was a disappointing tournament for the Italians after reaching the final itself four years earlier in the United States.

That match ended in the ultimate disappointment too as Italy lost to Brazil on penalties and it is now 20 years since the Italians ruled the world when they won the World Cup for the third time in Spain with a 3-1 victory over West Germany.

Italy now look capable of going all the way again this time around, when victory would not only mean they emulate Brazil's record of four World titles, but they would also become the first team since Brazil in 1958 to win the World Cup outside their own continent.

SQUAD

CHRISTIAN ABBIATI (AC MILAN) BORN: 08.07.77 CAPS: 0 GLS: 0
Italian U21 international keeper in the side that won the 2000 European U21 title, and then went straight into the Euro 2000 squad as cover after Gianluigi Buffon's injury. Pulled his club out of a hole following Sebastiano Rossi's misdemeanours in the 1999 title winning season. Played for Monza in B from 1994-98, but this is Milan's feeder team, so progress was monitored, and he has now overtaken Rossi at his club side.

DANIELE ADANI (FIORENTINA) BORN: 10.07.74 CAPS: 3 GLS: 0
Defender with a relegated club in 2002 – may be on the move. Bought by Fiorentina in summer 1999 from Brescia for £2 million – he was developed by Brescia and played in their teams in Serie A and B. Began his career in Serie B with Modena from 1991-94, then was snapped up by Lazio, who released him without a first team game in the mid-1990s so he went to Brescia and thence to Fiorentina. Played 150 games in Serie B before being established in Serie A.

MASSIMO AMBROSINI (AC MILAN) BORN:29.05.77 CAPS: 9 GLS: 0
Injured knee ligaments v in Februray 2001 and restarted too soon, only now starting to get back to full fitness. Superb 2000, played in Euro 2000 final, and was in the team that won the European U21 title - and then went to the Olympics. Arrived back at Milan in summer 1998 from Vicenza after being on loan for the 1997-98 season along with Coco. Played 7 times in Milan's 1996 Championship win and qualified for a medal. Thence to Vicenza on loan in 1997-98 and has been back in Milan's first team until his injuries.

GIANLUIGI BUFFON (JUVENTUS) BORN: 28.01.78 CAPS: 25 GLS: 0
World record fee for a keeper – £32 million from Parma to Juventus in summer 2001. Missed Euro 2000 with a broken hand – now back in contention as No 1. No 2 at 1998 World Cup, and developed via the U21 and Olympic squads. Came to prominence with Parma's 1999 UEFA Cup and Italian Cup successes.

ITALY

FABIO CANNAVARO (PARMA) BORN: 13.09.73 CAPS: 56 GLS: 0
Blossomed under Cesare Maldini and is a fixture in the heart of the national team's defence – played all five games at the 1998 World Cup, and five out of six at Euro 2000 in a superb tournament. Rated the best Italian defender (ahead of Maldini) and key player in 1999 UEFA and Italian Cup wins. Was in the team that won the 1996 European U21 championship and also went to the Olympics in Atlanta where he was the captain. Reluctant summer 1995 departure from cash-starved Napoli, for whom he had played since 1991 and made Serie A debut in 1993.

FRANCESCO COCO (BARCELONA, SPAIN) BORN: 08.01.77 CAPS: 11 GLS: 0
Moved in summer 2001 to Spain from AC Milan for £11 million Member of the team that won the 2000 European U21 championship for the fourth time in the last five attempts. Was Paolo Maldini's reserve at Milan but now pushed forward more often down the flanks. Played five times in Milan's championship team in 1996 and another six games in their 1999 success. Rated as one of Italy's best young wide players.

MARCO DELVECCHIO (ROMA) BORN: 07.04.73 CAPS: 15 GLS: 3
Italian scorer in final of Euro 2000. Championship medal 2001. Had been on the fringes of the national squad in 1998 under Dino Zoff along with team mate Totti – after an increasingly consistent spell, and then finally capped. Another from the European U21 Championship winning squad and Atlanta Olympic squad of 1996, and joined Roma in Nov 1995 from Inter Milan. Can play central or wide forward positions.

LUIGI DI BIAGIO (INTER MILAN) BORN: 03.06.71 CAPS: 25 GLS: 2
Superb 1998 World Cup – played every game – but will be remembered for his missed penalty vs France in the quarter-final shoot-out. Got back into national side also for last four games of Euro 2000. Has been with Inter since September 1999 when he signed from Roma. Signed by Roma from relegated Foggia in summer 1995 for £2 million , he is from Rome and played for Lazio in Serie A before being released to Monza and then played for Foggia in A from 1992-95.

ALESSANDRO DEL PIERO (JUVENTUS) BORN: 09.11.74 CAPS: 47 GLS: 16
Serious knee ligament injury in 1999. Now fit again but has not exactly played well since return though he did play at Euro 2000. Club top scorer in 1997 and 1998 title wins. Was a summer 1993 purchase for Juve from then Serie B club Padova, for whom he made his debut in 1992 and for whom he played just 14 league games before his move to Juve, where he first announced himself with crucial goals in the 1995 Championship win. Replaced Roberto Baggio at Juventus. Winning goal in 1996 World Club Cup final v River Plate (Nov 26 1996).

ANGELO DI LIVIO (FIORENTINA) BORN: 26.07.66 CAPS: 37 GLS: 0
Moved from Juventus to Fiorentina in summer 1999 for £1.5 million at supposedly the end of his career – can play anywhere down the flanks. Has come back into the international fold under coach Trapattoni who was his recent boss at Fiorentina. Also

one of Cesare Maldini's favourites – and was at Euro '96 and France '98 – but did not feature under Dino Zoff. Won 1995 Championship and 1996 Champions League with Juve and went into national squad at the age of 29. 1993-4 was his first Serie A season – he was a Roma reject who had been playing Serie B football for Padova from 1989-93, and was a surprise and late addition to Juventus 1993 ranks. Championship medals with Juve in '95, '97 and '98. Known as the 'Little Tin Soldier'.

CRISTIANO DONI (ATALANTA) BORN: 01.04.73 CAPS: 3 GLS: 1

Enjoying a fine season – he is currently up among the leading scorers in Serie A with a hatful of goals from midfield, and started against England at Leeds. Atalanta picked him up from Brescia in 1996 after he had spent his first six seasons drifting in the lower reaches, and he spent time in Serie B with the Atalanta club, but is a late developer and improved hugely on Atalanta's return to Serie A in 2000.

STEFANO FIORE (LAZIO) BORN: 17.04.75 CAPS: 22 GLS: 2

Has lost his way a little since joining Lazio in summer 2000 from Udinese. First capped in Feb 2000, and had an excellent run at Euro 2000. Joined Udinese from Parma in summer 1999 for £5.5 million. Joined Parma in 1994 and has been out at Padova and Chievo on loan while awaiting first team chances. Is one of the players whose chances were being held back by foreign players in Serie A. Name means Stephen Flower in English.

GENNARO GATTUSO (AC MILAN) BORN: 09.01.78 CAPS: 11 GLS: 1

Olympic Games 2000 – after winning the 2000 European U21 title with Italy. First capped in Euro 2000 warm up friendlies. Represented a gamble as he moved from relegated Salernitana to Milan in summer '99 for £7 million – but Milan knew what they were doing. Spent the previous 18 months at Glasgow Rangers – 40 games and 7 goals. First taste of Serie A was with Perugia aged 17.

MARK IULIANO (JUVENTUS) BORN: 12.08.73 CAPS: 14 GLS: 0

First cap vs Wales at Anfield in September 1998 – then not considered until just before Euro 2000, where he went on to have a superb tournament, playing every game including the final. Initially played at Juve as a reserve but gained first team place when Paolo Montero had knee surgery, and then Ciro Ferrara broke his leg. Another of Juve's dips into Serie B, they came up with a summer 1996 signing from Salernitana, who he joined in 1990. Iuliano is a defender, who settled in well to the 1997 Championship win and 1997 European Cup final loss in his first season. Won 1998 title also.

FILIPPO INZAGHI (AC MILAN) BORN: 09.08.73 CAPS: 37 GLS: 15

Moved summer 2001 from Juventus to AC Milan for £26.6 million – top scorer at Juventus for three seasons. Currently the national team's first choice striker. First came to prominence when he was the top scorer in Serie A in 1996-97 when at Atalanta with 24 goals in 33 games and moved to Juve in summer 1997 for £7.5 million from Parma (he was only at Atalanta on loan). 1997 Young Footballer of the Year. Brother Simone is also an international.

ITALY

MASSIMO MACCARONE (EMPOLI) BORN:06.09.79 CAPS: 1 GLS: 0
Was the sensation of the Italian win v England in March 2002 – he had scored in the U21 international the previous evening, and caused havoc with a late substitute appearance. First international since 1972 from Serie B – the last was Giorgio Chinaglia (Lazio via Swansea) and the 15th in all. A dozen goals for Empoli last season, and obvious future interest from the Serie A clubs.

PAOLO MALDINI (AC MILAN) BORN: 26.06.68 CAPS: 121 GLS: 7
Most capped Italian – captain of club and country since Franco Baresi retired. The best left back in the world, and has been around for Milan's six Championship wins, three European Cups and two World Club Cup wins since their first success in 1988. Played in 1994 World Cup final and Euro 2000 final. Son of Cesare Maldini, former captain of AC Milan's European Cup winning team in 1963 and Italian international, who is the 2002 Paraguay national coach. Paolo is a Milan player since day-one, he made his debut at 16, was an international at 18, was the youngest at the 1988 European Championships.

MARCO MATERAZZI (INTER MILAN) BORN: 19.08.73 CAPS: 5 GLS: 0
Former Everton man, now a full international, and signed by Inter in summer 2001 from Perugia for £6.3 million. Played 27 Premiership games for Everton in 1998-99 before his £3 million move back to Perugia in summer 1999. Was with Perugia for four seasons before his move to Merseyside in both A and B, and previous to Perugia had played all his football in the lower leagues. 6'4" tall and a late developer.

VINCENZO MONTELLA (ROMA) BORN: 18.06.74 CAPS: 13 GLS: 3
Was the form horse through spring 2002 and scored twice v England. Joined Roma from relegated Sampdoria in summer 1999 for £14 million – and scored 13 goals in Roma's 2001 title win, mainly from the bench. Been injured for much of 2001-2. The 1996-97 season was his first in Serie A and he made an amazing impact with 22 goals in just 28 games and finished runner up in the national scoring lists. His first club was Empoli, then Genoa, the 1996 Anglo-Italian Cup winners (he scored twice at Wembley) and then to Samp. 5'7" tall. Best Serie A rookie scorer of all-time in 96-97.

ALESSANDRO NESTA (LAZIO) BORN: 19.03.76 CAPS: 42 GLS: 0
Lazio club captain during outstanding 2000 with League and Cup success and superb displays at Euro 2000. Missed much of 1998-99 after being injured in France in World Cup (broken leg) – is the key defender, and outstanding for national side – he played three times at the 1998 World Cup finals. A last minute call up to the Euro '96 squad though he did not play in the finals and has been in the selectors eyes since then – went to the 1996 Olympics. This was the player with whom Gazza collided when he broke his leg in 1994 on the training ground. Local product, has come through the youth system – also won 1998 Italian Cup, and 1999 ECWC.

ITALY

GIUSEPPE PANCARO (LAZIO) BORN: 26.08.71 CAPS: 12 GLS: 0
League and Cup double with Lazio 2000, and ECWC 1999. Ex-Cagliari, and greatly
improved. Gained his first caps in spring 1999 to maintain progress. Saved by Lazio
from a fate in Serie B by a summer 1997 move from relegated Cagliari, for whom
he had played in A from 1992-97. One of those players favoured by the current
national coach.

CHRISTIAN PANUCCI (ROMA) BORN: 12.04.73 CAPS: 23 GLS: 1
Joined Roma just after the start of the 2001-02 season from Monaco where he had a
spat with their new coach Didier Deschamps. Played for AC Milan (who bought him
from Genoa) from 1993-97, then to Real Madrid from 1997-99 and back to Inter in
1999-2000. Then had short spells at Chelsea (17 games) and Monaco. Highly medalled
– won European Cup with two clubs: Milan in 1994 and Real in 1998 – and Serie A
medals in 1994 and 1996 with Milan and Primera Liga in 1997 with Real, with whom
he also won the World Club Cup in 1998. Links up again at Roma with his former coach
at AC Milan – Fabio Capello.

FRANCESCO TOLDO (INTER MILAN) BORN: 02.12.71 CAPS: 20 GLS: 0
Took over from the injured Gianluigi Buffon just before Euro 2000 and played in that
final. Buffon has now won his place back, but Toldo is pressurising him. Moved from
Fiorentina to Inter for £18.3 million in summer 2001. Tallest keeper in Serie A at 6'6".
First cap for Italy in October '95 v Croatia in strange circumstances when Luca Bucci
was sent off after nine mins and Toldo came on to play in goal with Zola being
sacrificed. Came to the fore in Fiorentina's 1993-94 promotion season when they
bounced straight back up to Serie A.

DAMIANO TOMMASI (ROMA) BORN: 17.05.74 CAPS: 12 GLS: 1
Now back in national team during Roma's 2001 title win – the only player to appear
in all 34 games in the 2001 title success. Was in the national squad for the 1998
World Cup qualifiers under Cesare Maldini, and then capped in 1998-99 under Dino
Zoff, but has only recently interested Trapattoni. Missed just one international
in 2001. Joined Roma in summer 1996 from Verona's Serie B championship
runners-up team. Was the star of the U21 side that won the 1996 European
Championship, and went to Atlanta with the Olympic team. Known for his charity
work. Nicknamed 'San Tomassi'.

FRANCESCO TOTTI (ROMA) BORN: 27.09.76 CAPS: 28 GLS: 5
Roma's playmaker in their championship win of 2001, and a star of Euro 2000. Played
as sub v the Swiss for his first cap in Oct 1998 in Euro 2000 qualifiers – after a rapidly
improving 1998. Roma debut at the age of 17 and comes from the city – he has moved
through the club's junior ranks. Was in the team that won the 1996 European U21
championship and is earmarked for the future.

ITALY

CHRISTIAN VIERI (INTER MILAN) BORN: 12.07.73 CAPS: 22 GLS: 10
Back after long term injury from autumn 2000, and finished with an excellent 18 goals in 27 Serie A games in 2000-01. Has, if anything, improved on that in 2001-02. Cost a then world record £32 million from Lazio in summer 1999. Hence No 32 presumably. Scored five times at '98 World Cup. Brought up in Australia – his hero is Allan Border! Championship medal with Juve in 1997 and then sold for £10 million to Atletico Madrid – moved back to Italy for £18.9 million in Aug 1998 after a season in Spain where he finished top of the Primera Liga scorers with 24 goals in just 24 games.

CHRISTIANO ZANETTI (INTER MILAN) BORN: 14.04.77 CAPS: 4 GLS: 0
Has become an established member of the squad since the Japan trip in November 2001 Played at the Olympic Games in Sydney 2000 Midfielder, and a former Fiorentina player, who spent 1994-96 with Fiorentina before moving to Venezia and Reggiana – he cost Inter £2 million in summer 1998 from Reggiana and then went on loan to Roma last season where he picked up a championship medal.

DAMIANO ZENONI (ATALANTA) BORN: 23.04.77 CAPS: 1 GLS: 0
Has a twin, Cristian, who was also in the Atalanta team and went in summer 2001 to Juventus and is also an international – Damiano is a midfielder, Cristian a defender. From the Bergamo region, both joined the club in 1994, and both were in the 2000 promotion team. Though Damiano was the first of the twins to make the national squad, Cristian was the first to play in Serie A and was the one who played for the national U21 side.

GIANLUCA ZAMBROTTA (JUVENTUS) BORN: 19.02.77 CAPS: 21 GLS: 0
Missed the Euro 2000 final after being sent off in the semi-final v Holland. Made a fine job of stand-in right wingback. Signed by Juventus from Bari for £10 million, he made the national squad in 1999 and won his first couple of caps in friendlies before the move to Juve. Originally with Como in Serie C, and left for Bari in 1997 – had two excellent seasons with Bari, culminating in summer 1999 move to Juve. Gained national attention via the U21 national team with Dino Zoff.

COACH

GIOVANNI TRAPATTONI BORN: 17.03.39
He won 17 caps for Italy and played in the 1966 World Cup and won '63. '68, '69 European Cup medal. He has coached the following: AC Milan 1972-74 youths, 1974-76 with first team, Juventus 1976-86 – won Serie A on six occasions and all three European competitions, the first club and the first trainer to win all three European Cups, Inter Milan 1986-91 – won 1989 Serie A and 1991 UEFA Cup. Juventus 1991-94 – won 1993 UEFA Cup. Then to Bayern for first time, and Cagliari (sacked) in poor period. Bayern 1996-98 – won 1997 title and 1998 German Cup, Fiorentina 1998-2000. Joined the national team after Euro 2000 when Dino Zoff resigned after being criticised by the media. Just signed an extension through to Euro 2004.

CROATIA

When Croatia beat the Netherlands 2-1 to clinch third place in the World Cup four years ago they achieved the best performance by a debutant nation since Portugal 34 years previously. In 1966, Portugal, with Eusebio (nine goals) finishing as the tournament's top scorer, took third place after losing to the hosts and eventual world champions (England) 2-1 in the semi-finals.

In 1998, Croatia, with Davor Suker (six goals) finishing as the tournament's top scorer, took third place after losing to the hosts and eventual world champions (France) 2-1 in the semi-finals.

As far as the Croatians are concerned the comparisons can end right there. Portugal did not return to the World Cup for another 20 years, and in fact this summer's finals will only be Portugal's third ever. Croatia have returned for a second successive appearance and with their promising blend of established stars and up-and-coming talent, are keen to prove that 1998 was not just a flash-in-the-pan.

And there are real causes for optimistically hoping it will not be. Croatia won a tricky qualifying group which included Belgium and Scotland with an unbeaten record of five wins and three draws in their eight matches. Pointedly they only conceded two goals in those games – the lowest of any team in the entire European qualifying campaign.

Their gamble in replacing coach Miroslav Blazevic in December 2000 after two opening draws against Belgium (0-0) and Scotland (1-1) also paid handsome dividends. Under replacement Mirko Jozic, Croatia won five of their remaining six qualifiers conceding just one more goal in a 4-1 win over Latvia.

Jozic makes no secret of his success. He stacks the team at the back, plays defensively and looks for goals on the counter. He is also fortunate that he has the players capable of employing his chosen system.

Jozic also laughs off comparisons with 1998 saying the current squad are under no pressure from him or anyone else to match that showing.

His goal, he says, it to get past the opening round and reach the knock-out stage and being drawn in the same group as Italy, Ecuador and Mexico, Croatia has a more than reasonable chance of doing just that. On paper at least, they should go through with Italy.

Jozic's caution is well-known among his countrymen and he has been reluctant to ditch some of the side that performed so heroically in France.

Veterans like Robert Prosinecki, Davor Suker and Robert Jarni, who have been playing together since winning the World Youth title in Chile in 1987, are still very much involved in his plans – even if they are now in the twilight of their first-class careers.

As Jozic said during the build-up to the finals: "We are not going to renounce the gold even if its shine has somewhat diminished."

And so far they have not let him down. It was the individual brilliance of the 32-year-old Prosinecki, now plying his trade with more than a modicum of success at first division side Portsmouth after a glittering career at Red Star Belgrade, Dinamo Zagreb and Real Madrid, that decided the crucial qualifying game against Belgium in Zagreb in October.

Prosinecki's measured 40-metre pass found Aston Villa striker Bosko Balaban in the

CROATIA

perfect position to serve Alen Boksic for the goal that secured Croatia a place in the World Cup finals. Jozic's main achievement in the last 18-months has been to rejuvenate largely the same group of players that failed to qualify for Euro 2000. Under Blazevic the defence began to leak some sloppy goals, but Jozic has worked hard to instill some discipline to the backline that was previously lacking. And it has not all been done by relying on the shoulders of the Old Guard.

He has brought in fresh legs including Balaban, Hajduk Split goalkeeper Stipe Pletikosa and 23-year-old central defender Igor Tudor of Juventus.

One worry is that the likes of Balaban, who scored five of Croatia's 15 goals in qualifying, has spent most of the season on the bench at Aston Villa, while Suker has only played a handful of games for TSV and Jarni has largely been sidelined at Las Palmas. But one new option is likely to be Tomislav Maric of Wolfsburg who has been scoring regularly in the Bundesliga this season. The good news too is that Boksic has had a good season at Middlesbrough and if not quite the dominant force he was in his youth, has still been playing regularly apart from injury.

While Tudor has become the focal point of the defence, newcomers like Dario Simic of Inter Milan and Robert Kovac of Bayern Munich have added some new steel at full-back.

In essence Croatia look a balanced, lively side that should survive the group phase and even if they do not reach the semi-finals again, they will probably leave the tournament with their reputation enhanced still further.

SQUAD

BOSKO BALABAN (ASTON VILLA) BORN: 15.10.78 CAPS: 12 GLS: 6
Moved in August 2001 to Villa for around £6 million but has been an onlooker. Another young player from the Dinamo club who is breaking into the national team – he was first capped on his home ground v France in a May 2000 friendly. In Dinamo's 2000 title win, after joining in 1999 from Rijeka. Been with the national U21 side in May 2000 and progressed after passing through that system.

IGOR BISCAN (LIVERPOOL) BORN: 04.05.78 CAPS: 16 GLS: 1
A utility player happy in defence or attack – signed by Liverpool from Dinamo Zagreb for £4 million in 2000-1. Was European cup-tied last season as Dinamo had played in the UCL qualifiers so he missed most of Liverpool's cup honours in 2001. First cap in game v Yugoslavia (sub) in the Euro 2000 qualifiers. Five seasons in the Dinamo club first team – title medals in 1997, 1998 and 2000. From club youths and through to first team in 1996.

NENAD BJELICA (KAISERSLAUTERN) BORN: 28.08.71 CAPS: 5 GLS: 0
Was the Croatian Footballer of the Year in 2000 in a surprise move, after a fine spell with his home club Osijek. An international only since 2001. Second move out of Croatia, he was in Spain for much of the 1990s with relegation-threatened sides Albacete, Betsi Seville, and Las Palmas, before returning to Osijek. Joined the Kaiserslautern club in the midwinter break 2000-1 from Osijek for £350,000.

CROATIA

ALEN BOKSIC (MIDDLESBROUGH) BORN: 21.01.70 CAPS: 36 GLS: 10
Joined Boro from Lazio in summer 2000 for £2.5 million after looking initially as though Galatasaray had signed him. Injured just before the 1998 World Cup finals – had to withdraw at last minute – operation on injured knee and hamstring. Never recovered form in six seasons with Lazio. Had previously figured in both the biggest buy and sell in Lazio's history – he was bought from Marseille in 1993 for a club record £7 million, then sold to Juventus for a club record £5 million in summer 1996. After a season at Juve where he won a Championship medal and played in the European Cup final, it was back to Lazio for another £7 million in summer 1997. Recent seasons have proved – regrettably – that his Achilles' heel is the inability to score enough goals. All of which was a stark contrast to his performance in Marseille's famous 1993 Championship and European Cup winning season, he was top of the French scorers in 1993 with 23 goals which put Lazio in for him. First club was Hajduk Split.

TOMISLAV BUTINA (DINAMO ZAGREB) BORN: 30.03.74 CAPS: 5 GLS: 0
Goalkeeper from the Dinamo club, who has replaced former national captain Drazen Ladic in the club goal. Has been with Dinamo for ten years having signed from a neighbouring club, but has lived in Ladic's shadow until 2000. Has played over 100 games for the club.

ROBERT JARNI (PANATHINAIKOS) BORN: 26.10.68 CAPS: 77 GLS: 2
Set new ongoing Croatian caps record in 2000. Moved in summer 1997 from Betis Seville – to Coventry for £2.5 million then onto Real Madrid without a Premiership game for £3.25 million, so at least Coventry made some money. Real Madrid squad for 1998 World Club Cup win. Class defender who fills the left back/midfield role. Won a 1995 Italian Championship medal with Juventus before a £3 million move to Betis in summer 1995. He was a member of the Yugoslavian team that won the World Junior Cup in 1987 and was in the 1990 World Cup squad for Yugoslavia. He also won seven caps for the old Yugoslavia. His home club was Hajduk Split and he left them in 1991 for Serie A duty with Bari, Juventus and a loan spell at Torino. Played all four at Euro '96 and all seven at the 1998 World Cup. Scored vs Germany in '98 quarter-final.

NICO KOVAC (BAYERN MUNICH) BORN: 15.10.71 CAPS: 19 GLS: 3
Re-united with his brother Robert at Bayern in summer 2001, signing from Hamburg for £3.6 million. Left his brother in summer 1999 to join Hamburg from Leverkusen on a Bosman transfer. Represents a new wave of Croatians – those eligible but born outside the country, his parents worked in Germany. Was not in the final 22 for the 1998 World Cup.

ROBERT KOVAC (BAYERN MUNICH) BORN: 06.04.74 CAPS: 19 GLS: 0
The younger of the Croatian brothers who have re-united in summer 2001 at Bayern, but the more expensive purchase at £5.5 million. Robert is a former U21 international for Croatia and was signed by Bayern from Leverkusen – he joined the Leverkusen club from Nurnberg during the 1995-96 season. Broke into the side on a regular basis towards the end of 1997-98 season, and was in the Leverkusen team for six seasons – including two that finished Bundesliga runners-up.

CROATIA

IVICA OLIC (NK ZAGREB) BORN: 14.09.79 CAPS: 3 GLS: 1
Is the one to watch in the future – a left-footed forward from the other club in the capital. Former U21 international who has moved into the full national team and gained his first caps from spring 2002.

STIPE PLETIKOSA (HAJDUK SPLIT) BORN: 08.01.79 CAPS: 18 GLS: 0
The current first choice national keeper – and from the national U21 side. Is from the Hajduk club and been first choice at the club for five years – won the 2001 title to end years of Dinamo dominance. Was said to have signed for Marseille all summer 2001 but then declined to move. First capped in March 1999 and has been national first choice since Drazen Ladic retired in Oct 1999. 6'3" tall.

ROBERT PROSINECKI (GRAMPUS EIGHT) BORN: 12.01.69 CAPS: 47 GLS: 11
Signed in summer 2001 for Pompey from Belgian club Standard Liege. Had been with Standard since Sept 2000 after Dinamo Zagreb let him go as they couldn't afford his wages. Father is a Croatian, mother is a Serb. He was in Red Star Belgrade's European Cup winning team in 1991 and then moved for £3 million in 1992 to Real Madrid. After a 1994-95 season with Oviedo on loan, he switched to Barcelona in summer 1995 and thence to Seville and Standard. Was in the 1987 World Junior Cup winning team for Yugoslavia, he went on to play in the 1990 World Cup finals for Yugoslavia, gaining 15 caps in all for that country. Played in first three games at Euro '96 then dropped, so needed a good 1998 World Cup and got it.

MILAN RAPAIJC (FENERBAHCE) BORN: 16.08.73 CAPS: 22 GLS: 1
Joined Fenerbahce from Perugia in Serie A in summer 2000 and was in the team that won the Turkish title – knocked Rangers out of the Champions League in August 2001. Four seasons with Perugia, and in 1997 relegation and 1998 promotion sides. Earned respect by staying when club was relegated though it cost him his international place temporarily. Had five seasons with Hajduk Split at the start of his career – and first capped at that club after their 1994 title win.

VEDRUN RUNJE (MARSEILLE) BORN: 10.02.76 CAPS: 1 GLS: 0
Recent addition to the squad – he joined Marseille in summer 2001 and previously had three seasons with Standard Liege. Won the Belgian league best keeper award during spell at Standard. His home club was Hajduk Split, and he was in the first team squad from 1995-98.

DANIJEL SARIC (PANATHINAIKOS) BORN: 04.08.72 CAPS: 24 GLS: 0
Now plays in Greece alongside Vlaovic. Was previously a key player in the Dinamo Zagreb league and cup double wins of 1996, 1997 and 1998 – and championship success in 1999 and 2000. Capped in World Cup warm up games 1998, but not in squad for finals. Formerly with Rijeka, then had a three season spell with Spain's Sporting Gijon 1993-96 before returning home with Dinamo.

CROATIA

ANTHONY SERIC (VERONA) BORN: 15.11.79 CAPS: 8 GLS: 0
Croatian U21 international and now won full caps, who joined Verona in summer 1999 from Hajduk Split via Parma who have loaned him to Verona for another season to see how he develops. Spent three seasons in Hajduk's first team, before moving to Serie A.

DARIO SIMIC (INTER MILAN) BORN: 12.11.75 CAPS: 48 GLS: 1
Moved to Inter in early 1999 for £6 million from Dinamo Zagreb. Known as Pitbull because he plays like one and owns several of them. His club won the League and Cup double in 1996, and repeated the dose in 1997 and 1998 and with Simic as an outstanding member. He was a Dinamo Zagreb junior – having come through their youth team to being a full international. Younger brother Josip is also an international.

JOSEP SIMIC (DINAMO ZAGREB) BORN: 16.09.77 CAPS: 3 GLS: 0
Younger brother of the international defender Dario Simic. Highly thought of and very promising after recovering from a rare muscle-spasm illness cured in a Swiss clinic. Excellent impression in 1999 title win.

JOSIP SIMUNIC (HERTHA BERLIN) BORN: 18.02.78 CAPS: 5 GLS: 0
Joined Hertha in Jan 2000 from Hamburg SV for £100,000. Registered as a Croatian, but arrived in Germany in 1997 from the Australian club Melbourne Knights. Born in Sydney and trained at the Australian Institute of Sport. Is 6'5" tall. Played twice for HSV but did not feature in the first part of the 1999-2000 season and so moved on.

TOMOSLAV SOKOTA (BENFICA) BORN: 08.04.77 CAPS: 2 GLS: 0
Joined Benfica in summer 2001 to replace Pierre van Hoojdonk who went back to Holland with Feyenoord. Was the Croatian League top scorer with Dinamo in 1999-2000 with 21 goals and then again in 2000-01 with 18 goals. Former youth and U21 international, he was from the Dinamo youth set up, and made his first team debut in 1995 as a teenager. Was around in the first team for four titles with increasing effect.

ZVONIMIR SOLDO (VFB STUTTGART) BORN: 02.11.67 CAPS: 59 GLS: 4
One of former coach Blazevic's favourites because of his versatility. League and Cup double with Dinamo Zagreb in 1996 before joining Stuttgart after Euro '96. sixth season with Stuttgart. Was a solid defender in the Croatian League and played in the old Yugoslav first Division with Dinamo since 1988. League title medal in 1992. Played in three of the four games at Euro 96 and six of seven at the 1998 World Cup.

IGOR STIMAC (HAJDUK SPLIT) BORN: 06.09.67 CAPS: 53 GLS: 2
Helped Derby back into Premiership 1995-96, before moving to West Ham in 1999. Retired in 2001 but returned to club and country due to injuries to other key players, lobbying his way back into the squad through the media. A member of the famous Yugoslav team that won the 1987 World Junior Cup, and former Hajduk Split captain. Has also played in Spain for Cadiz. Joined Derby in 1995 for £1.57 million after a move to Vicenza of Serie A fell through. Member of Hajduk's 1995 double winning team.

CROATIA

MARIO STANIC (CHELSEA) BORN: 10.04.72 CAPS: 43 GLS: 7
Joined Chelsea in summer 2000 for £6.5 million from Parma, then almost
immediately suffered the dreaded knee ligament injury. Utility player – anywhere
from wing back to striker, normally down right side. Won UEFA Cup and Italian Cup
medals in 1999 with Parma, and was there for three seasons 1997-2000 after
joining from Bruges. While at FC Bruges he became the Belgian League top scorer
in their title win of 1996 with 20 goals. His house in Sarajevo was flattened in the
War – family mostly escaped. He is a Bosnian-Croat. Before Bruges he was with
Zeleznicar Sarajevo and Dinamo Zagreb, then to Sporting Gijon and Benfica as he
searched for an identity in European football.

DAVOR SUKER (1860 MUNICH) BORN: 01.01.68 CAPS: 68 GLS: 45
Free agent after leaving West Ham in the summer of 2001 – has now moved to
Germany. Superb international record – top scorer in 1998 World Cup with six goals –
but goals drying up now for clubs and country. European Cup medal 1998 – played the
last 60 secs of the final in place of Mijatovic. Moved in summer 1996 to Real Madrid
on a four year contract and the fee was £3 million. He celebrated with 24 goals in their
1996-97 Championship win but lost his place to Fernando Morientes in 1997-98. Moved
to Arsenal from Real Madrid in summer 1999 with Anelka going the other way – Suker
was believed to be just £1.3 million (not £3 million). Moved again in summer 2000 to
West Ham on a free transfer. He was top scorer in the Euro '96 qualifiers with 12 goals
and scored two goals at Euro '96 against Portugal and once against Germany. Began
his career with Osijek then played for Croatia Zagreb until his move to Spain in 1991.
He was top scorer in the 1987 Yugoslav World Junior Cup winning team and was in the
squad for the 1990 World Cup but didn't play in the finals. Gained his two caps for the
old Yugoslavia (one goal) in 1991-92 before the wars.

MARIO TOKIC (DINAMO ZAGREB) BORN: 23.07.75 CAPS: 5 GLS: 0
Has joined the squad since the 1998 World Cup. He joined Dinamo Zagreb in summer
1998 from Rijeka of the Croatian League, where he had spent the previous four seasons
in their first team. Joined Rijeka in 1992, aged 17. Born in Bosnia, opted for Croatia.

STJEPAN TOMAS (VICENZA) BORN: 06.03.76 CAPS: 17 GLS: 1
Signed by Vicenza in summer 2000 for £1.3 million from Dinamo Zagreb. Joined
Dinamo in 1993 from D2 club Iskra, and was around for their last five championship
successes from 1996-2000. Then moved to nearby Italy. Was in the 1998 World Cup
squad but had to withdraw injured at last minute.

IGOR TUDOR (JUVENTUS) BORN: 16.04.78 CAPS: 25 GLS: 0
Joined Juventus for £4.5 million from Hajduk Split just before the 1998 World Cup finals
and has already created a fine impression. In Juventus team that were runners-up in
the 2000 and 2001 Serie A campaigns. Three full seasons with Hajduk's first team as
a teenager. Regular member of national U21 team then moved to full honours – is
around 6'3" tall.

CROATIA

GORAN VLAOVIC (PANATHINAIKOS) BORN: 07.08.72 CAPS: 50 GLS: 16
Happily recovered from a serious brain injury that threatened his life – and now beaten knee surgery. Moved to Greece from Valencia in summer 2000, played in the Champions League for both Valencia and Panathinaikos. Joined Valencia in summer 1996 after Euro '96, from Serie A relegated club Padova, for whom he scored 13 goals in a truncated season in 1995-96 after undergoing life threatening brain surgery. He joined Padova from Dinamo Zagreb where he was top scorer in 1993 in the Croatian league with 24 goals in Dinamo's title win. His Euro '96 was memorable for a fine goal against Turkey. Was the youngest to play for Croatia at 19.

JURICA VRANJES (BAYER LEVERKUSEN) BORN: 30.01.80 CAPS: 7 GLS: 0
Joined Leverkusen with Marko Babic for a combined £3.5 million from Osijek in Jan 2000, and made first team debut in spring 2000. Joined full national team in Aug 2000. West Ham and Arsenal had both expressed an interest in signing the midfielder, with Arsenal manager Arsene Wenger hoping Davor Suker, whose hometown club is Osijek, could have persuaded Vranjes to join Arsenal – Osijek told Wenger he would cost £6.5m! Billed as his country's eventual replacement for skipper Slaven Bilic but is often used in midfield where he is equally effective.

DAVOR VUGRINEC (LECCE) BORN: 24.03.75 CAPS: 19 GLS: 7
Moved in summer 2000 to Serie A with Lecce for a fee of £250,000 from Turkish club Trabzonspor. Played in the Turkish first Division from summer 1999 to 2000 after being a top scorer with Varteks Varazdin in the Croatian league. Capped as a sub just before Euro '96, but he didn't make the squad and was put out to grass for over two years. Came back after chronic list of injuries v Malta in 1998 as a sub.

BORIS ZIVKOVIC (BAYER LEVERKUSEN) BORN: 15.11.75 CAPS: 16 GLS: 1
In Leverkusen side and is often their right wing back. Signed in summer 1997 from Bosnian side FC Sarajevo – the former Yugoslav Division 1 team who had a back seat during the War. Originally from the Dinamo Zagreb club. Gained first full cap in away friendly v France (0-3) in Nov 1999.

COACH

MIRKO JOZIC BORN: 08.04.50
First game in charge was against Austria in March 2001, succeeded Miroslav Blazevic. Div 2 player in local leagues, and came into coaching via PE courses at Zagreb University. Was with the Yugoslav FA from 1972-1988, culminating in the winning of the 1987 World Junior U20 Cup with Yugoslavia with Suker, Boban, Prosinecki etc. Moved in 1989 to club coaching – in Chile with Colo Colo (had a year as their national coach) from 1989-95 winning a league and cup. Then to America, Mexico, then back home with Hajduk Split, over to Saudi Arabia with Al Hilal, and to Argentina with Newells Old Boys. A short spell from 1998-99 with Sporting Lisbon then, when sacked from that post, he became Croatia's youth development coach in 2000, and quickly moved on to the national job.

MEXICO

Mexico, the CONCACAF powerhouse, had their toughest time qualifying ever. It got so bad for the Tri Colores that they lost a qualifier in Mexico City for the first ever in 50 matches. The team went through two managers before Javier Aguirre came in, in July of 2001 and turned the squad around. He unloaded older players and gave the younger stars of the Mexican league a chance. It turned out to be a brilliant move as the team turned their fortunes around qualifying in the last match with a 3-0 win over Honduras.

At the back goalkeeper Oscar Perez was the star. He took over from the famous Jorge Campos and played spectacular football making the key saves giving his teammates the confidence to attack more.

The defence is led by the most capped player in FIFA history Claudio Suarez. 'The Emperor', as he is known is the team captain, and runs the team by leading on the field. He rarely speaks up, but his teammates believe and respect him.

The midfield was in shambles until World Cup veteran Alberto Garcia Aspe returned to the squad. His passion and mean streak helped the team become more potent in attack and stronger in defence.

Up front Cuahutemoc Blanco and Francisco Palencia are the stars. The two have international club experience playing in Spain. Blanco is a flashy striker who can score from anywhere and create space for others. Palencia is the smooth dribbler and passer who often drops deep to help bring the ball up or go out wide and send in good crosses to teammates.

SQUAD

SERGIO ALMAGUER (NECAXA) (31) CAPS: 16 GLS: 0
Has lost some of his speed as he is now 32 but not his savvy. Started his career in 1986 for Angeles, he has also played for Tigres, Puebla, Queretaro (scoring 11 times one season), Correcaminos, Necaxa and now Cruz Azul. Had an excellent season last season with the Mexico City club Necaxa, and after the year ended, he was immediately loaned to Cruz Azul to play in the second round and beyond of the Copa Libertadores.

JESUS ARELLANO (MONTERREY) (23) CAPS: 16 GLS: 0
Played in the World Cup in 1998, after being first capped by Lapuente in the Confederations Cup in 1997. Not a great scorer but Arellano has found his spot in the hole behind the forwards. He is an excellent dribbler and crosser of the ball. Is suspended for the first two World Cup matches for a fight in the Costa Rica match in qualifying.

SIDNEY BALDERAS (TIGRES) (25) CAPS: 2 GLS: 0
Came into the national team at the Gold Cup, and even though he got limited time at the tournament, Aguirre liked what he saw, and the 25-year-old is looking more and more like he will make the World Cup squad. Balderas is an outside full-back with plenty of pace. He plays for Tigres in Mexico, his only club in his short career.

MEXICO

CUAHUTEMOC BLANCO (VALLADOID) (27) CAPS: 68 GLS: 11

Impressive striker who has had a world of problems the last year and a half. The trouble started when he moved to Valladolid in Spain. Played well there but the travel back and forth was becoming a tug of war between club and country. Then in a first round qualifier versus Trinidad & Tobago he got tackled from behind and hurt his knee. Missed almost a year but returned and was the reason that Mexico started to play better. Scored two goals in the qualifying match versus Honduras. Then he quit the national team after he felt he was mistreated by the federation before moving back to Club America in Mexico in late March. He has returned to the side now.

ADOLFO BAUTISTA (TECOS) (22) CAPS: 4 GLS: 1

Bautista, like Ochoa, did not receive his first cap until this year at the Gold Cup. He was used by his club team UAG Tecos over the last few years. Then when given a chance last year scored five times in 29 matches, not a great strike rate but since most of them were scored with his head, he becomes a very valuable commodity. Netted twice in March of this year versus Albania to help his cause in making the squad.

JARED BORGUETTI (SANTOS LAGUNA) BORN: 14.08.73

A scoring phenomenon in the Mexican league with over 140 goals in 240 matches. However, after he started with a goal on his international debut he scored only one time in his next eight matches. Lost all confidence until Aguirre took over and now is back scoring with seven in his last 18 matches. Is an out and out striker who will sit in the box and when the ball falls to him it goes in. Can score with his head or feet.

MELVIN BROWN (CRUZ AZUL) (23) CAPS: 6 GLS: 0

Made a surprising debut in the World Cup qualifier versus the United States last year. Had just come back from a gruelling trip to Argentina, where he and his club team Cruz Azul lost in the second leg of the Copa Libertadores final. Brown was impressive, and Aguirre found the 23-year-old to have a wealth of talent and composure. Disappeared from the squad, but is now back in it and the full-back can play outside or as a stopper.

GABRIEL CABALLERO (PACHUCA) (30) CAPS: 3 GLS: 0

Has caused quite a stir over the last couple of months in Mexico. Caballero was born in Rosario Argentina, but has been playing in Mexico for the last seven years. Finally in early 2002 Caballero became a Mexican citizen, and Javier Aguirre called him up immediately. Many of the older and former players, criticised this move but Aguirre does not care. Caballero started with Santos in Mexico, before moving to Aguirre's former club Pachuca in 1998. He helped Pachuca to a title, and Aguirre rewarded him with his first cap versus Albania, in March. Has a good scoring touch and looks like he might link with Aspe in the midfield.

MEXICO

JORGE CAMPOS (ATLANTE) (34) CAPS: 140 GLS:0
One of the most exciting goalkeepers of the past decade but that might not be good enough for the wannabee striker to make the World Cup side. He is one of the most exciting players around, with his flair at making the big save and his desire to leave his line and play as another sweeper. Played in the 1994 and 1998 World Cups, where he performed admirably. He also played in the 1996 Olympics. Surprisingly received his first recall in almost a year, when Javier Aguirre called him up for the United States match.

DUILIO DAVINO (AMERICA F.C.) (26) CAPS: 47 GLS: 1
Another member of the lost bunch that Aguirre might still recall as the World Cup approaches. Davino, like Pardo, played in the 1996 Olympics, 1998 World Cup, and the 1999 and 2001 Confederations Cup. He is not as good as Pardo going forward but is equally strong defensively. He linked well with Claudio Suarez when they played for the national team. He is a tough customer when called upon, and has the ability to be a valuable asset on the defensive side.

MARCO A. GARCES (PACHUCA) (29) CAPS: 2 GLS: 1
Another player that Aguirre has called up from his former club team Pachuca. Garces is more of a winger, but can drop back into the defensive midfield role. Did not get his first look until earlier this year at the Gold Cup, but was one of the players to impress. Started his career with Cruz Azul and then to UAG and Chivas both of Guadalajara. Moved to Pachuca in 1999.

RAFAEL GARCIA (TOLUCA) (27) CAPS: 17 GLS: 2
Has been around the national team for a while now but does not have very many caps to show for it. Was first capped back in 1996, at the age of 22, but was rarely used after that. Then over the last two years, when his club manager Enrique Meza took over he became more and more involved. An attacking midfielder with good vision and touch. He has become an important player off the bench for the national side. Started his career at UNAM before moving to Toluca in 1998.

ALBERTO GARCIA ASPE (PUEBLA) (34) CAPS: 106 GLS: 22
One of the meanest and toughest players to come out of Mexico. Loves the confrontational aspect of the game. Has a rocket shot and plays the linking midfield position that Mexico had been missing for a while. Aguirre has said he wants players that would die to wear the Tricolores and he fits that picture. Aspe helped his club side, Puebla, to a strong performance last season and is playing well again this season.

VICTOR GUTIERREZ (CRUZ AZUL) (24) CAPS: 0 GLS: 0
Another member of Cruz Azul, who gained notoriety over the last year thanks to their historic run to the Copa Libertadores final. Can play either side in the midfield or wingback but because of his ability to cover so much ground he is used most often in the midfield.

MEXICO

RAFAEL MARQUEZ (MONACO) (23) CAPS: 34 GLS: 3
Quickly becoming one of the best players that Mexico has. He has improved immeasurably since he joined the French side AS Monaco. Has already gained over 20 caps at the age of 23. Marquez struggled with injuries last season, however he scored three times last year for the 2000 French Champions. Is good with the ball, strong in the air, and a nice passer out of the back. Playing in France has helped his overall game, and speed. Marquez has a temper, and has lost it on the field a few times causing him to miss key qualifiers.

JESUS MENDOZA (AMERICA F.C.) (23) CAPS: 8 GLS: 1
Received his first cap in late 1998, but was unimpressive and did not feature much again until Aguirre took over as manager. The 5'10" striker is good in the air, but is looked upon as a player that can play out wide or drop back and link the midfield to the forwards. Started his career at Leon and then moved to Chivas of Guadalajara, before moving to Club America. He is playing with Ivan Zamorano and has learned a lot over the last year from the Chilean star.

SIGIFREDO MERCADO (ATLAS) (33) CAPS: 17 GLS: 0
Mercado was first capped back in February of 1998, however, he was very seldom used by then manager Manuel Lapuente and after that Enrique Meza. When Aguirre took over Mercado moved into the mix. The 6'0" midfielder has a lot of club experience to call on, and his desire to win the ball does not hurt either. He has been playing in the Mexican league since 1987, having spells at Puebla, Toluca, and Leon along the way. Now with Atlas, and doing well in helping that club come back into the fray.

HERIBERTO MORALES (MORELIA) (26) CAPS: 15 GLS: 0
Not related to Ramon Morales another squad member. He is a centre back who has been in and out of the team since his first cap in late 2000. Morales is quite tall at 6'1" and seems to understand what he is on the field to do, which is to rough forwards up and clear his box. He is a good second half substitute as he does not try to do too much. Aguirre has faith in him late in the match when Mexico needs to hold onto a lead. Plays for Morelia in Mexico.

RAMON MORALES H. (CHIVAS) (26) CAPS: 17 GLS: 1
Did not get his first chance to play on a national team until last June, when Aguirre called him up for the Confederations Cup. A winger boasting good pace and the ability to score. Played at Monterrey until 1998, when he moved to Chivas of Guadalajara.

CARLOS OCHOA (LEON) (24) CAPS: 5 GLS: 1
Made his debut in the Gold Cup, where he played in a winger type role. The speedy winger is only 24, but has left a good mark on Aguirre. He started his career with Necaxa, but moved to UNL a year after. Aguirre likes Ochoa's speed, and desire to attack all the time.

MEXICO

OMAR ORTIZ (ATL. CELAYA) (26) CAPS: 1 GLS: 0
Tall goalkeeper who burst onto the scene during the Gold Cup 2002. He is good at commanding his box, and is a more than adequate shot blocker. Started his career with Monterrey, and moved to Celaya last winter. Seems to be well liked by Javier Aguirre, and looks to be the number three goalkeeper.

DANIEL OSORNO (CF ATLAS) (22)
A striker who plays a very direct game, which is very different than most Mexican players. The National team likes to knock the ball around and look for spots while Osorno likes to attack any chance without slowing down. He has good scoring ability with over 40 goals scored in 120 Mexican league games.

FRANCISCO PALENICIA (CRUZ AZUL) (28) CAPS: 66 GLS: 8
One of Mexico's most talented players who can play up front or in midfield. Can attack and defend with great pace and understanding of what needs to be done. Broke his jaw early in the season last year. He played in the 1996 Olympics, and 1998 World Cup. Has good speed, and will make good darting runs. He was a major reason that Cruz Azul became a power again in the late 1990s. Scored six times in the Copa Libertadores, and moved onto Espanyol of Spain where he is proving to be a valuable addition.

PAVEL PARDO (AMERICA F. C.) (25) CAPS: 76 GLS: 1
Was a certain starter before Javier Aguirre took over. Pardo has a deft right foot and is a dangerous playmaker from the back. His goal against Trinidad & Tobago early last year was a beauty. Aguirre has had some problems finding a quality right back, and Pardo might still get a look. He is a good man marker, strong with the ball, and can get involved offensively. Played in the 1996 Olympics, 1998 World Cup, and in the 1999 and 2001 Confederations Cup.

OSCAR PEREZ (CRUZ AZUL) (29) CAPS: 35 GLS: 0
Took over in goal once Aguirre became manager, and he proved Aguirre right. A small keeper like former No. 1 Jorge Campos but a much more adept shot blocker. Has played his whole career with Cruz Azul, which started in 1993. He has helped them to three titles since that time and has been world class in the team's run to the Copa Libertadores final.

ALBERTO RODRIGUEZ (PACHUCA) (28) CAPS: 11 GLS: 0
Another one of Aguirre's players from Pachuca. Links well with Manuel Vidrio and Rodriguez, who has been plying his trade in Mexico since 1992 starting with Pachuca. Has a serious chance at making the World Cup squad. He moved on to Monterrey for one season, and then back to Pachuca. Nicknamed, Beto, Rodriguez helped Pachuca get promoted and then lead them to the Title in 1999, and was a big factor in leading them back to the finals this season. Is the right back normally, but sometime plays in the centre when needed.

MEXICO

JOHAN RODRIGUEZ (SANTOS) (26) CAPS: 14 GLS: 1
Has for the most part been ignored at international level. Plays for Santos, one of the smaller sides in the Mexican league. Rodriguez has good talent, with a strong scoring rate for a midfielder. He has over 30 goals in 150 games in the Mexican league. His job is to feed striker Jared Borguetti at club level, and Rodriguez has excelled at that. Has a chance to be an attacking option off the bench especially with Jesus Arellano suspended for the first two World Cup games.

JUAN P. RODRIGUEZ (ATLAS) (22) CAPS: 12 GLS: 1
An attacking midfielder through and through. He has a problem playing in the unbalanced midfield, which Aguirre plays but is a valuable player off the bench. Likes to roam all over the midfield, but sometimes leaves his teammates in trouble as he is out of position. Rodriguez is a graduate from the famous Mexican Atlas football program. He has an accurate shot, and has two goals this season for the third place Atlas. Played in 2000 Olympic qualifying.

JAVIER SAAVEDRA (TIGRES) (28) CAPS: 11 GLS: 0
Was first discovered in June of 1999 by Mauel Lapuente, who thought the defensive midfielder had plenty of pace and ability to offer the national side. Unfortunately, Meza was not so impressed with him. Aguirre likes him, and he seems always to be in the mix come each call up. He is not very big, but he plays with hard tackles and a will to win that many Mexican players lack. Saavedra started his career with Deportivo Mexico before moving to Tigres.

OSWALDO SANCHEZ (CHIVAS) (28) CAPS: 19 GLS: 0
Was a member of the 1996 Mexican Olympic squad but never got a chance to play because Jorge Campos was there. A tall shot blocker who has been in the Mexican league since 1993. Sanchez is now behind Perez in the goalkeeping order, Sanchez has played for America, Atlas, before going home to Chivas of Guadalajara in the winter of '99. He has always played well for Mexico, but has the distinction of being the keeper that lost the first home game of qualifying in Mexican history.

CLAUDIO SUAREZ (TIGRES) (33) CAPS: 170 GLS: 8
Suarez, 'the Emperor,' as he is known is one of the best defenders Mexico has ever had. Made his debut in 1992, and has missed less than 20 matches that Mexico has played since. He was involved in the '94 and '98 World Cups, as well as the '96 Olympics. Is the most capped player in FIFA history. He is as good a centre back as he is a sweeper. Suarez started his career at Chivas in 1989, and then moved on to Pumas, and now Tigres. Was voted the best defender in Mexico last year. He led his team to the best defensive showing in Mexico in years with the team only conceding 13 goals in 17 matches. And this year Tigres are shutting down teams again. Suarez has scored four times for his club. Is strong in the air, moving forward, and winning the ball.

MEXICO

GERRADO TORRADO (TENERIFE) (22) CAPS: 26 GLS: 2
A midfield workhorse covering lots of ground and getting involved physically. He can be the ball winner or the link to the strikers. The defensive midfielder started his career with the UNAM Pumas but unlike many of his teammates he moved outside the country to Spain. Was instrumental in getting Tenerife promoted. Torrado was tremendous playing in 36 matches for the team. He scored once and is now with Sevilla in La Liga Primera.

OCTAVIO VALDEZ (AMERICA F. C.) CAPS: 0 GLS: 0
Made his debut in April of last year, and has claimed two more caps since. When his former club manager Aguirre took over Valdez, a left back, thought more caps would come. However, although he has been called in, he is yet to play for the national team under Aguirre. Attacks well and is a fine crosser of the ball. He started with Atletico Hidalgo but was quickly bought by Pachuca. Has since moved to Club America.

MANUEL VIDRIO (PACHUCA) (29) CAPS: 26 GLS: 1
A mean spirited full-back who never lets anyone get through without a fight. He started his career with Chivas of Guadalajara in 1992, before moving to Toluca after a short stint there onto UAG Tecos, and now Pachuca. Was instrumental in helping Pachuca become a power in the Mexican first division, and Aguirre is being very loyal to him. Vidrio is renownd for roughing up his opponents, just ask Francisco Palencia. Vidrio broke his jaw earlier this season in a clash for the ball. Has been in and out of the National team pool since the mid 1990s.

GERMAN VILLA (AMERICA F. C.) (29) CAPS: 45 GLS: 0
A player in the mold of the coach Aguirre. A committed tackler with a never-say-die spirit, Villa has played almost 50 times for his national team without scoring a goal. He does a lot of dirty work up and down the wings. Villa has played for America almost his whole career, although he did have one unsuccessful season at Espanyol in Spain.

COACH

JAVIER AGUIRRE
When Javier Aguirre took over as the Mexican National Team manager everything was in a shambles with the team. Aguirre immediately made changes, bringing in young hungry players, that "would die for the TriColores". He was able to most importantly bring Mexico to another World Cup, which looked so far away in July of last year. A very emotional manager, Aguirre brings a technical and tough minded approach to his job. He has playing experience, as he went through a World Cup in 1986, where as the hosts Mexico lost to the eventual runners-up West Germany on penalty kicks. Before he took over the team, Aguirre managed Pachuca. Pachuca were struggling in the Mexico 1A division, but quickly became a power in the top league and won the title in the winter of 1999. He has taken some abuse in the media for taking players that played for him, but he gets results, as a second place finish in the 2001 Copa America shows.

ECUADOR

Ecuador has been a struggling South American team that has always been on the outside looking in on the World Cup. However, Hernan Dario Gomez changed all that. The Colombian born coach has tightened the Ecuadorian's defence and that sparked a massive improvement. Ecuador only had a plus three goal differential in 18 matches of qualifying, yet finished second in the South American qualifying tournament above the likes of Brazil and Uraguay with 31 points. They conceded 20 goals, while scoring 23.

Jose Francisco Cevallos is the goalkeeper who kept everything together during qualifying keeping six clean sheets in his 16 matches. Ulises de la Cruz and Ivan Hurtado keep the backline together. De la Cruz is called upon to attack and help the midfield, while Hurtado does the dirty work.

The midfield has the ability to hold the ball for long stages, and wait for the right moment to push forward. The midfield is run by national hero Alex Aguinaga. He has a great shot, and nice touch to pick out the right player. He has played for Necaxa in Mexico for over ten years now, and played well in the FIFA Club Championship in Brazil.

Up front Agustin Delgado has become the superstar, while Ivan Kaviedes is the top scorer. Delgado scored in the win over Brazil and was unbelievable throughout qualifying. Kaviedes will be best known for scoring 43 goals at Emelec in one season in Ecuador. However, he should now also be known for scoring versus Venezuela in Ecuador's first qualifying win away from home since 1965.

SQUAD

ALEX AGUINAGA (NECAXA) (33) CAPS: 95 GLS: 22
Considered one of the best midfielders of the 1990s in the Americas. Can play all and any of the positions in the midfield, however, he now plays mostly as the attacking midfielder. Aguinaga is a dangerous customer and will mix it up with a rough tackle too. People might remember him from the CONCAF club championship in 1999, where he was the MVP. He was also instrumental in beating Manchester United in the World Club Championship. Aguinaga is one of the highest scoring midfielders in Mexican League history (with over 65).

JUAN FRANCISCO AGUINAGA (ESPOLI) (24) CAPS: 6 GLS: 0
The younger brother of Alex Aguinaga, and a lot is expected of him. Aguinaga has a cannon shot, and has been near the top of the scoring charts in the last year in Ecuador with Espoli. He is very quick, and dangerous with the ball, but has not been able to live with the pressure yet.

NICOLAS ASCENCIO (BARCELONA) (27) CAPS: 13 GLS: 0
Squad member who has never made his mark with only nine caps at the age of 25. He is a good club player as he finished in the top five with 12 goals scored last term. Has not played this year for the national side and only an injury to Angel Fernandez might give him the chance to impress.

ECUADOR

MARLON AYOVI (DEP. QUITO) (30) CAPS: 27 GLS: 0
A very versatile marking back who is right footed. He has been a mainstay since 1998 in the squad. Has played both outside positions in the back, as well as, moving up to a defensive midfield position. Ayovi plays at Deportivo Quito in Ecuador, and scored twice in last season's disappointing run. Has moved out to the left in matches this year.

WALTER AYOVI (NO CLUB) (22) CAPS: 3 GLS: 0
Played quite well last year for Emelec in his defensive midfield role. Walter Ayovi scored three times in helping them win the title. No longer with Emelec, and is looking for a club. A squad member rather than a starter.

RICHARD BORJA (EMELEQ) (21) CAPS: 1 GLS: 0
A defensive midfielder, he was a strong player last year in Emeleq's run to the championship and has been good again this year as Emeleq look for their second straight title. Fast and tough but lacks true international experience and touch.

MOISES CANDELARIO (EMELEQ) (25) CAPS: 6 GLS: 0
New player picking up his first cap versus Uruguay in a 4-0 loss during qualifying. He came on in the second half to play the attacking midfield role, but was not very successful. However, he played better for his club team, and has earned himself another call up. Scored eight times for Emeleq in their title season. Played versus Guatemala in January.

JOSE FRANCISCO CEVALLOS (BARCELONA) (30) CAPS: 61 GLS: 0
Moved to Barcelona of Ecuador in 1993, and that is when his international career took off. An athletic keeper who played brilliantly during the qualifiers. Cevallos was first capped in 1994, but did not really win the starting role until former Colombia coach Hernan Dario Gomez took over. Gomez' faith in Cevallos has paid off as the keeper has been key in Ecuador qualifying for the Finals. Has started every match this year, and looks like he will be the number one in Japan and South Korea.

KLEBER CHALA (SOUTHAMPTON) (30) CAPS: 63 GLS: 8
Chala's first cap came in the same match as Ivan Hurtado, and they have grown up together in the National team. Chala is a versatile player who can play in midfield, or attack when needed. Chala scored 30 goals for the U-23 squad in the early 1990s. He has eight goals for the full National team, scoring in qualifying versus Peru in June last year. Has moved onto Southampton from El Nacional, where he scored six times last season. Yet to play in the Premier League though.

ULISES DE LA CRUZ (HIBERNIAN) (30) CAPS: 51 GLS: 3
De la Cruz is one of the most versatile defenders in the world as he can play sweeper, stopper, and/or outside full-back. De la Cruz was courted by many teams in England and Italy before ending up in Scotland with Hibernian. He is tough in the air, and on the ground, and can make a great pass out of the back to start a counter attack, and will join the attack whenever he can. He made his debut at the tender age of 21, vs Japan.

ECUADOR

AGUSTIN DELGADO (SOUTHAMPTON) (27) CAPS: 45 GLS: 20

Came to prominence during the qualifying run. Delgado has been scoring from all over the place during CONMEBOL qualifying, and has nine overall, tied with Hernan Crespo of Argentina for top scorer. Equally dangerous in the air, with his shot, or dribbling at the player. Only scored four goals last season with Necaxa in Mexico, but the whole team struggled throughout the season. Southampton snapped him up, but 'Tin' only played one league game and FA Cup game before hurting his knee. Made a surprise debut in April. Was first capped in 1996 and scores in about every other match.

GEOVANNY ESPINOSA (MONTERREY) (24) CAPS: 20 GLS: 0

Has entered the mix within the last year, and although he has only had a limited role, he has impressed. So much so, that he has gotten into some key World Cup qualifiers to help preserve a lead. He plays at Aucus, where he marshals the defence. On the national squad, he is still working his way in, but looks like he will be a reserve, as he is yet to play this year. Good in the air and on set pieces. Scored two goals for his club last season as the team barely stayed up.

ANGEL FERNANDEZ (EL NACIONAL) (30) CAPS: 65 GLS: 13

An outside attacker who has good speed, but is not considered likely to score. He can, however, beat you on the counter attack, and will not miss an open chance. Fernandez has been with the National team since 1991, but has never been a mainstay – although he has amassed 64 caps, and 13 goals most of his time is spent on the bench. He scored ten goals for the El Nacional in a second place finish last year. Scored one time in qualifying in the Bolivia rout, and played eight times.

LUIS GOMEZ (BARCELONA) (29) CAPS: 8 GLS: 1

A right sided full-back, who won his first cap in the World Cup qualifying versus Bolivia where he scored a minute after walking on the pitch of a 5-1 thrashing. Likes to come forward and scored four goals last year for Barcelona. Has been used mostly as a second half substitute since he joined the club, but is moving into a starting role for the national team.

JORGE GUAGUA (EL NACIONAL) (19) CAPS: 2 GLS: 0

A young defender that burst on the scene last year, making his full debut for Ecuador versus Peru in June. He also played versus Argentina in qualifying. He is a central defender with good pace, but obviously lacks experience at the age of 19. Guagua is yet to play this year for Ecuador. Plays for El Nacional in Ecuador, scoring once last year.

RAUL GUERRON (DEP. QUITO) (25) CAPS: 21 GLS: 0

A teammate of Ayovi who has impressed with his hard nosed attitude and his defensive work ethic. He is very quick but will not attack very often from his left-sided position. Guerron scored two goals last term for Dep Quito. Played in the Turkey and Haiti internationals this year, where he was impressive.

ECUADOR

HUGO GUERRON (DEP QUITO) (24) CAPS: 2 GLS: 0
Shares the same club (Dep Quito) as brother Raul Guerron, but his style and flair are much different. Scored two goals last term for his club, and really came into his own playing in the middle. Played in the Guatemala match as a pre-Gold Cup warm-up.

IVAN HURTADO (LE PIADAD) (27) CAPS: 89 GLS: 4
One of the most experienced players in Ecuador history, this central defender has been with the National team since he was 18. Has a good relationship with de la Cruz, who plays as the floater for Ecuador, while Hurtado stays more at home in the centre. Good in the air, moved back to Ecuador from Mexico, so that he could play more in front of National team manager, Hernan Dario Gomez.

GEOVANNY IBARRA (EL NACIONAL) (32) CAPS: 10 GLS: 0
A long standing member of the national squad, however, because of Jose Cevallos, he has struggled to get many starts. Ibarra is good in the air, but has been known to struggle in big matches. He has been involved in Copa Libertadores, Copa America and World Cup qualifying. Looks like he will be the back-up for the World Cup. Only played one qualifier, and hasn't played for the national side this year.

IVAN KAVIEDES (BARCELONA) (24) CAPS: 26 GLS: 10
Striker who has struggled on the world stage. Kaviedes scored 43 goals for Emelec in a season (a record), and was immediately snapped up by Perugia of Italy. Could not get a regular start and went to Celta Vigo of Spain. Last year he played at Valladolid of Spain, where he scored four goals. His goal vs Venezuela that led to the away win earlier this year, was Ecuador's first away qualifying win since 1965. He scored three times in qualifying. Has moved back to Ecuador to play for Barcelona. On loan at Porto early 2002.

CRISTANA LARA (EL NACIONAL) (21) CAPS: 2 GLS: 0
Lara can play either the midfield or forward role, and did a nice job linking the two last season when his club team finished second. He scored 15 goals in the term. Lara got called up this year due to his impressive play, and he got his first cap versus Guatemala in January.

EDISON MENDEZ (DEP QUITO) (22) CAPS: 23 GLS: 2
Another of Gomez's finds, Mendez can attack and defend and most importantly run all day. Is close to displacing Obregon in the centre of midfield, but if needs be can move out wide normally on the left side, but he is equally strong with both feet. Was first capped in 2000, and has played almost every match for the Tricolores since, including all four this year. Four goals last term for Dep Quito. Scored versus Peru in qualifying.

ALFONSO OBREGON (DELFIN) (29) CAPS: 40 GLS: 0
Most of the midfield is made up of support players for the aging Aguinaga, who when on the team is a Valderrama type player in the sense of his movement on the defensive side. Obregon, is a workhorse in the mould of a Leonel Alvarez. Found his scoring touch last term with seven goals for Delfin.

ECUADOR

EVELIO ORDONEZ (EL NACIONAL) (30) CAPS: 7 GLS: 0
Another player from El Nacional, Ordonez has been in and out of Ecuador squads for years. Has a lot of pace, and has good awareness, but has never put it together on the international scene. Scored ten goals last term.

AUGUSTO POROSO (STANFORD) (27) CAPS: 18 GLS: 0
Porozo grew up in the youth system of Emelec, and is still there winning three championships with the squad, including last year's. PoroSo is a left-footed centre back who's good in the air. Not the most technically sound player, but has played well in qualifying. Scored four times last year. Received two reds during qualifying.

WELLINGTON SANCHEZ (NO CLUB) (27) CAPS: 35 GLS: 3
Sanchez was found by the MLS, when he scored vs the USA in Baltimore (1997). He is a good dribbler and distributor, but can drift out of games and does not like to mix it up. He played five qualifiers, scoring once and getting sent off. Scored eight goals last term for Emelec to help them win the title, but is without a club at the moment.

CARLOS TENORIO (LDI QUITO) (22) CAPS: 7 GLS: 2
Burst onto the scene last year scoring 11 goals in helping LDU Quito get promoted, and has been a major part of the team since. He has lightening speed and is a good dribbler. Prefers the right side but will play up top by himself when needed. Good in the air, he scored the winner versus Turkey in March.

EDWIN TENORIO (DEP QUITO) (25) CAPS: 33 GLS: 0
Plays as a linking midfielder for the defence and forwards. Very adept at moving the ball forward quickly. Tenorio has hardly played for the National team over the last two years. Was in second division Mexico but has moved home to Dep Quito in the hope of winning a place in the World Cup side.

DANIEL VITERI (EMELEQ) (21) CAPS: 0 GLS: 0
Came out of nowhere as he led the countries U-20 team to the second round in Argentina, and helped his club team, Emelec, to their first title since 1994. Good shot blocker but has a lot to learn about commanding his box.

COACH

HERNAN DARIO GOMEZ
Gomez is a national hero in Ecuador, having guided the National team to their first ever World Cup. He took over in 1999 and immediately things changed. The defence became much stronger only giving up 20 goals in 18 qualifiers. Gomez played in Colombia with Independiente Medellin and Atletico Nacional and for the Colombian National team in 1978. An assistant in the 1990 and 1994 World Cups for Colombia, he managed them himself in 1998. Gomez won championships as a manager with Atletico Nacional.

GROUP H

No host country in World Cup history has ever failed to qualify from the first stage and Japan can consider themselves fortunate to have been drawn in, possibly, the weakest group. As co-hosts, they did not have to qualify and, in Frenchman Philippe Troussier, they have a coach with a wealth of experience.

Nicknamed 'the Witch Doctor' after ten years in Africa, he led Japan's Under-20s to the final of the World Youth Cup and then helped the senior squad win the Asian Cup in 2000.

Their programme of friendlies has seen Japan draw 0-0 with Brazil, in the Confederations Cup, beat Australia 1-0 and, in November, hold Italy to a 1-1 draw. Now they believe they can improve on their first round failure in 1998 when they scored only one goal and lost all three games.

Japan have a young team; the expected average age in the Finals will be just 24. Troussier knows his players well after his involvement with the junior squad and likes to play attacking football with wingers.

The biggest names, Arsenal's Junichi Inamoto, Kashima Antlers's Atushi Yanagisawa, and Hidetoshi Nakata of Parma, are guaranteed their places while Feyenoord's Shinji Ono also offers great promise. With home advantage, Troussier is hopeful.

Another experienced coach is Belgium's Robert Waseige but it took a nervous play-off against the highly-fancied Czech Republic to see the country into their 11th Finals.

In the qualifying group Belgium had scored 25 goals but still finished behind Croatia. They beat the Czechs 1-0 at home and, in the return in Prague, stole another 1-0 victory to qualify, thanks to a late penalty from Marc Wilmots, his eighth goal in the competition.

The squad is getting old; Gert Verheyen is 31, Yves Vanderhaeghe is 32 and Wilmots is 33. Still, Waseige has younger players such as Celtic's Joos Valgaeren and the lively Wesley Sonck, who have shown much promise.

Russia won their group ahead of Slovenia and Yugoslavia and are turning to home-based players as the back bone of their squad. They have also shown a tendency to believe the rest of the world is against them.

When Premiership referee Graham Poll awarded a controversial, last-minute penalty to give Slovenia a 2-1 win over Russia, one of the Russian players, Alexander Mostovoi, called the official "a snivelling creep who robbed us".

Russia then went to the Faroe Islands with Siberian-born coach Oleg Romantsev, who also coached Spartak Moscow, pulling no punches. He said: "'If we can't beat teams from sheep-rearing islands we don't deserve to go to the World Cup Finals." They did beat them 3-0, and finished with a 4-0 victory over Switzerland.

Another experienced coach, Henri Michel, will take charge of Tunisia. The former

French national coach is going to the Finals for the fourth time, and with a fourth different team, after leading his own nation to third place, in 1986, Cameroon and Morocco.

But a poor showing in the African Nations Cup earlier this year, where Tunisia failed to score, has left the Frenchman to consider the make-up of his squad. Michel admitted his team needed a radical new approach to stand any chance of making an impression at the World Cup Finals after their early exit in Mali.

Michel came in for a German, Eckhard Krautzen, who had been been in charge for the majority of matches in Tunisia's impressive World Cup qualifying campaign.

Optimism, then, is not high. "It is true we were not properly prepared and that we did badly in Mali," says captain Chokri El Ouaer, the veteran goalkeeper who played at the last World Cup Finals. "There are many players now coming up from the Under-23 side but it takes time for them to get used to top level soccer."

JAPAN

"After the friendly draw against Italy, our confidence increased. We are one of the candidates in Group H to reach the last 16. In my mind, I feel that my players will surely show their potential looking forward to the World Cup. It is such an open group and we all have a chance." Japan coach **Philippe Trousier**

BELGIUM

"I see it as an open group where all teams can realize their ambitions. The cocktail is very interesting, with an Asian team (Japan), Russia, which is like its own continent, an African team (Tunisia) and one from Europe (Belgium). My sentiment is that the extra pressure will be on Japan, because the Japanese public and the Japanese press expect many things from their team. **Robert Waseige**, Belgian coach.

RUSSIA

"Reaching the quarter-finals is our minimum goal in Japan, where we play our first three games." **Oleg Romantsev**, Russian coach.

TUNISIA

"We're satisfied with the match up. We hope to make as much preparation as possible before the event, but the game against Japan will likely be a tough one." **Henri Michel**, Tunisia coach.

JAPAN

When Philippe Troussier took over as head coach of Japan in September 1998, many wondered what a man who had so much experience in Africa could do with one of Asia's most developed and progressive nations.

Millions had been spent on the J League and the development of the game since the Japanese decided to bid to host the World Cup, but no one was sure just how far the nation could go in the world game. The Japanese reached the Finals for the first time in France four years ago and failed to earn a single point, despite encouraging displays against Argentina and Croatia, but with then-coach Takeshi Okada resigning after the tournament, the way forward seemed uncertain.

In came Troussier, on the recommendation of Japan Football Association advisor Arsene Wenger, and, while the knives were out initially for the former South Africa, Burkina Faso and Nigeria coach, the Frenchman gradually won over the sceptics. Under Troussier, Japan's showing at international level – especially outside of Asia – has grown considerably over the last two years with solid results against Italy, Poland and Ukraine since the tail-end of 2001. Troussier's cause – and that of Japan – was helped by the fact that, since the birth of the J League in 1993, a technically sound and success-hungry group of youngsters have emerged and many of those have arrived in time to form the backbone of this summer's squad.

Japan's run of footballing success under Troussier started in Nigeria in 1999 when the nation's under-20 side reached the final of the World Youth Championship, losing out to Spain. From there the progression continued, with many of the Nigeria '99 squad helping Japan qualify for the Olympic Games in Sydney, where they eventually reached the quarter-finals, losing out to the United States on penalties.

The sign that Japan had moved forward quicker than many imagined came, however, in Lebanon in October 2000 when a team missing several top names – but again comprising the core which had made the last eight in Sydney – lifted the Asian Cup. That fact was underlined emphatically by reaching the final of the Confederations Cup in June 2001, where they lost 1-0 to France having beaten Cameroon, Canada and Australia and drawn with Brazil.

Troussier has successfully merged several generations of talented young players to create a top-class side that will impress and surprise many this year. He also has the likes of Parma's Hidetoshi Nakata at his disposal – the two-time Asian Player of the Year shining again against Poland in March after a disappointing season at club level – while Shinji Ono has blossomed since his move to Feyenoord last summer.

The Japanese have had problems, too, however. Both midfielder Junichi Inamoto and goalkeeper Yoshikatsu Kawaguchi – regulars in Troussier's starting line-up – have not had the same success as Nakata and Ono at Arsenal and Portsmouth respectively with neither settling in to first team football in England.

Injuries to the likes of Ryuzo Morioka, part of Troussier's controversial flat back three, have also hampered the team's preparations but, all-in-all, things have gone well. Expectations within Japan are high and when the draw was completed many felt the Asian Cup winners were given a good opportunity to qualify for the knockout stages. No doubt Belgium and Russia, in particular, would look to disagree but, with home advantage and an improving team, Japan's chances of taking a place in the second round look good.

SQUAD

TAKASHI FUKUNISHI (JUBILO IWATA) BORN: 01/09/76
Defensive midfielder who learned his trade under Brazilian legend Dunga. Hard in the tackle, Fukunishi has been the driving force behind much of Jubilo's success at national and Asian level but, with competition for places tough in his position, has rarely had the chance to shine for Japan.

YASUHIRO HATO (YOKOHAMA F MARINOS) BORN: 04/05/76
Impressed for Japan on the right side of midfield during the Confederations Cup when he was one of the revelations of the tournament for the Japanese. Has since come under pressure for a place in the starting line-up, however, from Daisuke Ichikawa.

TOSHIHIRO HATTORI (JUBILO IWATA) BORN: 23/09/73
A favourite of Troussier's for his work rate and defensive solidity. Hattori returned for the friendly match against Costa Rica in April after missing ten weeks due to intestinal surgery. Can play on the left side of the team's flat back three or in the left wingback position.

DAISUKE ICHIKAWA (SHIMIZU S-PULSE) BORN: 14/05/80
Ichikawa picked up his first cap for Japan back in April '98 as an 18-year-old and just missed out on selection for the France World Cup. Now, after several years building himself up, he is back in the reckoning and is battling with Hato for the place on the right wing.

JUNICHI INAMOTO (ARSENAL) BORN: 18/09/79
Was seen as Japan's great hope in the centre of midfield with his tough tackling and long, accurate passing before he became lost in Arsenal's reserves. A lack of first team football has already affected his performances for Japan but the tenacious tackler should pick up his form in time for the tournament.

YOSHIKATSU KAWAGUCHI (PORTSMOUTH) BORN: 10/08/73
Became a household name in Japan when his goalkeeping exploits helped Japan qualify for the Olympic Games in Atlanta in 1996 and shortly after established himself as the nation's number one. However, inconsistency has dogged him in the past and, while an impressive shot-stopper, Kawaguchi's weakness on crosses has seen him exposed in the past, none more so than following his move to England, where he has struggled in the First Division, losing his place in the starting line up to 42-year-old Dave Beassant.

NAOKI MATSUDA (YOKOHAMA F MARINOS) BORN: 14/03/77
After a shaky start, Matsuda has become one of the most stable of Japan's defenders. Can play in any position in the back three and was a member of the squad that easily won the Asian Cup in Lebanon in 2000.

JAPAN

TSUNEYASU MIYAMOTO (GAMBA OSAKA) BORN: 07/02/77
Deputised at the centre of Japan's defence for the injured Ryuzo Morioka but has failed to add the same stability given by the Shimizu S-Pulse defender. Came to international attention in 2000 when a proposed move to West Ham United fell through.

RYUZO MORIOKA (SHIMIZU S-PULSE) BORN: 07/10/75
Captained the team that won the Asian Cup in Lebanon in 2000 and looks set to lead the team this summer. Plays in the centre of Troussier's flat back three and will have just returned from a lengthy absence due to injury by the time the championship starts.

HIROAKI MORISHIMA (CEREZO OSAKA) BORN: 30/04/72
One of the elder statesmen of Troussier's team, Morishima came into his own as Japan won the Asian Cup in Lebanon two years ago. Usually fills the play-maker's role in the absence of Hidetoshi Nakata and regularly pitches in with a vital goal or two.

YUJI NAKAZAWA (YOKOHAMA F MARINOS) BORN: 25/02/78
Solid in the air but a little clumsy on the ground, Nakazawa has none the less done well for Japan at all levels. Moved to the Marinos during the close season after a poor year with Verdy last time around and has impressed alongside Matsuda.

HIDETOSHI NAKATA (PARMA) BORN: 25/01/77
The most high profile player in Japan, Nakata has had a troubled season at Parma, where he has struggled in a poor team. He has had his problems with Japan too, although his feud with Troussier appears to be over, a fact highlighted by his stirring performance in the 2-0 win against Poland. The key to Japan's success in many ways, the two-time Asian Player of the Year will be looking for a successful World Cup to kick start his own career.

KOJI NAKATA (KASHIMA ANTLERS) BORN: 09/07/79
Another player to have represented Japan at all levels. Plays on the left side but can also step into midfield. A fantastic long passer of the ball, Nakata has set up numerous fruitful forays into opposition territory for both Japan and Kashima, the current J League champions.

SHUNSUKE NAKAMURA (YOKOHAMA F MARINOS) BORN: 24/06/78
Said to be on his way to Real Madrid after the World Cup, Nakamura is something of an enigma. A top quality J League player who has yet to truly shine at international level. Has had more than a few run-ins with Troussier over his lack of defensive covering but can be deadly from set-pieces.

MASASHI NAKAYAMA (JUBILO IWATA) BORN: 23/09/67
Scored Japan's only goal in France '98 when he netted against Jamaica in the nation's 2-1 loss in Lyon. Had been a regular in the side under Troussier until the end of 2001, since when the Frenchman has failed to select him.

JAPAN

HIROSHI NANAMI (JUBILO IWATA) BORN: 28/11/72
Had a poor year in Italy after shining in both Japanese and Asian competitions for Jubilo and Japan. Nanami's famed left foot helped his club win the J League and the Asian Club Championship but his oft-criticised work rate made life difficult for him in Serie A. Missed much of 2001 due to a knee injury.

SEIGO NARAZAKI (NAGOYA GRAMPUS EIGHT) BORN: 15/04/76
Kicked off his career between the posts for Japan inauspiciously, conceding a soft goal against South Korea in March '98. Has struggled to establish himself since, although he did appear at one time to be Philippe Troussier's preferred choice before losing his place to Yoshikatsu Kawaguchi.

AKINORI NISHIZAWA (CEREZO OSAKA) BORN: 18/06/76
Had spells in Spain and England but failed to live up to expectations. Scored regularly for Japan but is unlikely to be given a starting place by Troussier unless one of his other forwards is hit by serious injury. Hard working but lacking in talent.

MITSUO OGASAWARA (KASHIMA ANTLERS) BORN: 05/04/79
Another of the young breed coming through at Kashima Antlers, Ogasawara is unlikely to make much of an impact on the squad this time around. If he is there for the Finals, it will be to prepare him for a greater role in four years' time.

DAISUKE OKU (YOKOHAMA F MARINOS) BORN: 07/02/76
Moved clubs during the close season in an attempt to win a place in Troussier's World Cup squad after his options appeared limited at Jubilo Iwata. Good enough at domestic and Asian level but yet to prove himself good enough for top class football.

SHINJI ONO (FEYENOORD)
With Nakata's poor form in Italy, Ono has moved into the spotlight with his performances in Holland. Moved to Rotterdam last summer and has steadily improved, underlining his rating as Japan's most naturally gifted player. Is likely to play wide either on the left or right for Japan as Nakata will occupy his usual central berth.

ALESSANDRO SANTOS (SHIMIZU S-PULSE) BORN: 20/07/77
Gained Japanese citizenship at the tail end of 2001 and was immediately selected for Troussier's squad. Known as Alex, the left wingback was named J League Player of the Year in 1999 and is known for his pace and skill.

TAKAYUKI SUZUKI (KASHIMA ANTLERS) BORN: 05/06/76
Came to the fore for Japan at the Confederations' Cup, scoring both goals in Japan's 2-0 win over Cameroon. A fiery character who has pace and physical presence, he is vying with club mate Atsushi Yanagisawa for a place in the forward line.

JAPAN

HITOSHI SOGAHATA (KASHIMA ANTLERS) BORN: 02/08/79
Young goalkeeper who made his name in Japan's Under-20s team that reached the final of the World Youth Championship in Nigeria in 1999. Has become the number one at J League champions Kashima Antlers and has a bright future.

NAOHIRO TAKAHARA (JUBILO IWATA) BORN: 04/06/79
Strong and physical striker who tried his luck in Argentina with disappointing results, playing only seven times and scoring just once. Returned to Japan because of the economic crisis in the South American nation. Regular scorer for Japan and Jubilo and should lead the line this summer.

KAZUYUKI TODA (SHIMIZU S-PULSE) BORN: 30/12/77
In the absence of Junichi Inamoto, who has only been able to play a handful of games for Japan since his move to Arsenal, Shimizu's Toda has stepped in to fill the position in front of the defence for Japan with great effect. Should operate alongside the former Gamba Osaka man at the World Cup.

ATSUSHI YANAGISAWA (KASHIMA ANTLERS) BORN: 27/05/77
Turned down a move to Italy's Perugia to stay in Japan in the months leading up to the World Cup. A strong physical striker, Yanagisawa has scored regularly for both club and country, although he hit a barren spell in the league at the start of 2002 as the pre-World Cup pressure began to mount.

YOSHITERU YAMASHITA (VEGALTA SENDA) BORN: 21/11/77
Was the key figure behind the success of his club side after their promotion to the top flight in Japan and his goalscoring record earned him a place in Troussier's squad ahead of the World Cup. Has improved significantly in recent seasons.

COACH

PHILIPPE TROUSSIER
Took over in September 1998 after working in Africa for a decade, where he earned the nickname 'White Witch Doctor' for his success with ASEC in Ivory Coast. Qualified Nigeria for the World Cup Finals in 1998 only to lose his job, then taking over as head coach in Burkina Faso for the African Nations Cup. He guided one of the world's poorest nations to the semi-finals before again packing his bags, this time heading to South Africa. He took the Bafana Bafana to France but the Frenchman had a troubled time as the team rebelled against his leadership and picked up only one point from three games – a draw against Saudi Arabia in the last round of matches. Despite an undistinguished playing career as a defender in France's lower divisions, Troussier is a student of the world game and counts Arrigo Sacchi among his heroes. Troussier has already made it clear he has no intention of staying in Japan after the World Cup, a fact that will no doubt please many within the Japan Football Association, who dislike his politicking and aggressive attitude.

BELGIUM

Ask most fans to name the only country ever to qualify for six successive World Cup finals without having the advantage of being either hosts or holders and the answer is unlikely to be Belgium.

But that is exactly who it is. Belgium created a little niche of their own as far as World Cup history is concerned when they beat the Czech Republic 1-0 home and away in the play-offs last November to become the first country ever to qualify for six successive World Cups.

What they have done when they have got there is another matter entirely. Apart from 1986 when they reached the semi-finals and lost the third-place play-off to France, Belgium usually travel more in hope than expectation, making up the numbers. Without being too dismissive of their chances this year, the same outcome is on the cards again.

But they should survive the first round at least. They are grouped with co-hosts Japan, Russia and Tunisia and have a reasonable chance of advancing from that section. Their most problematic game is likely to be their opening one against Japan in Saitama on June 4. The home team and fans will be fired up as never before. Although on paper Belgium would normally expect to beat the Japanese – these will be highly unusual circumstances, and as history has shown time and again, the hosts are almost always inspired by the World Cup, never usually daunted.

That of course, is more than can be said of Belgium themselves when they co-hosted Euro 2000 with the Netherlands and became the first hosts ever to be eliminated in the opening round.

They have gone some way into making amends for that by reaching the World Cup Finals. Unbeaten in seven matches until losing their last Group Six game 1-0 to Croatia – when they were assured of a place in the play-offs anyway – they duly completed their qualification with home and away victories over the fancied Czechs.

Belgium kept faith with coach Robert Waseige after the failure of Euro 2000 and he has largely retained the nucleus of that squad. His main problem in preparing for the World Cup was his lack of real cutting-edge strikers and a reliable safe pair of hands at the back.

Waseige, who has made a full recovery from a heart by-pass operation last year, is a strict adherent to 4-4-2 and could well deploy Gert Verheyen and the injury-riddled Emile Mpenza in attack. There was welcome news when Branko Strupar finally returned to the Derby County side late in the season after months out with injury – and he could provide some more potency in attack if called upon. There are also hopes that Wesley Sonck of Genk could add his pace to the front-line.

But the other worry is in goal. With Filip De Wilde in the cold after his woeful display when Belgium were eliminated from Euro 2000 losing 2-0 to Turkey in Brussels when he had a nightmare match ending with a late sending off, no-one has really emerged to fill the gap. Geert De Vlieger is now the incumbent, but doubts remain over his ability at the highest level.

Two years on from Euro 2000 and despite the lack of real class in attack, Waseige has managed to add some attacking flair to Belgium's traditional workmanlike industry.

The key to their success is undoubtedly the form and fitness of Schalke 04 midfielder

BELGIUM

Marc Wilmots, who is now 33. He was their top scorer in the qualifiers with eight goals and typically it was his late penalty against the Czechs in the second leg of the play-offs in Prague that secured Belgium's passage to Asia. He should take his tally of caps to nearly 70 by the time the World Cup is over.

Wilmots' most accomplished midfield partner is Hertha Berlin's Bart Goor, whose seven goals in his first 33 internationals prove his worth. Belgium also have an array of unremarkable but reliable defenders and midfielders in the shape of Yves Vanderhaeghe, Joos Valgaeren, Walter Baseggio and others, but everything points to another middle-ranking performance.

Since 1986 when Belgium reached the semi-finals, they have made it to the second round twice (1990 and 1994) and been eliminated in the first round once, in France, four years ago.

They are hopeful of improving on that performance this time around but are unlikely to go much further than the last 16, assuming they make it that far, again.

SQUAD

WALTER BASEGGIO (ANDERLECHT) BORN: 19.08.78 CAPS: 10 GLS: 1
Belgium's Young Footballer of the Year in both 1999 and 2000 – the last to win two in a row was Celestine Babayaro when he was at Anderlecht. Was third in the senior awards in 2000. Very close to Euro 2000 selection and a hot prospect. Gained first three caps before Euro 2000 - and first choice in squad since the Finals. Of Italian immigrant parents like Enzo Scifo, he has come through the club's juniors after joining aged 13.

GLEN DE BOECK (ANDERLECHT) BORN: 22.06.71 CAPS: 30 GLS: 0
Disappointed not to make the Euro 2000 squad – he must have been next on the list. Defender who can play defensive midfield, he is in his seventh season with Anderlecht, he arrived from Mechelen just after Anderlecht's previous title win in 1995, so had to wait until 2000 for his first championship medal. First choice in 2000 and 2001 title wins. Eight years in national team and squad.

DANNY BOFFIN (ST TRUIDEN) BORN: 10.07.65 CAPS: 50 GLS: 1
Recalled by coach Waseige after retiring from international football in 1999 - Waseige wanted a left-sided player after the failure at Euro 2000. Began his career with St Truiden then won a Cup medal under Waseige in his time at FC Liege, and was at Anderlecht from 1991-97 with whom he won three titles in 1993, 1994 and 1995. Spent three seasons with Metz in the French league, then returned to St Truiden in summer 2000. Was in charge of Belgium's left flank for much of the 1990s after winning first cap in 1989.

DANIEL VAN BUYTEN (MARSEILLE) BORN: 07.02.78 CAPS: 4 GLS: 1
Joined Marseille in summer 2001 from Standard Liege. His progression though has stalled in Marseille turmoil in 2001-2 season. Late equaliser in Scotland dented Scots chances of qualification. A first teamer at Standard since 1998, and nearly 6'5" tall.

BELGIUM

PHILIPPE CLEMENT (FC BRUGES) BORN: 22.03.74 CAPS: 17 GLS: 0
Joined Bruges in summer 1999 from Coventry for £770,000, a season after Coventry bought him from Genk for £600,000. Bruges were 2000 runners-up to Anderlecht. Just 12 Premiership games (six starts). Joined Coventry from Genk after being in their 1998 League runners-up team and Cup final success – missed '99 championship win when at Coventry instead. Nearly 6'3" tall and played two of three World Cup games in France.

BERTRAND CRASSON (ANDERLECHT) BORN: 05.10.71 CAPS: 26 GLS: 1
Captain of the Anderlecht team and won his fifth title in 2001 – recalled to national team in 2001. First played for Anderlecht aged 16, and is now in the fourth season of his second spell at the club after a time in Serie A with Napoli. First spell at club saw him as a teenage international full-back and club captain 1985-1996 when he won four titles in the 1990s. Settled in well at Napoli from 1996-98 until relegation.

ERIC DEFLANDRE (OLYMPIQUE LYON) BORN: 02.08.73 CAPS: 38 GLS: 0
£3.6 million move to Lyon in summer 2000. Is nominally the first choice right wing back – played in the 1998 World Cup where he came on after just 20 mins of the opener vs Holland to replace Bertrand Crasson and played well. Five seasons with Bruges – formerly FC Liege and Germinal Ekeren – and played key roles in their 1996 and 1998 title wins, 1996 was a double winning year. Regained place in national side after not getting on with Georges Leekens after World Cup.

DIDIER DHEEDENE (1860 MUNICH) BORN: 22.01.72 CAPS: 3 GLS: 0
Joined 1860 in summer 2001 on a Bosman transfer after being left wing back in the Anderlecht team that won the Belgian championship in 2000 and 2001 and was in the team that played in the second phase of the 2000-1 Champions League. Four seasons with Anderlecht, he arrived there in summer 1997 after being a star in the Belgian Cup final when his then club Germinal Ekeren beat Anderlecht. Reached 250 Division One games with Germinal and Anderlecht.

RONNY GASPERCIC (BETIS SEVILLE) BORN: 09.05.69 CAPS: 8 GLS: 0
Back-up keeper in the Belgian national squad, and in current squad – though not playing first team for Betis. Has been in Spain for four seasons – and moved in summer 2001 from Extremadura where the club was stagnating in Division Two. Former keeper for Genk (1990-96) and Harelbeke (1996-98) in the Belgian first division.

BART GOOR (HERTHA BERLIN) BORN: 09.04.73 CAPS: 35 GLS: 9
2000 and 2001 championship medals with Anderlecht – joined Hertha in summer 2001 from Anderlecht for £4.4 million. Former top scorer with Genk, he moved to Anderlecht in summer 1997 and was converted to a wide player operating down the left flank. Scored the first goal of Euro 2000 (vs Sweden).

BELGIUM

MARC HENDRIKX (ANDERLECHT) BORN: 02.07.74 CAPS: 15 GLS: 0
Changed clubs in 2001 when he moved from former champions Genk to Anderlecht –
to link up again with former coach Aime Anthuenis. Replaced Bart Goor at Anderlecht.
Was closely monitored for a couple of seasons by Ajax. In Genk side that won 1998 Cup
and were 1998 league runners-up, then became the 1999 champions. Four seasons
with Genk, ex-Lommel.

FREDERIC HERPOEL (GHENT) BORN:16.08.74 CAPS: 3 GLS: 0
First cap was as a sub in the memorable 5-5 draw with the Dutch in Sept '99 after injury
to van der Walle after just a few minutes. Not been trusted since. Former Anderlecht
junior from age of 14, he then moved moved to Ghent after a nine-year spell with
Anderlecht. Fifth season at Ghent.

PETER VAN HOUDT (BORUSSIA MONCHENGLADBACH) BORN: 04.11.76 CAPS: 3 GLS: 0
Two seasons with the German club, after joining from Dutch club Utrecht. Home club
was St Truiden but has spent most of his time outside the country. Reserve forward.

NICO VAN KERCKHOVEN (SCHALKE) BORN: 14.12.70 CAPS: 38 GLS: 3
Had another fine season with Schalke, the 2001 Bundesliga runners-up and 2001
German Cup winners. Joined Schalke for £1 million from Lierse after the 1998 World
Cup Finals and is a first choice in their side. Was the midfield hub of the Lierse club side
who won the 1997 championship and gained his first cap against Italy in summer 1996.
Born at Lier (Lierse) and was with the club for 12 seasons – played Champions League
1997-98. Operates almost exclusively down the left side – either in defence or attack –
but can fill in at central defence as he is 6'3" tall.

ERIC VAN MEIR (STANDARD LIEGE) BORN: 28.02.68 CAPS: 30 GLS: 1
Moved from Lierse to Standard in summer 2001 to replace Daniel van Buyten, who
went to Marseille. Was amazingly the top scorer for Lierse when they won the 1997
championship for the first time since 1961 with 16 goals from the sweeper's
position! Less success in an injured-plagued 1997-98 but popped up with another 14
goals in 1998-99 and another 16 goals to be club top scorer again in 1999-2000.
Was in the 1994 World Cup squad as a midfielder but has been switched to sweeper
when he moved in summer 1996 from his first club Charleroi to Lierse. Also in 1998
World Cup squad.

LOKONDA 'EMILE' MPENZA (SCHALKE) BORN: 04.07.78 CAPS: 35 GLS: 12
Known as Emile Mpenza, and is the younger of the brothers, born in Belgium of Zairean
parents. Moved from Standard to Schalke in Jan 2000 for £5 million. Super season in
2000-1 with 16 goals as the club was runner-up in the Bundesliga and won the German
Cup. First made the grade under former national coach Leekens when both were at
Mouscron in the 1996-97 season when he scored 12 goals.

BELGIUM

MBO MPENZA (MOUSCRON) BORN: 04.12.76 CAPS: 23 GLS: 0
The older of the brothers but less experienced internationally, also played in 1996-97 in breakthrough season at Mouscron under Georges Leekens – and like brother also scored 12 goals. He moved to Standard in the 2000 winter-break and then went to Sporting for £2 million and straight into a side that won the 2000 championship. Back from Sporting to first club Mouscron via a few brief months at Galatasaray where he was part of the Mario Jardel package. Is often used as a sub, he's very quick – but not as talented as Emile.

JACKY PEETERS (GHENT) BORN: 13.12.69 CAPS: 10 GLS: 0
First capped against Holland in the 5-5 draw, he was in Germany with the Bundesliga team Bielefeld, and was in their promotion team in 1999 as Div Two champions. However, in 2000 they were relegated. So returned to Belgium. Originally with Genk and left in 1998 after they won the Cup and were runners-up in the league. Likes to play as a full back. One of Waseige's additions to the squad.

BOB PEETERS (VITESSE ARNHEM) BORN: 10.01.74 CAPS: 11 GLS: 4
Plays his football in Holland for Vitesse. Began his career in Belgium with Lierse – he played for them from 1992 to 1997, and was in the team that won the 1997 championship. Moved from Lierse to Roda from 1997-2000 and was top scorer in the three seasons with them, which alerted Vitesse.

TIMMY SIMONS (FC BRUGES) BORN: 11.12.76 CAPS: 9 GLS: 0
Defensive midfielder with FC Bruges, close runners-up to Anderlecht in 2001. Joined Bruges in summer 2000 from Lommel, who were relegated. Had two seasons in the Lommel first team from 1998-2000 and was an U21 international, and continued improvement at Bruges.

WESLEY SONCK (RC GENK) BORN: 09.08.78 CAPS: 10 GLS: 2
Former U21 striker. Plays for Genk, and is in his second season with them after signing in summer 2000 from GB Antwerp, who are an amalgamation of three clubs in 1999 including Germinal Ekeren, with whom he played. Moved to Standard in summer 1997 when AC Milan and Barcelona also had a look at him – but the father, who is their agent, insisted that the brothers gain a full education first. Played in 1998 World Cup.

BRANKO STRUPAR (DERBY COUNTY) BORN: 09.02.70 CAPS: 13 GLS: 5
Belgian Footballer of the Year 1999 and a Belgian national since July 1999. Moved to Derby for £3 million in December 1999. A Croatian from the NK Zagreb club, born in Zagreb, and arrived at Genk in 1994 and gained citizenship. Was Belgian League top scorer in 1997-98 with 22 goals in a side that won the Cup and were second in the league, and was club top scorer with another 22 goals in 1998-99 when Genk won the title. Was also watched closely by Leverkusen, but Derby beat them to his signature. Formed an instant partnership with Emile Mpenza but it was broken up through injury.

BELGIUM

STEFAN TANGHE (UTRECHT) BORN: 15.01.72 CAPS: 9 GLS: 2
Recalled to the squad in March 2002 and is now with Dutch club Utrecht since summer 2000. Midfielder who played in Belgium for Kortrijk (1992-97) and then under former national coach Georges Leekens at Mouscron from 1997-2000. From the south of Belgium, his clubs are close to Lille in Northern France.

JOOS VALGAEREN (CELTIC) BORN: 03.03.76 CAPS: 13 GLS: 0
Might struggle to be fit for the Finals. Missed Celtic 2002 title run-in. First season with Celtic was when he won the treble of League, Cup and League Cup in 2000-1 after a £3 million move from Dutch club Roda JC in summer 2000. Also won 2000 Dutch Cup with Roda. Three seasons with Roda, and was signed from Mechelen for whom he played from teenage years to U21 honours – leaving when Mechelen hit hard times in 1997.

YVES VANDERHAEGHE (ANDERLECHT) BORN: 30.01.70 CAPS: 27 GLS: 2
A brave man who has recovered from cancer as a child. Joined Anderlecht from Mouscron in summer 2000 and won the title in first season with them. Another championship in 2001. Defensive midfielder also from Leekens former club Mouscron. Two spells at Mouscron, in between three seasons at Aalst from 1994-97. Plays in front of back four for club. Often said to play better for country than for his club, and has never let Belgium down. Has slotted into the role Franky van der Elst had for 12 years.

GERT VERHEYEN (FC BRUGES) BORN: 20.09.70 CAPS: 44 GLS: 10
Useful 15-20 goals a season winger who has started scoring at national level. Key player in Bruges' 1996 and 1998 title wins, he has been at Bruges for ten seasons now. Started as a Lierse junior, then to Anderlecht from 1988-92 but was moved on to Bruges for more chances in the top flight. Eight seasons in national squad.

SVEN VERMANT (SCHALKE) BORN: 04.04.73 CAPS: 11 GLS: 0
Joined the Belgian enclave in summer 2001 from FC Bruges, and cost £1.3 million. Few caps since 1995 is poor reward for some steady football down Bruges left flank. Eight seasons at Bruges after joining from Mechelen – with championship medals in 1996 and 1998, and runners-up in 2000 and 2001. Nearly 300 Belgian Div One games.

GEERT DE VLIEGER (WILLEM II TILBURG) BORN: 16.10.71 CAPS: 22 GLS: 0
Amazing run to the top in 1999 – he was formerly the Anderlecht No 2 to Filip de Wilde, the World Cup keeper, so was loaned out to Harelbeke, where he played so well on loan that he was capped. Anderlecht promptly got him back in summer 1999 and made him their No 1, then dropped him, and he moved to Dutch club Willem on extended loan. Six seasons on Anderlecht books, former Beveren keeper, and won 2000 title medal.

JOHAN WALEM (STANDARD LIEGE) BORN: 01.02.72 CAPS: 30 GLS: 1
After a couple of switchback seasons between Parma and Udinese from 1999-2001, he then joined Standard in 2001. Left-sided player and named after Johan Cruyff. Joined Udinese from Anderlecht in summer 1997 under the Bosman ruling, and was in Italy for

four seasons. At Anderlecht since the age of seven, and was a first team player at 18, and an international at 19. Won four championships with Anderlecht and was club captain. Missed the '98 World Cup but recalled by coach Georges Leekens for Euro 2000 warm up games and retained place under Waseige.

MARC WILMOTS (SCHALKE) BORN: 22.02.69 CAPS: 63 GLS: 24
Returned for £1.2 million to Schalke for second spell there after just the 2000-01 season with top French club Bordeaux, where he did not settle. Plays behind the front men in the attacking midfield role once held down by Enzo Scifo. Known as '1,000 Volts' by Schalke fans. Won UEFA Cup medal with Schalke in 1997 and was one of the Belgian colony at Schalke. Formerly with Mechelen (1988-91) and Standard (1991-96) and first time with Schalke (1996-2000). Improved dramatically with Schalke – played in 1994 World Cup, then came back for 1998 in France. Is often the national captain.

COACH

ROBERT WASEIGE BORN: 26.08.39
Took the national coaching post in 1999 to replace Georges Leekens when the preparation for Euro 2000 was not going well. Tidied up the whole set up despite the disappointments of Euro 2000. Three times the Belgian Trainer of the Year in 1986, 1994 and 1995, though never won the title. Coach of Winterslag (now Genk) from 1971-76, Standard Liege (1976-79), Winterslag again (1979-81), Lokeren (1981-83), FC Liege (1983-92) and Standard again from 1994-96. Then went to Sporting Lisbon 1996-97 which did not work out, so back to Charleroi from 1997-99. Former player with FC Liege, RWDM, and Winterslag in the top flight but uncapped at full level.

WORLD CUP FACTS

Robbie Rensenbrink of Holland scored the 1000th goal in the World Cup finals when he converted a penalty against Scotland in Argentina in 1978.

Louis Laurent of France against Mexico netted the first goal scored in the World Cup Finals on July 13 in Montevideo, Uruguay in the 4-1 win in 1930.

The lowest attendance for any world cup match was the 300 for Romania v Peru on July 14 1930 in Montevideo, Uruguay.

Inter Milan's Gerry Hitchens became the first 'overseas' star to play a World Cup game for England in 1962. Ray Wilkins and Mark Hateley of AC Milan followed in his footsteps.

RUSSIA

No-one, not even the Russians themselves, expects them to win the World Cup, but a place in the quarter-finals will be the next best thing. It will also be a big improvement on their last performance in the Finals when they were eliminated in the first phase of USA '94.

Coach Oleg Romantsev is realistic to know that a place in the semi-finals is probably beyond his men, but after failing even to reach the Finals in France four years ago, making the last eight would be acceptable.

"One benefit for us is that because our season runs from spring to autumn, our home-based players would only have played around 12 matches by the time the World Cup starts," says Romantsev, who also coaches Spartak Moscow.

"That means they will not be too tired at the end of a long season like a lot of other European players. I am optimistic we will do better than in 1994. I think we are better prepared and I think we have a good mix of youth and experience.

"We face hosts Japan, Belgium and Tunisia, and while I am deeply respectful of all of our opponents, I also think we are good enough to finish either first or second in the group and go on from there." Brazil or Turkey are likely to be their second round opponents if they get that far.

Russia were impressive enough in the qualifiers, winning seven of their ten matches in European Group One, drawing twice and losing just once to Slovenia. They finished three points clear at the top.

Spearheading Russia's assault on the Finals was the ever-improving Vladimir Beschastnykh, one of a number of key players who returned from abroad to re-join domestic clubs last year after Romantsev pronounced that those playing in Russia, who he could watch more closely, would have a better chance of making the party for Asia.

Beschastnykh, who had slipped in the pecking order at Racing Santander in Spain, returned to Moscow Spartak and finished as Russia's top scorer in the qualifiers with seven goals including two diving headers that brought six points.

Just 28, he could well catch the eye of the inevitable scouts again and gain a lucrative move back to one of Europe's top clubs after the Finals.

Forward Alexander Panov (from St Etienne), Defender Omari Tetradze (PAOK Salonica) and goalkeeper Sergei Ovchinnikov (Porto) also returned home and their good club form enhanced the strength of the squad, even if Panov and Ovchinnikov made almost no contribution to the qualifying campaign.

Panov missed almost all of it apart from one substitute appearance because of injury, but, along with Ovchinnikov should be included in the 23 for the Finals.

Romantsev, who was in charge of Russia at their last major Finals at Euro '96 in England before quitting after they went out in the first round in that tournament – returned as national coach for a second time after the failure to reach France '98.

He has changed their style of play from a short-passing game to one that is at once more varied and effective. The Russian national side is now more likely to play wider going forward, and use a more direct, longer ball for Beschastnykh to chase. This greater variety has brought greater success and with the likes of the experienced Yuri Kovtun and Yuri Nikiforov at the back, Russia are that much harder to break down.

Also standing in the way of opponents is the impressive No 1 Ruslan Nigmatullin, who, along with captain and defender Victor Onopko and midfielder Yegor Titov, was ever-present throughout the qualifying campaign. Nigmatullin, voted Russia's Player of the Year in 2001 caught Verona's eye playing impressively for Lokomotiv Moscow in the Champions League earlier in the season, and is now plying his trade in Serie A. Although his form dipped over the second half of the season, at least he has been facing some world class strikers which can only benefit Russia in Japan.

However, there are various reasons why Russia are no world-beaters. One is that although the squad does have experience, the defence, which has largely been together for the last eight years, lacks pace, and can be turned by quick, top-class strikers.

Also, while the overall approach of the team is more expansive, a tendency to over-elaborate in midfield allows opponents to take the initiative. These are areas Romantsev must work on if Russia are to go as far as they hope.

Russia have a poor record in major tournaments since the break-up of the old Soviet Union – and even the Soviet Union's World Cup record doesn't exactly make for wildly impressive reading with a best-ever finish of fourth in 1966.

SQUAD

DIMITRI ALEINICHEV (FC PORTO) BORN: 29.09.73 CAPS: 41 GLS: 6
Now playing in Portugal since summer 2000 after a spell in Serie A with Roma, and then with Perugia. 1997 Russian Footballer of the Year – moved from Spartak Moscow in summer 1998 for £4 million to Roma saying he could earn 20-times as much with Roma as playing for Spartak in Champions League. Played outstanding role in Spartak's 1997 championship win – diminutive midfielder. Settled in well at Roma – crowd favourite, though not given many chances. In the end he was slightly disappointing and has not really hit the headlines in Portugal as yet.

VLADIMIR BESTATCHNIYKH (SPARTAK MOSCOW) BORN: 01.04.74 CAPS: 63 GLS: 24
Top scorer in the qualifiers and top scorer for the new Russia. Rejoined former club Spartak in summer 2001 after six seasons with Racing Santander in the Primera Liga, only for Racing to be relegated in 2001. Joined Bremen for £2million in summer 1994 from Spartak Moscow to start his travels. He was ill just before the 1994 World Cup, and only played one game as sub, and has often been unavailable because of club commitments. Scored fine goal vs Czechs in Euro '96. Won two league titles with Spartak to set up moves abroad to Germany and Spain. Not sure of place under previous coach Anatoly Byshovets – now No 1 under Romantsev.

ANTON BOBYOR (KYRLYA SOVETOV SAMARA) BORN: 28.09.82 CAPS: 1 GLS: 0
Called up for the first time to the squad to play in the March 2002 friendly with Latvia. Youth international, who moved into his club first team in 2000 and is already attracting interest from the bigger clubs. Also moving into the national U21 squad.

RUSSIA

MAXIM BUZNIKIN (LOKOMOTIV MOSCOW) BORN: 01.03.77 CAPS: 8 GLS: 5
Was allowed to leave Spartak in 2000 and has developed well since then. Had a fine start to his international career, but not a damaging scorer yet in the domestic league. Spartak signed him from a junior club, and he was there from 1997-2000 but failed to crack first team on regular basis.

IGOR CHUGAINOV (URALAN ELISTA) BORN: 06.04.70 CAPS: 29 GLS: 0
Moved in January 2002 to Uralan after being long-time captain with Lokomotiv Moscow. Failed dope test after 1997 Russian Cup final – but second test proved negative. Key defender in Loko's fine run to the 1998 and 1999 ECWC semis. Former Torpedo Moscow defender. A regular choice in Russian squad now, and good in the air.

VIACHESLAV DAYEV (CSKA MOSCOW) BORN: 06.09.72 CAPS: 6 GLS: 0
Defender from the CSKA club who is in his first season with them after leaving Torpedo Moscow at the end of the 2001 season. Played in the Premier League since 1995, with Krylya and Baltika, who are not such good sides, then upgraded to Torpedo.

YURI DROZDOV (LOKOMOTIV MOSCOW) BORN: 16.04.72 CAPS: 10 GLS: 0
Into squad in spring 1998 on the back of Loko's run to the 1999 ECWC semis. Midfielder, who can also play in defence, capped first vs Armenia in March 1999. Good form in domestic league – though cover for national team. In tenth season with Loko in 2002.

ALEXANDER FILIMONOV (DYNAMO KIEV) BORN: 15.10.73 CAPS: 15 GLS: 0
Reckoned to be the No 1 keeper, especially after the retirements of Cherchasov and Kharine, but has not really claimed the spot – though he is always in the squad. First teamer at Spartak for five seasons, was in the 1996-2001 Championship wins, he won six titles in his five seasons at Spartak. Signed by Spartak from Fakel Voronezh also of the First Division. Still a bit erratic according to the critics, though very talented.

ROLAN GUSEV (CSKA MOSCOW) BORN: 17.09.77 CAPS: 9 GLS: 0
Has moved into the national team in the last two years – plays normally down the left side. Was the only one in the squad from the famous old Dinamo Moscow club until moving to CSKA a few months ago. Had been with Dinamo since his teens in 1994, and made first team debut aged 19 in 1996. Reputed not to get on with the national coach.

SERGEI IGNASHEVICH (LOKOMOTIV MOSOW) BORN: 14.07.79 CAPS: 0 GLS: 0
Recent U21 international who is in his second season with Loko. Previously played for Kryla Sovietov Samara. Played well in the 2001-02 Champions League.

MARAT ISMAILOV (LOKOMOTIV MOSCOW) BORN: 21.09.82 CAPS: 7 GLS: 0
His first season with the Loko first team was in 2001, and indicates the lack of forwards, by being propelled straight into the national squad as a teenager. Third season with Loko, was not in first team in 2000, made the grade into the first team in 2001 – played no more than 20 first team games for club before first cap.

RUSSIA

VALERY KARPIN (CELTA VIGO) BORN: 02.02.69 CAPS: 68 GLS: 16
Joined Celta on a free transfer after being released by Valencia, who sold him for £2.8 million in summer 1997 after he had been at Celta on loan initially. Had previously gained an excellent reputation with Real Sociedad from 1994-96. Eight seasons in Spain. Played at the 1994 World Cup and Euro '92 and Euro '96, and is in the current side again. Born in Estonia but opted for Russia with Spartak Moscow, with whom he won three national titles before leaving for Spain.

ANDREI KARYAKA (KRYLYA SOVIETOV SAMARA) BORN: 01.04.78 CAPS: 4 GLS: 0
His first call up was for the Greece game in 2001, where he won his first cap. Breakthrough season in 2001. Used down the left flank which is a problem role for Russia.

ALEXANDER KERZHAKOV (ZENIT ST PETERSBURG) BORN: 16.10.81 CAPS: 1 GLS: 0
Called up for the first time to the squad to play in the March 2002 friendly with Latvia.

DIMITRI KHLESTOV (BESIKTAS) BORN: 21.01.71 CAPS: 49 GLS: 0
Moved from Spartak Moscow to Besiktas in summer 2000. Recalled since 1998 by Russia following superb club form. Broke his leg just before Euro '96, when first choice right back, and never really got back his place on a regular basis until 1998. Played all three games in 1994 World Cup and Euro '92. Has won his eighth Championship in nine seasons with Spartak in 2000, and was their captain – is a product of Spartak's youth academy and never been anywhere else until the move to Turkey.

DIMITRY KOKHLOV (REAL SOCIEDAD) BORN: 22.12.75 CAPS: 37 GLS: 4
Utility player from PSV's Dutch 1999 title win who moved to Spain with Sociedad in 2000 after a loan spell. Is a useful man to have in squad – can operate almost anywhere. Joined PSV in October 1997 season after finishing the Russian season with Torpedo, and established himself as a first choice for Russia also from autumn 1997. In Euro '96 squad. International debut at Old Trafford in Umbro Cup in 1995.

YURI KOVTUN (SPARTAK MOSCOW) BORN: 05.01.70 CAPS: 43 GLS: 3
In his second season with Spartak after playing all his career for Dinamo Moscow – he came across to fill the right back vacancy at the club vacated by Sergei Gorlukovich. Had been in the Dynamo team since the age of 19 and was in the national team for the past six seasons. Recently been sent off twice in the group games in the 1999-2000 UCL, first for two yellows, second was a direct red. Has tried to get into the Premiership but failed to impress both Southampton and West Ham in the late 1990s.

ALEXANDER MOSTOVOI (CELTA VIGO) BORN: 22.08.68 CAPS: 58 GLS: 12
He was a fine player at Spartak Moscow where he first caught attention. From 1991, he played for Benfica, Caen, Strasbourg and now six seasons with Celta since 1996 – intermittently either brilliant or erratic until he reached Celta. Set piece expert, and still playing well in the Primera Liga.

RUSSIA

RUSLAN NIGMATULLIN (VERONA) BORN: 07.11.74 CAPS: 18 GLS: 0
Moved from Lokomotiv Moscow to Verona in December 2001 and is the current 2001 Russian Footballer of the Year, who played in all the qualifiers. Took over from Filimonov as No 1 in 2000. Debut vs USA in April 2000. From the Loko Moscow side that were runners-up to Spartak in 1999-2001 and were 2000 Cup winners, as well as 1998 and 1999 European semi-finalists. Was reserve keeper at Spartak from 1995-97 before joining Loko so well known to coach Romantsev.

YURI NIKIFOROV (PSV EINDHOVEN) BORN: 16.09.70 CAPS: 54 GLS: 6
Recalled in 2001 after a three-year absence when he refused to play internationally because he was accused of tax evasion in 1998 by the Russian police. From the PSV 1999 and 2001 title winning sides, and showed fine form in the UCL in last two seasons. Replaced Jaap Stam at PSV. Former five times champion with Spartak Moscow, he joined Sporting Gijon in summer 1996 - but left in 1998 after Gijon were relegated. Had actually played for Ukraine (two caps) before the country became affiliated to UEFA and FIFA - then left Chernomorets Odessa for Spartak. Played well in 1994 World Cup and at Euro '96.

VICTOR ONOPKO (OVIEDO) BORN: 14.10.69 CAPS: 96 GLS: 6
Most capped of the modern Russian team. Plays central defence or defensive midfield. Russian captain and midfield anchor man - and most capped of the new Russia, and was voted in as captain from 1999 by teammates. Joined Oviedo in midwinter break 1995-96 after Atletico Madrid had thought they'd bought him and Newcastle and Everton expressed interest in him. Moved to Spartak and opted to play for Russia rather than his native Ukraine after being picked for the Russian 1992 European Championship team. Was the captain in Moscow Spartak's 1992, 1993 and 1994 Championship wins. Delayed playing in Spain because his mother-in-law couldn't get a visa! Twice Russian Footballer of the Year.

SERGEI OVCHINNIKOV (LOKOMOTIV MOSCOW) BORN: 10.11.70 CAPS: 18 GLS: 0
Returned to Russia in December 2001 to replace Nigmatullin in the club side. Had been in Portugal for the previous four years with Benfica and then Porto. Originally with Loko from 1991-97 and first played for Russia in 1993.

ALEXANDR PANOV (DINAMO MOSCOW) BORN: 21.09.75 CAPS: 16 GLS: 4
Now back home in Russia after a short spell with French club St Etienne, whom he joined from Zenit St Petersburg. Recently injured. Came on as sub in international vs Brazil in Nov '98 when home-based players only were picked. Picked up a couple of useful goals and is getting a run up front.

RUSLAN PIMENOV (LOKOMOTIV MOSCOW) BORN: 25.11.81 CAPS: 0 GLS: 0
U21 international and recent youth international, who is on the verge of the World Cup squad. Two seasons in the club first team squad, and from the club's juniors. Also played well in the 2001-2 Champions League.

RUSSIA

ALEXANDR SCHIRKO (TORPEDO MOSCOW) BORN: 24.11.76 CAPS: 7 GLS: 1
Recalled in 2001 for the first time since 1999 by coach Romantsev who, in his role as Spartak coach, off-loaded him to Torpedo! Originally from the Spartak youth academy, he was in the B team from 1993-97 and had been in their first team for five seasons. All previous caps prior to 2001 were in 1999.

SERGEI SEMAK (CSKA MOSCOW) BORN: 27.02.76 CAPS: 30 GLS: 1
First call up to national squad for the second play-off game vs Italy in November 1997 before the World Cup, coming on as sub. Has come through nationally as captain of the CSKA side since 1998. Fine domestic form with one of the top domestic sides. Was developed in the CSKA (army) youth set up, and in tenth season with the CSKA first team squad.

DIMITRI SENNIKOV (LOKOMOTIV MOSCOW) BORN: 24.06.74 CAPS: 2 GLS: 0
Released as a junior by CSKA Moscow, the army team. Joined Loko in 1999, and now in his fourth season in first team squad. Another on the fringe of World Cup selection.

ALEXEI SMERTIN (BORDEAUX) BORN: 01.05.75 CAPS: 24 GLS: 0
Joined Bordeaux from Lokomotiv Moscow in summer 2000 for £2 million. Into national squad in 1998 – from unfashionable provincial club Uralan Elista, he joined Lokomotiv Moscow in 1999 after becoming an international. In Loko team that reached 1999 ECWC semis. Sent off on international debut vs Iceland in an embarrassing defeat.

OMARI TETRADZE (ALANYA VLADIKAVKAZ) BORN: 13.10.69 CAPS: 39 GLS: 1
Back to Russia in December 2001 from Greek club PAOK of Salonica. Had been playing in Greece for a year after leaving Serie A club Roma, where he was often injured and failed to claim a regular place in his four years at the club 1996-2000. Has been an international for most of the 1990s. His best season was as captain of the 1995 Alania Vladikavkaz side that dented Spartak's run by winning the championship, which earned a ticket to Italy.

YEGOR TITOV (SPARTAK MOSCOW) BORN: 29.05.76 CAPS: 29 GLS: 5
Russia's Footballer of the Year for 1999 and 2000 – he plays just behind the strikers and is the Spartak captain from 2000. Now key man for club and country since the turn of the century. Won seven titles in a row with Spartak. Has been in Spartak's first team squad for nine seasons. Called into the national squad in autumn 1998 after impressing in the Champions League.

COACH

OLEG ROMANTSEV BORN: 04.01.54
President and head coach of Spartak Moscow, the champions, he took over the national side again after Anatoli Byshovets was sacked in November '98. He combines the club and country roles. Coached Russia previously at Euro '96. Capped ten times for USSR as player – bronze medal in 1980 Olympics, and played for Spartak from 1976-83. Coached Spartak 1989-95, and from 1997 to the present. Won nine championships with Spartak.

TUNISIA

Of the five African qualifiers, it's ironic that Tunisia should get what is arguably the easiest draw. The team which failed to score, let alone impress, in the Nations Cup in Mali doesn't look in any shape to take advantage. Like Nigeria and South Africa, Tunisia have made a late coaching change, with Amman Souayah's collective replacing the vastly experienced Henri Michel.

The players, with a couple of exceptions, are the same ones who disappointed in Mali, and Souayah will have to be every bit as tactically aware as they say he is for the sole North African representatives to go further. Having not even made the quarter-finals of the Nations Cup, how can we expect them to get out of World Cup Group H?

Tunisian football is in such a mess that it's hard to pinpoint strengths and weaknesses. Many of the squad have experience from France '98 which can only count in the team's favour, and Zoubeir Baya and Hassen Gabsi have it in them to be surprise summer stars, but the benefits of experience may be outweighed by tired legs.

This squad has been around, and is ageing, with Ali Zitouni and Slim Benachour the only youngsters seemingly assured of notable international futures. After the Nations Cup, the former coach Michel issued the following indictment: "We have weaknesses everywhere – tactically, technically, mentally and physically." Nothing much has changed in four months and Tunisia must be rank outsiders. The country which became the first from Africa to win a match at the World Cup finals will do very well to emulate that this time round.

SQUAD

ADAILTON (ESPERANCE)
Naturalised Brazilian who operates best from wide on the left. Was controversially dropped by Michel (and replaced by Benachour) just before the Nations Cup finals, after the former coach criticised him for his work rate. No relation to his much better paid namesake who plays for Verona in Serie A.

WALID AZAIEZ (ESPERANCE) BORN: 25/4/76
Notorious for his sending off, and punching of a policeman, at the 2000 Champions League final. Not an international regular, but does have five years experience as an international player.

KHALED BADRA (ESPERANCE) BORN: 8/4/73
Experience of France '98 and four Nations cups. Played briefly at Genoa with Chokri, before returning to Esperance. He was on the shortlist for the African Footballer of the Year award in 1999, and is arguably Tunisia's most accomplished player. Can play wide down the right or as a sweeper. Also a useful goalscorer, particularly from free kicks. Got the CAF Cup final winner for Esperance in 1997.

ZOUBEIR BAYA (BESIKTAS) BORN: 15/5/71
A class act in the midfield. Adaptable player who has spent seven years in the national team.

TUNISIA

Played also at Freiburg. Hit the headlines for his excellent performances in the '96 Nations Cup, and has always had a knack of scoring crucial goals, never more so than in that '96 tournament when he scored in the quarter-final and semi-final. Was given the award for the best goal in African World Cup qualifying after his 70-yarder (no exaggeration) against DR Congo.

HASSEM BEJAOUI (CA BIZERTE) BORN: 14/2/75
Likely to travel merely as backup to Chokri. Went to Mali in a similar role. Has been in excellent form this season for his club side and is seen as the successor to the legendary Chokri.

SLIM BENACHOUR (MARTIGUES) BORN: 8/9/81
A late addition to the Nations Cup squad as a replacement for Adailton. He performed well when given the chance in Mali, but missed a crucial penalty in the game against Senegal. It's a sign of his confidence, though, that he volunteered to take it.

RIADH BOUAZIZI (BURSASPOR) BORN: 8/4/73
Before moving to Turkey, he won two CAF Cups and one Cup Winners' Cup with the Tunisian giants Etoile Du Sahel. Also played in France '98 and the '96 Olympics. Has a history of problems with referees. Can play in the defence or in midfield.

ANIS BOUJELBENE (CS SFAXIEN) BORN: 6/2/78
Only a handful of caps so far, and they've all been as a substitute. His performances in the domestic league for Club Sfaxien have impressed.

MOUNIR BOUKADIDA (WALDHOF MANNHEIM) BORN: 24/10/67
Twice won African honours with Etoile du Sahel in Tunisia, but currently playing in the German Second Division. Experience of France '98 and four Nations Cups, including a final in 1996. During qualifying, he asked to be left out of the team because of his part in Mannheim's relegation struggle.

RAOUF BOUZAIENE (GENOA) BORN: 16/8/70
Another of the six Tunisians who went with the former national coach Scoglio when he took over at Genoa. Had several years out of the national side after being involved in the terrible '94 Nations Cup showing. Spent a great deal of his career in the French Second Division with Laval, and had a brief spell back in Tunisia with Club Africain.

SIRAJEDDINE CHIHI (ESPERANCE) BORN: 16/4/70
Veteran and stylish midfielder. Played in France '98. Was in the Esperance side that lost the now infamous 2000 Champions League final against Hearts of Oak.

JOSE CLAYTON (ETOILE DU SAHEL)
Naturalised Brazilian who went to France '98. Hasn't been heavily involved recently, but there have been suggestions that the new coach may recall him for his experience.

TUNISIA

CHOKRI EL OUAER (ESPERANCE) BORN: 15/8/66
After such an outstanding career for club and country, it's sad that Chokri will mainly be remembered as the player who deliberately cut himself above the eye in the 2000 Champions League final against Hearts of Oak. His plan to stop the match failed, and he was banned for one year. Became the fourth African player, and the first non-Egyptian, to win 100 caps. Scored the decisive penalty in the '96 Nations Cup quarter-final against Gabon. Has recently returned to Tunisian domestic football after a disappointing spell at Genoa. Played in all three matches in France '98.

HASSEN GABSI (GENOA) BORN: 23/2/74
Another who went with Scoglio to Genoa. Had a cruciate ligament injury just before the '98 World Cup that threatened to end his career, and despite further injuries, has still made over 20 appearances for the Italian club this season. Won two African titles with his old club Esperance. A definite starter if fit.

KAIES GHODBAIENE (ETOILE SAHEL) BORN: 7/1/76
Played in all three games in France '98, and has appeared in four Nations Cups. Captained Etoile to the CAF Cup final last year. Played in every game in the '96 Olympics. Scored in the '96 Nations Cup semi-final against Zambia.

HABIB JAOUACHI (ESS)
Travelled to his first Nations Cup in Mali as a number three, and is favourite to occupy the same position at the World Cup.

RADHI JAIDI (ESPERANCE) BORN: 30/8/75
Huge centre back, immensely reliable defender. Has the knack of scoring important goals from set pieces. Member of the Atlanta Olympics squad.

ZIAD JAZIRI (ETOILE SAHEL) BORN: 12/7/78
Missed the Nations Cup through injury. Was the top scorer in World Cup qualifying with six goals and is likely to start up front. On the shortlist for the African footballer of the Year award but a major disappointment at the Nations Cup.

HAMDI MARZOUKI (CLUB AFRICAIN) BORN: 23/1/77
Played in Mali, but certainly not a regular. Captain of his club side.

MOURAD MELKI (ESPERANCE) BORN: 9/5/75
A fringe player, he was a squad member at France '98 but failed to get a game. Moved to Esperance from Olympique Beja in Tunisia.

IMED MHADHEBI (GENOA) BORN: 22/3/76
Bags of pace, but still needs to work on his finishing. He is favourite to start up front alongside Jaziri, if Zitouni is unfit.

TUNISIA

EMIR MKADEMI (ETOILE SAHEL) BORN: 20/8/78
Left back who was a surprise call up for the Nations Cup after showing very solid form for his Tunisian club side.

MEHDI NAFTI (RACING SANTANDER) BORN: 28/11/78
Born in France, he played for four seasons in Toulouse before moving to Spain in 2000. Yet to score for his Spanish club. Was a late replacement in Mali.

ADEL SELLIMI (FREIBURG) BORN: 16/11/72
Was suspended for the end of qualifying after being sent off in the match against the Ivory Coast. Dropped from the Nations Cup squad for refusing to travel home for a friendly match against Spain. Has over 70 caps, and has spent four seasons in the Bundesliga with Freiburg. Not been in his best goalscoring form this season, where he has been stuck in single figures. Formerly with Nantes.

HATEM TRABELSI (AJAX) BORN: 25/1/77
Former CS Sfaxien player who was signed by Ajax at the start of the season. Played once in France '98, and will probably be the first choice right back. No relation to the former international Sami Trabelsi. Was man of the match in his first Ajax appearance against Celtic and has impressed when selected this season.

JAMEL ZABI (CA BIZERTE) BORN: 19/6/75
Hat-trick on debut against Liberia in November, but started all three Nations Cup games and failed to score. Has played all his career for Bizerte and enjoyed relative success as a goalscorer, but will be little more than a replacement in the summer.

ALI ZITOUNI (ESPERANCE) BORN: 11/1/81
The great young hope for Tunisian football who has a marvellous partnership with Jaziri. Six months out with an injury have set him back, though, and having missed the Nations Cup, he faces a battle to be fit for the World Cup. The management will do anything to get him fit.

COACH

AMMAN SOUAYAH
Has a reputation as being the master tactician, and his recent appointment following the resignation of Henri Michel has been seen as a boost for the national side. Michel gave up the job after Souayah was appointed as his assistant. Souayah himself will be strongly supported by his coaching partner Khemaies Laabidi. If the rumours about players deliberately underperforming to get Michel the sack are true, Souayah may have more work to do than is currently apparent.

SEOUL

SEOUL WORLD CUP STADIUM.
CAPACITY: 64,640.
OPENED: NOVEMBER 2001.
FRIDAY MAY 31 KO 2030 (1230 BST): FRANCE V SENEGAL (GROUP A)
THURSDAY JUNE 13 KO 1530 (0730 BST): TURKEY V CHINA (GROUP C)
TUESDAY JUNE 25 KO 2030 (1230 BST): SEMI-FINAL

The capital of Korea since 1392 has risen from the ashes of the Korean War and emerged as one of the fastest-growing cities on the planet. Since the economic boom of the 1960s Seoul's population has increased to 10.4 million and is estimated to be the fifth-largest city in the world. It is a place of marked contrast with ancient tombs and royal palaces sitting alongside the modern skyscrapers and 21st century designs built by the 'tiger' economy.

The Han River runs through the centre of Seoul creating somewhat of a north-south divide, a scenario which is not uncommon in Korea! South of the river are classic boutiques and trendy hang-outs like the Myeongdong shopping precinct. To the north are historic palaces, Confucian shrines and Buddhist pagodas. Of note are the Gyeonbokgung palace dating back to the start of the ruling Joseon Dynasty in 1392 and the Jogyesa temple, the headquarters of the Korean Buddhist Order Jogye, the country's largest religious sect.

The major leisure attraction in Seoul is Lotte World, an amusement park which features a gigantic indoor arcade, an island, a model village and a huge lake for water sports.

The stadium has been built from scratch on the site of a former rubbish dump ten miles from the centre of the bustling city. The roof design represents a traditional Korean kite called Bangpaeyeon, which expresses the hope of all mankind. From above, the stadium looks like an octagonal plate overlaid on a typical circle tray, to say 'welcome'. The pitch is imported Kentucky Blue Grass.

INCHEON

MUNHAK STADIUM.
CAPACITY: 50,256.
OPENED: MARCH 2002.
SUNDAY JUNE 9 KO 1800 (1000 BST): TURKEY V COSTA RICA (GROUP C)
TUESDAY JUNE 11 KO 1530 (0730 BST): DENMARK V FRANCE (GROUP A)
FRIDAY JUNE 14 KO 2030 (1230 BST): S KOREA V PORTUGAL (GROUP D)

In the late 19th century, as the Joseon Dynasty was reaching its end, free trade was introduced to Korea. Incheon was a chief beneficiary. It has since evolved into a prominent international port with a population of 2.6 million. Cargo ships from around the world dock at the port, while its massive new airport has made Incheon an important terminal for international air freight.

With so many visitors it is no surprise that Incheon has developed into a cosmopolitan town. It is thought to be the place where modern football was introduced to Korea – probably by traders using the port.

The city's major trading partner is China and ferries are available linking Korea to neighbouring Chinese cities such as Tianjin, Shanghai and Weihai. The Chinese influence on Incheon is pronounced as illustrated by the city's Chinatown. Founded in 1883, it was once a flourishing commercial centre for silk and herbal medicines but now it has become a popular location for authentic Chinese cuisine. Another example of the foreign flavour to the city is the Freedom Park. This Western-style park features a statue of General Douglas MacArthur, the American commander who successfully led the Incheon landing operation during the Korean War. Check out an episode of the US television show MASH to get a feel for Korea's modern history.

The Munhak Stadium emphasises Incheon's identity as a port, with a design echoing "a sailing vessel ploughing through the raging sea". One of three stadiums with a running track.

SUWON

SUWON WORLD CUP STADIUM.
CAPACITY: 43,138.
OPENED: MAY 2001.
WEDNESDAY JUNE 5 KO 1800 (1000 BST): UNITED STATES V PORTUGAL (GROUP D)
TUESDAY JUNE 11 KO 1530 (0730 BST): SENEGAL V URUGUAY (GROUP A)
THURSDAY JUNE 13 KO 1530 (0730 BST): COSTA RICA V BRAZIL (GROUP C)
SUNDAY JUNE 16 KO 2030 (1230 BST): WINNER B V RUNNER-UP E

Suwon can be found in the heart of Korea. It was the country's first planned city, built around the imposing Hwaseong fortress during the Korean renaissance in the 18th century.

King Jeongjo of the ruling Josean Dynasty wanted to move the capital from Seoul to Suwon to be closer to the tomb of his father and to carry out political reforms. He built the Hwaseong fortress and relocated a large number of people to the area and in doing so created a city. The king also constructed the Yongjusa temple which can still be visited today.

Suwon is proud of its heritage and one of its major tourist attractions is a reconstructed traditional Korean folk village. Staffed by actors in traditional costumes, the village replicates 18th century Korean life and is often used as the setting for historical TV dramas. More renaissance-themed entertainment can be found at nearby

Yeonmudae which every June hosts a martial arts festival featuring demonstrations of 18th century fighting skills.

Elsewhere, the Everland theme park is the seventh largest in the world consisting of a zoo, a water park, a motor racing track and botanical gardens.

The city is also well-known for its food and a particular delicacy is Suwon galbi – marinated beef rib grilled over a charcoal fire.

The people of Suwon helped pay for the stadium themselves and the design reflects the images of the nearby Hwaeseong Fortress and the wings of a giant bird soaring into the sky. Suwon was the first planned city in Korea, created in the 18th century. It is now a centre of transportation and home to universities and corporate research facilities.

DAEJEON

DAEJEON WORLD CUP STADIUM.
CAPACITY: 41,024.
OPENED: SEPTEMBER 2001.
WEDNESDAY JUNE 12 KO 2030 (1230 BST): SOUTH AFRICA V SPAIN (GROUP B)
FRIDAY JUNE 14 KO 2030 (1230 BST): POLAND V UNITED STATES (GROUP D)
TUESDAY JUNE 18 KO 2030 (1230 BST): 2ND ROUND: WINNER GROUP D V RUNNER-UP GROUP G

The central Korea city of Daejeon has a population of 1.5 million. It has become Korea's technological capital and centre for scientific research and hosted the International Expo science fair in 1993. The science park built for the Expo still holds exhibitions of the latest technological developments and features the distinctive Hanbit Tower. The Daedeok Valley is comparable to America's Silicon Valley and houses state-of-the-art science and technology companies.

In contrast to the cutting-edge modernity of the Daedeok Valley are historical sites such as Buyeo and Gongju, ancient capitals of the Baekje kingdom (18BC-660AD). Museums dedicated to these cities include well-preserved treasures from that period.

Also worth a visit is the Geusman Ginseng market. This was where the popular Goryeo ginseng was first grown and is Korea's largest ginseng market. Herbal buffs can get a taste for the stuff at a special sampling stall.

Ginseng is a key ingredient in two of the region's most popular dishes samgyetang and dolsotbab. The former is a ginseng-stuffed chicken stew known to boost stamina and the latter is a rice dish heated in a special stone pot.

Daejeon is also famous for the Yuseong Hot Springs which are known for their effective treatment of skin disorders.

The simple design of the stadium represents the city's scientific background – straight lines and planes. The stainless steel roof is semi-retractable, moving 15 metres. Underneath, the inside represents the courtyard of a traditional Korean house.

JEONJU

JEONJU WORLD CUP STADIUM.
CAPACITY: 42,477.
OPENED: NOVEMBER 2001.
FRIDAY JUNE 7 1800 (1000 BST): SPAIN V PARAGUAY (GROUP B)
MONDAY JUNE 10 KO 2030 (1230 BST): PORTUGAL V POLAND (GROUP D)
MONDAY JUNE 17 KO 1530 (0730 BST): 2ND ROUND: WINNER GROUP G V
RUNNER-UP GROUP D

One of the smaller towns to be hosting World Cup matches, Jeonju is famous among Koreans as a place of culture and cuisine.

Relatively under-developed compared with the rest of South Korea, the town traces its history back to 757AD and contains many relics from its past as a capital of the Yi Dynasty. Jeonju is also home to one of the most beautiful Catholic churches in Korea, the Jeondong Cathedral. The Jeonju Daessaseupnori, a traditional classical music festival, has been held here for the past 200 years and on the back of it Jeonju has developed as a popular festival venue. The town is the setting for an international film festival, a paper festival and a festival of sound.

Food is another central pillar of Jeonju life and its famous bibimbab – cooked rice mixed with vegetables – can be sampled, in one of the town's many speciality restaurants. Another favourite dish is kongnamulgukbab – steamed rice mixed with bean sprout soup – which is said to help hangovers. To get a real taste of the local diet try a hanjeongsik, a traditional full-course Korean meal.

During the World Cup, the Pungnam Festival will take place featuring a food court, poetry readings and a sijo (three-verse Korean ode) writing contest. The four roofs represent folding bamboo fans, with the tension cables modelled after the 12 strings of the traditional gayageum musical instrument – fittingly in the City of Song.

GWANGJU

GWANGJU WORLD CUP STADIUM.
CAPACITY: 43,121.
OPENED: NOVEMBER 2001.
SUNDAY JUNE 2 KO 2030 (1230 BST): SPAIN V SLOVENIA (GROUP B)
TUESDAY JUNE 4 KO 1530 (0730 BST): CHINA V COSTA RICA (GROUP C)
SATURDAY JUNE 22 KO 1530 (0730 BST): QUARTER-FINAL

Gwangju is a liberal, artistic city with a long-cherished tradition of freedom of thought and democracy. Korea's fifth largest city, with a population of 1.4 million, has a reputation for exquisite locally-produced food. This is largely thanks to rich harvests in the nearby farmland and a mild climate. It is also viewed as an important cultural and artistic centre. The city will host the Gwangju Biennale international arts festival for the fourth time to coincide with the World Cup. This cultural showcase has a growing worldwide reputation. Visiting fans will be able to enjoy authentic performances of a traditional form of Korean folk music known as Gwangsan Nongak and watch experts demonstrate their skills in calligraphy and handicrafts. It's a bit like the Generation Game as festival-goers are then invited to have a go afterwards. On the outskirts of the city, Mount Mudeung is renowned for its magnificent scenery and hidden temples.

The surrounding areas contain several national parks and other places of outstanding natural beauty. You can also take a boat trip out to one of the exotic islands situated in the Dadhoae, 'the Many Islands Seas'. The curve of the stadium roof echoes the gentle curve of Mount Medeung, which overlooks the 'City of Art, Chivalry and Beauty'. Gwangju is the cultural capital of Korea but the masts holding up the roof have been designed in a Y-shape to resemble the head of the straw rope chariots used in the traditional folk game of gossaum nori, in which two teams ram the chariots at each other. The stadium has been designed as environment-friendly and adjacent to Yeomju Park.

DAEGU

DAEGU WORLD CUP STADIUM.
CAPACITY: 70,140.
OPENED: JULY 2001.
THURSDAY JUNE 6 KO 1530 (0730 BST): DENMARK V SENEGAL (GROUP A)
SATURDAY JUNE 8 KO 1530 (0730 BST): SOUTH AFRICA V SLOVENIA (GROUP B)
MONDAY JUNE 10 KO 1530 (0730 BST): SOUTH KOREA V UNITED STATES (GROUP D)
SATURDAY JUNE 29 KO 2000 (1200 BST): THIRD-PLACE PLAY-OFF

Behind Seoul and Busan, Daegu is the third largest city in Korea with a population of 2.5 million. Known locally as the 'Korean Milan', not due to the presence of two superpower football clubs, but because it is home to Korea's resurgent fashion industry.

Daegu specialises in the manufacture of synthetic fibres and textiles and is rapidly developing as one of the leading centres for fashion in Asia. The trendier residents of the city tend to be found strutting their stuff in the shopping malls, cafes and restaurants of Dongseongno, the busiest street in Daegu. Historically, Daegu has always been a focal point for the Buddhist and Confucian religions. The Hyanggo Confucian Academy, which is based there, is an important seat of learning for the teachings of Confucious. Visitors to the academy are asked to behave themselves and join in classes on traditional Chinese and Korean manners.

Elsewhere, there are some interesting ancient relics within striking distance of town, including the Bulguksa Temple and Seokguram Buddhist Grotto. Both feature impressive monuments and pagodas dating back to the ancient Silla Kingdom.

Ahead of the World Cup, 204,000 trees of 56 different species have been planted to form a big wood around the host stadium.

ULSAN

MUNSU FOOTBALL STADIUM.
CAPACITY: 43,512.
OPENED: APRIL 2001.
SATURDAY JUNE 1 KO 1800 (1000 BST): URUGUAY V DENMARK (GROUP A)
MONDAY JUNE 3 KO 1800 (1000 BST): BRAZIL V TURKEY (GROUP C)
FRIDAY JUNE 21 KO 2030 (1230 BST): QUARTER-FINAL

Ulsan is a port city in the industrial heartland of Korea and a centre for shipbuilding and car making. It is home to the biggest shipyard in the world, plus several large industrial complexes manufacturing such things as chemicals, equipment for oil and gas exploration and heavy-duty machinery. Hyundai Motors, which produces 1.4 million cars every year across the world, is also based in Ulsan.

However, the city is more than just one long production line. Its location, so close to Japan, has led to strong cultural links. All the latest Japanese fads and fashions hit Ulsan before the rest of Korea and there is a distinctly Japanese flavour to the local cuisine. A particular speciality is a raw fish dish called sashami. For some Koreans the sole purpose of their visit to Ulsan is for the quality of the sashami, made from fresh fish caught off the east coast.

The same part of the ocean often features some bigger fish not to fry, so to speak, as it is the annual migration patch of the grey whale. Although it is unlikely any of these creatures will be seen in the summer as Wales have not reached the World Cup finals since 1958. The simple stadium – known locally as 'The Big Crown' after the gold crown of the ancient kingdom of Silla, symbolises Ulsan's industrial present and future.

BUSAN

ASIAD MAIN STADIUM.
CAPACITY: 62,686.
OPENED: SEPTEMBER 2001.
SUNDAY JUNE 2 KO 1630 (0830 BST): PARAGUAY V SOUTH AFRICA (GROUP B)
TUESDAY JUNE 4 KO 2030 (1230 BST): SOUTH KOREA V POLAND (GROUP D)
THURSDAY JUNE 6: KO 2030 (1230 BST): FRANCE V URUGUAY (GROUP A)

With a population of four million, Busan is Korea's second city behind Seoul. With its huge, modern port, Busan has become a major centre for Korea's international trade.

Exotic beaches, warm waters and nearby islands have also made it a popular tourist destination. The coastal area provides the perfect location for boating, wind surfing and other water sports as well as just lounging about in the sun.

Busan is also South-East Asia's equivalent of Cannes, hosting an international film festival every year. The glitz and glamour of the film world descends on the city as its

Cinema Zone screens more than 200 entries. Away from the big screen, the people of Busan love their sport. The city has already successfully hosted the 1986 Asian Games and the 1988 Olympic football tournament and, after the World Cup, it will be staging another Asian Games at more than 30 different venues in the area. On the food front, every day is pancake day in Busan as one of the most popular local dishes is Dongnae Pajeon, a traditional seafood pancake cooked with green onions, oysters and clams. Other delicacies include a seafood soup, barbecued goat and roasted eel.

One of only three Korean stadia built with a running track. Designed like an upturned saucer with a hole cut in the middle. The roof represents a boat with all sails up and headed for the ocean. It took five and a half years to build the stadium which will also host the Asian Games in September and October this year after the World Cup is over. The roof design is symbolic in a city which is Korea's largest port – the third largest container harbour in the world – and known as the 'Gateway to Korea'.

SEOGWIPO

JEJU WORLD CUP STADIUM.
CAPACITY: 42, 256.
OPENED: DECEMBER 2001.
SATURDAY JUNE 8 KO 2030 (1230 BST): BRAZIL V CHINA (GROUP C)
WED JUNE 12 KO 2030 (1230 BST): SLOVENIA V PARAGUAY (GROUP B)
SATURDAY JUNE 15 KO 1530 (0730 BST): 2ND ROUND: WINNER GROUP E V RUNNER-UP GROUP B

Seogwipo is a tourist resort on Jejudo Island off the south coast of Korea. Known as the 'Island of Mystery', Jejudo is a famous honeymoon destination enjoying a sub-tropical climate, superb facilities and beautiful beaches.

The scenery is magnificent featuring everything you would imagine there to be on a tropical island paradise. Beyond the sun-drenched sands and deep blue ocean are cascading water falls, spectacular rock faces and clouded mountain tops. The many tangerine farms on the island create a 'golden glow' to the fields while more colour exudes from the spring azalea blossoms. Jejudo does not sound like the sort of place you will want to leave in a hurry,

It would also be no surprise if Seogwipo witnesses some explosive action during the World Cup – and not just because Brazil play there – as rising from the centre of Jejudo is the Mount Hallasan volcano. Hallasan, which is dormant, is the highest peak in Korea, stretching some 1950 metres above sea level.

The nearby Cheonjeyeon Falls sound worth a visit. Cheonjeyeon means 'the Sky Emperor's pond' and legend has it that the seven nymphs who guarded the Sky Emperor – an ancient mystical figure and not Rupert Murdoch – used to bathe there.

The stadium is reminiscent of the 360 parasite volcanoes scattered through the island while the roof reflects the fishing heritage of the islanders, based on the design of the local small vessels called Te-u and a traditional fishing net.

SAPPORO

SAPPORO DOME.
CAPACITY: 42,585.
OPENED: MAY 2001.
SAT JUNE 1 KO 2030 (1230 BST): GERMANY V SAUDI ARABIA (GROUP E)
MONDAY JUNE 3 KO 2030 (1230 BST): ITALY V ECUADOR (GROUP G)
FRIDAY JUNE 7 KO 2030 (1230 BST): ENGLAND V ARGENTINA (GROUP F)

Sapporo is the capital of Hokkaido, the northern-most of the four main islands of Japan. A relatively new place, it is less than 150 years old and the equivalent of a British new town. Yet unlike Stevenage or Milton Keynes, its growth has been extraordinary and the city is now Japan's fifth-largest with a population of 1.8 million.

With 5,000 shops in the city centre as well as the Susukino entertainment district, featuring a range wide range of restaurants, bars and "adult-orientated" establishments, there is plenty to do. And for anyone who gets fed up with the football, there is always the opportunity to blow some yen at the Sapporo race course. The eponymous beer has been brewed in Sapporo since 1867 and is exported worldwide. With an England game scheduled, the local stocks are bound to take a bit of a pounding. A grilled mutton and vegetable dish known as "Genghis Khan" is viewed as the perfect accompaniment to a pint of Sapporo in the city's vibrant beer halls.

Indeed you can go on the piste in all sorts of ways in Sapporo with ski slopes less than two hours drive from the city centre. The city was the venue for 1972 Winter Olympics and hosts a popular snow festival every year. The grass to be used in the futuristic dome stadium is grown outside and then transferred under the huge roof by means of an air-hovering mobile system. An observatory at the stadium gives a panoramic view of the city four miles away.

MIYAGI

MIYAGI STADIUM.
CAPACITY: 49,133.
OPENED: MARCH 2000.
SUNDAY JUNE 9 KO 1530 (0730 BST): MEXICO V ECUADOR (GROUP G)
WEDNESDAY JUNE 12 KO 1530 (0730 BST): SWEDEN V ARGENTINA
TUESDAY JUNE 18 2ND ROUND: WINNER GROUP H V RUNNER-UP GROUP C

The district of Miyagi is located in the southern part of the Tohoku region of north Japan. Its capital Sendai, where the World Cup matches take place, boasts a population of more than a million people. The area is a popular tourist destination with a colourful history. During the 16th century, a Samurai warlord called General Date Masamune won control of Miyagi and under his rule the region prospered enormously. Known as the "one-eyed dragon" due to the fact he lost an eye as a child. The General's heritage is represented by the main roof having a crescent-shaped design, resembling the Kabuto battle dress helmet he wore to his victories. It is designed to "harmonise with nature" with the secondary roof aligned with the ridge line of the hill behind it.

IBARAKI

KASHIMA STADIUM.
CAPACITY: 41,800.
OPENED: MAY 2001.
SUNDAY JUNE 2 KO 1430 (0630 BST): ARGENTINA V NIGERIA (GROUP F)
WEDNESDAY JUNE 5 KO 2030 (1230 BST): GERMANY V REPUBLIC OF IRELAND (GROUP E)
SATURDAY JUNE 8 KO 1800 (1000 BST): ITALY V CROATIA (GROUP G)

The Ibaraki region lies in the middle of Japan, about an hour north-east of Tokyo.

Its economy is based around scientific research and the development of cutting-edge modern technology. The massive Tsukuba Science City houses around 300 different companies and institutes, employing 13,000 researchers. Some of the more exciting projects take place at the Tsukuba Space Centre where boffins develop equipment for satellites and rockets.

In contrast to the laboratories and research stations, Ibaraki also features some of the most outstanding areas of natural beauty to be found in Japan. Lake Kasumigaura is the country's largest lagoon and a centre for fishing and sailing, while the twin-peaked Mount Tsukuba offers spectacular views and can be scaled by foot or cable car. Ibaraki's Pacific coastline contains miles of glorious, sandy beaches and the tides have made the area a surfers' paradise.

The locals are football crazy in Ibaraki's main city of Kashima. In his twilight years, Brazilian legend Zico played for Kashima Antlers and became so popular that the city erected a statue in his honour.

SAITAMA

SAITAMA STADIUM 2002.
CAPACITY: 63,700.
OPENED: JULY 2001.
SUNDAY JUNE 2 KO 1830 (1030 BST): ENGLAND V SWEDEN (GROUP F)
TUESDAY JUNE 4 KO 1800 (1000 BST): JAPAN V BELGIUM (GROUP H)
THURSDAY JUNE 6 KO 1800 (1000 BST): CAMEROON V SAUDI ARABIA (GROUP E)
WEDNESDAY JUNE 26 KO 2030 (1230 BST): SEMI-FINAL

In May last year, the cities of Urawa, Omiya and Yono merged to form Saitama City, on the outskirts of Greater Tokyo.

Full of shiny, new buildings, it is an important centre for Japanese business and commerce and has a population of more than a million people.

Pride of place in the new city is the Saitama Super Arena, one of the world's largest indoor venues capable of holding anything from pop concerts to basketball championships. The Arena building also houses the official John Lennon Museum which chronicles the former Beatle's life and music.

England fans will be hoping Sven-Göran Eriksson's side can avoid a hard day's night against Sweden in Saitama on 2 June and book their ticket to ride into the second round.

Football has been played in Saitama since 1908 and the area is home to the fanatically-supported Red Diamonds of the J-League.

Beyond the city limits, the Saitama region is known as the 'land of colour' due to the variety of flowers and blossoms that punctuate the landscape. The tree-crafting art of bonsai is also practised in Saitama and some excellent examples are on show at the Bonsai Village in Omiya.

One of the football-only stadia built for the tournament, the structure has been designed to be earthquake-resistant – up to Scale Seven. It is the new home for the Urawa Reds, one of the best-supported teams in the J-League.

YOKOHAMA

INTERNATIONAL STADIUM YOKOHAMA.
CAPACITY: 72,370.
OPENED: MARCH 1998.
SUNDAY JUNE 9 KO 2030 (1230 BST): JAPAN V RUSSIA (GROUP H)
TUESDAY JUNE 11 KO 2030 (1230 BST): SAUDI ARABIA V REPUBLIC OF IRELAND (GROUP E)
THURSDAY JUNE 13 KO 2030 (1230 BST): ECUADOR V CROATIA (GROUP G)
SUNDAY JUNE 30 KO 2000 (1200 BST): WORLD CUP FINAL

Once a small fishing village of just 600 people, Yokohama has been transformed over the past 140 years. Its port was opened to the Western world in 1859 after 250 years of isolation and since then, on the back of foreign trade, Yokohama has developed into Japan's second largest city with a population of 3.4 million.

Located around 18 miles south of Tokyo, its pioneering history has given rise to the nickname, 'The City of Firsts'. Japan's first railway linking Yokohama to Tokyo was opened there in 1872 soon to be followed by the country's first newspaper and brewery. Yokohama will achieve another first on 30 June when it hosts Asia's first-ever World Cup final. A combination of the Great Kanto Earthquake in 1923 and large-scale bombing during the Second World War forced Yokohama into a major rebuilding programme after 1945. A typical example is the state-of-the-art seafront development of Minato Mirai 21. It contains hundreds of offices, restaurants and shops as well as the Yokohama

CITY GUIDE JAPAN

Landmark Tower, Japan's tallest building, which offers visitors a panoramic view from downtown Tokyo to Mount Fuji.

As a centre for the silk trade, Yokohama has also emerged as one of the world's principal scarf producing centres though football's acrylic variety is not seen as particularly sought after.

Not the prettiest ground used in the tournament by any means, although the biggest capacity of any stadium and the nearest to Tokyo – the capital is 15 miles away from the country's second-largest city. Yokohama is even more westernised than Tokyo, perhaps unsurprising given its port status and it will also host the World Cup International Media Centre.

NIIGATA

BIG SWAN STADIUM.
CAPACITY: 42,300.
OPENED: MARCH 2001.
SATURDAY JUNE 1 KO 1530 (0730 BST): REPUBLIC OF IRELAND V CAMEROON (GROUP E)
MONDAY JUNE 3 KO 1530 (0730 BST): CROATIA V MEXICO (GROUP G)
SATURDAY JUNE 15 KO 2030 (1230 BST): 2ND ROUND: WINNER GROUP A V RUNNER-UP GROUP F

Niigata is in a mountainous and remote area to the north-west of Tokyo on Japan's main island. The region features some of Japan's most picturesque countryside including rugged coastlines, snow-capped mountains, tranquil lagoons and hot springs.

Like Yokohama, the key to the area's prosperity is its port, located in Niigata City, which was opened up to foreign trade in the mid-19th century.

Water is central to life in Niigata with Japan's longest river, the Shinano, flowing through the centre of the city. A network of canals was originally built as the main means of transport, but now creates a stylish atmosphere with willow trees lining the routes. Niigata City has opulence as well as elegance and the downtown Furumachi Arcade features top restaurants and high-class boutiques. In certain areas, you can still find geigi girls, a throwback to Japan's imperial past. The girls are professional entertainers who dress in traditional costumes to perform songs, dances and tea ceremonies for tourists.

Anyone seeking something stronger than tea is in the right place as Niigata is also well known for its rice wine or sake. To produce the best sake, the Japanese say it is crucial to have high quality rice and pure water and Niigata has an abundance of both.

The roof is designed to resemble the image of white swans alighting for the nearby Toyanogata lagoon and has been christened 'Big Swan' locally. Seats in the upper two levels overhang the pitch. Niigata Prefecture is Japan's biggest producer of rice, cut tulips and pears, and a leading sake producer as well. Its location bordering the Sea of Japan has made it a major trading port.

SHIZUOKA

SHIZUOKA STADIUM ECOPA.
CAPACITY: 51,349.
OPENED: MARCH 2001.
TUESDAY JUNE 11 KO 2030 (1230 BST): GERMANY V CAMEROON (GROUP E)
FRIDAY JUNE 14 KO 1530 (0730 BST): BELGIUM V RUSSIA (GROUP H)
FRIDAY JUNE 21 KO 1530 (0730 BST): QUARTER-FINAL

On the Pacific coast about an hour's drive from Tokyo, the Shizuoka region lies in the shadow of one of Japan's most recognisable landmarks, Mount Fuji. The highest mountain in Japan, its 3,800 feet or so are said to symbolise the pride of the Japanese people. Shizuoka is a ramblers' paradise as also nearby are the Fuji-Hakone-Izu and the Southern alps national parks so anyone thinking about a trip should remember their hiking boots and compass. But when they're not trekking up and down mountains, the locals are more than likely to be playing or watching football as Shizuoka is the undisputed soccer capital of Japan. There are thousands of active teams involved with more than 50,000 registered players and the game is so popular that there is a museum dedicated to it. With a well-developed coaching structure in both clubs and schools, Shizuoka is a breeding ground for young talent and has produced more J-League players than any other region in Japan. The area is also home to two of the J-League's most successful clubs. Jubilo Iwata are the current Asian champions, while rivals Shimuzu S-Pulse are also highly regarded. With Fuji so close both clubs are at an advantage in home games as visiting teams always seem to have the proverbial mountain to climb!

Newly built in the Ogasayama Sports Park the seats are fully covered by a retractable roof. The stadium is designed to unify with the surrounding picturesque mountains and the Shinkansen bullet train from Tokyo goes past Mount Fuji en route. Shizuoka, near the centre of Japan, is noted for its fruit and marine products, and tea production. The home of Japanese football. It's still to be decided which of the two local J-League sides, Shimizu S-Pulse near Shimizu – most famous former managers Ossie Ardiles and Steve Perryman – or Jubilo Iwata will play here after the World Cup.

OSAKA

NAGAI STADIUM.
CAPACITY: 50,000.
OPENED: MAY 1996.
WEDNESDAY JUNE 12 KO 1530 (0730 BST): ENGLAND V NIGERIA (GROUP F)
FRIDAY JUNE 14 KO 1530 (0730 BST): JAPAN V TUNISIA (GROUP H)
SATURDAY JUNE 22 KO 2030 (1230 BST): QUARTER-FINAL

Osaka, Japan's third biggest city, is known as the 'City of Waters' due to its many rivers and network of canals.

It was once the capital of Japan and the principal centre for trade with neighbouring China. The city's proud heritage is reflected in the lavish 16th century Osaka Castle and the Shitennoji Temple, the oldest state Buddhist temple in Japan.

Modern-day Osaka is a bustling, happening city with an array of tourist attractions. A Universal Studios theme park has recently opened featuring rides and shows based on Hollywood movies such as ET, Back To The Future and Jaws, though perhaps a Godzilla-based attraction would be more in keeping with the location.

More sea creatures can be found in the Kaiyukan Osaka Aquarium, one of the largest in the world, where the highlight is a giant whale shark.

Shopping is also big in Osaka and pride of place goes to Nagahori, a former lumber yard which is now the world's largest underground shopping centre. The loftiest high fashion can be found in the America Mura district while Den-Den Town sells all the latest hi-tech gadgetry.

In terms of nightlife, England fans can practice their terrace chants at one of Osaka's many karaoke bars and restaurants.

The only World Cup stadium to include a youth hostel on site, it has been renovated for the tournament. The distinctive roof covers two thirds of the seats, which could prove very useful given the rain expected every day in Japan during the tournament. Osaka, a handful of miles from Kobe, is Japan's second city and a major port and business centre, dating back to the 16th century.

KOBE

KOBE WING STADIUM.
CAPACITY: 42,000.
OPENED: OCTOBER 2001.
WEDNESDAY JUNE 5 KO 1530 (0730 BST): RUSSIA V TUNISIA (GROUP H)
FRIDAY JUNE 7 KO 1530 (0730 BST): SWEDEN V NIGERIA (GROUP F)
MONDAY JUNE 17 KO 2030 (1230 BST): 2ND ROUND: WINNER GROUP C V RUNNER-UP GROUP H

Kobe is making steady progress in recovering from the devastating effects of the Great Hanshin-Awaji Earthquake of 1995. The first major tremor to directly hit a Japanese city, destroyed lives, homes and infrastructure, but, seven years on, the signs of recovery are there for all to see. The international port of Kobe has been completely rebuilt while its business as usual in the economically important Kinki area. A lasting tribute to the victims of the disaster has been created in the Kobe Port Earthquake Memorial Park.

Situated to the south of Tokyo on an island, Kobe remains a chic, cosmopolitan city which became prosperous after its port was opened up to foreign trade in the 19th century. Key products associated with Kobe are pearls, beef, wine and rubber shoes. Away from commerce, the city is also famous for its suspension bridge – the longest in the world stretching 3,911 metres – and its thriving Chinatown complete with trendy shops and bars.

On the outskirts of the city lies Mount Rokko where English trader Arthur H Groom constructed Japan's first golf course. But for those who don't wish to have a good walk spoiled, the national park surrounding the mountain offers some challenging hiking trails.

The Wing Stadium gets its name from the front-on view. It is the new home of J-League Vissel Kobe. One of just three football-only venues in Japan.

OITA

BIG EYE STADIUM.
CAPACITY: 43,000.
OPENED: MARCH 2001.
MONDAY JUNE 10 KO 1800 (1000 BST): TUNISIA V BELGIUM (GROUP H)
THURSDAY JUNE 13 KO 2030 (1230 BST): MEXICO V ITALY (GROUP G)
SUNDAY JUNE 16 KO 1530 (0730 BST): 2ND ROUND: WINNER GROUP F V RUNNER-UP GROUP A

Oita is a rural region situated at the eastern end of the island of Kyushu. Its capital is Oita City – where the World Cup games will be held – but the area is probably best known for the hot springs of Beppu and Yufulin, two of the world's biggest spa resorts, and its breathtaking countryside.

The hot springs are known locally as 'hells' although they are supposed to be heaven for anyone suffering from troublesome aches and pains. One spring near Beppu City is particularly eye-catching as it is deep red in colour and goes by the wonderful title of 'Blood Pond Hell'.

A short detour on the road to the hills from Oita City is the beautiful Takasaki Mountain, home of the biggest monkey population in Japan, while more wild animals, including giraffes and tigers, can be found at the nearby Kyushi African Safari park.

One absolute must for anyone making the trip out to Oita are the spectacular Harajiri Falls, also known as the 'Niagra of the Orient' due to the 20-metre high cascades of water.

Yet Oita is not only about tranquillity, the region also contains a Formula One-accredited motor racing circuit and a huge amusement park based on the life of a children's doll called 'Kitty-Chan'.

The most easterly stadium used in Japan, on Kyusyu island, Oita is perhaps the most spectacular stadium in the country, with its teflon membrane retractable roof – which takes 20 minutes to open and close – and elliptical exterior. The name is obvious from the design, fitting in an area of outstanding natural beauty.

ABSENT FRIENDS

Spare a thought for the players – and the fans – missing out on the unfolding drama in South Korea and Japan. The most notable absentees are Holland and their glittering array of stars like Patrick Kluivert, Marc Overmars, Edgar Davids, Jaap Stam and Ruud Van Nistelrooy who had already plundered more than 30 goals in his debut season for Manchester United by the middle of March.

The Dutch, semi-finalists in 1998 and co-hosts and semi-finalists at Euro 2000, seemed likely qualifiers when they were grouped with Portugal, Ireland, Estonia, Cyprus and Andorra, but a 2-0 home defeat to Portugal in October 2000 was always likely to prove costly. With Portugal and Ireland going through the group stage unbeaten, the Dutch could not afford a second defeat so when it came against Ireland, who beat them 1-0 in Dublin last September, their fate was sealed. Ironically only Portugal (33 goals) scored more than Holland (30) in the entire European qualification tournament.

Also missing will be the familiar yellow strip of Romania, worn with such distinction by the likes of Gheorghe Hagi, Gica Popescu and Dan Petrescu in major tournaments over the last decade. With Hagi and Petrescu now out of the international picture – Romania's current stars trailed home four points behind Italy in their group – but then lost out to Slovenia 3-2 on aggregate in the play-offs.

There is also no place for the Czech Republic and Bulgaria, who have both graced major tournaments in recent years. Bulgaria, who famously beat Germany and made it through to the semi-finals of the World Cup in the United States eight years ago, trailed home in third place behind Denmark and the Czech Republic in their group. And even though they finished second behind the Danes, the Czechs, prompted throughout by the sublime skills of Pavel Nedved, slid out of the World Cup losing 1-0 home and away to Belgium in the play-offs.

Liberia and former World Player of the Year, George Weah, also came close to their first-ever World Cup appearance, but a 2-1 home defeat by Ghana last July finally put paid to their chances and Weah, one of the greatest footballing ambassadors Africa has ever produced, lost his last chance of appearing in the finals. He finally quit the international scene after Liberia's disappointing showing in the African Nations Cup in Mali in February.

For a long time during the seemingly never-ending South American qualifying competition, Brazil flirted dangerously with elimination, but eventually took the third of the four automatic qualifying places. In the end Colombia agonisingly missed out on even a play-off spot on goal difference. Bolivia, Peru and Chile were the other big-name South American casualties and although Venezuela also failed, as usual, to qualify, they had a tournament to remember – winning five matches – the first five qualifying matches they have ever won.

While Argentina, debutants Ecuador, Brazil and Paraguay booked their automatic spots, Uruguay had to see off Australia in a two-legged play-off.

So the likes of Mark Viduka and Harry Kewell, who flew thousands of miles back to Australia to help the cause ended up on the sidelines. They will be in good company along with the likes of Van Nistelrooy, Davids, Nedved, and all the others who failed to make it. The only consolation for them is: there should be some great matches to watch on the telly this summer.

EUROPE - GROUP ONE

Group winners qualified automatically for finals. Eight of the nine runners-up played
each other in a two-legged home and away playoff with the winners qualifying.
Ireland met Iran in the Europe/Asian playoff and qualified.

SWITZERLAND	0	RUSSIA	1
LUXEMBOURG	0	YUGOSLAVIA	2
FAROE ISLANDS	2	SLOVENIA	2
SWITZERLAND	5	FAROE ISLANDS	1
LUXEMBOURG	1	SLOVENIA	2
RUSSIA	3	LUXEMBOURG	0
SLOVENIA	2	SWITZERLAND	2
YUGOSLAVIA	1	SWITZERLAND	1
RUSSIA	1	SLOVENIA	1
LUXEMBOURG	0	FAROE ISLANDS	2
SWITZERLAND	5	LUXEMBOURG	0
SLOVENIA	1	YUGOSLAVIA	1
RUSSIA	1	FAROE ISLANDS	0
YUGOSLAVIA	0	RUSSIA	1
RUSSIA	1	YUGOSLAVIA	1
FAROE ISLANDS	0	SWITZERLAND	1
SLOVENIA	2	LUXEMBOURG	0
SWITZERLAND	0	SLOVENIA	1
LUXEMBOURG	1	RUSSIA	2
FAROE ISLANDS	0	YUGOSLAVIA	6
YUGOSLAVIA	2	FAROE ISLANDS	0
SWITZERLAND	1	YUGOSLAVIA	1
SLOVENIA	2	RUSSIA	1
FAROE ISLANDS	1	LUXEMBOURG	0
YUGOSLAVIA	1	SLOVENIA	1
LUXEMBOURG	0	SWITZERLAND	3
FAROE ISLANDS	0	RUSSIA	3
YUGOSLAVIA	6	LUXEMBOURG	2
RUSSIA	4	SWITZERLAND	0
SLOVENIA	3	FAROE ISLANDS	0

FINAL TABLE	P	W	D	L	F	A	PTS
1. RUSSIA	10	7	2	1	18	5	23
2. SLOVENIA	10	5	5	0	17	9	20
3. YUGOSLAVIA	10	5	4	1	22	8	19
4. SWITZERLAND	10	4	2	4	18	12	14
5. FAROE ISLANDS	10	2	1	7	6	23	7
6. LUXEMBOURG	10	0	0	10	4	28	0

EUROPE - GROUP TWO

ESTONIA	1	ANDORRA	0
ANDORRA	2	CYPRUS	3
NETHERLANDS	2	IRELAND	2
ESTONIA	1	PORTUGAL	3
ANDORRA	1	ESTONIA	2
CYPRUS	0	NETHERLANDS	4
PORTUGAL	1	IRELAND	1
IRELAND	2	ESTONIA	0
NETHERLANDS	0	PORTUGAL	2
CYPRUS	5	ANDORRA	0
PORTUGAL	3	ANDORRA	0
ANDORRA	0	NETHERLANDS	5
CYPRUS	0	IRELAND	4
ANDORRA	0	IRELAND	3
PORTUGAL	2	NETHERLANDS	2

CYPRUS	2	ESTONIA	2
NETHERLANDS	4	CYPRUS	0
IRELAND	3	ANDORRA	1
IRELAND	1	PORTUGAL	1
ESTONIA	2	NETHERLANDS	4
ESTONIA	0	IRELAND	2
PORTUGAL	6	CYPRUS	0
ESTONIA	2	CYPRUS	2
ANDORRA	1	PORTUGAL	7
IRELAND	1	NETHERLANDS	0
NETHERLANDS	5	ESTONIA	0
CYPRUS	1	PORTUGAL	3
NETHERLANDS	4	ANDORRA	0
PORTUGAL	5	ESTONIA	0
IRELAND	4	CYPRUS	0

FINAL TABLE	P	W	D	L	F	A	PTS
1. PORTUGAL	10	6	3	0	33	7	24
2. IRELAND	10	6	3	0	23	5	24
3. NETHERLANDS	10	6	2	2	30	9	20
4. ESTONIA	10	2	2	6	10	26	8
5. CYPRUS	10	2	2	6	13	31	8
6. ANDORRA	10	0	0	10	5	36	0

EUROPE - GROUP THREE

N. IRELAND	1	MALTA	0
BULGARIA	0	CZECH REPUBLIC	1
ICELAND	1	DENMARK	2
N. IRELAND	1	DENMARK	1
CZECH REPUBLIC	4	ICELAND	0
BULGARIA	3	MALTA	0
ICELAND	1	N. IRELAND	0
DENMARK	1	BULGARIA	1
MALTA	0	CZECH REPUBLIC	0
N. IRELAND	0	CZECH REPUBLIC	1
BULGARIA	2	ICELAND	1
MALTA	0	DENMARK	5
BULGARIA	4	N. IRELAND	3
CZECH REPUBLIC	0	DENMARK	0
MALTA	1	ICELAND	4
ICELAND	3	MALTA	0
N. IRELAND	0	BULGARIA	1
DENMARK	2	CZECH REPUBLIC	1
ICELAND	1	BULGARIA	1
DENMARK	2	MALTA	0
CZECH REPUBLIC	3	N. IRELAND	0
ICELAND	3	CZECH REPUBLIC	1
MALTA	0	BULGARIA	2
DENMARK	1	N. IRELAND	0
CZECH REPUBLIC	3	MALTA	2
BULGARIA	0	DENMARK	2
N. IRELAND	3	ICELAND	0
CZECH REPUBLIC	6	BULGARIA	0
DENMARK	6	ICELAND	0
MALTA	0	N.IRELAND	1

FINAL TABLE	P	W	D	L	F	A	PTS
1. DENMARK	10	6	4	0	22	6	22
2. CZECH REPUBLIC	10	6	2	2	20	8	20
3. BULGARIA	10	5	2	3	14	15	17
4. ICELAND	10	4	1	5	14	20	13
5. N. IRELAND	10	3	2	5	11	12	11
6. MALTA	10	0	1	9	4	24	1

EUROPE - GROUP FOUR

AZERBAIJAN	0	SWEDEN	1
TURKEY	2	MOLDOVA	0
SLOVAKIA	2	MACEDONIA	0
MACEDONIA	3	AZERBAIJAN	0
SWEDEN	1	TURKEY	1
MOLDOVA	0	SLOVAKIA	1
SLOVAKIA	0	SWEDEN	0
AZERBAIJAN	0	TURKEY	1
MOLDOVA	0	MACEDONIA	0
SWEDEN	1	MACEDONIA	0
TURKEY	1	SLOVAKIA	1
AZERBAIJAN	0	MOLDOVA	0
MOLDOVA	0	SWEDEN	2
SLOVAKIA	3	AZERBAIJAN	1
MACEDONIA	1	TURKEY	2
TURKEY	3	AZERBAIJAN	0
MACEDONIA	2	MOLDOVA	2
SWEDEN	2	SLOVAKIA	0
TURKEY	3	MACEDONIA	3
SWEDEN	6	MOLDOVA	0
AZERBAIJAN	2	SLOVAKIA	0
MACEDONIA	1	SWEDEN	2
MOLDOVA	2	AZERBAIJAN	0
SLOVAKIA	0	TURKEY	1
TURKEY	1	SWEDEN	2
SLOVAKIA	4	MOLDOVA	2
AZERBAIJAN	1	MACEDONIA	1
MOLDOVA	0	TURKEY	3
MACEDONIA	0	SLOVAKIA	5
SWEDEN	3	AZERBAIJAN	0

FINAL TABLE	P	W	D	L	F	A	PTS
1. SWEDEN	10	8	2	0	20	3	26
2. TURKEY	10	6	3	1	18	8	21
3. SLOVAKIA	10	5	2	3	16	9	17
4. MACEDONIA	10	1	4	5	11	18	7
5. MOLDOVA	10	1	3	6	6	20	6
6. AZERBAIJAN	10	1	2	7	4	17	5

EUROPE - GROUP FIVE

BELARUS	2	WALES	1
NORWAY	0	ARMENIA	0
UKRAINE	1	POLAND	3
WALES	1	NORWAY	1
ARMENIA	2	UKRAINE	3
POLAND	3	BELARUS	1
POLAND	0	WALES	0
NORWAY	0	UKRAINE	1
BELARUS	2	ARMENIA	1
UKRAINE	0	BELARUS	0
NORWAY	2	POLAND	3
ARMENIA	2	WALES	2
BELARUS	2	NORWAY	1
POLAND	4	ARMENIA	0
WALES	1	UKRAINE	1

ARMENIA	0	BELARUS	0
WALES	1	POLAND	2
UKRAINE	0	NORWAY	0
NORWAY	1	BELARUS	1
UKRAINE	1	WALES	1
ARMENIA	1	POLAND	1
BELARUS	0	UKRAINE	2
WALES	0	ARMENIA	0
POLAND	3	NORWAY	0
UKRAINE	3	ARMENIA	0
BELARUS	4	POLAND	1
NORWAY	3	WALES	2
WALES	1	BELARUS	0
ARMENIA	1	NORWAY	4
POLAND	1	UKRAINE	1

FINAL TABLE	P	W	D	L	F	A	PTS
1. POLAND	10	6	3	1	21	11	21
2. UKRAINE	10	4	5	1	13	8	17
3. BELARUS	10	4	3	3	12	11	15
4. NORWAY	10	2	4	4	12	14	10
5. WALES	10	1	6	3	10	12	9
6. ARMENIA	10	0	5	5	7	19	5

EUROPE - GROUP SIX

LATVIA	0	SCOTLAND	1
BELGIUM	0	CROATIA	0
SAN MARINO	0	SCOTLAND	2
LATVIA	0	BELGIUM	4
CROATIA	1	SCOTLAND	1
SAN MARINO	0	LATVIA	1
BELGIUM	10	SAN MARINO	1
CROATIA	4	LATVIA	1
SCOTLAND	2	BELGIUM	2
SCOTLAND	4	SAN MARINO	0

LATVIA	1	SAN MARINO	1
CROATIA	4	SAN MARINO	0
BELGIUM	3	LATVIA	1
LATVIA	0	CROATIA	1
SAN MARINO	1	BELGIUM	4
SCOTLAND	0	CROATIA	0
SAN MARINO	0	CROATIA	4
BELGIUM	2	SCOTLAND	0
CROATIA	1	BELGIUM	0
SCOTLAND	2	LATVIA	1

FINAL TABLE	P	W	D	L	F	A	PTS
1. CROATIA	8	5	3	0	15	2	18
2. BELGIUM	8	5	2	1	25	6	17
3. SCOTLAND	8	4	3	1	12	6	15
4. LATVIA	8	1	1	6	5	16	4
5. SAN MARINO	8	0	1	7	3	30	1

EUROPE - GROUP SEVEN

BOSNIA	1	SPAIN	2
ISRAEL	2	LIECHTENSTEIN	0
LIECHTENSTEIN	0	AUSTRIA	1
SPAIN	2	ISRAEL	0
ISRAEL	3	BOSNIA	1
AUSTRIA	1	SPAIN	1
BOSNIA	1	AUSTRIA	1
SPAIN	5	LIECHTENSTEIN	0
AUSTRIA	2	ISRAEL	1
LIECHTENSTEIN	0	BOSNIA	3

AUSTRIA	2	LIECHTENSTEIN	0
SPAIN	4	BOSNIA	1
LIECHTENSTEIN	0	ISRAEL	3
ISRAEL	1	SPAIN	1
BOSNIA	0	ISRAEL	0
SPAIN	4	AUSTRIA	0
LIECHTENSTEIN	0	SPAIN	2
AUSTRIA	2	BOSNIA	0
BOSNIA	5	LIECHTENSTEIN	0
ISRAEL	1	AUSTRIA	1

FINAL TABLE	P	W	D	L	F	A	PTS
1. SPAIN	8	6	2	0	21	4	20
2. AUSTRIA	8	4	3	1	10	8	15
3. ISRAEL	8	3	3	2	11	7	12
4. BOSNIA	8	2	2	4	12	12	8
5. LIECHTENSTEIN	8	0	0	8	0	23	0

EUROPE - GROUP EIGHT

ROMANIA	1	LITHUANIA	0
HUNGARY	2	ITALY	2
LITHUANIA	0	GEORGIA	4
ITALY	3	ROMANIA	0
LITHUANIA	1	HUNGARY	6
ITALY	2	GEORGIA	0
HUNGARY	1	LITHUANIA	1
ROMANIA	0	ITALY	2
GEORGIA	0	ROMANIA	2
ITALY	4	LITHUANIA	0

ROMANIA	2	HUNGARY	0
GEORGIA	1	ITALY	2
LITHUANIA	1	ROMANIA	2
HUNGARY	4	GEORGIA	1
GEORGIA	3	HUNGARY	1
LITHUANIA	0	ITALY	0
GEORGIA	3	LITHUANIA	1
HUNGARY	0	ROMANIA	2
ITALY	1	HUNGARY	0
ROMANIA	1	GEORGIA	1

FINAL TABLE	P	W	D	L	F	A	PTS
1. ITALY	8	6	2	0	16	3	20
2. ROMANIA	8	5	1	2	10	7	16
3. GEORGIA	8	3	1	4	12	12	10
4. HUNGARY	8	2	2	4	14	13	8
5. LITHUANIA	8	0	2	6	3	20	2

EUROPE - GROUP NINE

FINLAND	2	ALBANIA	1
GERMANY	2	GREECE	0
ENGLAND	0	GERMANY	1
GREECE	1	FINLAND	0
ALBANIA	2	GREECE	0
FINLAND	0	ENGLAND	0
ENGLAND	2	FINLAND	1
GERMANY	2	ALBANIA	1
ALBANIA	1	ENGLAND	3
GREECE	2	GERMANY	4
GREECE	1	ALBANIA	0
FINLAND	2	GERMANY	2
GREECE	0	ENGLAND	2
ALBANIA	0	GERMANY	2
GERMANY	1	ENGLAND	5
ALBANIA	0	FINLAND	2
ENGLAND	2	ALBANIA	0
FINLAND	5	GREECE	1
GERMANY	0	FINLAND	0
ENGLAND	2	GREECE	2

FINAL TABLE	P	W	D	L	F	A	PTS
1. ENGLAND	8	5	2	1	16	6	17
2. GERMANY	8	5	2	1	14	10	17
3. FINLAND	8	3	3	2	12	7	12
4. GREECE	8	2	1	5	7	17	7
5. ALBANIA	8	1	0	7	5	14	3

EUROPEAN PLAY-OFFS

GAME ONE

| SLOVENIA | 2 | ROMANIA | 1 |
| ROMANIA | 1 | SLOVENIA | 1 |

GAME TWO

| UKRAINE | 1 | GERMANY | 1 |
| GERMANY | 4 | UKRAINE | 1 |

GAME THREE

| BELGIUM | 1 | CZECH REPUBLIC | 0 |
| CZECH REPUBLIC | 0 | BELGIUM | 1 |

GAME FOUR

| AUSTRIA | 0 | TURKEY | 1 |
| TURKEY | 5 | AUSTRIA | 0 |

EUROPEAN/ASIAN PLAY-OFF

| IRELAND | 2 | IRAN | 0 |
| IRAN | 1 | IRELAND | 0 |

SOUTH AMERICA

COLOMBIA	0	BRAZIL	0	COLOMBIA	1	URUGUAY	0
ECUADOR	2	VENEZUELA	0	CHILE	3	BRAZIL	0
URUGUAY	1	BOLIVIA	0	ECUADOR	2	BOLIVIA	0
ARGENTINA	4	CHILE	1	ARGENTINA	1	PARAGUAY	1
PERU	2	PARAGUAY	0	PERU	1	VENEZUELA	0
BOLIVIA	1	COLOMBIA	1	PARAGUAY	3	VENEZUELA	0
PARAGUAY	1	URUGUAY	0	CHILE	0	COLOMBIA	0
VENEZUELA	0	ARGENTINA	4	URUGUAY	4	ECUADOR	0
CHILE	1	PERU	1	PERU	1	ARGENTINA	2
BRAZIL	3	ECUADOR	2	BRAZIL	5	BOLIVIA	0
URUGUAY	2	CHILE	1	COLOMBIA	0	PARAGUAY	2
PARAGUAY	3	ECUADOR	1	VENEZUELA	0	BRAZIL	6
ARGENTINA	1	BOLIVIA	0	BOLIVIA	1	PERU	0
PERU	0	BRAZIL	1	ECUADOR	1	CHILE	0
COLOMBIA	3	VENEZUELA	0	ARGENTINA	2	URUGUAY	1
VENEZUELA	4	BRAZIL	2	BRAZIL	1	COLOMBIA	0
BRAZIL	1	URUGUAY	1	PARAGUAY	5	PERU	1
ECUADOR	2	PERU	1	BOLIVIA	0	URUGUAY	0
CHILE	3	PARAGUAY	1	VENEZUELA	1	ECUADOR	2
COLOMBIA	1	ARGENTINA	3	CHILE	0	ARGENTINA	2
URUGUAY	3	VENEZUELA	1	COLOMBIA	2	BOLIVIA	0
PARAGUAY	2	BRAZIL	1	PERU	3	CHILE	1
BOLIVIA	1	CHILE	0	ECUADOR	1	BRAZIL	0
PERU	0	COLOMBIA	1	ARGENTINA	5	VENEZUELA	0
ARGENTINA	2	ECUADOR	0	URUGUAY	0	PARAGUAY	1
ECUADOR	0	COLOMBIA	0	ECUADOR	2	PARAGUAY	1
VENEZUELA	0	CHILE	2	VENEZUELA	2	COLOMBIA	2
URUGUAY	0	PERU	0	CHILE	0	URUGUAY	1
BRAZIL	3	ARGENTINA	1	BOLIVIA	3	ARGENTINA	3
BOLIVIA	0	PARAGUAY	0	BRAZIL	1	PERU	1

QUALIFICATION ROUTE

COLOMBIA	0	BRAZIL	0
ECUADOR	2	VENEZUELA	0
URUGUAY	1	BOLIVIA	0
ARGENTINA	4	CHILE	1
PERU	2	PARAGUAY	0
BOLIVIA	1	COLOMBIA	1
PARAGUAY	1	URUGUAY	0
VENEZUELA	0	ARGENTINA	4
CHILE	1	PERU	1
BRAZIL	3	ECUADOR	2
URUGUAY	2	CHILE	1
PARAGUAY	3	ECUADOR	1
ARGENTINA	1	BOLIVIA	0
PERU	0	BRAZIL	1

COLOMBIA	3	VENEZUELA	0
VENEZUELA	4	BRAZIL	2
BRAZIL	1	URUGUAY	1
ECUADOR	2	PERU	1
CHILE	3	PARAGUAY	1
COLOMBIA	1	ARGENTINA	3
URUGUAY	3	VENEZUELA	1
PARAGUAY	2	BRAZIL	1
BOLIVIA	1	CHILE	0
PERU	0	COLOMBIA	1
ARGENTINA	2	ECUADOR	0
ECUADOR	0	COLOMBIA	0
VENEZUELA	0	CHILE	2
URUGUAY	0	PERU	0
BRAZIL	3	ARGENTINA	1

FINAL TABLE	P	W	D	L	F	A	PTS
1. ARGENTINA	18	13	4	1	42	15	44
2. ECUADOR	18	9	4	5	23	20	31
3. BRAZIL	18	9	3	6	31	17	30
4. PARAGUAY	18	9	3	6	29	23	30
5. URUGUAY	18	7	6	5	19	13	27
6. COLOMBIA	18	7	6	5	20	15	27
7. BOLIVIA	17	4	5	8	20	32	17
8. VENEZUELA	17	5	1	11	18	41	16
9. PERU	17	4	3	10	13	24	15
10. CHILE	17	3	2	12	15	27	11

PRELIMINARY ROUND
ASIA - GROUP ONE

SYRIA	12	PHILLIPINES	0	PHILIPPINES	0	OMAN	2
OMAN	12	LAOS	0	LAOS	0	SYRIA	9
OMAN	7	LAOS	0	SYRIA	3	OMAN	3
PHILIPPINES	1	SYRIA	5	LAOS	2	PHILLIPINES	0
OMAN	7	PHILLIPINES	0	OMAN	2	SYRIA	0
SYRIA	11	LAOS	0	PHILIPPINES	1	LAOS	1

FINAL TABLE	P	W	D	L	F	A	PTS
1. OMAN	6	5	1	0	33	3	16
2. SYRIA	6	4	1	1	40	6	13
3. LAOS	6	1	1	4	3	40	4
4. PHILIPPINES	6	0	1	5	2	29	1

ASIA - GROUP TWO

IRAN	19	GUAM	0	IRAN	2	TAJIKISTAN	0
TAJIKISTAN	16	GUAM	0				

FINAL TABLE	P	W	D	L	F	A	PTS
1. IRAN	2	2	0	0	21	0	6
2. TAJIKISTAN	2	1	0	1	16	2	3
3. GUAM	2	0	0	2	0	35	0

ASIA - GROUP THREE

QATAR	5	MALAYSIA	1
HONG KONG	1	PALESTINE	1
QATAR	2	PALESTINE	1
HONG KONG	0	MALAYSIA	2
PALESTINE	1	MALAYSIA	0
HONG KONG	0	QATAR	2

PALESTINE	1	HONG KONG	0
QATAR	0	MALAYSIA	0
HONG KONG	2	MALAYSIA	1
QATAR	2	PALESTINE	1
QATAR	3	HONG KONG	1
MALAYSIA	4	PALESTINE	3

FINAL TABLE	P	W	D	L	F	A	PTS
1. QATAR	6	5	1	0	14	3	16
2. PALESTINE	6	2	1	3	8	9	7
3. MALAYSIA	6	2	1	3	8	11	7
4. HONG KONG	6	1	1	4	3	10	4

ASIA - GROUP FOUR

BAHRAIN	1	KUWAIT	2
SINGAPORE	0	KYRGYZSTAN	1
BAHRAIN	1	KYRGYZSTAN	0
KUWAIT	1	SINGAPORE	1
KYRGYZSTAN	0	KUWAIT	3
SINGAPORE	1	BAHRAIN	2

BAHRAIN	2	KYRGYZSTAN	1
KUWAIT	1	SINGAPORE	0
KUWAIT	2	KYRGYZSTAN	0
BAHRAIN	2	SINGAPORE	0
KYRGYZSTAN	1	SINGAPORE	1
KUWAIT	0	BAHRAIN	1

FINAL TABLE	P	W	D	L	F	A	PTS
1. BAHRAIN	6	5	0	1	9	4	15
2. KUWAIT	6	4	1	1	9	3	13
3. KYRGYZSTAN	6	1	1	4	3	9	4
4. SINGAPORE	6	0	2	4	3	8	2

ASIA - GROUP FIVE

THAILAND	2	SRI LANKA	4	
LEBANON	6	PAKISTAN	0	
THAILAND	3	PAKISTAN	0	
LEBANON	4	SRI LANKA	0	
PAKISTAN	3	SRI LANKA	3	
LEBANON	1	THAILAND	2	
LEBANON	8	PAKISTAN	1	
THAILAND	3	SRI LANKA	0	
LEBANON	4	SRI LANKA	0	
THAILAND	3	PAKISTAIN	0	
PAKISTAN	3	SRI LANKA	3	
LEBANON	1	THAILAND	2	

FINAL TABLE	P	W	D	L	F	A	PTS
1. THAILAND	6	5	1	0	20	5	16
2. LEBANON	6	4	1	1	26	5	13
3. SRI LANKA	6	1	1	4	8	20	4
4. PAKISTAN	6	0	1	5	5	29	1

ASIA - GROUP SIX

KAZAKHSTAN	6	NEPAL	0
MACAO	0	IRAQ	8
KAZAKHSTAN	3	MACAO	0
IRAQ	9	NEPAL	1
MACAO	1	NEPAL	4
IRAQ	1	KAZAKHSTAN	1
KAZAKHSTAN	4	NEPAL	0
MACAO	0	IRAQ	5
MACAO	0	KAZAKHSTAN	5
IRAQ	4	NEPAL	2
MACAO	1	NEPAL	6
IRAQ	1	KAZAKHSTAN	1

FINAL TABLE	P	W	D	L	F	A	PTS
1. IRAQ	6	4	2	0	28	5	14
2. KAZAKHSTAN	6	4	2	0	20	2	14
3. NEPAL	6	2	0	4	13	25	6
4. MACAO	6	0	0	6	2	31	0

ASIA - GROUP SEVEN

TURKMENISTAN 2	JORDAN		0
UZBEKISTAN	7	TAIWAN	0
TAIWAN	0	JORDAN	2
UZBEKISTAN	1	TURKMENISTAN	0
TAIWAN	0	TURKMENISTAN	5
UZBEKISTAN	2	JORDAN	2

JORDAN	6	TAIWAN	0
TURKMENISTAN 2	UZBEKISTAN		5
TAIWAN	0	UZBEKISTAN	4
JORDAN	1	TURKMENISTAN	1
TURKMENISTAN 1	TAIWAN		0
JORDAN	1	UZBEKISTAN	1

FINAL TABLE	P	W	D	L	F	A	PTS
1. UZBEKISTAN	6	4	2	0	20	5	14
2. TURKMENISTAN	6	4	0	2	12	7	12
3. JORDAN	6	2	2	2	14	7	8
4. TAIWAN	6	0	0	6	0	25	0

ASIA - GROUP EIGHT

BRUNEI	0	YEMEN	5
INDIA	1	UAE	0
BRUNEI	0	UAE	12
INDIA	1	YEMEN	1
UAE	1	INDIA	0
YEMEN	1	BRUNEI	0

YEMEN	3	INDIA	3
UAE	4	BRUNEI	0
YEMEN	2	UAE	1
BRUNEI	0	INDIA	1
UAE	3	YEMEN	2
INDIA	5	BRUNEI	0

FINAL TABLE	P	W	D	L	F	A	PTS
1. U. ARAB EMIRATES	6	4	0	2	21	5	12
2. YEMEN	6	3	2	1	14	8	11
3. INDIA	6	3	2	1	11	5	11
4. BRUNEI	6	0	0	6	0	28	0

ASIA - GROUP NINE

MALDIVES	6	CAMBODIA	0
INDONESIA	5	MALDIVES	0
CAMBODIA	1	MALDIVES	1
INDONESIA	6	CAMBODIA	0
CHINA	10	MALDIVES	1
MALDIVES	0	CHINA	1

CAMBODIA	0	INDONESIA	2
CAMBODIA	0	CHINA	4
MALDIVES	0	INDONESIA	2
CHINA	5	INDONESIA	1
CHINA	3	CAMBODIA	1
INDONESIA	0	CHINA	2

FINAL TABLE	P	W	D	L	F	A	PTS
1. CHINA	6	6	0	0	25	3	18
2. INDONESIA	6	4	0	2	16	7	12
3. MALDIVES	6	1	1	4	8	19	4
4. CAMBODIA	6	0	1	5	2	21	1

ASIA - GROUP TEN

VIETNAM	0	BANGLADESH	0
SAUDI ARABIA	6	MONGOLIA	0
MONGOLIA	0	VIETNAM	1
BANGLADESH	0	SAUDI ARABIA	3
MONGOLIA	0	BANGLADESH	3
SAUDI ARABIA	5	VIETNAM	0

SAUDI ARABIA	6	MONGOLIA	0
BANGLADESH	0	VIETNAM	4
VIETNAM	4	MONGOLIA	0
SAUDI ARABIA	6	BANGLADESH	0
MONGOLIA	2	BANGLADESH	2
SAUDI ARABIA	4	VIETNAM	0

FINAL TABLE	P	W	D	L	F	A	PTS
1. SAUDI ARABIA	6	6	0	0	30	0	18
2. VIETNAM	6	3	1	2	9	9	10
3. BANGLADESH	6	1	2	3	5	15	5
4. MONGOLIA	6	0	1	5	2	22	1

FINAL ROUND
ASIA - GROUP A

IRAQ	4	THAILAND	0
SAUDI ARABIA	1	BAHRAIN	1
BAHRAIN	2	IRAQ	0
IRAN	2	SAUDI ARABIA	0
SAUDI ARABIA	1	IRAQ	0
THAILAND	0	IRAN	0
BAHRAIN	1	THAILAND	1
IRAQ	1	IRAN	2
IRAN	0	BAHRAIN	0
THAILAND	1	SAUDI ARABIA	3

BAHRAIN	0	SAUDI ARABIA	4
THAILAND	1	IRAQ	1
IRAQ	1	BAHRAIN	0
SAUDI ARABIA	2	IRAN	2
IRAN	1	THAILAND	0
IRAQ	1	SAUDI ARABIA	2
IRAN	2	IRAQ	0
THAILAND	1	BAHRAIN	0
BAHRAIN	3	IRAN	0
SAUDI ARABIA	4	THAILAND	1

FINAL TABLE	P	W	D	L	F	A	PTS
1. SAUDI ARABIA	8	5	2	1	17	8	17
2. IRAN	8	4	3	1	10	7	15
3. BAHRAIN	8	2	4	2	8	9	10
4. IRAQ	8	2	1	5	9	10	7
5. THAILAND	8	0	4	4	5	15	4

FINAL ROUND
ASIA - GROUP B

QATAR	0	OMAN	0		OMAN	0	QATAR	3
UAE	4	UZBEKISTAN	1		UZBEKISTAN	0	UAE	1
CHINA	3	UAE	0		UAE	0	CHINA	1
UZBEKISTAN	2	QATAR	1		QATAR	2	UZBEKISTAN	2
UAE	0	QATAR	2		QATAR	1	UAE	2
OMAN	0	CHINA	2		CHINA	1	OMAN	0
QATAR	1	CHINA	1		OMAN	4	UZBEKISTAN	2
UZBEKISTAN	5	OMAN	0		CHINA	3	QATAR	0
OMAN	1	UAE	1		UAE	2	OMAN	2
CHINA	2	UZBEKISTAN	0		UZBEKISTAN	1	CHINA	0

FINAL TABLE	P	W	D	L	F	A	PTS
1. CHINA	8	6	1	1	13	2	19
2. U. ARAB EMIRATES	8	3	2	3	10	11	11
3. UZBEKISTAN	8	3	1	4	13	14	10
4. QATAR	8	2	3	3	10	10	9
5. OMAN	8	1	3	4	7	16	6

Saudi Arabia and China qualify
automatically for the finals.
Iran and the UAE played off for the
right to meet Ireland for a
place in the finals.

ASIAN RUNNERS-UP PLAY-OFFS

IRAN	1	UAE	0
UAE	0	IRAN	3

(IRAN WON 4-0 ON AGGREGATE)

EUROPEAN/ASIAN PLAY-OFF

IRELAND	2	IRAN	0
IRAN	1	IRELAND	0

(IRELAND WON 2-1 ON AGGREGATE AND
QUALIFY FOR THE FINALS

QUALIFICATION ROUTE

FIRST ROUND
AFRICA

MAURITANIA	1	TUNISIA	2	ZIMBABWE	3	C. AFRICAN REP.	1
TUNISIA	3	MAURITANIA	0	CONGO	2	EQ. GUINEA	1
GUINEA-BISSAU	0	TOGO	0	EQ. GUINEA	1	CONGO	3
TOGO	3	GUINEA-BISSAU	0	MALI	3	LIBYA	1
GAMBIA	0	MOROCCO	1	LIBYA	3	MALI	0
MOROCCO	2	GAMBIA	0	DJIBOUTI	1	DR CONGO	1
BENIN	1	SENEGAL	1	DR CONGO	9	DJIBOUTI	1
SENEGAL	1	BENIN	0	SEYCHELLES	1	NAMIBIA	1
CAPE VERDE ISL.	0	ALGERIA	0	NAMIBIA	3	SEYCHELLES	0
ALGERIA	2	CAPE VERDE ISL.	0	ERITREA	0	NIGERIA	0
MADAGASCAR	2	GABON	0	NIGERIA	4	ERITREA	0
GABON	1	MADAGASCAR	0	SOMALIA	0	CAMEROON	3
BOTSWANA	0	ZAMBIA	1	CAMEROON	3	SOMALIA	0
ZAMBIA	1	BOTSWANA	0	MAURITIUS	0	EGYPT	2
SWAZILAND	0	ANGOLA	0	EGYPT	4	MAURITIUS	2
ANGOLA	7	SWAZILAND	1	TANZANIA	0	GHANA	1
LESOTHO	0	SOUTH AFRICA	2	GHANA	3	TANZANIA	2
SOUTH AFRICA	1	LESOTHO	0	UGANDA	4	GUINEA	4
SUDAN	1	MOZAMBIQUE	0	GUINEA	3	UGANDA	0
MOZAMBIQUE	2	SUDAN	1	MALAWI	2	KENYA	0
SAO TOME E P.	2	SIERRA LEONE	1	KENYA	0	MALAWI	0
SIERRA LEONE	4	SAO TOME E P.	0	CHAD	0	LIBERIA	1
RWANDA	2	IVORY COAST	2	LIBERIA	0	CHAD	0
IVORY COAST	2	RWANDA	0	ETHIOPIA	2	BURKINA FASO	1
C. AFRICAN REP.	0	ZIMBABWE	1	BURKINA FASO	3	ETHIOPIA	0

SECOND ROUND
AFRICA - GROUP A

ANGOLA	2	ZAMBIA	1
LIBYA	0	CAMEROON	3
ZAMBIA	2	TOGO	0
CAMEROON	3	ANGOLA	0
ANGOLA	3	LIBYA	1
TOGO	0	CAMEROON	2
LIBYA	3	TOGO	3
CAMEROON	1	ZAMBIA	0
ZAMBIA	2	LIBYA	0
TOGO	1	ANGOLA	1

ZAMBIA	1	ANGOLA	1
CAMEROON	1	LIBYA	0
ANGOLA	2	CAMEROON	0
TOGO	3	ZAMBIA	2
LIBYA	1	ANGOLA	1
CAMEROON	2	TOGO	0
ZAMBIA	2	CAMEROON	2
TOGO	2	LIBYA	0
ANGOLA	1	TOGO	1
LIBYA	2	ZAMBIA	4

FINAL TABLE	P	W	D	L	F	A	PTS
1. CAMEROON	8	6	1	1	14	4	19
2. ANGOLA	8	3	4	1	11	9	13
3. ZAMBIA	8	3	2	3	14	11	11
4. TOGO	8	2	3	3	10	13	9
5. LIBYA	8	0	2	6	7	19	2

CAMEROON QUALIFY FOR FINALS

SECOND ROUND
AFRICA - GROUP B

NIGERIA	2	SIERRA LEONE	0
SUDAN	2	LIBERIA	0
LIBERIA	2	NIGERIA	1
SIERRA LEONE	0	GHANA	5
NIGERIA	3	SUDAN	0
GHANA	1	LIBERIA	3
SUDAN	1	GHANA	0
LIBERIA	1	SIERRA LEONE	0
SIERRA LEONE	0	SUDAN	2
GHANA	0	NIGERIA	0

SIERRA LEONE	1	NIGERIA	0
LIBERIA	2	SUDAN	0
SIERRA LEONE	1	GHANA	1
NIGERIA	2	LIBERIA	0
LIBERIA	1	GHANA	2
SUDAN	0	NIGERIA	4
SIERRA LEONE	0	LIBERIA	1
GHANA	1	SUDAN	0
NIGERIA	3	GHANA	0
SUDAN	3	SIERRA LEONE	0

FINAL TABLE	P	W	D	L	F	A	PTS
1. NIGERIA	8	5	1	2	15	3	16
2. LIBERIA	8	5	0	3	10	8	15
3. SUDAN	8	4	0	4	8	10	12
4. GHANA	8	3	2	3	10	9	11
5. SIERRA LEONE	8	1	1	6	2	15	4

NIGERIA QUALIFY FOR FINALS

SECOND ROUND
AFRICA - GROUP C

ALGERIA	1	SENEGAL	1
NAMIBIA	0	MOROCCO	0
SENEGAL	0	EGYPT	0
MOROCCO	2	ALGERIA	1
ALGERIA	1	NAMIBIA	0
EGYPT	0	MOROCCO	0
NAMIBIA	1	EGYPT	1
MOROCCO	0	SENEGAL	0
SENEGAL	4	NAMIBIA	0
EGYPT	5	ALGERIA	2
SENEGAL	3	ALGERIA	0
MOROCCO	3	NAMIBIA	0
ALGERIA	1	MOROCCO	2
EGYPT	1	SENEGAL	0
NAMIBIA	0	ALGERIA	4
MOROCCO	1	EGYPT	0
EGYPT	8	NAMIBIA	2
SENEGAL	1	MOROCCO	0
ALGERIA	1	EGYPT	1
NAMIBIA	0	SENEGAL	5

FINAL TABLE	P	W	D	L	F	A	PTS
1. SENEGAL	8	4	3	1	14	2	15
2. MOROCCO	8	4	3	1	8	3	15
3. EGYPT	8	3	4	1	16	7	13
4. ALGERIA	8	2	2	4	11	14	8
5. NAMIBIA	8	0	6	2	3	26	2

SENEGAL QUALIFY FOR FINALS

SECOND ROUND
AFRICA - GROUP D

MADAGASCAR	3	CONGO DR	0
IVORY COAST	2	TUNISIA	2
TUNISIA	1	MADAGASCAR	0
CONGO DR	2	CONGO	0
MADAGASCAR	1	IVORY COAST	3
CONGO	1	TUNISIA	2
TUNISIA	6	CONGO DR	0
CONGO DR	1	IVORY COAST	2
CONGO	2	MADAGASCAR	0
IVORY COAST	2	CONGO	0

CONGO DR	1	MADAGASCAR	0
MADAGASCAR	0	TUNISIA	2
CONGO	1	DR CONGO	1
TUNISIA	1	IVORY COAST	1
TUNISIA	6	CONGO	0
IVORY COAST	6	MADAGASCAR	0
DR CONGO	0	TUNISIA	3
CONGO	1	IVORY COAST	1
MADAGASCAR	1	CONGO	0
IVORY COAST	1	DR CONGO	2

FINAL TABLE	P	W	D	L	F	A	PTS
1. TUNISIA	8	6	2	0	23	4	20
2. IVORY COAST	8	4	3	1	18	8	15
3. DR CONGO	8	3	1	4	7	16	10
4. MADAGASCAR	8	2	0	6	5	15	6
5. CONGO	8	1	2	5	5	15	5

TUNISIA QUALIFY FOR FINALS

SECOND ROUND
AFRICA - GROUP E

MALAWI	1	BURKINA FASO	1	
GUINEA	3	ZIMBABWE	0	
ZIMBABWE	0	SOUTH AFRICA	2	
BURKINA FASO	2	GUINEA	3	
GUINEA	1	MALAWI	1	
SOUTH AFRICA	1	BURKINA FASO	0	
BURKINA FASO	1	ZIMBABWE	2	
MALAWI	1	SOUTH AFRICA	2	

ZIMBABWE	2	MALAWI	0
BURKINA FASO	4	MALAWI	2
SOUTH AFRICA	2	ZIMBABWE	1
BURKINA FASO	1	SOUTH AFRICA	1
SOUTH AFRICA	2	MALAWI	0
ZIMBABWE	1	BURKINA FASO	0
MALAWI	0	ZIMBABWE	1

Note: Guinea expelled from World Cup by Fifa on 19/03/01 and results of matches against Guinea expunged from records

FINAL TABLE	P	W	D	L	F	A	PTS
1. SOUTH AFRICA	6	5	1	0	10	3	16
2. ZIMBABWE	6	4	0	2	7	5	12
3. BURKINA FASO	6	1	2	3	7	8	5
4. MALAWI	6	0	1	5	4	12	1

SOUTH AFRICA QUALIFY FOR FINALS

FIRST ROUND
OCEANIA - GROUP ONE

SAMOA	0	TONGA	1		AUSTRALIA	31	AMERICAN SAMOA	0
FIJI	13	AMERICAN SAMOA	0		AUSTRALIA	2	FIJI	0
AUSTRALIA	22	TONGA	0		TONGA	5	AMERICAN SAMOA	0
AMERICAN SAMOA	0	SAMOA	8		AUSTRALIA	11	SAMOA	0
SAMOA	1	FIJI	6		TONGA	1	FIJI	8

FINAL TABLE	P	W	D	L	F	A	PTS
1. AUSTRALIA	4	4	0	0	66	0	12
2. FIJI	4	3	0	1	27	4	9
3. TONGA	4	2	0	2	7	30	6
4. SAMOA	4	1	0	3	9	18	3
5. AMERICAN SAMOA	4	0	0	4	0	57	0

FIRST ROUND
OCEANIA - GROUP TWO

TAHITI	6	VANUATU	1		NEW ZEALAND	2	COOK ISLANDS	0
SOLOMON ISLANDS	9	COOK ISLANDS	1		SOLOMON ISLANDS	1	NEW ZEALAND	5
TAHITI	0	NEW ZEALAND	5		COOK ISLANDS	0	TAHITI	6
COOK ISLANDS	1	VANUATU	8		NEW ZEALAND	7	VANUATU	0
VANUATU	2	SOLOMON ISLANDS	7		TAHITI	2	SOLOMON ISLANDS	0

FINAL TABLE	P	W	D	L	F	A	PTS
1. NEW ZEALAND	4	4	0	0	19	1	12
2. TAHITI	4	3	0	1	14	6	9
3. SOLOMON ISLANDS	4	2	0	2	17	10	6
4. VANUATU	4	1	0	3	11	21	3
5. COOK ISLANDS	4	0	0	4	2	25	0

Australia and New Zealand played off
for the right to meet Uruguay for a
place in the finals.

OCEANIA PLAY-OFFS

NEW ZEALAND	0	AUSTRALIA	2
AUSTRALIA	4	NEW ZEALAND	1

(AUSTRALIA WON 6-1 ON AGGREGATE TO
QUALIFY FOR A FINAL PLAY-OFF
AGAINST URUGUAY)

SOUTH AMERICA/OCEANIA PLAY-OFFS

AUSTRALIA	1	URUGUAY	0
URUGUAY	3	AUSTRALIA	0

(URUGUAY WON 3-1 ON AGGREGATE AND
QUALIFY FOR THE FINALS

PRELIMINARY ROUND
CEN. AMERICA ZONE - GROUP A

EL SALVADOR	3	BELIZE	0
BELIZE	1	GUATEMALA	2
GUATEMALA	0	EL SALVADOR	1

BELIZE	1	EL SALVADOR	3
EL SALVADOR	1	GUATEMALA	1
GUATEMALA	0	BELIZE	0

FINAL TABLE	P	W	D	L	F	A	PTS
1. EL SALVADOR	4	3	1	0	10	2	10
2. GUATEMALA	4	1	2	1	3	3	5
3. BELIZE	4	0	1	3	2	10	1

PRELIMINARY ROUND
CEN. AMERICA ZONE - GROUP B

HONDURAS	3	NICARAGUA	0
NICARAGUA	0	PANAMA	2
PANAMA	1	HONDURAS	0

NICARAGUA	0	HONDURAS	1
HONDURAS	3	PANAMA	1
PANAMA	4	NICARAGUA	0

FINAL TABLE	P	W	D	L	F	A	PTS
1. PANAMA	4	3	0	1	8	3	9
2. HONDURAS	4	3	0	1	7	2	9
3. NICARAGUA	4	0	0	4	0	10	0

QUALIFICATION ROUTE

FIRST ROUND
CARIBBEAN ZONE

CUBA	4	CAYMAN ISLANDS	0
CAYMAN ISLANDS	0	CUBA	0
ST LUCIA	1	SURINAM	0
SURINAM	1	ST LUCIA	0
BARBADOS	2	GRENADA	2
GRENADA	2	BARBADOS	3
ARUBA	4	PUERTO RICO	2
PUERTO RICO	2	ARUBA	2
ST VINCENT	9	US VIRG. ISLANDS	0
US VIRG. ISLANDS	1	ST VINCENT	5
BRITISH VIRG. IS.	1	BERMUDA	5

BERMUDA	9	BRITISH VIRG. IS.	0
ST KITTS	8	TURKS & CALCOS IS.	0
TURKS & CALCOS IS.	0	ST KITTS	6
TRIN. & TOB.	5	DUTCH ANTILLES	0
DUTCH ANTILLES	1	TRIN. & TOB.	1
ANGUILLA	1	BAHAMAS	3
BAHAMAS	2	ANGUILLA	1
DOMINICAN REP	3	MONTSERRAT	0
MONTSERRAT	1	DOMINICAN REP	3
HAITI	4	DOMINICA	0
DOMINICA	1	HAITI	3

SECOND ROUND
CARIBBEAN ZONE

ARUBA	1	BARBADOS	3
BARBADOS	4	ARUBA	0
CUBA	1	SURINAM	0
SURINAM	0	CUBA	0
ANTIGUA & BARBUDA	0	BERMUDA	0
BERMUDA	1	ANTIGUA & BARBUDA	1

ST VINCENT	1	ST KITTS	0
ST KITS	1	ST VINCENT	2
HAITI	9	BAHAMAS	0
BAHAMAS	0	HAITI	4
TRINIDAD & TOBAGO	3	DOMINICAN REP.	0
DOMINICAN REP.	0	TRINIDAD & TOBAGO	1

QUALIFICATION ROUTE

FINALS
CARIBBEAN ZONE

CUBA	1	BARBADOS	1
BARBADOS	1	CUBA	1
(BARBADOS WON 5-4 ON PENALTIES)			

ANTIGUA & BARBUDA	2	ST VINCENT	1
ST VINCENT	4	ANTIGUA & BARBUDA	0
TRINIDAD & TOBAGO	3	HAITI	1
HAITI	1	TRINIDAD & TOBAGO	1

PLAY-OFFS
CARIBBEAN ZONE

CUBA	0	CANADA	1
CANADA	0	CUBA	0

ANTIGUA & BARBUDA	0	GUATEMALA	1
GUATEMALA	8	ANTIGUA & BARBUDA	1
HONDURAS	4	HAITI	0
HAITI	1	HONDURAS	3

WORLD CUP FACTS

Liverpool's Ian Callaghan played in the 1966 World Cup group game against France – and it was 12 years before he won his next cap!

Michael Owen was only 18yrs, 183 days when he played against Tunisia in 1998, our youngest World Cup player. Peter Shilton is the oldest; a grand 40yrs 295 days v Italy in 1990

Lawrence Hughes of Liverpool never played for England before or after the 1950 World Cup. But he won three caps during the tournament; including the infamous defeat against the USA.

Paul Gascoigne is the only member of the Italia 90 squad who has appeared in the Premiership this season – playing for Everton before moving to Burnley.

GROUP C

CANADA	0	TRINIDAD	2		MEXICO	7	PANAMA	1
PANAMA	0	MEXICO	1		TRINIDAD	4	CANADA	0
PANAMA	0	CANADA	0		MEXICO	7	TRINIDAD	0
TRINIDAD	1	MEXICO	0		CANADA	1	PANAMA	0
MEXICO	2	CANADA	0		CANADA	0	MEXICO	0
TRINIDAD	6	PANAMA	0		PANAMA	0	TRINIDAD	1

FINAL TABLE	P	W	D	L	F	A	PTS
1. TRINIDAD & TOBAGO	6	5	0	1	14	7	15
2. MEXICO	6	4	1	1	17	2	13
3. CANADA	6	1	2	3	1	8	5
4. PANAMA	6	0	1	5	1	16	1

TRINIDAD & TOBAGO AND MEXICO QUALIFIED FOR THE FINAL STAGE
OF QUALIFYING TOURNAMENT

GROUP D

EL SALVADOR	2	HONDURAS	5		HONDURAS	5	EL SALVADOR	0
ST VINCENT	0	JAMAICA	1		JAMAICA	2	ST VINCENT	0
EL SALVADOR	7	ST VINCENT	1		ST VINCENT	1	EL SALVADOR	2
JAMAICA	3	HONDURAS	1		HONDURAS	1	JAMAICA	0
JAMAICA	1	EL SALVADOR	0		ST VINCENT	0	HONDURAS	7
HONDURAS	6	ST VINCENT	0		EL SALVADOR	2	JAMAICA	0

FINAL TABLE	P	W	D	L	F	A	PTS
1. HONDURAS	6	5	0	1	25	5	15
2. JAMAICA	6	4	0	2	7	4	12
3. EL SALVADOR	6	3	0	3	13	13	9
4. ST VINCENT	6	0	0	6	2	25	0

HONDURAS AND JAMAICA QUALIFIED FOR THE FINAL STAGE OF
QUALIFYING TOURNAMENT

Jay Jay Okocha of Nigeria, who are drawn in Group F, the 'Group of Death'

Raul could become Spain's all-time top scorer during this World Cup

GROUP E

GUATEMALA	1	UNITED STATES	1
BARBADOS	2	COSTA RICA	1
GUATEMALA	2	BARBADOS	0
COSTA RICA	2	UNITED STATES	1
COSTA RICA	2	GUATEMALA	1
UNITED STATES	7	BARBADOS	0

COSTA RICA	3	BARBADOS	0
UNITED STATES	1	GUATEMALA	0
BARBADOS	1	GUATEMALA	3
UNITED STATES	0	COSTA RICA	0
GUATEMALA	2	COSTA RICA	1
BARBADOS	0	UNITED STATES	4

FINAL TABLE	P	W	D	L	F	A	PTS
1. UNITED STATES	6	3	2	1	14	3	11
2. COSTA RICA	6	3	1	2	9	6	10
3. GUATEMALA	6	3	1	2	9	6	10
4. BARBADOS	6	1	0	5	3	20	3

UNITED STATES QUALIFIED FOR THE FINAL STAGE
OF QUALIFYING TOURNAMENT

COSTA RICA AND GUATEMALA PLAY-OFF FOR A PLACE IN THE FINAL STAGE

PLAY-OFF

COSTA RICA	5	GUATAMALA	2

QUALIFICATION ROUTE

FINAL STAGE

COSTA RICA	2	HONDURAS	2
UNITED STATES	2	MEXICO	0
JAMAICA	1	TRINIDAD	0
MEXICO	4	JAMAICA	0
COSTA RICA	3	TRINIDAD	0
HONDURAS	1	UNITED STATES	2
UNITED STATES	1	COSTA RICA	0
JAMAICA	1	HONDURAS	1
TRINIDAD	1	MEXICO	1
JAMAICA	0	UNITED STATES	0
TRINIDAD	2	HONDURAS	4
MEXICO	1	COSTA RICA	2
UNITED STATES	2	TRINIDAD	0
HONDURAS	3	MEXICO	1
COSTA RICA	2	JAMAICA	1

TRINIDAD	1	JAMAICA	2
MEXICO	1	UNITED STATES	0
HONDURAS	2	COSTA RICA	3
TRINIDAD	0	COSTA RICA	2
UNITED STATES	2	HONDURAS	3
JAMAICA	1	MEXICO	2
HONDURAS	1	JAMAICA	0
MEXICO	3	TRINIDAD	0
COSTA RICA	2	UNITED STATES	0
HONDURAS	0	TRINIDAD	1
UNITED STATES	2	JAMAICA	1
COSTA RICA	0	MEXICO	0
JAMAICA	0	COSTA RICA	1
TRINIDAD	0	UNITED STATES	0
MEXICO	3	HONDURAS	0

FINAL TABLE	P	W	D	L	F	A	PTS
1. COSTA RICA	10	7	2	1	17	7	23
2. MEXICO	10	5	2	3	16	9	17
3. UNITED STATES	10	5	2	3	11	8	17
4. HONDURAS	10	4	2	4	17	17	14
5. JAMAICA	10	2	2	6	7	14	8
6. TRINIDAD	10	1	2	7	5	18	5

COSTA RICA, MEXICO AND U.S. QUALIFIED FOR THE FINALS

292

GOAL STATS

TOP SCORERS

YEAR	HOST COUNTRY	PLAYER	GOALS
1930	URUGUAY	**GUILLERMO STABILE** (ARGENTINA)	8
1934	ITALY	**ANGELO SCHIAVO** (ITALY)	4
		OLDRICH NEJEDLY (CZECHOSLOVAKIA)	4
		EDMUND CONEN (GERMANY)	4
1938	FRANCE	**LEONIDAS** (BRAZIL)	8
1950	BRAZIL	**ADEMIR** (BRAZIL)	9
1954	SWITZERLAND	**SANDOR KOCSIS** (HUNGARY)	11
1958	SWEDEN	**JUSTE FONTAINE** (FRANCE)	13
1962	CHILE	**GARRINCHA** (BRAZIL)	4
		VAVA (BRAZIL)	4
		LEONEL SANCHEZ (CHILE)	4
		DRAZAN JERKOVIC (YUGOSLAVIA)	4
		FLORIAN ALBERT (HUNGARY)	4
		VALETIN IVANOV (SOVIET UNION)	4
1966	ENGLAND	**EUSEBIO** (PORTUGAL)	9
1970	MEXICO	**GERD MUELLER** (WEST GERMANY)	10
1974	WEST GERMANY	**GRZEGORZ LATO** (POLAND)	7
1978	ARGENTINA	**MARIO KEMPES** (ARGENTINA)	6
1982	SPAIN	**PAOLO ROSSI** (ITALY)	6
1986	MEXICO	**GARY LINEKER** (ENGLAND)	6
1990	ITALY	**SALVATORE SCHILACHI** (ITALY)	6
1994	UNITED STATES	**HRISTO STOITCHKOV** (BULGARIA)	6
		OLEG SALENKO (RUSSIA)	6
1998	FRANCE	**DAVOR SUKER** (CROATIA)	6

WORLD CUP GOAL SCORERS

MOST SUCCESSFUL SCORERS

GLS	PLAYER	COUNTRY	YR/GLS	YR/GLS	YR/GLS	YR/GLS
14	GERD MULLER	W.GERMANY	1970/10	1974/4		
13	JUSTE FONTAINE	FRANCE	1958/13			
12	PELE	BRAZIL	1958/6	1962/1	1966/1	1970/4
11	SANDOR KOCSIS	HUNGARY	1954/11			
11	JUERGEN KLINSMANN	W.GERMANY	1990/3	1994/5	1998/3	
10	HELMUT RAHN	W.GERMANY	1954/4	1958/6		
10	TEOFILIO CUBILLAS	PERU	1970/5	1978/5		
10	GRZEGORZ LATO	POLAND	1974/7	1978/2	1982/1	
10	GARY LINEKER	ENGLAND	1986/6	1990/4		
9	LEONIDAS	BRAZIL	1934/1	1938/8		
9	ADEMIR	BRAZIL	1950/9			
9	VAVA	BRAZIL	1958/5	1962/4		
9	UWE SEELER	W.GERMANY	1958/2	1962/2	1966/2	1970/3
9	EUSEBIO	PORTUGAL	1966/9			
9	JAIRZINHO	BRAZIL	1970/7	1974/2		
9	PAOLO ROSSI	ITALY	1978/3	1982/6		
9	K-H RUMMENIGGE	W.GERMANY	1978/3	1982/5	1986/1	

GOALS AND GOAL AVERAGES

The total number of goals scored in each tournament and the number of goals on average scored per tournament:

DATE	GAMES	TOTAL GOALS	AVERAGE PER GAME
1930	18	70	3.89
1934	17	70	4.12
1938	18	84	4.67
1950	22	88	4.00
1954	26	140	5.38
1958	35	126	3.60
1962	32	89	2.78
1966	32	89	2.78
1970	32	95	2.97
1974	38	97	2.55
1978	38	102	2.68
1982	52	146	2.81
1986	52	132	2.54
1990	52	115	2.21
1994	52	141	2.71
1998	64	171	2.67

PLAYER OF THE TOURNAMENT

The official Player of the Tournament award (also known as the Most Valuable Player) was introduced at the 1982 finals and is selected by vote cast by some of the thousands of reporters who cover the World Cup. The previous winners have been:

1982	PAOLO ROSSI (ITALY)
1986	DIEGO MARADONA (ARGENTINA)
1990	SALVATORE SCHILACHI (ITALY)
1994	ROMARIO (BRAZIL)
1998	RONALDO (BRAZIL)

WORLD CUP GOAL SCORERS

MILESTONE GOALS

GOAL	PLAYER	MATCH	GOAL	RESULT	DATE
1ST	**LAURENT** (FRANCE)	FRANCE V MEXICO	1-0	4-1	13/7/30
100TH	**SCHIAVO** (ITALY)	ITALY V USA	5-1	7-1	5/5/34
200TH	**KELLER** (SWEDEN)	SWEDEN V CUBA	8-0	8-0	12/6/38
300TH	**CHICO** (BRAZIL)	BRAZIL V SPAIN	3-0	6-1	13/7/50
400TH	**MORLOCK** (W.GERMANY)	W.GERMANY V TURKEY	5-1	7-2	23/6/54
500TH	**COLLINS** (SCOTLAND)	SCOTLAND V PARAGUAY	2-3	2-3	11/6/58
600TH	**JERKOVIC** (YUGOSLAVIA)	YUGOSLAVIA V URUGUAY	3-1	3-1	2/6/62
700TH	**PAK SEUNG ZIN** (N.KOREA)	N.KOREA V CHILE	1-1	1-1	15/7/66
800TH	**MULLER** (W. GERMANY)	W.GERMANY V BULGARIA	5-2	5-2	7/6/70
900TH	**YAZALDE** (ARGENTINA)	ARGENTINA V HAITI	1-0	4-1	23/6/74
1000TH	**RENSENBRINK** (HOLLAND)	HOLLAND V SCOTLAND	1-0	3-2	11/6/78
1100TH	**BALTACHA** (SOVIET UNION)	SOVIET UNION V N.ZEALAND	3-0	3-0	19/6/82
1200TH	**PAPIN** (FRANCE)	FRANCE V CANADA	1-0	1-0	1/6/86
1300TH	**LINEKER** (ENGLAND)	ENGLAND V PARAGUAY	3-0	3-0	18/6/86
1400TH	**EKSTROM** (SWEDEN)	SWEDEN V COSTA RICA	1-0	2-1	20/6/90
1500TH	**CANIGGIA** (ARGENTINA)	ARGENTINA V NIGERIA	1-1	2-1	6/6/94
1600TH	**ISSA** (SOUTH AFRICA OG)	SOUTH AFRICA V FRANCE	0-2	0-3	12/6/98
1700TH	**KOMLJENOVIC** (YUGOSLAVIA)	YUGOSLAVIA V USA	1-0	1-0	25/6/98
1755TH	**PETIT** (FRANCE)	FRANCE V BRAZIL	3-0	3-0	12/7/98

Goals in penalty shoot-outs not included

FINALS STATS

GOAL TIMES

Totals	GAMES	1ST GOAL*	2ND GOAL**	LAST GOAL	TOTAL GOAL MINUTES
FRANCE 98	64	2641	3861	2790	8749
USA 94	52	1838	3161	2113	6653
ITALIA 90	52	2587	3847	2689	6051
MEXICO 86	52	1796	3254	2337	6232
SPAIN 82	52	1966	3267	2319	7340

Averages	GAMES	1ST GOAL*	2ND GOAL**	LAST GOAL	TOTAL GOAL MINUTES
FRANCE 98	64	41	60	44	137
USA 94	52	35	61	41	128
ITALIA 90	52	50	74	52	116
MEXICO 86	52	35	63	45	120
SPAIN 82	52	38	63	45	141

*Treated as 90 when no goal scored **Treated as 90 when only one goal scored

CARDS, CORNERS, FOULS & OFFSIDES

Totals	GAMES	YELLOW CARDS	RED CARDS	CORNERS	FOULS	OFFSIDES
USA 94	52	227	13	540	1476	346
FRANCE 98	64	248	22	664	2121	371

Averages	GAMES	YELLOW CARDS	RED CARDS	CORNERS	FOULS	OFFSIDES
USA 94	52	4.4	0.3	10.4	28.4	6.7
FRANCE 98	64	3.9	0.3	10.4	33.1	5.8

AVERAGE TIME OF FIRST YELLOW & RED CARDS*

	YELLOW CARDS	RED CARDS	
USA 94	26	82	*Treated as 90 when no card issued.
FRANCE 98	24	83	All figures are for 90 minutes of play only (ie, extra-time not included)

PENALTY SHOOT-OUT SEQUENCES

YEAR	STAGE	TEAMS	SHOOT-OUT SCORE	1st	2nd	3rd	4th	5th	6th	7th
1998	SF	BRAZIL	4	1	1	1	1			
		HOLLAND	2	1	1	0	0			
1998	QF	FRANCE	4	1	0	1	1	1		
		ITALY	3	1	0	1	1	0		
1998	RD 2	ARGENTINA	4	1	0	1	1	1		
		ENGLAND	3	1	0	1	1	0		
1994	F	ITALY	2	0	1	1	0	0		
		BRAZIL	3	0	1	1	1			
1994	QF	SWEDEN	5	0	1	1	1	1	1	
		ROMANIA	4	1	1	1	0	1	0	
1994	RD 2	MEXICO	1	0	0	0	1			
		BULGARIA	3	0	1	1	1			
1990	SF	ENGLAND	1	1	1	1	0	0		
		GERMANY	1	1	1	1	1			
1990	SF	ITALY	1	1	1	1	0	0		
		ARGENTINA	1	1	1	1	1			
1990	QF	ARGENTINA	0	3	1	1	0	0	1	
		YUGOSLAVIA	0	2	0	1	1	0	0	
1990	QF	FRANCE	1	4	1	1	1	0	1	
		BRAZIL	1	2	0	0	1	1	0	
1990	2nd Rd	REP. OF IRELAND	0	1	1	1	1	1		
		ROMANIA	0	1	0	1	1	1		
1986	QF	WEST GERMANY	0	4	1	1	1	1		
		MEXICO	1	1	1	0	0			
1986	2nd Rd	BELGIUM	1	4	1	0	1	1	1	
		SPAIN	1	5	1	1	1	1	1	
1982	SF	WEST GERMANY	3	5	1	1	0	1	1	1
		FRANCE	3	4	1	1	1	0	1	0

USA 1994 AND FRANCE
DETAILED BREAKDOWN FOR ALL COUNTRIES ALSO PARTICIPATING

USA '94	Games	Red cards	Yellow cards	Corners for	Corners against	Fouls committed	Fouls by opponents	Offsides	Offsides by opponents
ARGENTINA	4	0	9	16	16	51	68	9	17
BELGIUM	4	0	5	21	25	39	73	14	14
BRAZIL	7	1	7	34	22	86	92	29	16
CAMEROON	3	1	5	13	18	38	28	10	11
DENMARK	-	-	-	-	-	-	-	-	-
ENGLAND	-	-	-	-	-	-	-	-	-
FRANCE	-	-	-	-	-	-	-	-	-
GERMANY	5	0	14	34	27	81	70	19	7
ITALY	7	2	11	35	30	97	137	24	42
JAPAN	-	-	-	-	-	-	-	-	-
MEXICO	4	1	10	23	27	65	54	17	9
NIGERIA	4	0	9	20	20	77	45	16	7
PARAGUAY	-	-	-	-	-	-	-	-	-
REPUBLIC OF IRELAND	4	0	8	21	21	55	58	24	9
RUSSIA	3	1	8	11	10	34	30	8	13
SAUDI ARABIA	3	0	7	16	15	36	35	3	7
SOUTH AFRICA	-	-	-	-	-	-	-	-	-
SOUTH KOREA	3	0	6	19	10	45	41	8	11
SPAIN	5	1	13	27	43	96	67	19	10
SWEDEN	7	1	13	20	22	68	89	24	19
TUNISIA	-	-	-	-	-	-	-	-	-
UNITED STATES	4	1	8	23	25	46	52	8	12

1998 STATISTICS
IN JAPAN AND SOUTH KOREA 2002

FRANCE '98	Games	Red cards	Yellow cards	Corners for	Corners against	Fouls committed	Fouls by opponents	Offsides	Offsides by opponents
ARGENTINA	5	1	10	22	25	97	110	20	5
BELGIUM	3	1	4	11	21	59	39	4	16
BRAZIL	7	0	12	32	39	95	131	32	19
CAMEROON	3	3	6	19	22	42	45	7	18
DENMARK	5	2	12	28	23	71	85	11	15
ENGLAND	4	1	5	21	18	60	84	4	14
FRANCE	7	3	12	65	21	126	118	18	26
GERMANY	5	1	12	24	24	84	93	9	14
ITALY	5	0	10	19	36	83	91	35	9
JAPAN	3	0	7	20	10	69	59	5	16
MEXICO	4	2	9	19	11	48	69	14	2
NIGERIA	4	0	8	27	22	51	56	2	13
PARAGUAY	4	0	7	26	42	66	64	12	5
REPUBLIC OF IRELAND	-	-	-	-	-	-	-	-	-
RUSSIA	-	-	-	-	-	-	-	-	-
SAUDI ARABIA	3	1	4	8	24	34	48	6	9
SOUTH AFRICA	3	1	7	13	16	54	36	12	10
SOUTH KOREA	3	1	7	12	19	46	45	7	10
SPAIN	3	0	7	19	17	55	51	9	3
SWEDEN	-	-	-	-	-	-	-	-	-
TUNISIA	3	0	7	17	25	65	40	9	12
UNITED STATES	3	0	4	18	11	43	60	6	2

URUGUAY 1930

GROUP 1
France 4 (Laurent, Langiller, Maschinot 2), Mexico 1 (Carreno)
Argentina 1 (Monti), France 0
Chile 3 (Subiare 2, Vidal), Mexico 0
Argentina 6 (Stabile 3, Zumelzu, Varallo 2), Mexico 3 (M Rosas, F Rosas, Lopez)
Chile 1 (Subiare), France 0
Argentina 3 (Stabile 2, M Evaristo), Chile 1 (Subiabre)

GROUP 2
Yugoslavia 2 (Tirnanic, Bek), Brazil 1 (Preguinho)
Yugoslavia 4 (Bek 2, Marjanovic, Vujadnovic), Bolivia 0
Brazil 4 (Carvalho Leite, Preguinho 3), Bolivia 0

GROUP 3
Romania 3 (Desu, Sanciu, Kovacs), Peru 1 (Souza)
Uruguay 1 (Castro), Peru 0
Uruguay 4 (Dorado, H Scarone, Anselmo, Cea), Romania 0

GROUP 4
USA 3 (McGhee 2, Patenaude), Belgium 0
USA 3 (Patenaude 2, Flori), Paraguay 0
Paraguay 1 (Pena), Belgium 0

SEMI-FINALS
Argentina 6 (Stabile 2, Peucelle 2, Monti, Scopelli), USA 1 (Brown)
Uruguay 6 (Cea 3, Anselmo 2, Iriarte), Yugoslavia 1 (Sekulic)

FINAL
Uruguay 4 (Dorado, Cea, Iriarte, Castro), Argentina 2 (Peucelle, Stabile)

ITALY 1934

FIRST ROUND
Sweden 3 (Jonasson 2, Kroon), Argentina 2 (Belis, Galateo)
Germany 5 (Kobierski, Conen 3, Siffling), Belgium 2 (Voorhoof 2)
Spain 3 (Iraragorri, Langara 2), Brazil 1 (Leonidas)
Switzerland 3 (Kielholz 2, A Abegglen), Holland 2 (Smit, Vente)
Hungary 4 (Teleki, Toldi 2, Vincze), Egypt 2 (Fawzi 2)
Italy 7 (Schiavio 3, Orsi 2, Ferrari, Meazza), United States 1 (Donelli)
Czechoslovakia 2 (Puc, Nejedly), Romania 1 (Dobai)
Austria 3 (Sindelar, Schall, Bican), France 2 (Nicolas, Verriest) aet

PREVIOUS FINALS

QUARTER-FINALS
Austria 2 (Horvath, Zischek), Hungary 1 (Sarosi)
Italy 1 (Ferrari), Spain 1 (Regueiro) aet; replay: Italy 1 (Meazza), Spain 0
Germany 2 (Hohmann 2), Sweden 1 (Dunker)
Czechoslovakia 3 (Svoboda, Sobotka, Nejedly), Switzerland 2 (Kielholz, A Abegglen)

SEMI-FINALS
Italy 1 (Guaita), Austria 0
Czechoslovakia 3 (Nejedly 3), Germany 1 (Noack)
Third place Germany 3 (Lehner 2, Conen), Austria 2 (Horvath, Sesta)

FINAL
Italy 2 (Orsi, Schiavio), Czechoslovakia 1 (Puc) aet

FRANCE 1938

FIRST ROUND
Switzerland 1 (A Abegglen), Germany 1 (Gauchel) aet. Replay: Switzerland 4 (A Abegglen 2, Walaschek, Bickel), Germany 2 (B Hahnemann, Loertscher og)
Cuba 3 (Socorro 2, Maquina), Romania 3 (Bindea, Baratki, Dobai) aet. Replay: Cuba 2 (Socorro, Maquina), Romania 1 (Dobai)
Sweden -, Austria -. Austria withdrew
Hungary 6 (G Sarosi 2, Zsengeller 2, Kohut, Toldi), Dutch East Indies 0
France 3 (Nicolas 2, Veinante), Belgium 1 (Isemborghs)
Czechoslovakia 3 (Kostalek, Nejedly, Zeman), Holland 0 aet
Brazil 6 (Leonidas 4, Peracio, Romeo), Poland 5 (Willimowski 4, Piontek) aet
Italy 2 (Ferraris, Piola), Norway 1 (Brustad) aet

SECOND ROUND
Sweden 8 (Wetterstrom 4, Andersson, Jonasson, Keller, Nyberg), Cuba 0
Hungary 2 (Zsengeller 2), Switzerland 0
Italy 3 (Piola 2, Colaussi), France 1 (Heisserer)
Brazil 1 (Leonidas), Czechoslovakia 1 (Nejedly) aet. Replay: Brazil 2 (Leonidas, Roberto), Czechoslovakia 1 (Kopecky)

SEMI-FINALS
Italy 2 (Colaussi, Meazza), Brazil 1 (Romeo)
Hungary 5 (Zsengeller 3, Titkos, Sarosi), Sweden 1 (Nyberg)

THIRD PLACE PLAY-OFF
Brazil 4 (Leonidas 2, Romeo, Peracio), Sweden 2 (Jonasson, Nyberg)

FINAL
Italy 4 (Colaussi 2, Peiola 2), Hungary 2 (Titkos, G Sarosi)

BRAZIL 1950

FIRST ROUND
GROUP 1
Brazil 4 (Ademir 2, Jair R Pinto, Baltazar), Mexico 0
Yugoslavia 3 (Tomasevic 2, Ognjanov), Switzerland 0
Brazil 2 (Alfredo, Baltazar), Switzerland 2 (Fatton 2)
Yugoslavia 4 (Ciakowski 2, Bobek, Tomasevic), Mexico 1 (Casarin)
Brazil 2 (Ademir, Zizinho), Yugoslavia 0
Switzerland 2 (Bader, Antenen), Mexico 1 (Casarin)

GROUP 2
England 2 (Mortensen, Mannion), Chile 0
Spain 3 (Basora 2, Zarra), USA 1 (J Souza)
Spain 2 (Basora, Zarra), Chile 0
USA 1 (Gaetjens), England 0
Spain 1 (Zarra), England 0
Chile 5 (Cremaschi 3, G Robledo, Prieto), USA 2 (Pariani, E Souza)

GROUP 3
Sweden 3 (Jeppson 2, Andersson), Italy 2 (Carapellese, Muccinelli)
Sweden 2 (Sundqvist, Palmer), Paraguay 2 (Lopez, Lopez Fretas)
Italy 2 (Carapellese, Pandolfini), Paraguay 0

GROUP 4
Uruguay 8 (Schiaffino 4, Miguez 2, Ghiggia, Vidal), Bolivia 0

FINAL ROUND
Brazil 7 (Ademir 4, Chico 2, Maneca), Sweden 1 (Andersson)
Spain 2 (Basora 2), Uruguay 2 (Ghiggia, Varela)
Brazil 6 (Ademir 2, Jair R Pinto, Chico 2, Zizinho), Spain 1 (Igoa)
Uruguay 3 (Ghiggia, Miguez 2), Sweden 2 (Palmer, Sundqvist)
Sweden 3 (Sundqvist, Mellberg, Palmer), Spain 1 (Zarra)

FINAL
Uruguay 2 (Schiaffino, Ghiggia), Brazil 1 (Friaca)

SWITZERLAND 1954

FIRST ROUND
GROUP 1
Yugoslavia 1 (Milutinovic), France 0

PREVIOUS FINALS

Brazil 5 (Baltazar, Didi, Pinga 2, Julinho), Mexico 0
Brazil 1 (Didi), Yugoslavia 1 (Zebec)
France 3 (Vincent, Gardenas og, Kopa), Mexico 2 (Naranjo, Balcazar)

GROUP 2
Hungary 9 (Kocsis 3, Puskas 2, Palotas 2, Lantos, Czibor), South Korea 0
West Germany 4 (Scafer, Klodt, O Walter, Morlock), Turkey 1 (Suat)
Hungary 8 (Kocsis 4, Hidegkuti 2, Puskas, Toth), West Germany 3 (Pfaff, Rahn, Hermann)
Turkey 7 (Burhan 3, Suat 2, Erol, Lefter), South Korea 0
Play-off West Germany 7 (Morlock 3, Schafer 2, O Walter, F Walter), Turkey 2 (Mustafa, Lefter)

GROUP 3
Austria 1 (Probst), Scotland 0
Uruguay 2 (Miguez, Schiaffino), Czechoslovakia 0
Austria 5 (Probst 3, Stojaspal 2), Czechoslovakia 0
Uruguay 7 (Borges 3, Miguez 2, Abbadie 2), Scotland 0

GROUP 4
England 4 (Broadis 2, Lofthouse 2), Belgium 4 (Anoul 2, Coppens, Dickinson og)
Switzerland 2 (Ballaman, Hugi), Italy 1 (Boniperti)
England 2 (Mullen, Wilshaw), Switzerland 0
Italy 4 (Penadolfini, Galli, Frigani, Lorenzi), Belgium 1 (Anoul)
Play-off Switzerland 4 (Hugi 2, Ballaman, Fatton), Italy 1 (Nesti)

QUARTER-FINALS
West Germany 2 (Horvat og, Rahn), Yugoslavia 0
Austria 7 (Wagner 3, Korner 2, Ocwirk, Probst), Switzerland 5 (Hugi 3, Ballaman 2)
Uruguay 4 (Borges, Varela, Schiaffino, Ambrois), England 2 (Lofthouse, Finney)
Hungary 4 (Kocsis 2, Hidegkuti, Lantos), Brazil 2 (D Santos, Julinho)

SEMI-FINALS
West Germany 6 (O Walter 2, F Walter 2, Schafer, Morlock), Austria 1 (Probst)
Hungary 4 (Kocsis 2, Czibor, Hidegkuti), Uruguay 2 (Hohberg 2)

THIRD PLACE PLAY-OFF
Austria 3 (Stojaspal, Ocwirk, Cruz og), Uruguay 1 (Hohberg)

FINAL
West Germany 3 (Rahn 2, Morlock), Hungary 2 (Puskas, Czibor)

SWEDEN 1958

FIRST ROUND
GROUP 1
Northern Ireland 1 (Cush), Czechoslovakia 0
West Germany 3 (Rahn 2, Seeler), Argentina 1 (Corbatta)
Argentina 3 (Corbatta, Menendez, Avio), Northern Ireland 1 (McParland)
Czechoslovakia 2 (Dvorak, Zikan), West Germany 2 (Schafer, Rahn)
Northern Ireland 2 (McParland 2), West Germany 2 (Rahn, Seeler)
Czechoslovakia 6 (Zikan 2, Hovorka 2, Dvorak, Feureisi), Argentina 1 (Corbatta)
Play-off Northern Ireland 2 (McParland 2), Czechoslovakia 1 (Zikan)

GROUP 2
Scotland 1 (Murray), Yugoslavia 1 (Petakovic)
France 7 (Fontaine 3, Piantoni, Wisnieski, Kopa, Vincent), Paraguay 3 (Amarilla 2, Romero)
Paraguay 3 (Aguero, Re, Parodi), Scotland 2 (Mudie, Collins)
Yugoslavia 3 (Veselinovic 2, Petakovic), France 2 (Fontaine 2)
France 2 (Kopa, Fontaine), Scotland 1 (Baird)
Paraguay 3 (Parodi, Aguero, Romero), Yugoslavia 3 (Ognjanovic, Veselinovic, Rajkov)

GROUP 3
Sweden 3 (Simonsson 2, Liedholm), Mexico 0
Hungary 1 (Bozsik), Wales 1 (Charles)
Wales 1 (Allchurch), Mexico 1 (Belmonte)
Sweden 2 (Hamrin 2), Hungary 1 (Tichy)
Sweden 0, Wales 0
Hungary 4 (Tichy 2, Sander, Gonzalez og), Mexico 0
Play-off
Wales 2 (Allchurch, Medwin), Hungary 1 (Tichy)

GROUP 4
Brazil 3 (Altafini 2, Nilton Santos), Austria 0
England 2 (Kevan, Finney), Soviet Union 2 (Simonian, A Ivanov)
Soviet Union 2 (Ilyin, A Ivanov), Austria 0
Brazil 0, England 0
England 2 (Haynes, Kevan), Austria 2 (Koller, Korner)
Brazil 2 (Vava), Soviet Union 0
Play-off
Soviet Union 1 (Ilyin), England 0

QUARTER-FINALS
Brazil 1 (Pele), Wales 0

PREVIOUS FINALS

France 4 (Fontaine 2, Wisnieski, Piantoni), Northern Ireland 0
West Germany 1 (Rahn), Yugoslavia 0
Sweden 2 (Hamrin, Simonsson), Soviet Union 0

SEMI-FINALS
Brazil 5 (Pele 3, Vava, Didi), France 2 (Fontaine, Piantoni)

THIRD PLACE PLAY-OFF
France 6 (Fontaine 4, Kopa, Douis), West Germany 3 (Cieslarczyk, Rahn, Schafer)

FINAL
Brazil 5 (Vava 2, Pele 2, Zagalo), Sweden 2 (Liedholm, Simonsson)

CHILE 1962

FIRST ROUND
GROUP 1
Uruguay 2 (Sacia, Cubilla), Colombia 1 (Zuluaga)
Soviet Union 2 (V Ivanov, Ponedelnik), Yugoslavia 0
Yugoslavia 3 (Skoblar, Galic, Jerkovic), Uruguay 1 (Cabrera)
Soviet Union 4 (V Ivanov 2, Chislenko, Ponedelnik), Colombia 4 (Aceros, Coll, Rada, Klinger)
Soviet Union 2 (Mamikin, V Ivanov), Uruguay 1 (Sacia)
Yugoslavia 5 (Galic 2, Jerkovic 2, Melic), Colombia 0

GROUP 2
Chile 3 (L Sanchez 2, Ramirez), Switzerland 1 (Wuthrich)
West Germany 0, Italy 0
Chile 2 (Ramirez, Toro), Italy 0
West Germany 2 (Brulls, Seeler), Switzerland 1 (Antenen)
West Germany 2 (Szymaniak, Seeler), Chile 0
Italy 3 (Bulgarelli 2, Mora), Switzerland 0

GROUP 3
Brazil 2 (Zagalo, Pele), Mexico 0
Czechoslovakia 1 (Stibranyi), Spain 0
Brazil 0, Czechoslovakia 0
Spain 1 (Peiro), Mexico 0
Brazil 2 (Amarildo 2), Spain 1 (Adelrado)
Mexico 3 (Diaz, Del Aguila, H Hernandez), Czechoslovakia 1 (Masek)

GROUP 4
Argentina 1 (Facundo), Bulgaria 0

PREVIOUS FINALS

Hungary 2 (Tichy, Albert), England 1 (Flowers)
England 3 (Flowers, R Charlton, Greaves), Argentina 1 (Sanfilippo)
Hungary 6 (Albert 3, Tichy 2, Solymosi), Bulgaria 1 (Sokolov)
Hungary 0, Austria 0
England 0, Bulgaria 0

QUARTER-FINALS
Brazil 3 (Garrincha 2, Vava), England 1 (Hitchens)
Chile 2 (Sanchez, Rojas), Soviet Union 1 (Chislenko)
Yugoslavia 1 (Radakovic), West Germany 0
Czechoslovakia 1 (Scherer), Hungary 0

SEMI-FINALS
Brazil 4 (Garrincha 2, Vava 2), Chile 2 (Toro, Sanchez)
Czechoslovakia 3 (Schere 2, Kadraba) Yugoslavia 1 (Jerkovic)

THIRD PLACE PLAY-OFF
Chile 1 (Rojaz), Yugoslavia 0

FINAL
Brazil 3 (Amarildo, Zito, Vava), Czechoslovakia 1 (Masopust)

ENGLAND 1966

FIRST ROUND
GROUP 1
England 0, Uruguay 0
France 1 (Hausser), Mexico (Borja)
Uruguay 2 (Rocha, Cortes), France 1 (De Bourgoing)
England 2 (R Charlton, Hurst), Mexico 0
Uruguay 0, Mexico 0
England 2 (Hunt 2), France 0

GROUP 2
West Germany 5 (Beckenbauer 2, Haller 2, Held), Switzerland 0
Argentina 2 (Artime 2), Spain 1 (Pirri)
Spain 2 (Sanchis, Amancio), Switzerland 1 (Quentin)
Argentina 2, Switzerland 0
West Germany 2 (Emmerich, Seeler), Spain (Fuste)

GROUP 3
Brazil 2 (Pele, Garrincha). Bulgaria 0
Portugal 3 (Augusto 2, Torres), Hungary 1 (Bene)

Hungary 3 (Bene, Farkas, Meszoloy), Brazil 1 (Tostao)
Portugal 3 (Eusebio 2, og), Bulgaria 0
Portugal 3 (Eusebio 2, Simoes), Brazil 1 (Rildo)
Hungary 3 (og, Meszoly, Bene), Bulgaria 1 (Asparukov)

GROUP 4
Soviet Union 3 (Malafeev 2, Banichevski), North Korea 0
Italy 2 (Mazzola, Barison), Chile 0
North Korea 1 (Seung-zin), Chile 1 (Marcos)
Soviet Union 1 (Chislenko), Italy 0
North Korea 1 (Doo-ik), Italy 0
Soviet Union 2 (Porkujan), Chile 1 (Marcos)

QUARTER-FINALS
England 1 (Hurst), Argentina 0
Portugal 5 (Eusebio 4, Augusto), North Korea 3 (Seung-zin, Dong-woon, Seung-kook)
Soviet Union 2 (Chislenko, Porkujan), Hungary 1 (Bene)
West Germany 4 (Held, Beckenbaur, Seeler, Haller), Uruguay 0

SEMI-FINALS
England 2 (R Charlton 2), Portugal 1 (Eusebio)
West Germany 2 (Haller, Beckenbauer), Soviet Union 1 (Porkjuan)

THIRD PLACE PLAY-OFF
Portugal 2 (Eusebio, Torres), Soviet Union 1 (Metreveli)

FINAL
England 4 (Hurst 3, Peters), West Germany 2 (Haller, Weber) aet

MEXICO 1970

FIRST ROUND
GROUP 1
Mexico 0, Soviet Union 0
Belgium 3 (van Moer 2, Lambert), El Salvador 0
Soviet Union 4 (Bishovets 2, Asatiani, Khmelnitski), Belgium 1 (Lambert)
Mexico 4 (Valdivia 2, Fragoso, Basaguren), El Salvador 0
Soviet Union 2 (Bishovets 2), El Salvador 0
Mexico 1 (Pena), Belgium 0

GROUP 2
Uruguay 2 (Maneiro, Mujica), Israel 0
Italy 1 (Domenghini), Sweden 0

Uruguay 0, Italy 0
Israel 1 (Spiegler), Sweden 1 (Turesson)
Sweden 1 (Grahn), Uruguay 0
Italy 0, Israel 0

GROUP 3
England 1 (Hurst), Romania 0
Brazil 4 (Jairzinho 2, Rivelino, Pele), Czechoslovakia 1 (Petras)
Brazil 1 (Jairzinho), England 0
Brazil 3 (Pele 2, Jairzinho), Romania 2 (Dumitrache, Dembrovski)
England 1 (Clarke), Czechoslovakia 0

GROUP 4
Peru 3 (Gallardo, Chumpitaz, Cubillas), Bulgaria 2 (Dermendjev, Bonev)
West Germany 2 (Seeler, Muller), Morocco 1 (Houmane Jarir)
Peru 3 (Cubillas 2, Challe), Morocco 0
West Germany 5 (Muller 3, Libuda, Seeler), Bulgaria 2 (Nikodimov, T Kolev)
West Germany 3 (Muller 3), Peru 1 (Cubillas)
Bulgaria 1 (Jechev), Morocca 1 (Ghazouani)

QUARTER-FINALS
Brazil 4 (Tostao 2, Rivelino, Jairzinho), Peru 2 (Gallardo, Cubillas)
Uruguay 1 (Esparrago), Soviet Union 0 aet
West Germany 3 (Beckenbauer, Seeler, Muller), England 2 (Mullery, Peters) aet
Italy 4 (Riva 2, Domenghini, Rivera), Mexico 1 (Gonzalez)

SEMI-FINALS
Brazil 3 (Clodoaldo, Jairzinho, Rivelino), Uruguay 1 (Cubilla)
Italy 4 (Boninsegna, Burgnich, Riva, Rivera), West Germany 3 (Muller 2, Schnellinger) aet

THIRD PLACE PLAY-OFF
West Germany 1 (Overath), Uruguay 0

FINAL
Brazil 4 (Pele, Gerson, Jairzinho, Carlos Alberto), Italy 1 (Boninsegna)

WEST GERMANY 1974

FIRST ROUND
GROUP ONE
West Germany 1 (Breitner), Chile 0
East Germany 2 (og, Streich), Australia 0

PREVIOUS FINALS

West Germany 3 (Overath, Cullmann, Muller), Australia 0
Chile 1 (Ahumada), East Germany 1 (Hoffmann)
Australia 0, Chile 0
East Germany 1 (Sparwasser), West Germany 0

GROUP TWO

Brazil 0, Yugoslavia 0
Scotland 2 (Lorimer, Jordan), Zaire 0
Brazil 0, Scotland 0
Yugoslavia 9 (Bajevic 3, Dzajic, Surjak, Katalinski, Bogicevic, Oblak, Petkovic), Zaire 0
Yugoslavia 1 (Karasi), Scotland 1 (Jordan)
Brazil 3 (Jairzinho, Rivelino, Valdomiro), Zaire 0

GROUP THREE

Holland 2 (Rep 2), Uruguay 0
Bulgaria 0, Sweden 0
Holland 0, Sweden 0
Bulgaria 1 (Bonev), Uruguay 1 (Pavoni)
Holland 4 (Neeskens 2, Rep, de Jong), Bulgaria 1 (og)
Sweden 3 (Edstrom 2, Sandberg), Uruguay 0

GROUP FOUR

Italy 3 (Rivera, og, Anastasi), Haiti 1 (Sanon)
Poland 3 (Lato 2, Szarmach), Argentina 2 (Heredia, Babington)
Argentina 1 (Houseman), Italy 1 (og)
Poland 7 (Szarmach 3, Lato 2, Deyna, Gorgon), Haiti 0
Argentina 4 (Yazalde 2, Houseman, Ayala), Haiti 1 (Sanon)
Poland 2 (Szarmach, Deyna), Italy 1 (Capello)

SECOND ROUND
GROUP A

Brazil 1 (Rivelino), East Germany 0
Holland 4 (Cruyff 2, Krol, Rep), Argentina 0
Holland 2 (Neeskens, Rensenbrink), East Germany 0
Brazil 2 (Rivelino, Jairzinho), Argentina 1 (Brindisi)
East Germany 1 (Streich), Argentina 1 (Houseman)
Holland 2 (Neeskens, Cruyff), Brazil 0

GROUP B

Poland 1 (Lato), Sweden 0
West Germany 2 (Breitner, Muller), Yugoslavia 0
Poland 2 (Deyna, Lato), Yugoslavia 1 (Karasi)
West Germany 4 (Overath, Bonhof, Grabowski, Hoeness), Sweden 2 (Edstrom, Sandberg)

Sweden 2 (Edstrom, Torstensson), Yugoslavia 1 (Surjak)
West Germany 1 (Muller), Poland 0

THIRD PLACE PLAY-OFF
Poland 1 (Lato), Brazil 0

FINAL
West Germany 2 (Breitner, Muller), Holland 1 (Neeskens)

ARGENTINA 1978

FIRST ROUND
GROUP 1
Italy 2 (Rossi, Zaccarelli), France 1 (Lacombe)
Argentina 2 (Luque, Bertoni), Hungary 1 (Csapo)
Italy 3 (Rossi, Bettega, Benetti), Hungary 1 (A Toth)
Argentina 2 (Passarella, Luque), France 1 (Platini)
Italy 1 (Bettega), Argentina 0
France 3 (Lopez, Berdoll, Rocheteau), Hungary 1 (Zombori)

GROUP 2
Poland 0, West Germany 0
Tunisia 3 (Kaabi, Ghommidh, Dhouieb), Mexico 1 (Ayala)
Poland 1 (Lato), Tunisia 0
West Germany 6 (Rumenigge 2, Flohe 2, D Muller, H Muller), Mexico 0
West Germany 0, Tunisia 0
Poland 3 (Boniek 2, Deyna), Mexico 1 (Rangel)

GROUP 3
Brazil 1 (Reinaldo), Sweden 1 (Sjoberg)
Austria 2 (Schachner, Krankl), Spain 1 (Dani)
Austria 1 (Krankl), Sweden 0
Brazil 0, Spain 0
Brazil 1 (Roberto Dinamite), Austria 0
Spain 1 (Asensi), Sweden 0

GROUP 4
Holland 3 (Rensenbrink 3), Iran 0
Peru 3 (Cubillas 2, Cueto), Scotland 1 (Jordan)
Holland 0, Peru 0
Scotland 1 (og), Iran 1 (Danaifar)
Scotland 3 (Gemmill 2, Dalglish), Holland 2 (Rensenbrink, Rep)
Peru 4 (Cubillas 3, Velasquez), Iran 1 (Rowshan)

SECOND ROUND
GROUP A
Italy 0, West Germany 0
Holland 5 (Rep 2, Brandts, Rensenbrink, W van der Kerkof), Austria 1 (Obermayer)
Holland 2 (Haan, R van de Kerkof), West Germany 2 (Abramczik, D Muller)
Italy 1 (Rossi), Austria 0
Austria 3 (Krankl 2, og), West Germany 2 (Rummenigge, Holzbein)
Holland 2 (Brandts, Haan), Italy 1 (og)

GROUP B
Brazil 3 (Dirceu 2, Zico), Peru 0
Argentina 2 (Kempes 2), Poland 0
Poland 1 (Szarmach), Peru 0
Argentina 0, Brazil 0
Brazil 3 (Roberto 2, Nelinho), Poland 1 (Lato)
Argentina 6 (Kempes 2, Luque 2, Tarantini, Housemann), Peru 0

THIRD PLACE PLAY-OFF
Brazil 2 (Nelinho, Dirceu), Italy 1 (Causio)

FINAL
Argentina 3 (Kempes 2, Bertoni), Holland 1 (Nanninga) aet

SPAIN 1982

FIRST ROUND
GROUP 1
Italy 0, Poland 0
Peru 0, Cameroon 0
Italy 1 (Conti), Peru 1 (og)
Cameroon 0, Poland 0
Poland 5 (Smolarek, Lato, Boniek, Buncol, Ciolek), Peru 1 (La Rosa)
Italy 1 (Graziani), Cameroon 1 (M'Bida)

GROUP 2
Algeria 2 (Madjer, Belloumi), West Germany 1 (Rummenigge)
Austria 1 (Schachner), Chile 0
West Germany 4 (Rummenigge 3, Reinders), Chile 1 (Moscoso)
Austria 2 (Schachner, Krankl), Algeria 0
Algeria 3 (Assad 2, Bensaoula), Chile 2 (Neira, Letelier)
West Germany 1 (Hrubesch), Austria 0

PREVIOUS FINALS

GROUP 3
Belgium 1 (Vandenbergh), Argentina 0
Hungary 10 (Fazekas 3, Kiss 3, Nvilasi 2, Poloskei, Szentes), El Salvador 1 (Ramirez Zapata)
Argentina 4 (Maradona 2, Ardiles, Bertoni), Hungary 1 (Poloskei)
Belgium 1 (Coeck), El Salvador 0
Belgium 1 (Czerniatynski), Hungary 1 (Varga)
Argentina 2 (Passarella, Bertoni), El Salvador 0

GROUP 4
England 3 (Robson 2, Mariner), France 1 (Soler)
Czechoslovakia 1 (Panenka), Kuwait 1 (Al Dakhil)
England 2 (Francis, og), Czechoslovakia 0
France 4 (Genghini, Platini, Six, Bossis), Kuwait 1 (Al Blouloshi)
France 1 (Six), Czechoslovakia 1 (Panenka)
England 1 (Francis), Kuwait 0

GROUP 5
Spain 1 (Lopez Ufarte), Honduras 1 (Zelaya)
Northern Ireland 0, Yugoslavia 0
Spain 2 (Juanito, Saura), Yugoslavia 1 (Gudelj)
Northern Ireland 1 (Armstrong), Honduras 1 (Laing)
Yugoslavia 1 (Petrovic), Honduras 0
Northern Ireland 1 (Armstrong), Spain 0

GROUP 6
Brazil 2 (Socrates, Eder), Soviet Union 1 (Bal)
Scotland 5 (Wark 2, Robertson, Dalglish, Archibald), New Zealand 2 (Sumner, Wooddin)
Brazil 4 (Zico, Oscar, Eder, Falcao), Scotland 1 (Narey)
Soviet Union 3 (Gavrilov, Blokhin, Baltacha), New Zealand 0
Soviet Union 2 (Chivadze, Shengelia), Scotland 2 (Jordan, Souness)
Brazil 4 (Zico 2, Falcao, Serginho), New Zealand 0

SECOND ROUND
GROUP A
Poland 3 (Boniek 3), Belgium 0
Soviet Union 1 (Oganesian), Belgium 0
Poland 0, Soviet Union 0

GROUP B
West Germany 0, England 0
West Germany 2 (Littbarski, Fischer), Spain 1 (Zamora)
England 0, Spain 0

GROUP C
Italy 2 (Tardelli, Cabrini), Argentina 1 (Passarella)
Brazil 3 (Zico, Serginho, Junior), Argentina 1 (Diaz)
Italy 3 (Rossi 3), Brazil 2 (Socrates, Falcao)

GROUP D
France 1 (Genghini), Austria 0
Austria 2 (Pezzey, Hintermaier), Northern Ireland 2 (Hamilton 2)
France 4 (Giresse 2, Rocheteau 2), Northern Ireland 1 (Armstrong)

SEMI-FINALS
Italy 2 (Rossi 2), Poland 0
West Germany 3 (Littbarski, Rummenigge, Fischer), France 3 (Platini, Tresor, Giresse)
aet (West Germany won 5-4 on penalties)

THIRD PLACE PLAY-OFF
Poland 3 (Szarmach, Majewski, Kupcewicz), France 2 (Girard, Couriol)

FINAL
Italy 3 (Rossi, Tardelli, Altobelli), West Germany 1 (Breitner)

MEXICO 1986

FIRST ROUND
GROUP 1
Italy 1 (Altobelli), Bulgaria 1 (Sirakov)
Argentina 3 (Valdano 2, Ruggeri), South Korea 1 (Park Chang-sun)
Argentina 1 (Maradona), Italy 1 (Altobelli)
South Korea 1 (Kim Jong-boo), Bulgaria 1 (Getov)
Argentina 2 (Valdano, Burruchaga), Bulgaria 0
Italy 3 (Altobelli 2, og), South Korea 2 (Choi Soon-ho, Hoh Jung-moo)

GROUP 2
Mexico 2 (Quirarte, Sanchez), Belgium 1 (Vandenbergh)
Parguay 1 (Romero), Iraq 0
Mexico 1 (Flores), Paraguay 1 (Romero)
Belgium 2 (Scifo, Claesen), Iraq (Rhadi)
Belgium 2 (Vercauteren, Veyt), Paraguay 2 (Cabanas 2)
Mexico 1 (Quirarte), Iraq 0

GROUP 3
France 1 (Papin), Canada 0
Soviet Union 6 (Yaremchuk 2, Yakovenko, Aleinkov, Belanov, Rodionov), Hungary 0

PREVIOUS FINALS

France 1 (Fernandez), Soviet Union 1 (Rats)
Hungary 2 (Esterhazy, Detari), Canada 0
France 3 (Stopyra, Tigana, Rocheteau), Hungary 0
Soviet Union 2 (Blokhin, Zavarov), Canada 0

GROUP 4
Brazil 1 (Socrates), Spain 0
Algeria 1 (Zidane), Northern Ireland 1 (Whiteside)
Brazil 1 (Careca), Algeria 0
Spain 2 (Butragueno, Salinas), Northern Ireland 1 (Clarke)
Brazil 3 (Careca, Josimar), Northern Ireland 0
Spain 3 (Caldere 2, Eloy), Algeria 0

GROUP 5
West Germany 1 (Allofs), Uruguay 1 (Alzamendi)
Denmark 1 (Elkjaer-Larsen), Scotland 0
West Germany 2 (Voller, Allofs), Scotland 1 (Strachan)
Denmark 6 (Elkjaer-Larsen 3, Lerby, M Laudrup, J Olsen), Uruguay 1 (Francescoli)
Denmark 2 (J Olsen, Eriksen), West Germany 0
Uruguay 0, Scotland 0

GROUP 6
Morocco 0, Poland 0
Portugal 1 (Carlos Manuel), England 0
Morocco 0, England 0
Poland 1 (Smolarek), Portugal 0
England 3 (Lineker 3), Poland 0
Morocco 3 (Khairi 2, Krimau), Portugal 1 (Diamantino)

SECOND ROUND
Argentina 1 (Pasculli), Uruguay 0
England 3 (Lineker 2, Beardsley), Paraguay 0
Spain 5 (Butragueno 4, Goicoechea), Denmark 1 (J Olsen)
Belgium 4 (Scifo, Ceulemans, Demol, Claesen), Soviet Union 3 (Belanov 3) aet
France 2 (Platini, Stopyra), Italy 0
Brazil 4 (Socrates, Josimar, Edinho, Careca), Poland 0
Mexico 2 (Negrete, Servin), Bulgaria 0
West Germany 1 (Matthaus), Morocco 0

QUARTER-FINALS
Argentina 2 (Maradona 2), England 1 (Lineker)
Belgium 1 (Ceulemans), Spain 1 (Senor) aet (Belgium won 5-4 on penalties)
France 1 (Platini), Brazil 1 (Careca) aet (France won 4-3 on penalties)
West Germany 0, Mexico 0 aet (West Germany won 4-1 on penalties)

PREVIOUS FINALS

SEMI-FINALS
Argentina 2 (Maradona 2), Belgium 0
West Germany 2 (Brehme, Voller), France 0

THIRD PLACE PLAY-OFF
France 4 (Ferreri, Papin, Genghini. Amoros), Belgium 2 (Ceulemans, Claesen) aet

FINAL
Argentina 3 (Brown, Valdano, Burruchaga), West Germany 2 (Rummenigge, Voller)

ITALY 1990

FIRST ROUND
GROUP A
Italy 1 (Schillaci), Austria 0
Czechoslovakia 5 (Skuhravy 2, Bilek, Hasek, Luhovy), USA 1 (Caligiuri)
Italy 1 (Giannini), USA 0
Czechoslovakia 1 (Bilek), Austria 0
Austria 2 (Ogris, Rodax), USA 1 (Murray)
Italy 2 (Schillaci, R Baggio), Czechoslovakia 0

GROUP B
Cameroon 1 (Omam Biyik), Argentina 0
Romania 2 (Lacatus), Soviet Union 0
Argentina 2 (Troglio, Burruchaga), Soviet Union 0
Cameroon 2 (Milla 2), Romania 1 (Balint)
Soviet Union 4 (Protasov, Zygmantovich, Zavarov, Dobrovolski), Cameroon 0
Argentina 1 (Monzon), Romania 1 (Balint)

GROUP C
Brazil 2 (Careca 2), Sweden 1 (Brolin)
Costa Rica 1 (Cayasso), Scotland 0
Brazil 1 (Muller), Costa Rica 0
Scotland 2 (McCall, Johnston), Sweden 1 (Stromberg)
Costa Rica 2 (Flores, Medford), Sweden 1 (Ekstrom)
Brazil 1 (Muller), Scotland 0

GROUP D
Colombia 2 (Redin, Valderrama), UAE 0
West Germany 4 (Matthaus 2, Klinsmann, Voller), Yugoslavia 1 (Jozic)
Yugoslavia 1 (Jozic), Colombia 0
West Germany 5 (Voller 2, Klinsmann, Matthaus, Bein), UAE 1 (Khalid Mubarak)
Yugoslavia 4 (Pancev 2, Susic, Prosinecki), UAE 1 (Jumaa)

PREVIOUS FINALS

West Germany 1 (Littbarski), Colombia 1 (Rincon)

GROUP E
Belgium 2 (Degryse, de Wolf), South Korea 0
Spain 0, Uruguay 0
Spain 3 (Michel 3), South Korea 1 (Bo-Kwan)
Belgium 3 (Clijsters, Scifo, Ceulemans), Uruguay 1 (Bengoechea)
Uruguay 1 (Fonseca), South Korea 0
Spain 2 (Michel, Gorriz), Belgium 1 (Vervoort)

GROUP F
England 1 (Lineker), Republic of Ireland 1 (Sheedy)
Holand 1 (Kieft), Egypt 1 (Abdelghani)
England 0, Holland 0
Republic of Ireland 0, Egypt 0
Republic of Ireland 1 (Quinn), Holland 1 (Gullit)
England 1 (M Wright), Egypt 0

SECOND ROUND
West Germany 2 (Klinsmann, Brehme), Holland 1 (R Koeman)
Czechoslovakia 4 (Skuhravy 3, Kubik), Costa Rica 1 (Gonzalez)
Cameroon 2 (Milla 2), Colombia 1 (Redin) aet
England 1 (Platt), Belgium 0 aet
Italy 2 (Schillaci, Serena), Uruguay 0
Republic of Ireland 0, Romania 0 aet (Ireland won 5-4 on penalties)
Yugoslavia 2 (Stojkovic 2), Spain 1 (Salinas)
Argentina 1 (Caniggia), Brazil 0

QUARTER-FINALS
West Germany 1 (Matthaus), Czechoslovakia 0
England 3 (Lineker 2, Platt), Cameroon 2 (Kunde, Ekeke) aet
Italy 1 (Schillaci), Republic of Ireland 0
Argentina 0, Yugoslavia 0 aet (Argentina won 3-2 on penalties)

SEMI-FINALS
West Germany 1 (Brehme), England 1 (Lineker) aet (West Germany won 4-3 on penalties)
Argentina 1 (Caniggia), Italy 1 (Schillaci) aet (Argentina won 4-3 on penalties)

THIRD PLACE PLAY-OFF
Italy 2 (R Baggio, Schillaci), England 1 (Platt)

FINAL
West Germany 1 (Brehme), Argentina 0

USA 1994

FIRST ROUND
GROUP A
USA 1 (Wynalda), Switzerland 1 (Bregy)
Romania 3 (Raducioiu 2, Hagi), Colombia 1 (Valencia)
Switzerland 4 (A Sutter, Chapuisat, Knup, Bregy), Romania 1 (Hagi)
USA 2 (og, Stewart), Columbia 1 (Valencia)
Romania 1 (Petrescu), USA 0
Colombia 2 (Gaviria, Lazano), Switzerland 0

GROUP B
Cameroon 2 (Embe, Oman-Biyik), Sweden 2 (Ljung, Dahlin)
Brazil 2 (Romario, Rai), Russia 0
Brazil 3 (Romario, Marcio Santos, Bebeto), Cameroon 0
Sweden 3 (Dahlin 2, Brolin), Russia 1 (Salenko)
Russia 6 (Salenko 5, Radchenko), Cameroon 1 (Milla)
Brazil 1 (Romario), Sweden 1 (K Andersson)

GROUP C
Germany 1 (Klinsmann), Bolivia 0
Spain 2 (Salinas, Goikoetxea), South Korea 2 (Myong-bo, Jung-won)
Germany 1 (Klinsmann), Spain 1 (Goikoetxea)
South Korea 0, Bolivia 0
Spain 3 (Caminero 2, Guardiola), Bolivia 1 (Sanchez)
Germany 3 (Klinsmann 2, Riedle), South Korea 2 (Sun-hong, Myong-bo)

GROUP D
Argentina 4 (Batitusta 3, Maradona), Greece 0
Nigeria 3 (Yekini, Amokachi, Amunike), Bulgaria 0
Argentina 2 (Caniggia 2), Nigeria 1 (Siasia)
Bulgaria 4 (Stoichkov 2, Lechkov, Boromirov), Greece 0
Nigeria 2 (George, Amokachi), Greece 0
Bulgaria 2 (Stoichkov, Sirakov), Argentina 0

GROUP E
Republic of Ireland 1 (Houghton), Italy 0
Norway 1 (Rekdal), Mexico 0
Italy 1 (D Baggio), Norway 0
Mexico 2 (Garcia 2), Republic of Ireland 1 (Aldridge)
Italy 1 (Massaro), Mexico 1 (Bernal)
Republic of Ireland 0, Norway 0

PREVIOUS FINALS

GROUP F
Belgium 1 (Degryse), Morocco 0
Holland 2 (Jonk, Taument), Saudi Arabia 1 (Amin)
Saudi Arabia 2 (Al-Jaber, Amin), Morocco 1 (Chauch)
Belgium 1 (Albert), Holland 0
Holland 2 (Bergkamp. Roy), Morocco 1 (Nader)
Saudi Arabia 1 (Owairan), Belgium 0

SECOND ROUND
Brazil 1 (Bebeto), USA 0
Holland 2 (Bergkamp, Jonk), Republic of Ireland 0
Romania 3 (Dumitrescu 2, Hagi), Argentina 2 (Batistuta, Balbo)
Sweden 3 (K Andersson 2, Dahlin), Saudi Arabia 1 (Al Ghashiyan)
Bulgaria 1 (Stoichkov), Mexico 1 (Garcia Aspe) aet (Bulgaria won 3-1 on penalties)
Germany 3 (Voller 2, Klinsmann), Belgium 2 (Grun, Albert)
Spain 3 (Hierro, Luis Enrique, Beguiristain), Switzerland 0
Italy 2 (R Baggio 2), Nigeria 1 (Amunike)

QUARTER-FINALS
Brazil 3 (Romario, Bebeto, Branco), Holland 2 (Bergkamp, Winter)
Sweden 2 (Brolin, K Andersson), Romania 2 (Raducioiu 2) aet (Sweden won 5-4 on penalties)
Bulgaria 2 (Stoichkov, Letchkov), Germany 1 (Matthaus)
Italy 2 (D Baggio, R Baggio), Spain 1 (Caminero)

SEMI-FINALS
Brazil 1 (Romario), Sweden 0
Italy 2 (R Baggio 2), Bulgaria 1 (Stoichkov)

THIRD PLACE PLAY-OFF
Sweden 4 (Brolin, Mild, H Larsson, K Andersson), Bulgaria 0

FINAL
Brazil 0, Italy 0 aet (Brazil won 3-2 on penalties)

FRANCE 1998

GROUP A
Brazil 2 (Cesar Sampaio, Boyd og), Scotland 1 (Collins)
Morocco 2 (Hadji, Hadda), Norway 2 (Chippo og, Eggen)
Brazil 3 (Ronaldo, Rivaldo, Bebeto), Morocco 0
Scotland 1 (Burley), Norway 1 (H Flo)
Brazil 1 (Bebeto), Norway 2 (T Flo, Rekdal)

PREVIOUS FINALS

Scotland 0, Morocco 3 (Bassir 2, Hadda)

GROUP B
Cameroon 1 (Njanka), Austria 1 (Polster)
Italy 2 (Vieri, R Baggio), Chile 2 (Salas 2)
Chile 1 (Salas), Austria 1 (Vastic)
Italy 3 (Vieri 2, Di Biagio), Cameroon 0
Chile 1 (Sierra), Cameroon 1 (Mboma)
Italy 2 (Vieri, R Baggio), Austria 1 (Herzog)

GROUP C
France 3 (Dugarry, Isa 2 og), South Africa 0
Saudi Arabia 0, Denmark 1 (Rieper)
France 4 (Henry 2, Trezeguet, Lizarazu), Saudi Arabia 0
South Africa 1 (McCarthy), Denmark 1 (Nielsen)
France 2 (Djorkaeff, Petit), Denmark 1 (M Laudrup)
South Africa 2 (Bartlett 2), Saudi Arabia 2 (al Jaber, al Thynyan)

GROUP D
Paraguay 0, Bulgaria 0
Spain 2 (Hierro, Raul), Nigeria 3 (Adepoju, Zubizarreta og, Oliseh)
Nigeria 1 (Ikpeba), Bulgaria 0
Spain 0, Paraguay 0
Nigeria 1 (Oruma), Paraguay 3 (Ayala, Benitez, Cardozo)
Spain 6 (Morientes 2, Kiko 2, Hierro, Luis Enrique), Bulgaria 1 (Kostadinov)

GROUP E
Holland 0, Belgium 0
South Korea 1 (Ha), Mexico 3 (Hernandez 2, Pelaez)
Belgium 2 (Wilmots), Mexico 2 (Garcia Aspe, Blanco)
Holland 5 (Cocu, Overmars, Bergkamp, Van Hooijdonk, R De Boer), South Korea 0
Belgium 1 (Nilis), South Korea 1 (Yoo)
Holland 2 (Cocu, R De Boer), Mexico 2 (Pelaez, Hernandez)

GROUP F
Yugoslavia 1 (Mihajlovic), Iran 0
Germany 2 (Moller, Klinsmann), USA 1
Germany 2 (Mihaljovic og, Bierhoff), Yugoslavia 2 (Mijatovic, Stojkovic)
USA 1 (McBride), Iran 2 (Estili, Mahdavikia)
Germany 2 (Bierhoff, Klinsmann), Iran 0
USA 0, Yugoslavia 1 (Komljenovic)

GROUP G
England 2 (Shearer, Scholes), Tunisia 0

PREVIOUS FINALS

Romania 1 (Ilie), Colombia 0
Colombia 1 (Preciado), Tunisia 0
Romania 2 (Moldovan, Petrescu), England 1 (Owen)
Colombia 0, England 2 (Anderton, Beckham)
Romania 1 (Moldovan), Tunisia 1 (Souayah)

GROUP H
Argentina 1 (Batistuta), Japan 0
Jamaica 1 (Earle), Croatia 3 (Stanic, Prosinecki, Suker)
Japan 0, Croatia 1 (Suker)
Argentina 5 (Batistuta 3, Ortega 2), Jamaica 0
Argentina 1 (Pineda), Croatia 0
Japan 1 (Nakayama), Jamaica 2 (Whitmore 2)

SECOND ROUND
Brazil 4 (Cesar Sampaio 2, Ronaldo 2), Chile 1 (Salas)
Italy 1 (Vieri), Norway 0
France 1 (Blanc), Paraguay 0 aet
Nigeria 1 (Babangida), Denmark 4 (Moller, B Laudrup, Sand, Helveg)
Germany 2 (Klinsmann, Bierhoff), Mexico 1 (Hernandez)
Holland 2 (Bergkamp, Davids), Yugoslavia 1 (Komljenovic)
Argentina 2 (Batistuta, Zanetti), England 2 (Shearer, Owen) aet (Argentina won 4-3 on penalties)
Romania 0, Croatia 1 (Suker)

QUARTER-FINALS
Brazil 3 (Rivaldo 2, Bebeto), Denmark 2 (Jorgensen, B Laudrup)
France 0, Italy 0 aet (France won 4-3 on penalties)
Germany 0, Croatia 3 (Jarni, Vlaovic, Suker)
Holland 2 (Kluivert, Bergkamp), Argentina 1 (Lopez)

SEMI-FINALS
Brazil 1 (Ronaldo), Holland 1 (Kluivert) aet (Brazil won 4-2 on penalties)
France 2 (Thuram 2), Croatia 1 (Suker)

THIRD PLACE PLAY-OFF
Holland 1 (Zenden), Croatia 2 (Prosinecki, Suker)

FINAL
Brazil 0, France 3 (Zidane 2, Petit)

PREVIOUS MEETINGS

RESULTS OF PREVIOUS MEETINGS AT WORLD CUP FINALS BETWEEN
TEAMS DRAWN IN THE SAME FIRST ROUND GROUP AS ONE ANOTHER

GROUP A

FRANCE v SENEGAL - No previous meetings
FRANCE v URUGUAY - 1966, France 1 Uruguay 2
FRANCE v DENMARK - 1998, France 2 Denmark 1
SENEGAL v URUGUAY - No previous meetings
SENEGAL v DENMARK - No previous meetings
DENMARK v URUGUAY - 1986, Denmark 6 Uruguay 1

GROUP B

SPAIN v SLOVENIA - No previous meetings
SPAIN v PARAGUAY - 1998, Spain 0 Paraguay 0
SPAIN v SOUTH AFRICA - No previous meetings
SLOVENIA v PARAGUAY - No previous meetings
SLOVENIA v SOUTH AFRICA - No previous meetings
PARAGUAY v SOUTH AFRICA - No previous meetings

GROUP C

BRAZIL v TURKEY - No previous meetings
BRAZIL v CHINA - No previous meetings
BRAZIL v COSTA RICA - 1990, Brazil 1 Costa Rica 0
TURKEY v CHINA - No previous meetings
TURKEY v COSTA RICA - No previous meetings
CHINA v COSTA RICA - No previous meetings

GROUP D

SOUTH KOREA v POLAND - No previous meetings
SOUTH KOREA v UNITED STATES - No previous meetings
SOUTH KOREA v PORTUGAL - No previous meetings
POLAND v UNITED STATES - No previous meetings
POLAND v PORTUGAL - 1986, Poland 1 Portugal 0
UNITED STATES v PORTUGAL - No previous meetings

PAST WORLD CUP MEETINGS

GROUP E

GERMANY v SAUDI ARABIA - No previous meetings
GERMANY v IRELAND - No previous meetings
GERMANY v CAMEROON - No previous meetings
SAUDI ARABIA v IRELAND - No previous meetings
SAUDI ARABIA v CAMEROON - No previous meetings
IRELAND v CAMEROON - No previous meetings

GROUP F

ARGENTINA v NIGERIA - 1994, Argentina 2 Nigeria 1
ARGENTINA v ENGLAND - 1962, Argentina 1 England 3
- 1966, Argentina 0 England 1
- 1986, Argentina 2 England 1
- 1998, Argentina 2 England 2
(Argentina won 4-3 on penalties)
ARGENTINA v SWEDEN - 1934, Argentina 2 Sweden 3
NIGERIA v ENGLAND - No previous meetings
NIGERIA v SWEDEN - No previous meetings
ENGLAND v SWEDEN - No previous meetings

GROUP G

ITALY v ECUADOR - No previous meetings
ITALY v CROATIA - No previous meetings
ITALY v MEXICO - 1970, Italy 4 Mexico 1
- 1994, Italy 1 Mexico 1
ECUADOR v CROATIA - No previous meetings
ECUADOR v MEXICO - No previous meetings
CROATIA v MEXICO - No previous meetings

GROUP H

JAPAN v BELGIUM - No previous meetings
JAPAN v RUSSIA - No previous meetings
JAPAN v TUNISIA - No previous meetings
BELGIUM v RUSSIA - No previous meetings
BELGIUM v TUNISIA - No previous meetings
RUSSIA v TUNISIA - No previous meetings

HISTORY

PAST RECORDS

Tournament histories for this year's teams except China, Ecuador, Senegal and Slovenia, who will be appearing in the World Cup finals for the first time.

ARGENTINA

PREVIOUS APPEARANCES: 1930, 1934, 1958, 1962, 1966, 1974, 1978, 1982, 1986, 1990, 1994, 1998
BEST PERFORMANCE: WINNERS 1978, 1986 RUNNERS UP: 1930, 1990
HOSTS: 1978
RECORD: P91 W48 D10 L33 F101 A65

1930 URUGUAY
R1	FRANCE	W 1-0 Luis Monti
R1	MEXICO	W 6-3 Guillermo Stabile 3, Adolfo Zumelzu 2, Francisco Varallo
R1	CHILE	W 3-1 Guillermo Stabile 2, Marino Evaristo
SF	UNITED STATES	W 6-1 Luis Monti, Alejandro Scopelli, Guillermo Stabile 2, Carlos Peucelle 2
F	URUGUAY	L 2-4 Carlos Peucelle, Guillermo Stabile

1934 ITALY
R1	SWEDEN	L 2-3 Ernesto Belis, Alberto Galateo

1958 SWEDEN
R1	WEST GERMANY	L 1-3 Orestes Corbatta
R1	NORTHERN IRELAND	W 3-1 Orestes Corbatta 2 (1pen), Ludovico Avio
R1	CZECHOSLOVAKIA	L 1-6 Orestes Corbatta pen

1962 CHILE
R1	BULGARIA	W 1-0 Hector Facundo
R1	ENGLAND	L 1-3 Jose Sanfilippo
R1	HUNGARY	D 0-0

1966 ENGLAND
R1	SPAIN	W 2-1 Luis Artime 2
R1	SWITZERLAND	W 2-0 Luis Artime, Ermindo Onega
R1	WEST GERMANY	D 0-0
QF	ENGLAND	L 0-1

1974 WEST GERMANY
R1	POLAND	L 2-3 Ramon Heredia, Carlos Babington
R1	ITALY	D 1-1 Rene Houseman
R1	HAITI	W 4-1 Hector Yazalde 2, Rene Houseman, Ruben Ayala
R2	NETHERLANDS	L 0-4
R2	BRAZIL	L 1-2 Miguel Brindisi
R2	EAST GERMANY	D 1-1 Rene Houseman

HISTORY

1978 ARGENTINA

R1	HUNGARY	W 2-1 Leopoldo Luque, Ricardo Bertoni
R1	FRANCE	W 2-1 Daniel Passarella, Leopoldo Luque
R1	ITALY	L 0-1
R2	POLAND	W 2-0 Mario Kempes 2
R2	BRAZIL	D 0-0
R2	PERU	W 6-0 Mario Kempes 2, Alberto Tarantini, Leopoldo Luque 2, Rene Houseman
F	NETHERLANDS	W 3-1aet Mario Kempes 2, Ricardo Bertoni

1982 SPAIN

R1	BELGIUM	L 0-1
R1	HUNGARY	W 4-1 Ricardo Bertoni, Diego Maradona 2, Ossie Ardiles
R1	EL SALVADOR	W 2-0 Daniel Passarella pen, Ricardo Bertoni
R2	ITALY	L 1-2 Daniel Passarella
R2	BRAZIL	L 1-3 Ramon Diaz

1986 MEXICO

R1	SOUTH KOREA	W 3-1 Jorge Valdano 2, Oscar Ruggeri
R1	ITALY	D 1-1 Diego Maradona
R1	BULGARIA	W 2-0 Jorge Valdano Jose Luis Burruchaga
R2	URUGUAY	W 1-0 Pedro Pasculli
QF	ENGLAND	W 2-1 Diego Maradona 2
SF	BELGIUM	W 2-0 Diego Maradona 2
F	WEST GERMANY	W 3-2 Jose Luis Brown, Jorge Valdano, Jose Luis Burruchaga

1990 ITALY

R1	CAMEROON	L 0-1
R1	SOVIET UNION	W 2-0 Pedro Troglio, Jose Luis Burruchaga
R1	ROMANIA	D 1-1 Pedro Monzon
R2	BRAZIL	W 1-0 Claudio Cannigia
QF	YUGOSLAVIA	D 0-0aet (Argentina won 3-2 on penalties)
SF	ITALY	D 1-1aet Claudio Cannigia (Argentina won 4-3 on penalties)
F	WEST GERMANY	L 0-1

1994 UNITED STATES

R1	GREECE	W 4-0 Gabriel Batistuta 3 (1pen), Diego Maradona
R1	NIGERIA	W 2-1 Claudio Cannigia 2
R1	BULGARIA	L 0-2
R2	ROMANIA	L 2-3 Gabriel Batistuta pen, Abel Balbo

1998 FRANCE

R1	JAPAN	W 1-0 Gabriel Batistuta
R1	JAMAICA	W 5-0 Ariel Ortega 2, Gabriel Batistuta 3 (1pen)
R1	CROATIA	W 1-0 Hector Pineda
R2	ENGLAND	D 2-2aet Gabriel Batistuta pen, Javier Zanetti (Argentina win 4-3 on penalties)
QF	NETHERLANDS	L 1-2 Claudio Lopez

BELGIUM

PREVIOUS APPEARANCES 1930, 1934, 1938, 1954, 1970, 1982, 1986, 1990, 1994, 1998
BEST PERFORMANCE SEMI FINALISTS 1986 (4th)
RECORD P32, W9, D7, L16, F40, A56

1930 URUGUAY
| R1 | UNITED STATES | L 0-3 |
| R1 | PARAGUAY | L 0-1 |

1934 ITALY
| R1 | GERMANY | L 2-5 Bernard Voorhoof 2 |

1938 FRANCE
| R1 | FRANCE | L 1-3 Henri Isemborghs |

1954 SWITZERLAND
| R1 | ENGLAND | D 4-4 Leopold Anoul 2, Henri Coppens, Jimmy Dickenson og |
| R1 | ITALY | L 1-4 Leopold Anoul |

1970 MEXICO
R1	EL SALVADOR	W 3-0 Wilfried Van Moer 2, Raoul Lambert
R1	SOVIET UNION	L 1-4 Raoul Lambert
R1	MEXICO	L 0-1

1982 SPAIN
R1	ARGENTINA	W 1-0 Erwin Vandenbergh
R1	EL SALVADOR	W 1-0 Ludo Coeck
R1	HUNGARY	D 1-1 Alex Czerniatynski
R2	POLAND	L 0-3
R2	SOVIET UNION	L 0-1

1986 MEXICO
R1	MEXICO	L 1-2 Erwin Vandenbergh
R1	IRAQ	W 2-1 Enzo Scifo, Nico Claesen
R1	PARAGUAY	D 2-2 Frank Vercauterern, Danny Veyt
R2	SOVIET UNION	W 4-3aet Enzo Scifo, Jan Ceulemans, Stephane Demol, Nico Claesen
QF	SPAIN	D 1-1aet Jan Ceulemans
		(Belgium won 5-4 on penalties)
SF	ARGENTINA	L 0-2
3/4	FRANCE	L 2-4 Jan Ceulemans, Nico Claesen

1990 ITALY
R1	SOUTH KOREA	W 2-0 Marc Degryse, Jean De Wolf
R1	URUGUAY	W 3-1 Leo Clijsters, Enzo Scifo, Jan Ceulemans
R1	SPAIN	L 1-2 Patrick Vervoort
R2	ENGLAND	L 0-1 aet

1994 UNITED STATES
R1	MOROCCO	W 1-0 Marc Degryse
R1	NETHERLANDS	W 1-0 Philippe Albert
R1	SAUDI ARABIA	L 0-1
R2	GERMANY	L 2-3 Georges Grun, Philippe Albert

1998 FRANCE

R1	NETHERLANDS	D 0-0
R1	MEXICO	D 2-2 Marc Wilmots 2
R1	SOUTH KOREA	D 1-1 Luc Nilis

BRAZIL

PREVIOUS APPEARANCES 16 (Brazil are the only nation to have taken part in the finals of every World Cup 1930-1998)
BEST PERFORMANCE WINNERS 1958, 1962, 1970, 1994
RUNNERS-UP 1950, 1998
HOSTS 1950
RECORD P80, W53, D14 , L13, F173, A78

1930 URUGUAY

R1	YUGOSLAVIA	L 1-2 Preguinho
R1	BOLIVIA	W 4-0 Preguinho 3, Carvalho Leite

1934 ITALY

R1	SPAIN	L 1-3 Leonidas

1938 FRANCE

R1	POLAND	W 6-5aet Leonidas 4, Peracio, Romeo
QF	CZECHOSLOVAKIA	D 1-1 Leonidas
QF	CZECHOSLOVAKIA	W 2-1 Leonidas, Roberto
SF	ITALY	L 1-2 Romeo
3/4	SWEDEN	W 4-2 Leonidas 2, Romeo, Peracio

1950 BRAZIL

R1	MEXICO	W 4-0 Ademir Menezes 2, Baltazar, Jair Pinto
R1	SWITZERLAND	D 2-2 Alfredo, Baltazar
R1	YUGOSLAVIA	W 2-0 Ademir Menezes, Zizinho
R2	SWEDEN	W 7-1 Ademir Menezes 4, Chico 2, Maneca
R2	SPAIN	W 6-1 Ademir Menezes 2, Chico 2, Jair Pinto, Zizinho
F	URUGUAY	L 1-2 Friaca

1954 SWITZERLAND

R1	MEXICO	W 5-0 Pinga 2, Baltazar, Didi, Julinho
R1	YUGOSLAVIA	D 1-1 Didi
QF	HUNGARY	L 2-4 D.Santos, Julinho

1958 SWEDEN

R1	AUSTRIA	W 3-0 Altafini 2, Nilton Santos
R1	ENGLAND	D 0-0
R1	SOVIET UNION	W 2-0 Vava 2
QF	WALES	W 1-0 Pele
SF	FRANCE	W 5-2 Pele 3, Vava, Didi
F	SWEDEN	W 5-2 Pele 2, Vava 2, Zagallo

HISTORY

1962 CHILE
R1	MEXICO	W 2-0 Zagallo, Pele
R1	CZECHOSLOVAKIA	D 0-0
R1	SPAIN	W 2-1 Amarildo 2
QF	ENGLAND	W 3-1 Garrincha 2, Vava
SF	CHILE	W 4-2 Garrincha 2, Vava 2
F	CZECHOSLOVAKIA	W 3-1 Amarildo, Zito, Vava

1966 ENGLAND
R1	BULGARIA	W 2-0 Pele, Garrincha
R1	HUNGARY	L 1-3 Tostao
R1	PORTUGAL	L 1-3 Rildo

1970 MEXICO
R1	CZECHOSLOVAKIA	W 4-1 Jairzinho 2, Rivelino, Pele
R1	ENGLAND	W 1-0 Jairzinho
R1	ROMANIA	W 3-2 Jairzinho, Pele 2
QF	PERU	W 4-2 Jairzinho, Tostao 2, Rivelino
SF	URUGUAY	W 3-1 Jairzinho, Clodoaldo, Rivelino
F	ITALY	W 4-1 Jairzinho, Pele, Gerson, Carlos Alberto

1974 WEST GERMANY
R1	YUGOSLAVIA	D 0-0
R1	SCOTLAND	D 0-0
R1	ZAIRE	W 3-0 Rivelino, Jairzinho, Valdomiro
R2	EAST GERMANY	W 1-0 Rivelino
R2	ARGENTINA	W 2-1 Rivelino, Jairzinho
R2	NETHERLANDS	L 0-2

1978 ARGENTINA
R1	SWEDEN	D 1-1 Reinaldo
R1	SPAIN	D 0-0
R1	AUSTRIA	W 1-0 Roberto Dinamite
R2	PERU	W 3-0 Dirceu 2, Zico
R2	ARGENTINA	D 0-0
R2	POLAND	W 3-1 Nelinho, Roberto 2
3/4	ITALY	W 2-1 Nelinho, Dirceu

1982 SPAIN
R1	SOVIET UNION	W 2-1 Socrates, Eder
R1	SCOTLAND	W 4-1 Zico, Oscar, Eder, Falcao
R1	NEW ZEALAND	W 4-0 Zico 2, Falcao, Serginho
R2	ARGENTINA	W 3-1 Zico, Serginho, Junior
R2	ITALY	L 2-3 Socrates, Falcao

1986 MEXICO
R1	SPAIN	W 1-0 Socrates
R1	ALGERIA	W 1-0 Careca
R1	N. IRELAND	W 3-0 Careca 2, Josimar
R2	POLAND	W 4-0 Socrates, Josimar, Edinho, Careca
QF	FRANCE	D 1-1aet Careca **(France won 4-3 on penalties)**

HISTORY

1990 ITALY
R1	SWEDEN	W 2-1 Careca 2
R1	COSTA RICA	W 1-0 Muller
R1	SCOTLAND	W 1-0 Muller
R2	ARGENTINA	L 0-1

1994 UNITED STATES
R1	RUSSIA	W 2-0 Romario, Rai
R1	CAMEROON	W 3-0 Romario, Marcio Santos, Bebeto
R1	SWEDEN	D 1-1 Romario
R2	UNITED STATES	W 1-0 Bebeto
QF	NETHERLANDS	W 3-2 Romario, Bebeto, Branco
SF	SWEDEN	W 1-0 Romario
F	ITALY	D 0-0 aet (Brazil won 3-2 on penalties)

1998 FRANCE
R1	Scotland	W 2-1 Cesar Sampaio, Boyd og
R1	Morocco	W 3-0 Ronaldo, Rivaldo, Bebeto
R1	Norway	L 1-2 Bebeto
R2	Chile	W 4-1 Cesar Sampaio 2, Ronaldo 2 (1 pen)
QF	Denmark	W 3-2 Bebeto, Rivaldo 2
SF	Netherlands	D 1-1 aet Ronaldo (Brazil won 4-2 on penalties)
F	France	L 0-3

CAMEROON

PREVIOUS WORLD CUP APPEARANCES 1982, 1990, 1994, 1998
BEST PERFORMANCE QUARTER-FINALS 1990
WORLD CUP FINALS RECORD P14, W3, D6, L5, F13, A26

1982 SPAIN
R1	PERU	D 0-0
R1	POLAND	D 0-0
R1	ITALY	D 1-1 Gregoire M'bida

1990 ITALY
R1	ARGENTINA	W 1-0 Francois Omam Biyik
R1	ROMANIA	W 2-1 Roger Milla 2
R1	USSR	L 0-4
R2	COLOMBIA	W 2-1 aet Roger Milla 2
QF	ENGLAND	L 2-3 aet Emmanuel Kunde pen, Eugene Ekete

1994 UNITED STATES
R1	SWEDEN	D 2-2 David Embe, Francois Omam Biyik
R1	BRAZIL	L 0-3
R1	RUSSIA	L 1-6 Roger Milla

1998 FRANCE
R1	AUSTRIA	D 1-1 Pierre Njanka

| R1 | ITALY | L 0-3 |
| R1 | CHILE | D 1-1 Patrick Mboma 55 |

COSTA RICA
PREVIOUS WORLD CUP APPEARANCES 1990
BEST PERFORMANCE SECOND ROUND 1990
WORLD CUP RECORD P4, W2, D0, L2, F4, A6

1990 ITALY

R1	SCOTLAND	W 1-0 Juan Cayasso
R1	BRAZIL	L 0-1
R1	SWEDEN	W 2-1 Roger Flores, Hernan Medford
R2	CZECHOSLOVAKIA	L 1-4 Ronald Gonzalez

CROATIA
PREVIOUS WORLD CUP APPEARANCES 1998
BEST PERFORMANCE THIRD PLACE 1998
WORLD CUP RECORD P7, W5, D0, L2, F11, A5

1998 FRANCE

R1	JAMAICA	W 3-1 Mario Stanic, Robert Prosinecki, Davor Suker
R1	JAPAN	W 1-0 Davor Suker
R1	ARGENTINA	L 0-1
R2	ROMANIA	W 1-0 Davor Suker pen
QF	GERMANY	W 3-0 Robert Jarni, Goran Vlaovic, Davor Suker
SF	FRANCE	L 1-2 Davor Suker
3/4	NETHERLANDS	W 2-1 Robert Prosinecki, Davor Suker

DENMARK
PREVIOUS WORLD CUP APPEARANCES 1986, 1998
BEST PERFORMANCE QUARTER-FINALS 1998
WORLD CUP FINALS RECORD P9, W5, D1, L3, F19, A13

1986 MEXICO

R1	SCOTLAND	W 1-0 Preben Elkjaer-Larsen
R1	URUGUAY	W 6-1 Preben Elkjaer-Larsen 3, Soren Lerby, Michael Laudrup, Jesper Olsen
R1	WEST GERMANY	W 2-0 Jesper Olsen pen, John Eriksen
R2	SPAIN	L 1-5 Jesper Olsen pen

1998 FRANCE

R1	SAUDI ARABIA	W 1-0 Marc Rieper
R1	SOUTH AFRICA	D 1-1 Allan Nielsen
R1	FRANCE	L 1-2 Michael Laudrup pen
R2	NIGERIA	W 4-1 Peter Moller, Brian Laudrup, Ebbe Sand, Thomas Helveg
QF	BRAZIL	L 2-3 Martin Jorgensen, Brian Laudrup

ENGLAND

PREVIOUS WORLD CUP APPEARANCES 1950, 1954, 1958, 1962, 1966, 1970, 1982, 1986, 1990, 1998
BEST PERFORMANCE WINNERS 1966
HOSTS 1966
WORLD CUP FINALS RECORD P45, W20, D13, L12, F62, A42

1950 BRAZIL

R1	CHILE	W 2-0 Stan Mortensen, Wilf Mannion
R1	UNITED STATES	L 0-1
R1	SPAIN	L 0-1

1954 SWITZERLAND

R1	BELGIUM	D 4-4 aet Ivor Broadis 2, Nat Lofthouse
R1	SWITZERLAND	W 2-0 Jimmy Mullen, Denis Wilshaw
QF	URUGUAY	L 2-4 Nat Lofthouse, Tom Finney

1958 SWEDEN

R1	USSR	D 2-2 Derek Kevan, Tom Finney pen
R1	BRAZIL	D 0-0
R1	AUSTRIA	D 2-2 Johnny Haynes, Derek Kevan
PO	USSR	L 0-1

1962 CHILE

R1	HUNGARY	L 1-2 Ron Flowers pen
R1	ARGENTINA	W 3-1 Ron Flowers pen, Bobby Charlton, Jimmy Greaves
R1	BULGARIA	D 0-0
QF	BRAZIL	L 1-3 Gerry Hitchens

1966 ENGLAND

R1	URUGUAY	D 0-0
R1	MEXICO	W 2-0 Bobby Charlton, Roger Hunt
R1	FRANCE	W 2-0 Roger Hunt 2
QF	ARGENTINA	W 1-0 Geoff Hurst
SF	PORTUGAL	W 2-1 Bobby Charlton 2
F	WEST GERMANY	W 4-2 aet Geoff Hurst 3, Martin Peters

1970 MEXICO

R1	ROMANIA	W 1-0 Geoff Hurst
R1	BRAZIL	L 0-1
R1	CZECHOSLOVAKIA	W 1-0 Allan Clarke pen

QF	WEST GERMANY	L 2-3 aet	Alan Mullery, Martin Peters

1982 SPAIN

R1	FRANCE	W 3-1	Bryan Robson 2, Paul Mariner
R1	CZECHOSLOVAKIA	W 2-0	Trevor Francis, Jozef Barmos og
R1	KUWAIT	W 1-0	Trevor Francis
R2	WEST GERMANY	D 0-0	
R2	SPAIN	D 0-0	

1986 MEXICO

R1	PORTUGAL	L 0-1	
R1	MOROCCO	D 0-0	
R1	POLAND	W 3-0	Gary Lineker 3
R2	PARAGUAY	W 3-0	Gary Lineker 2, Peter Beardsley
QF	ARGENTINA	L 1-2	Gary Lineker

1990 ITALY

R1	IRELAND	D 1-1	Gary Lineker
R1	NETHERLANDS	D 0-0	
R1	EGYPT	W 1-0	Mark Wright
R2	BELGIUM	W 1-0aet	David Platt
QF	CAMEROON	W 3-2aet	David Platt, Gary Lineker 2 pens
SF	WEST GERMANY	D 1-1aet	Gary Lineker
		(West Germany won 4-3 on penalties)	
3/4	ITALY	L 1-2	David Platt

1998 FRANCE

R1	TUNISIA	W 2-0	Alan Shearer, Paul Scholes
R1	ROMANIA	L 1-2	Michael Owen
R1	COLOMBIA	W 2-0	Darren Anderton, David Beckham
R2	ARGENTINA	D 2-2aet	Alan Shearer pen, Michael Owen
		(Argentina won 4-3 on penalties)	

FRANCE

PREVIOUS APPEARANCES 1930, 1934, 1938, 1954, 1958, 1966, 1978, 1982, 1986, 1998
BEST PERFORMANCE WINNERS 1998
HOSTS 1938, 1998
WORLD CUP FINALS RECORD P41, W23, D3, L15, F86, A58

1930 URUGUAY

R1	MEXICO	W 4-1	Lucien Laurent, Marcel Langiller, Andre Maschinot 2
R1	ARGENTINA	L 0-1	
R1	CHILE	L 0-1	

1934 ITALY

R1	AUSTRIA	L 2-3aet	Jean Nicolas, Georges Verriest pen

1938 FRANCE

R1	BELGIUM	W 3-1	Emil Veinante, Jean Nicolas 2

HISTORY

QF   ITALY   L 1-3 Oscar Heisserer

1954 SWITZERLAND

R1   YUGOSLAVIA   L 0-1

R1   MEXICO   W 3-2 Jean Vincent, Raymond Kopa pen, Raul Cardenas og

1958 SWEDEN

R1   PARAGUAY   W 7-3 Juste Fontaine 3, Roger Piantoni, Maryan Wisnieski, Raymond Kopa, Jean Vincent

R1   YUGOSLAVIA   L 2-3 Juste Fontaine 2

R1   SCOTLAND   W 2-1 Raymond Kopa, Juste Fontaine

QF   N. IRELAND   W 4-0 Maryan Wisnieski, Juste Fontaine 2, Roger Piantoni

SF   BRAZIL   L 2-5 Juste Fontaine, Roger Piantoni

3/4 WEST GERMANY W 6-3 Juste Fontaine 4, Raymond Kopa, Maryan Wisnieski

1966 ENGLAND

R1   MEXICO   D 1-1 Gerard Hausser

R1   URUGUAY   L 1-2 Hector De Bourgoing pen

R1   ENGLAND   L 0-2

1978 ARGENTINA

R1   ITALY   L 1-2 Bernard Lacombe

R1   ARGENTINA   L 1-2 Michel Platini

R1   HUNGARY   W 3-1 Christian Lopez, Marc Berdoll, DominiqueRochetau

1982 SPAIN

R1   ENGLAND   L 1-3 Gerard Soler

R1   KUWAIT   W 4-1 Bernard Genghini, Michel Platini, Didier Six, Maxime Bossis

R1   CZECHOSLOVAKIA D 1-1 Didier Six

R2   AUSTRIA   W 1-0 Bernard Genghini

R2   N. IRELAND   W 4-1 Alain Giresse 2, Dominique Rocheteau 2

SF   WEST GERMANY D 3-3 aet Michel Platini pen, Marius Tresor, Alain Giresse **(West Germany won 5-4 on penalties)**

3/4 POLAND   L 2-3 Rene Girard, Alain Couriol

1986 MEXICO

R1   CANADA   W 1-0 Jean-Pierre Papin

R1   USSR   D 1-1 Luis Fernandez

R1   HUNGARY   W 3-0 Yannick Stopyra, Jean Tigana, Dominique Rocheteau

R2   ITALY   W 2-0 Michel Platini, Yannick Stopyra

QF   BRAZIL   D 1-1aet Michel Platini (**France won 4-3 on penalties)**

SF   WEST GERMANY L 0-2

3/4 BELGIUM   W 4-2 Jean-Marc Ferreri, Jean-Pierre Papin, Bernard Genghini, Manuel Amoros

1998 FRANCE

R1   SOUTH AFRICA   W 3-0 Christophe Dugarry, Pierre Issa og, Thierry Henry

R1   SAUDI ARABIA   W 4-0 Thierry Henry 2, David Trezeguet, Bixente Lizarazu

R1   DENMARK   W 2-1 Youri Djorkaeff pen, Emmanuel Petit

R2   PARAGUAY   W 1-0 aet Laurent Blanc

QF   ITALY   D 0-0 aet **(France won 4-3 on penalties)**

SF   CROATIA   W 2-1 Lilian Thuram 2

F   BRAZIL   W 3-0 Zinedine Zidane 2, Emmanuel Petit

HISTORY

GERMANY
APPEARED AS GERMANY 1934-38, WEST GERMANY 1954-90 GERMANY SINCE 1994
PREVIOUS WORLD CUP APPEARANCES 1934, 1938, 1954, 1958, 1962, 1966,1970, 1974, 1978, 1982, 1986, 1990, 1994, 1998
BEST PERFORMANCE WINNERS 1954, 1974, 1990 RUNNERS-UP 1966, 1982, 1986
HOSTS 1974; DESIGNATED HOSTS OF 2006 FINALS
WORLD CUP FINALS RECORD P78, W45, D17, L16, F164, A104

1934 ITALY
R1	BELGIUM	W 5-2 Edmund Conen 3, Stanislaus Kobierski, Otto Siffling
QF	SWEDEN	W 2-1 Karl Hohmann 2
SF	CZECHOSLOVAKIA	L 1-3 Rudolf Noack
3/4	AUSTRIA	W 3-2 Ernst Lehner 2, Edmund Conen

1938 FRANCE
R1	SWITZERLAND	D 1-1aet Josef Gauchel
R1	SWITZERLAND	L 2-4 Wilhelm Hahnemann, Ernst Lortschner og

1954 SWITZERLAND
R1	TURKEY	W 4-1 Hans Schaefer, Bernhard Klodt, Ottmar Walter, Max Morlock
R1	HUNGARY	L 3-8 Albert Pfaff, Helmut Rahn, Richard Herrmann
p/o	TURKEY	W 7-2 Max Morlock 3, Hans Schaefer 2, Ottmar Walter, Fritz Walter
QF	YUGOSLAVIA	W 2-0 Horvat og, Helmu Rahn
SF	AUSTRIA	W 6-1 Fritz Walter 2, Ottmar Walter 2, Hans Schaefer, Max Morlock
F	HUNGARY	W 3-2 Helmut Rahn 2, Max Morlock

1958 SWEDEN
R1	ARGENTINA	W 3-1 Helmut Rahn 2, Uwe Seeler
R1	CZECHOSLOVAKIA	D 2-2 Hans Schaefer, Helmut Rahn
R1	N.IRELAND	D 2-2 Helmut Rahn, Uwe Seeler
QF	YUGOSLAVIA	W 1-0 Helmut Rahn
SF	SWEDEN	L 1-3 Hans Scharfer
3/4	FRANCE	L 3-6 Hans Cieslarczyk, Helmut Rahn, Hans Schaefer

1962 CHILE
R1	ITALY	D 0-0
R1	SWITZERLAND	W 2-1 Albert Brulls, Uwe Seeler
R1	CHILE	W 2-0 Horst Szymaniak, Uwe Seeler
QF	YUGOSLAVIA	L 0-1

1966 ENGLAND
R1	SWITZERLAND	W 5-0 Helmut Haller 2, Franz Beckenbauer 2,Siggi Held
R1	ARGENTINA	D 0-0
R1	SPAIN	W 2-1 Lothar Emmerich, Uwe Seeler
QF	URUGUAY	W 4-0 Siggi Held, Franz Beckenbauer, Helmut Haller
SF	SOVIET UNION	W 2-1 Helmut Haller, Franz Beckenbauer
F	ENGLAND	L 2-4 Helmut Haller, Wolfgang Weber **(aet 2-2 at 90 minutes)**

1970 MEXICO
R1	MOROCCO	W 2-1 Uwe Seeler, Gerd Muller

HISTORY

R1	BULGARIA	W 5-2 Gerd Muller 3, Reinhard Libuda, Uwe Seeler
R1	PERU	W 3-1 Gerd Muller 3
QF	ENGLAND	W 3-2 aet Franz Beckenbauer, Uwe Seeler, Gerd Muller
SF	ITALY	L 3-4 aet Karl-Heinz Schnellinger, Gerd Muller 2
3/4	URUGUAY	W 1-0 Wolfgang Overath

1974 WEST GERMANY

R1	CHILE	W 1-0 Paul Breitner
R1	AUSTRALIA	W 3-0 Wolfgang Overath, Bernhard Cullmann, Gerd Muller
R1	EAST GERMANY	L 0-1
R2	YUGOSLAVIA	W 2-0 Paul Breitner, Gerd Muller
R2	SWEDEN	W 4-2 Wolfgang Overath, Rainer Bonhof, Juergen Grabowski, Uli Hoeness
R2	POLAND	W 1-0 Gerd Muller
F	NETHERLANDS	W 2-1 Paul Breitner pen, Gerd Muller

1978 ARGENTINA

R1	POLAND	D 0-0
R1	MEXICO	W 6-0 Karl-Heinz Rummenigge 2, Heinz Flohe 2, Dieter Muller, Hansi Muller
R1	TUNISIA	D 0-0
R2	ITALY	D 0-0
R2	NETHERLANDS	D 2-2 Rudiger Abramczik, Dieter Muller
R2	AUSTRIA	L 2-3 K-H Rummenigge, Hans Holzenbein

1982 SPAIN

R1	ALGERIA	L 1-2 K-H Rummenigge
R1	CHILE	W 4-1 K-H Rummenigge 3, Uwe Reinders
R1	AUSTRIA	W 1-0 Hans Hrubesch
R2	ENGLAND	D 0-0
R2	SPAIN	W 2-1 Pierre Littbarski, Klaus Fischer
SF	FRANCE	D 3-3 aet Pierre Littbarski, K-H Rummenigge, Klaus Fischer **(West Germany won 5-4 on penalties)**
F	ITALY	L 1-3 Paul Breitner

1986 MEXICO

R1	URUGUAY	D 1-1 Klaus Allofs
R1	SCOTLAND	W 2-1 Rudi Voller, Klaus Allofs
R1	DENMARK	L 0-2
R2	MOROCCO	W 1-0 Lothar Matthaeus
QF	MEXICO	D 0-0 aet (aet, West Germany won 4-1 on penalties)
SF	FRANCE	W 2-0 Andreas Brehme, Rudi Voller
F	ARGENTINA	L 2-3 K-H Rummenigge, Rudi Voller

1990 ITALY

R1	YUGOSLAVIA	W 4-1 Lothar Matthaeus 2, Juergen Klinsmann, Rudi Voller
R1	UAE	W 5-1 Rudi Voller 2, Juergen Klinsmann, Lothar Matthaeus, Uwe Bein
R1	COLOMBIA	D 1-1 Pierre Littbarski
R2	NETHERLANDS	W 2-1 Juergen Klinsmann, Andreas Brehme
QF	CZECHOSLOVAKIA	W 1-0 Lothar Matthaeus
SF	ENGLAND	D 1-1 Andreas Brehme **(West Germany won 4-3 on penalties)**
F	ARGENTINA	W 1-0 Brehme pen

1994 UNITED STATES

R1	BOLIVIA	W 1-0 Juergen Klinsmann
R1	SPAIN	D 1-1 Juergen Klinsmann
R1	SOUTH KOREA	W 3-2 Juergen Klinsmann 2, Karl-Heinz Riedle
R2	BELGIUM	W 3-2 Juergen Klinsmann, Rudi Voller 2
QF	BULGARIA	L 1-2 Lothar Matthaeus pen

1998 FRANCE

R1	UNITED STATES	W 2-0 Andreas Moeller, Juergen Klinsmann
R1	YUGOSLAVIA	D 2-2 Slavisa Mihaljovic og, Oliver Bierhoff
R1	IRAN	W 2-0 Oliver Bierhoff, Juergen Klinsmann
R2	MEXICO	W 2-1 Juergen Klinsmann, Oliver Bierhoff
QF	CROATIA	L 0-3

ITALY

PREVIOUS WORLD CUP APPEARANCES 1934, 1938, 1950, 1954, 1962, 1966, 1970, 1974, 1978, 1982, 1986, 1990, 1994, 1998
BEST PERFORMANCE WINNERS 1934, 1938, 1982
HOSTS 1934, 1990
WORLD CUP FINALS RECORD P66, W38, D16, L12, F105, A62

1934 ITALY

R1	UNITED STATES	W 7-1 Angelo Schiavio 3, Raymundo Orsi 2, Giovanni Ferrari, Giuseppe Meazza
QF	SPAIN	D 1-1aet Giovanni Ferrari
QF	SPAIN	W 1-0 Giuseppe Meazza
SF	AUSTRIA	W 1-0 Enrique Guaita
F	CZECHOSLOVAKIA	W 2-1aet Raymundo Orsi, Angelo Schiavio

1938 FRANCE

R1	NORWAY	W 2-1aet Pietro Ferraris, Silvio Piola
QF	FRANCE	W 3-1 Gino Colaussi, Silvio Piola 2
SF	BRAZIL	W 2-1 Gino Colaussi, Giuseppe Meazza pen
F	HUNGARY	W 4-2 Gino Colaussi 2, Silvio Piola 2

1950 BRAZIL

R1	SWEDEN	L 2-3 Riccardo Carapellese, Ermes Muccinelli
R1	PARAGUAY	W 2-0 Carapellese, Egisto Pandolfini

1954 SWITZERLAND

R1	SWITZERLAND	L 1-2 Gianpiero Boniperti
R1	BELGIUM	W 4-1 Egisto Pandolfini en, Carlo Galli, Amleto Frignani, Benito Lorenzi
PO	SWITZERLAND	L 1-4 Fulvio Nesti

1962 CHILE

R1	WEST GERMANY	D 0-0
R1	CHILE	L 0-2
R1	SWITZERLAND	W 3-0 Bruno Mora, Giacomo Bulgarelli 2

HISTORY

1966 ENGLAND

R1	CHILE	W 2-0 Sandro Mazzola, Paolo Barison
R1	SOVIET UNION	L 0-1
R1	NORTH KOREA	L 0-1

1970 MEXICO

R1	SWEDEN	W 1-0 Angelo Domenghini
R1	URUGUAY	D 0-0
R1	ISRAEL	D 0-0
QF	MEXICO	W 4-1 Gustavo Pena og, Luigi Riva 2, Gianni Rivera
SF	WEST GERMANY	W 4-3 aet Roberto Boninsenga, Tarcisio Burgnich, Luigi Riva, Gianni Rivera
F	BRAZIL	L 1-4 Roberto Boninsenga

1974 WEST GERMANY

R1	HAITI	W 3-1 Gianni Rivera, Romeo Benetti, Pietro Anastasi
R1	ARGENTINA	D 1-1 Roberto Perfumo og
R1	POLAND	L 1-2 Fabio Capello

1978 ARGENTINA

R1	FRANCE	W 2-1 Paolo Rossi, Renato Zaccarelli
R1	HUNGARY	W 3-1 Paolo Rossi, Roberto Bettega, Romeo Benetti
R1	ARGENTINA	W 1-0 Roberto Bettega
R2	WEST GERMANY	D 0-0
R2	AUSTRIA	W 1-0 Paolo Rossi
R2	NETHERLANDS	L 1-2 Ernie Brandts og
3/4	BRAZIL	L 1-2 Franco Causio

1982 SPAIN

R1	POLAND	D 0-0
R1	PERU	D 1-1 Bruno Conti
R1	CAMEROON	D 1-1 Francesco Graziani
R2	ARGENTINA	W 2-1 Marco Tardelli, Antonio Cabrini
R2	BRAZIL	W 3-2 Paolo Rossi 3
SF	POLAND	W 2-0 Paolo Rossi 2
F	WEST GERMANY	W 3-1 Paolo Rossi, Marco Tardelli, Alessandro Altobelli

1986 MEXICO

R1	BULGARIA	D 1-1 Alessandro Altobelli
R1	ARGENTINA	D 1-1 Alessandro Altobelli pen
R1	SOUTH KOREA	W 3-2 Alessandro Altobelli 2, Cho Kwang Rae og
R2	FRANCE	L 0-2

1990 ITALY

R1	AUSTRIA	W 1-0 Salvatore Schillaci
R1	UNITED STATES	W 1-0 Giuseppe Giannini
R1	CZECHOSLOVAKIA	W 2-0 Salvatore Schillaci, Roberto Baggio
R2	URUGUAY	W 2-0 Salvatore Schillaci, Aldo Serena
QF	IRELAND	W 1-0 Salvatore Schillaci
SF	ARGENTINA	D 1-1aet Salvatore Schillaci (**Argentina won 4-3 on penalties**)
3/4	ENGLAND	W 2-1 Roberto Baggio, Salvatore Schillachi

HISTORY

1994 UNITED STATES
R1	IRELAND	L 0-1
R1	NORWAY	W 1-0 Dino Baggio
R1	MEXICO	D 1-1 Daniele Massaro
R2	NIGERIA	W 2-1aet Roberto Baggio 2 (1pen)
QF	SPAIN	W 2-1 Dino Baggio, Roberto Baggio
SF	BULGARIA	W 2-1 Roberto Baggio 2
F	BRAZIL	D 0-0 aet **(Brazil won 3-2 on penalties)**

1998 FRANCE
R1	CHILE	D 2-2 Christian Vieri, Roberto Baggio pen
R1	CAMEROON	W 3-0 Luigi Di Biagio, Christian Vieri 2
R1	AUSTRIA	W 2-1 Christian Vieri, Roberto Baggio
R2	NORWAY	W 1-0 Christian Vieri
QF	FRANCE	D 0-0 aet **(France won 4-3 on penalties)**

JAPAN
PREVIOUS WORLD CUP APPEARANCES 1998
BEST PERFORMANCE FIRST ROUND 1998
WORLD CUP FINALS RECORD P3, W0, D0, L3, F1, A4

1998 FRANCE
R1	ARGENTINA	L 0-1
R1	CROATIA	L 0-1
R1	JAMAICA	L 1-2 Nakayama

MEXICO
PREVIOUS WORLD CUP APPEARANCES 1930, 1950, 1954, 1958, 1962, 1966, 1970, 1978, 1986, 1994, 1998
BEST PERFORMANCE QUARTER FINALS 1970, 1986 **HOSTS** 1970, 1986
WORLD CUP FINALS RECORD P37, W9, D9, L19, F40, A75

1930 URUGUAY
R1	FRANCE	L 1-4 Juan Carreno
R1	CHILE	L 0-3
R1	ARGENTINA	L 3-6 Manuel Rosas, Felipe Rosas, Hilario Lopez

1950 BRAZIL
R1	BRAZIL	L 0-4
R1	YUGOSLAVIA	L 1-4 Horacio Casarin
R1	SWITZERLAND	L 1-2 Horacio Casarin

1954 SWITZERLAND
R1	BRAZIL	L 0-5

HISTORY

R1	FRANCE	L 2-3 Jose Naranjo, Tomas Balcazar

1958 SWEDEN

R1	SWEDEN	L 0-3
R1	WALES	D 1-1 Jaime Belmonte
R1	HUNGARY	L 0-4

1962 CHILE

R1	BRAZIL	L 0-2
R1	SPAIN	L 0-1
R1	CZECHOSLOVAKIA	W 3-1 Isidoro Diaz, Alfredo Del Aguila, Hector Hernandez

1966 ENGLAND

R1	FRANCE	D 1-1 Enrique Borja
R1	ENGLAND	L 0-2
R1	URUGUAY	D 0-0

1970 MEXICO

R1	SOVIET UNION	D 0-0
R1	EL SALVADOR	W 4-0 Javier Valdivia 2, Javier Fragoso, Juan Basaguren
R1	BELGIUM	W 1-0 Gustavo Pena
QF	ITALY	L 1-4 Luis Gonzalez

1978 ARGENTINA

R1	TUNISIA	L 1-3 Arturo Ayala
R1	WEST GERMANY	L 0-6
R1	POLAND	L 1-3 Victor Rangel

1986 MEXICO

R1	BELGIUM	W 2-1 Fernando Quirate, Hugo Sanchez
R1	PARAGUAY	D 1-1 Luis Flores
R1	IRAQ	W 1-0 Fernando Quirate
R2	BULGARIA	W 2-0 Manuel Negrete, Raul Servin
QF	WEST GERMANY	D 0-0aet (after extra-time, West Germany won 4-1 on pens)

1994 UNITED STATES

R1	NORWAY	L 0-1
R1	IRELAND	W 2-1 Luis Garcia 2
R1	ITALY	D 1-1 Marcelino Bernal
R2	BULGARIA	D 1-1 Alberto Garcia Aspe pen
		(after extra-time, Bulgaria won 3-1 on pens)

1998 FRANCE

R1	SOUTH KOREA	W 3-1 Ricardo Pelaez, Luis Hernandez 2
R1	BELGIUM	D 2-2 Alberto Garcia Aspe pen, Cuauhtemoc Blanco
R1	NETHERLANDS	D 2-2 Ricardo Pelaez, Luis Hernandez
R2	GERMANY	L 1-2 Luis Hernandez

NIGERIA

PREVIOUS WORLD CUP APPEARANCES 1994, 1998
BEST PERFORMANCE SECOND ROUND 1994, 1998
WORLD CUP FINALS RECORD P8, W4, D0, L4, F13, A13

1994 UNITED STATES
R1	BULGARIA	W 3-0 Rasheed Yekini, Daniel Amokachi, Emmanuel Amunike
R1	ARGENTINA	L 1-2 Samson Siasia
R1	GREECE	W 2-0 Finidi George, Rasheed Yekini
R2	ITALY	L 1-2aet Emmanuel Amunike

1998 FRANCE
R1	SPAIN	W 3-2 Mutiu Adepoju, Garba Lawal, Sunday Oliseh
R1	BULGARIA	W 1-0 Victor Ikpeba
R1	PARAGUAY	L 1-3 Wilson Oruma
R2	DENMARK	L 1-4 Tijani Babangida

PARAGUAY

PREVIOUS WORLD CUP APPEARANCES 1930, 1950, 1958, 1986, 1998
BEST PERFORMANCE SECOND ROUND 1986, 1998
WORLD CUP FINALS RECORD P15, W4, D6, L5, F19, A27

1930 URUGUAY
| R1 | UNITED STATES | L 0-3 |
| R1 | BELGIUM | W 1-0 Luis Vargas Pena |

1950 BRAZIL
| R1 | SWEDEN | D 2-2 Atilio Lopez, Cesar Lopez Fretes |
| R1 | ITALY | L 0-2 |

1958 SWEDEN
R1	FRANCE	L 3-7 Florencio Amarilla 2 (1pen), Jorgelino Romero
R1	SCOTLAND	W 3-2 Juan Bautista Aguero, Cavetano Re, Jose Parodi
R1	YUGOSLAVIA	D 3-3 Jose Parodi, Juan Bautista Aguero, Jorgelino Romero

1986 MEXICO
R1	IRAQ	W 1-0 Julio Cesar Romero
R1	MEXICO	D 1-1 Julio Cesar Romero
R1	BELGIUM	D 2-2 Roberto Cabanas 2
R2	ENGLAND	L 0-3

1998 FRANCE
R1	BULGARIA	D 0-0
R1	SPAIN	D 0-0
R1	NIGERIA	W 3-1 Celso Ayala, Miguel Benitez, Jose Cardozo
R2	FRANCE	L 0-1

POLAND

PREVIOUS WORLD CUP APPEARANCES 1938, 1974, 1978, 1982, 1986
BEST PERFORMANCE THIRD PLACE 1974, 1982
WORLD CUP FINALS RECORD P25, W13, D5, L7, F39, A29

HISTORY

1938 FRANCE
| R1 | BRAZIL | L 5-6 aet Ernest Willimowski 4 (1pen), Fryderyk Scherfke 50 |

1974 WEST GERMANY
R1	ARGENTINA	W 3-2 Grzegorz Lato 2, Andrzej Szarmach
R1	HAITI	W 7-0 Grzegorz Lato 2, Kazimierz Deyna, Andrzej Szarmach 3, Jerzy Gorgon
R1	ITALY	W 2-1 Andrzej Szarmach, Kazimierz Deyna
R2	SWEDEN	W 1-0 Grzegorz Lato
R2	YUGOSLAVIA	W 2-1 Kazimierz Deyna pen, Grzegorz Lato
R2	WEST GERMANY	L 0-1
3/4	BRAZIL	W 1-0 Grzegorz Lato

1978 ARGENTINA
R1	WEST GERMANY	D 0-0
R1	TUNISIA	W 1-0 Grzegorz Lato
R1	MEXICO	W 3-1 Zbigniew Boniek 2, KazimierzDeyna
R2	ARGENTINA	L 0-2
R2	PERU	W 1-0 Andrzej Szarmach
R2	BRAZIL	L 1-3 Grzegorz Lato

1982 SPAIN
R1	ITALY	D 0-0
R1	CAMEROON	D 0-0
R1	PERU	W 5-1 Wlodzimierz Smolarek, Grzegorz Lato, Zbigniew Boniek, Andrzej Buncol, Wlodzimierz Ciolek
R2	BELGIUM	W 3-0 Zbigniew Boniek 3
R2	USSR	D 0-0
SF	ITALY	L 0-2
3/4	FRANCE	W 3-2 Andrzej Szarmach, Stefan Majewski, Janusz Kupcewicz

1986 MEXICO
R1	MOROCCO	D 0-0
R1	PORTUGAL	W 1-0 Wlodzimierz Smolarek
R1	ENGLAND	L 0-3
R2	BRAZIL	L 0-4

PORTUGAL

PREVIOUS WORLD CUP APPEARANCES 1966, 1986
BEST PERFORMANCE THIRD PLACE 1966
WORLD CUP FINALS RECORD P9, W6, D0, L3, F19, A12

1966 ENGLAND
R1	HUNGARY	W 3-1 Jose Augusto 2, Jose Torres
R1	BULGARIA	W 3-0 Ivan Vutzov og, Eusebio, Jose Torres
R1	BRAZIL	W 3-1 Simoes, Eusebio 2
QF	NORTH KOREA	W 5-3 Eusebio 4 (1pen), Jose Augusto

SF	ENGLAND	L 1-2 Eusebio pen
3/4	USSR	W 2-1 Eusebio pen, Jose Torres

1986 MEXICO

R1	ENGLAND	W 1-0 Carlos Manuel
R1	POLAND	L 0-1
R1	MOROCCO	L 1-3 Diamantino

REPUBLIC OF IRELAND

PREVIOUS WORLD CUP APPEARANCES 1990, 1994
BEST PERFORMANCE QUARTERFINALS 1990
WORLD CUP FINALS RECORD P9, W1, D5, L3, F4, A7

1990 ITALY

R1	ENGLAND	D 1-1 Kevin Sheedy
R1	EGYPT	D 0-0
R1	NETHERLANDS	D 1-1 Niall Quinn
R2	ROMANIA	D 0-0aet (Ireland won 5-4 on penalties)
QF	ITALY	L 0-1

1994 UNITED STATES

R1	ITALY	W 1-0 Ray Houghton
R1	MEXICO	L 1-2 John Aldridge
R1	NORWAY	D 0-0
R2	NETHERLANDS	L 0-2

RUSSIA

SOVIET UNION 1958-1990
PREVIOUS WORLD CUP APPEARANCES 1958, 1962, 1966, 1970, 1982, 1986, 1990, 1994
BEST PERFORMANCE 4TH PLACE 1966
WORLD CUP FINALS RECORD P34, W16, D6, L12, F60, A40

1958 SWEDEN

R1	ENGLAND	D 2-2 Nikita Simonyan, Alexander Ivanov
R1	AUSTRIA	W 2-0 Alexander Ivanov, Anatoli Ilyin
R1	BRAZIL	L 0-2
QF	SWEDEN	L 0-2

1962 CHILE

R1	YUGOSLAVIA	W 2-0 Valentin Ivanov, Viktor Ponedelnik
R1	COLOMBIA	D 4-4 Valentin Ivanov 2, Igor Chislenko, Viktor Pondelik
R1	URUGUAY	W 2-1 Alexei Mamykin, Valentin Ivanov
QF	CHILE	L 1-2 Igor Chislenko

1966 ENGLAND

R1	NORTH KOREA	W 3-0 Eduard Malofeev 2, Anatoli Banishevski

R1	ITALY	W 1-0 Igor Chislenko
R1	CHILE	W 2-1 Valeri Porkuyan 2
QF	HUNGARY	W 2-1 Igor Chislenko, Valeri Porkuyan
SF	WEST GERMANY	L 1-2 Valeri Porkuyan
3/4	PORTUGAL	L 1-2 Eduard Malofeev

1970 MEXICO

R1	MEXICO	D 0-0
R1	BELGIUM	W 4-1 Anatoli Byshovets 2, Kakhi Asatiani, Vitali Kmelnitski
R1	EL SALVADOR	W 2-0 Anatoli Byshovets 2
QF	URUGUAY	L 0-1aet

1982 SPAIN

R1	BRAZIL	L 1-2 Andrei Bal
R1	NEW ZEALAND	W 3-0 Yuri Gavrilov, Oleg Blokhin, Sergey Baltacha
R1	SCOTLAND	D 2-2 Alexandr Chivadze, Ramaz Shengelia
R2	BELGIUM	W 1-0 Khoren Oganesian
R2	POLAND	D 0-0

1986 MEXICO

R1	HUNGARY	W 6-0 Pavel Yakovenko, Sergei Aleinikov, Igor Belanov pen, Ivan Yaremchuk 2, Sergei Rodionov
R1	FRANCE	D 1-1 Vasili Rats
R1	CANADA	W 2-0 Oleg Blokhin, Alexandr Zavarov
R2	BELGIUM	L 3-4aet Igor Belanov 3 (1pen)

1990 ITALY

R1	ROMANIA	L 0-2
R1	ARGENTINA	L 0-2
R1	CAMEROON	W 4-0 Oleg Protasov, Andrei Zygmantovich, Alexandr Zavarov, Igor Dobrovolski

1994 UNITED STATES

R1	BRAZIL	L 0-2
R1	SWEDEN	L 1-3 Oleg Salenko pen
R1	CAMEROON	W 6-1 Oleg Salenko 5 (1pen), Dmitri Radchenko

SAUDI ARABIA

PREVIOUS WORLD CUP APPEARANCES 1994, 1998
BEST PERFORMANCE SECOND ROUND 1994
WORLD CUP FINALS RECORD P7, W2, D1, L4, F7, A13

1994 UNITED STATES

R1	NETHERLANDS	L 1-2 Fuad Amin
R1	MOROCCO	W 2-1 Sami Al-Jaber, Fuad Amin
R1	BELGIUM	W 1-0 Saeed Al-Owairan
R2	SWEDEN	L 1-3 Fahad Al Ghesheyan

1998 FRANCE

| R1 | DENMARK | L 0-1 |

R1	FRANCE	L 0-4
R1	SOUTH AFRICA	D 2-2 Sami Al-Jaber pen, Youssef Al-Thynyan pen

---

SOUTH AFRICA

PREVIOUS WORLD CUP APPEARANCES 1998
BEST PERFORMANCE FIRST ROUND 1998
WORLD CUP FINALS RECORD P3, W0, D2, L1, F3, A6

1998 FRANCE

R1	FRANCE	L 0-3
R1	DENMARK	D 1-1 Benni McCarthy
R1	SAUDI ARABIA	D 2-2 Shaun Bartlett 2 (1pen)

SOUTH KOREA

PREVIOUS WORLD CUP APPEARANCES 1954, 1986, 1990, 1994, 1998
BEST PERFORMANCE NEVER PAST FIRST ROUND
CO-HOSTS 2002
WORLD CUP FINALS RECORD P14, W0, D4, L10, F11, A43

1954 SWITZERLAND

R1	HUNGARY	L 0-9
R1	TURKEY	L 0-7

1986 MEXICO

R1	ARGENTINA	L 1-3 Chang Sun Park
R1	BULGARIA	D 1-1 Jong Boo Kim
R1	ITALY	L 2-3 Soon Ho Choi, Jung Moo Huh

1990 ITALY

R1	BELGIUM	L 0-2
R1	SPAIN	L 1-3 Kwan Hwang Bo
R1	URUGUAY	L 0-1

1994 UNITED STATES

R1	SPAIN	D 2-2 Myung Bo Hong, Jung Woon Seo
R1	BOLIVIA	D 0-0
R1	GERMANY	L 2-3 Sun Hong Hwang, Myung Bo Hong

1998 FRANCE

R1	MEXICO	L 1-3 Seok Ju Ha
R1	NETHERLANDS	L 0-5
R1	BELGIUM	D 1-1 Sang Chul Yoo

SPAIN

PREVIOUS WORLD CUP APPEARANCES 1934, 1950, 1962, 1966, 1978, 1982, 1986, 1990, 1994, 1998
BEST PERFORMANCE FINAL GROUP 1950 (FINISHED 4TH)
HOSTS 1982
WORLD CUP FINALS RECORD P40, W16, D10, L14, F65, A47

1934 ITALY
R1	BRAZIL	W 3-1 Jose Iraragorri pen, Isidro Langara 2
QF	ITALY	D 1-1aet Luis Regueiro
QF	ITALY	L 0-1

1950 BRAZIL
R1	UNITED STATES	W 3-1 Estanislao Basora 2, Telmo Zarra
R1	CHILE	W 2-0 Estanislao Basora, Telmo Zarra
R1	ENGLAND	W 1-0 Telmo Zarra
FP	URUGUAY	D 2-2 Basora 2
FP	BRAZIL	L 1-6 Silvestre Igoa
FP	SWEDEN	L 1-3 Telmo Zarra

1962 CHILE
R1	CZECHOSLOVAKIA	L 0-1
R1	MEXICO	W 1-0 Joaquin Peiro
R1	BRAZIL	L 1-2 Rodriguez Abelardo

1966 ENGLAND
R1	ARGENTINA	L 1-2 Pirri
R1	SWITZERLAND	W 2-1 Manuel Sanchis, Amancio Amaro
R1	WEST GERMANY	L 1-2 Jose Fuste

1978 ARGENTINA
R1	AUSTRIA	L 1-2 Ruiz Dani
R1	BRAZIL	D 0-0
R1	SWEDEN	W 1-0 Juan Manuel Asensi

1982 SPAIN
R1	HONDURAS	D 1-1 Roberto Lopez Ufarte pen
R1	YUGOSLAVIA	W 2-1 Juan Gomez Juanito, Enrique Saura
R1	N.IRELAND	L 0-1
R2	WEST GERMANY	L 1-2 Jesus Maria Zamora
R2	ENGLAND	D 0-0

1986 MEXICO
R1	BRAZIL	L 0-1
R1	N.IRELAND	W 2-1 Emilio Butragueno, Julio Salinas
R1	ALGERIA	W 3-0 Ramon Caldere 2, Jose Eloy
R2	DENMARK	W 5-1 Emilio Butragueno 4, Andoni Goikoetxea pen
QF	BELGIUM	D 1-1aet Juan Antonio Senor (Belgium won 5-4 pens)

1990 ITALY
| R1 | URUGUAY | D 0-0 |

R1	SOUTH KOREA	W 3-1 Michel 3
R1	BELGIUM	W 2-1 Michel pen, Alberto Gorriz
R2	YUGOSLAVIA	L 1-2aet Julio Salinas

1994 UNITED STATES

R1	SOUTH KOREA	D 2-2 Julio Salinas, Andoni Goikoetxea
R1	GERMANY	D 1-1 Andoni Goikoetxea
R1	BOLIVIA	W 3-1 Josep Guardiola pen, Jose Caminero 2
R2	SWITZERLAND	W 3-0 Fernando Hierro, Luis Enrique, Aitor Begiristain
QF	ITALY	L 1-2 Jose Caminero

1998 FRANCE

R1	NIGERIA	L 2-3 Fernando Hierro, Raul
R1	PARAGUAY	D 0-0
R1	BULGARIA	W 6-1 Fernando Hierro pen, Luis Enrique, Fernando Morientes 2,Kiko 2

SWEDEN

PREVIOUS WORLD CUP APPEARANCES 1934, 1938, 1950, 1958, 1970, 1974, 1978, 1990, 1994
BEST PERFORMANCE RUNNERS-UP 1958
HOSTS 1958
WORLD CUP FINALS RECORD P38, W16, D8, L14, F66, A60

1934 ITALY

R1	BYE	
R2	ARGENTINA	W 3-2 Sven Jonasson 2, Kurt Kroon
QF	GERMANY	L 1-2 Gosta Dunker

1938 FRANCE

R1	BYE	
R2	CUBA	W 8-0 Tore Keller 3, Gustav Wettersrom 3, Arne Nyberg, Harry Andersson
SF	HUNGARY	L 1-5 Arne Nyberg
3/4	BRAZIL	L 2-4 Sven Jonasson, Arne Nyberg

1950 BRAZIL

R1	ITALY	W 3-2 Hans Jeppson 2, Sune Andersson
R1	PARAGUAY	D 2-2 Stig Sundqvist, Karl-Erik Palmer
FP	BRAZIL	L 1-7 Sune Andersson pen
FP	URUGUAY	L 2-3 Karl Erik Palmer, Stig Sunqvist
FP	SPAIN	W 3-1 Stig Sundqvist, Bror Mellberg, Karl Erik Palmer

1958 SWEDEN

R1	MEXICO	W 3-0 Agne Simonsson 2, Nils Liedholm pen
R1	HUNGARY	W 2-1 Kurt Hamrin 2
R1	WALES	D 0-0
QF	USSR	W 2-0 Kurt Hamrin, Agne Simonsson
SF	WEST GERMANY	W 3-1 Lennart Skoglund, Gunnar Gren, Kurt Hamrin
F	BRAZIL	L 2-5 Nils Liedholm, Agne Simonsson

1970 MEXICO
R1	ITALY	L	0-1	
R1	ISRAEL	D	1-1	Tom Turesson
R1	URUGUAY	W	1-0	Ove Grahn

1974 WEST GERMANY
R1	BULGARIA	D	0-0	
R1	NETHERLANDS	D	0-0	
R1	URUGUAY	W	3-0	Ralf Edstrom 2, Roland Sandberg
R2	POLAND	L	0-1	
R2	WEST GERMANY	L	2-4	Ralf Edstrom, Roland Sandberg
R2	YUGOSLAVIA	W	2-1	Ralf Edstrom, Conny Torstensson

1978 ARGENTINA
R1	BRAZIL	D	1-1	Thomas Sjoberg
R1	AUSTRIA	D	0-1	
R1	SPAIN	L	0-1	

1990 ITALY
R1	BRAZIL	L	1-2	Thomas Brolin
R1	SCOTLAND	L	1-2	Glenn Stromberg
R1	COSTA RICA	L	1-2	Johnny Ekstrom

1994 UNITED STATES
R1	CAMEROON	D	2-2	Roger Ljung, Martin Dahlin
R1	RUSSIA	W	3-1	Thomas Brolin pen, Martin Dahlin 2
R1	BRAZIL	D	1-1	Kennet Andersson
R2	SAUDI ARABIA	W	3-1	Martin Dahlin, Kennet Andersson 2
QF	ROMANIA	D	2-2 aet	Thomas Brolin, Kennet Andersson
		(Sweden won 5-4 on penalties)		
SF	BRAZIL	L	0-1	
3/4	BULGARIA	W	4-0	Thomas Brolin, Hakan Mild, Henrik Larsson, Kennet Andersson

TUNISIA

PREVIOUS WORLD CUP APPEARANCES 1978, 1998
BEST PERFORMANCE FIRST ROUND 1978, 1998
WORLD CUP FINALS RECORD P6, W1, D2, L3, F4, A6

1978 ARGENTINA
R1	MEXICO	W	3-1	Ali Kaabi, Nejib Ghommida, Moktar Dhouieb
R1	POLAND	L	0-1	
R1	WEST GERMANY	D	0-0	

1998 FRANCE
R1	ENGLAND	L	0-2	
R1	COLOMBIA	L	0-1	
R1	ROMANIA	D	1-1	Skander Souayah

TURKEY
PREVIOUS WORLD CUP APPEARANCES 1954
BEST PERFORMANCE 1ST ROUND
WORLD CUP FINALS RECORD P3, W1, D0, L2, F10, A11

1954 SWITZERLAND
R1	WEST GERMANY	L 1-4 Mamat Suat
R1	SOUTH KOREA	W 7-0 Sargun Burhan 3 Mamat Suat 2 Kucu Lefter, Ertan Mustafa
PO	WEST GERMANY	L 2-7 Ertan Mustafa, Kucu Lefter

UNITED STATES
PREVIOUS WORLD CUP APPEARANCES 1930, 1934, 1950, 1990, 1994, 1998
BEST PERFORMANCE SEMI-FINALS 1930
HOSTS 1994
WORLD CUP FINALS RECORD P17, W4, D1, L12, F18, A38

1930 URUGUAY
R1	BELGIUM	W 3-0 Bart McGhee 2, Bart Patenaude
R1	PARAGUAY	W 3-0 Bart Patenaude 3
SF	ARGENTINA	L 1-6 James Brown

1934 ITALY
R1	ITALY	L 1-7 Aldo Donelli

1950 BRAZIL
R1	SPAIN	L 1-3 John Souza
R1	ENGLAND	W 1-0 Larry Gaetjens
R1	CHILE	L 2-5 Gino Pariani, John Souza pen

1990 ITALY
R1	CZECHOSLOVAKIA	L 1-5 Paul Caligiuri
R1	ITALY	L 0-1
R1	AUSTRIA	L 1-2 Bruce Murray

1994 UNITED STATES
R1	SWITZERLAND	D 1-1 Eric Wynalda
R1	COLOMBIA	W 2-1 Andres Escobar og, Ernie Stewart
R1	ROMANIA	L 0-1
R2	BRAZIL	L 0-1

1998 FRANCE
R1	GERMANY	L 0-2
R1	IRAN	L 1-2
R1	YUGOALSVIA	L 0-1

URUGUAY

PREVIOUS WORLD CUP APPEARANCES 1930, 1950, 1954, 1962, 1966, 1970, 1974, 1986, 1990
BEST PERFORMANCE WINNERS 1930, 1950
HOSTS 1930 (first World Cup)
WORLD CUP FINALS RECORD P37, W15, D8, L14, F61, A52

1930 URUGUAY
R1	PERU	W 1-0 Hector Castro
R1	ROMANIA	W 4-0 Pablo Dorado, Hector Scarone, Peregrino Anselmo, Pedro Cea
SF	YUGOSLAVIA	W 6-1 Pedro Cea 3, Anselmo 2, santos Iriarte
F	ARGENTINA	W 4-2 Pablo Dorado, Pedro Cea, Santos Iriarte, Hector Castro

1950 BRAZIL
R1	BOLIVIA	W 8-0 Juan Schiaffino 4, Omar Miguez 2, Ernesto Vidal, Alcide Ghiggia
FP	SPAIN	D 2-2 Alcides Ghiggia, Obdulio Varela
FP	SWEDEN	W 3-2 Omar Miguez 2, Alcides Ghiggia
FP	BRAZIL	W 2-1 Juan Schiaffino, Alcides Ghiggia

1954 SWITZERLAND
R1	CZECHOSLOVAKIA	W 2-0 Omar Miguez, Juan Schiaffino
R1	SCOTLAND	W 7-0 Carlos Borges 3, Omar Miguez 2, Julio Cesar Abbadie 2
QF	ENGLAND	W 4-2 Carlos Borges, Obdulio Varela, Juan Schiaffino, Javier Ambrois
SF	HUNGARY	L 2-4 Juan Eduardo Hohberg 2
3/4	AUSTRIA	L 1-3 Juan Eduardo Hohberg

1962 CHILE
R1	COLOMBIA	W 2-1 Luis Cubilla, Jose Sacia
R1	YUGOSLAVIA	L 1-3 Ruben Cabrera
R1	USSR	L 1-2 Jose Sacia

1966 ENGLAND
R1	ENGLAND	D 0-0
R1	FRANCE	W 2-1 Pedro Rocha, Julio Cortes
R1	MEXICO	D 0-0
QF	WEST GERMANY	L 0-4

1970 MEXICO
R1	ISRAEL	W 2-0 Ildo Maneiro, Juan Martin Mujica
R1	ITALY	D 0-0
R1	SWEDEN	L 0-1
QF	USSR	W 1-0 aet Victor Esparrago
SF	BRAZIL	L 1-3 Luis Cubilla
3/4	WEST GERMANY	L 0-1

1974 WEST GERMANY
R1	NETHERLANDS	L 0-2
R1	BULGARIA	D 1-1 Ricardo Pavoni
R1	SWEDEN	L 0-3

1986 MEXICO

R1	WEST GERMANY	D 1-1 Antonio Alzamendi
R1	DENMARK	L 1-6 Enzo Francescoli (pen)
R1	SCOTLAND	D 0-0
R2	ARGENTINA	L 0-1

1990 ITALY

R1	SPAIN	D 0-0
R1	BELGIUM	L 1-3 Pablo Bengoechea
R1	SOUTH KOREA	W 1-0 Daniel Fonseca
R2	ITALY	L 0-2

FINAL THOUGHTS

by henry winter

The world is on fever-pitch footing as the greatest show on earth looms. Millions will attend the games live, billions will tune in from afar, huddling around television sets from Rio to Rochdale to marvel at the flickering deeds of Owen, Raul, Zidane, Veron, Totti and Roberto Carlos. But the wild and widespread sense of anticipation is tempered by the reality that the Yokohama final will not be contested by the best two sides.

The draw is far too lop-sided. Italy are worth a decent wager simply because their path is relatively straightforward compared to other heavyweights. Poor France. They must feel that the world is really against them. The world champions must negotiate an unbelievable obstacle course to defend their title. No favours for the favourites, then. France should win their group which will see them play, in all probability, England in the first knockout round. If that was not tough enough on the masterful Zinedine Zidane and his French musketeers, their projected quarter-final opponents are Brazil with Argentina as scheduled foe in the final four. France's easiest knockout match of the tournament could prove the actual final itself. The nightmare scenario for France, let alone television producers praying for the big box-office attractions to stay on the screens, is for the world's elite pair, Argentina and France, to duel in the first knockout stage as could happen if Veron and company slip up against England in Sapporo on June 7. France-Argentina would be an epic encounter contrasting with minor meetings elsewhere in the second-round.

The incentive for England and Argentina to finish top of their group is immense - anything to avoid France in the next round. It is a World Cup of two halves. One Japan-based competition resembles a high-wire act where France, Argentina and England could tumble at a solitary, cruel blast from a referee's penalty-signalling whistle. The other, centred around South Korea, promises good teams like Italy an extended stay in the spotlight. Whereas the quarter-final line-up is usually made up of familiar faces, spread between Europe and Latin America, opportunity knocks for wild-cards because of the imbalanced draw. Do not bet against an African or Asian side reaching the last eight. But do bet on the delighted Italians travelling far. The real drama, though, will be in the Argentina/England/France/Brazil jousting arena.

REFEREES

THE 36 REFEREES REPRESENT ALL OF THE VARIOUS CONFEDERATIONS FROM AROUND THE WORLD. THE OFFICIALS FOR THE LATTER STAGES OF THE TOURNAMENT DEPEND ON WHICH TEAMS ADVANCE FROM THE GROUPS

UBALDO AQUINO
D.O.B. 02.05.1958
HEIGHT/WEIGHT
179cm/77kg
INTERNATIONAL SINCE 01.01.94
LIVES Paraguay
OCCUPATION
Dentist, University Lecturer
HOBBIES Nature documentaries, travelling, music

CARLOS BATRES
D.O.B. 02.04.1968
HEIGHT/WEIGHT
178cm/81kg
INTERNATIONAL SINCE 01.01.96
LIVES Guatemala
OCCUPATION
Bachelor of Science
HOBBIES Sport and reading

ALI BUJSAIM
D.O.B. 09.09.1959
HEIGHT/WEIGHT
180cm/80kg
INTERNATIONAL SINCE 01.01.90
LIVES UAE
OCCUPATION
Immigration Officer
HOBBIES
Watersports

COFFI CODJIA
D.O.B. 09.12.1967
HEIGHT/WEIGHT
174cm/74kg
INTERNATIONAL SINCE 01.01.94
LIVES Benin
OCCUPATION
Inspector
HOBBIES Cycling

PIERLUIGI COLLINA
D.O.B. 13.02.1960
HEIGHT/WEIGHT
188cm/75kg
INTERNATIONAL SINCE 01.01.95
LIVES Italy
OCCUPATION
Financial Consultant
HOBBIES Reading, basketball and Internet

MOURAD DAAMI
D.O.B. 15.08.1962
HEIGHT/WEIGHT
184cm/82kg
INTERNATIONAL SINCE 01.01.96
LIVES Tunisia
OCCUPATION
Merchant
HOBBIES Music and swimming

HUGH DALLAS
D.O.B. 26.10.1957
HEIGHT/WEIGHT
180cm/77kg
INTERNATIONAL SINCE 01.01.93
LIVES Scotland
OCCUPATION
Company Director
HOBBIES
Keeping fit

ANDERS FRISK
D.O.B. 18.02.1963
HEIGHT/WEIGHT
184cm/74kg
INTERNATIONAL SINCE 01.01.91
LIVES Sweden
OCCUPATION
Sales Manager
HOBBIES Sports and film

MATCH OFFICIALS

GAMAL GHANDOUR
D.O.B. 12.6.1957
HEIGHT/WEIGHT 187cm/87kg
INTERNATIONAL SINCE 01.01.93
LIVES Egypt
OCCUPATION Accountant
HOBBIES Swimming and reading

MOHAMED GUEZZAZ
D.O.B. 01.10.1962
HEIGHT/WEIGHT 178cm/75kg
INTERNATIONAL SINCE 01.01.97
LIVES Morocco
OCCUPATION Professor History & Geography
HOBBIES Sports, travelling & reading

BRIAN HALL
D.O.B. 05.06.1961
HEIGHT/WEIGHT 185cm/92kg
INTERNATIONAL SINCE 01.01.92
LIVES USA
OCCUPATION Vice President Purchaser
HOBBIES Coaching football & photography

TERJE HAUGE
D.O.B. 05.10.1965
HEIGHT/WEIGHT 186cm/90kg
INTERNATIONAL SINCE 01.01.93
LIVES Norway
OCCUPATION Referee Adviser
HOBBIES Sport, angling and music

TORU KAMIKAWA
D.O.B. 08.06.1963
HEIGHT/WEIGHT 181cm/76kg
INTERNATIONAL SINCE 01.01.98
LIVES Japan
OCCUPATION Clerk
HOBBIES Reading and music

YOUNG JOO KIM
D.O.B. 30.12.1957
HEIGHT/WEIGHT 172cm/65kg
INTERNATIONAL SINCE 01.01.94
LIVES Korea Republic
OCCUPATION Business (Sports Marketing)
HOBBIES Music

ANTONIO LOPEZ NIETO
D.O.B. 25.01.1958
HEIGHT/WEIGHT 176cm/82kg
INTERNATIONAL SINCE 01.01.93
LIVES Spain
OCCUPATION Industrial Worker
HOBBIES Playing netball, music and reading

JUN LU
D.O.B. 19.03.1959
HEIGHT/WEIGHT 175cm/74kg
INTERNATIONAL SINCE 01.01.91
LIVES Egypt
OCCUPATION Businessman
HOBBIES Football

SAAD MANE
D.O.B. 06.01.1963
HEIGHT/WEIGHT 173cm/70kg
INTERNATIONAL SINCE 01.01.94
LIVES Kuwait
OCCUPATION Sergeant, Ministry of Interior
HOBBIES Football, swimming and tennis

WILLIAM MATTUS
D.O.B. 17.04.1964
HEIGHT/WEIGHT 169cm/75kg
INTERNATIONAL SINCE 01.01.97
LIVES Costa Rica
OCCUPATION Medical Data Manager
HOBBIES Athletics, music and football

URS MEIER
D.O.B. 22.01.1959
HEIGHT/WEIGHT 179cm/74kg
INTERNATIONAL SINCE 01.01.94
LIVES Switzerland
OCCUPATION Independent Businessman
HOBBIES Skiing, motorbiking and reading

MARKUS MERK
D.O.B. 15.03.1962
HEIGHT/WEIGHT 181cm/75kg
INTERNATIONAL SINCE 01.01.92
LIVES Germany
OCCUPATION Dentist
HOBBIES Triathlon, marathon, cross-country skiing and travelling

MATCH OFFICIALS

LUBOS MICHEL
D.O.B. 16.05.1968
HEIGHT/WEIGHT
178cm/75kg
INTERNATIONAL SINCE 01.01.93
LIVES Slovakia
OCCUPATION Teacher
HOBBIES Tennis and reading

BYRON MORENO
D.O.B. 23.11.1969
HEIGHT/WEIGHT
176cm/78kg
INTERNATIONAL SINCE 01.01.96
LIVES Ecuador
OCCUPATION Football Ref, Student of Law
HOBBIES Reading, football & basketball

FALLA NDOYE
D.O.B. 04.03.1960
HEIGHT/WEIGHT
187cm/75kg
INTERNATIONAL SINCE 01.01.93
LIVES Senegal
OCCUPATION Administrator
HOBBIES Music and football

KIM MILTON NIELSEN
D.O.B. 03.08.1960
HEIGHT/WEIGHT
196cm/98kg
INTERNATIONAL SINCE 01.01.88
LIVES Denmark
OCCUPATION IT Manager
HOBBIES Tennis

RENE ORTUBE
D.O.B. 26.12.1964
HEIGHT/WEIGHT
171cm/75kg
INTERNATIONAL SINCE 01.01.92
LIVES Bolivia
OCCUPATION Public Accountant
HOBBIES Travel, music and reading

VITOR MELO PEREIRA
D.O.B. 21.04.1957
HEIGHT/WEIGHT
176cm/72kg
INTERNATIONAL SINCE 01.01.92
LIVES Portugal
OCCUPATION Telecomunication Expert
HOBBIES Sports

GRAHAM POLL
D.O.B. 29.07.1963
HEIGHT/WEIGHT
184cm/88kg
INTERNATIONAL SINCE 01.01.96
LIVES England
OCCUPATION Football Referee
HOBBIES Golf

PETER PRENDERGAST
D.O.B. 23.09.1963
HEIGHT/WEIGHT
175cm/78kg
INTERNATIONAL SINCE 01.01.94
LIVES Jamaica
OCCUPATION Businessman
HOBBIES Watching football and playing squash

FELIPE RAMOS RIZO
D.O.B. 10.03.1963
HEIGHT/WEIGHT
181cm/81kg
INTERNATIONAL SINCE 01.01.97
LIVES Mexico
OCCUPATION Accountant
HOBBIES Films and computer

OSCAR RUIZ
D.O.B. 01.11.1969
HEIGHT/WEIGHT
185cm/83kg
INTERNATIONAL SINCE 01.01.95
LIVES Colombia
OCCUPATION Lawyer
HOBBIES Music and reading

ANGEL SANCHEZ
D.O.B. 03.03.1957
HEIGHT/WEIGHT
180cm/83kg
INTERNATIONAL SINCE 01.01.94
LIVES Argentina
OCCUPATION Radiologist Technician
HOBBIES Playing football

MARK SHIELD
D.O.B. 02.09.1973
HEIGHT/WEIGHT
187cm/82kg
INTERNATIONAL SINCE 01.01.99
LIVES Australia
OCCUPATION Company Director
HOBBIES Squash and fishing